GW01367115

TEACHING AND TEACHER EDUCATION IN INTERNATIONAL CONTEXTS

ADVANCES IN RESEARCH ON TEACHING

Series Editor: Cheryl J. Craig & Stefinee Pinnegar

Recent Volumes:

Volume 25:	Exploring Pedagogies for Diverse Learners Online
Volume 26:	Knowing, Becoming, Doing as Teacher Educators: Identity, Intimate Scholarship, Inquiry
Volume 27:	Innovations in English Language Arts Teacher Education
Volume 28:	Crossroads of the Classroom: Narrative Intersections of Teacher Knowledge and Subject Matter
Volume 29:	Culturally Sustaining and Revitalizing Pedagogies
Volume 30:	Self-study of Language and Literacy Teacher Education Practices
Volume 31:	Decentering the Researcher in Intimate Scholarship: Critical Posthuman Methodological Perspectives in Education
Volume 32:	Essays on Teaching Education and the Inner Drama of Teaching: Where Biography and History Meet
Volume 33:	Landscapes, Edges, and Identity-Making
Volume 34:	Exploring Self Toward Expanding Teaching, Teacher Education and Practitioner Research
Volume 35:	Preparing Teachers to Teach the STEM Disciplines in America's Urban Schools
Volume 36:	Luminous Literacies: Localized Teaching and Teacher Education
Volume 37:	Developing Knowledge Communities Through Partnerships for Literacy
Volume 38:	Understanding Excessive Teacher and Faculty Entitlement: Digging at the Roots
Volume 39:	Global Meaning Making: Disrupting and Interrogating International Language and Literacy Research and Teaching
Volume 40:	Making Meaning With Readers and Texts: Beginning Teachers' Meaning-Making From Classroom Events
Volume 41:	Teacher Education in the Wake of Covid-19: ISATT 40th Anniversary Yearbook

"Tilburg Dawn," a photo by Christopher Clark, was taken in 1984 at the second conference of the International Study Association on Teacher Thinking.*

---

*For additional details, see *A History of ISATT 2013-2023: Internationalization*, by Frances O'Connell Rust & Christopher M. Clark in Volume I of this series.

ADVANCES IN RESEARCH ON TEACHING   VOLUME 42

TEACHING AND TEACHER EDUCATION IN INTERNATIONAL CONTEXTS: ISATT 40TH ANNIVERSARY YEARBOOK

EDITED BY

CHERYL J. CRAIG
Texas A&M University, USA

JUANJO MENA
University of Salamanca, Spain

And

RUTH G. KANE
University of Ottawa, Canada

emerald PUBLISHING

United Kingdom – North America – Japan
India – Malaysia – China

Emerald Publishing Limited
Howard House, Wagon Lane, Bingley BD16 1WA, UK

First edition 2023

Editorial Matter and Selection © 2023 Cheryl J. Craig, Juanjo Mena and Ruth G. Kane.
Individual chapters 1, 3, 4, 5, 6, 13–20 and 22–27 © 2023 the respective Author/s.
Published under exclusive licence by Emerald Publishing Limited.

Individual chapters 2, 7, 9, 10, 11 and 12 © 2023 Emerald Publishing Limited.
Copyright © 2023 Emerald Publishing Limited, with the exception of Tensions and Paradoxes in Teaching: Implications for Teacher Education © Taylor & Francis, InFo-TED: Bringing Policy, Research, and Practice Together Around Teacher Educator Development © Emerald Publishing, "Data is [G]od": The influence of cumulative policy reforms on teachers' knowledge in an urban middle school in the United States © Elsevier.

Reprints and permissions service
Contact: permissions@emeraldinsight.com

No part of this book may be reproduced, stored in a retrieval system, transmitted in any form or by any means electronic, mechanical, photocopying, recording or otherwise without either the prior written permission of the publisher or a licence permitting restricted copying issued in the UK by The Copyright Licensing Agency and in the USA by The Copyright Clearance Center. Any opinions expressed in the chapters are those of the authors. Whilst Emerald makes every effort to ensure the quality and accuracy of its content, Emerald makes no representation implied or otherwise, as to the chapters' suitability and application and disclaims any warranties, express or implied, to their use.

British Library Cataloguing in Publication Data
A catalogue record for this book is available from the British Library

ISBN: 978-1-80455-471-5 (Print)
ISBN: 978-1-80455-470-8 (Online)
ISBN: 978-1-80455-472-2 (Epub)

ISSN: 1479-3687 (Series)

Printed and bound by CPI Group (UK) Ltd, Croydon, CR0 4YY

INVESTOR IN PEOPLE

CONTENTS

List of Figures and Tables	xi
About the Authors	xiii
Foreword	xix

SECTION 1: TRIBUTES

Tribute to John Loughran — 3
Amanda Berry

Tribute to Jean Clandinin — 7
Eliza Pinnegar and Cheryl J. Craig

Tribute to Geert Kelchtermans — 11
Maria Assunção Flores and Lily Orland-Barak

Tribute to Theo Wubbels — 15
Luce Claessens and Tim Mainhard

Tribute to Christopher Day — 19
Maria Assunção Flores

Tribute to Judith Warren Little — 23
Rebecca Cheung

SECTION 2: TEACHER EDUCATION REFORM

Introduction — 29
Diane Yendol-Hoppey

Tensions and Paradoxes in Teaching: Implications for Teacher Education — 33
Miriam Ben-Peretz and Maria Assunção Flores

Teacher Education Reforms in Kenya: The Past, the Present, and Mapping the Future *39*
Samuel Ouma Oyoo, Maureen Atieno Olel, Maurine Kang'ahi and Francis Chisikwa Indoshi

Teacher Education Reform in Scotland *51*
Margery McMahon

Teacher Education Reform in the United States: Colliding Forces? *61*
Diane Yendol-Hoppey, Madalina Tanase and Jennifer Jacobs

Innovative Research Training in Higher Education for LSP Teachers: From Institutional Policy to the Development of Custom-Made Projects *83*
M.A. Châteaureynaud and M.C. Deyrich

SECTION 3: SCHOOL REFORM SECTION

Introduction *101*
Maria Assunção Flores

Listening as a Basis of Reforming Schools in Asia: From Hostility to Trust *105*
Eisuke Saito

School Reform in South Africa: A Struggle for Mobility *117*
Maropeng Modiba and Sandra Stewart

"Data Is [G]od": The Influence of Cumulative Policy Reforms on Teachers' Knowledge in an Urban Middle School in the United States *131*
Cheryl J. Craig

Principals' Views in a Context of Reform: The Case of School Curriculum Policy in Portugal *161*
Maria Assunção Flores

SECTION 4: PREPARING TEACHER EDUCATORS (InFo-TED) SECTION

Introduction *177*
Amanda Berry

Looking Back and Looking Forward at InFo-TED—Reflecting on Purpose, Progress, and Challenges *181*
Kari Smith and Ruben Vanderlinde

InFo-TED, North America: Addressing a Problem of Practice *195*
Frances Rust and Diane Yendol-Hoppey

InFo-TED: Bringing Policy, Research, and Practice Together Around Teacher Educator Development *211*
Eline Vanassche, Frances Rust, Paul F. Conway, Kari Smith, Hanne Tack and Ruben Vanderlinde

SECTION 5: PARTNERSHIPS

Introduction *233*
Özge Hacıfazlıoğlu

Communities of Practice With Visiting Scholars *235*
Paul J. Magnuson, Özge Hacıfazlıoğlu, Steven Carber and Rae Newman

Collaborative Reflection, Knowledge, and Growth: Exploring Ongoing Teacher Learning Within Knowledge Communities *255*
Michaelann Kelley and Gayle A. Curtis

Multinational Policy Analyses: Third Time Around *273*
Maria Assunção Flores, Darlene Ciuffetelli Parker, Maria Inês Marcondes and Cheryl J. Craig

International Forum on Teacher Education as an Educational Research Partnership *289*
Roza Valeeva, Aydar Kalimullin and Tatiana Baklashova

Cultivating Teacher Resilience Through Intercultural Interaction and Collaboration *307*
Özge Hacıfazlıoğlu, Bilge Kalkavan, Chunyan Yang, Gökçe Ünlü and Serra Gürün

Afterword *327*

Index *329*

LIST OF FIGURES AND TABLES

Chapter 12
Figure 1.	Research Process Outlined in the TRAILS Erasmus+ Grant Award.	92
Figure 2.	Mind Map Commented on Collectively.	94

Chapter 16
Figure 1.	Literacy Meeting Agenda and Truncated Notes-to-File (Craig, 2014).	146

Chapter 20
Figure 1.	The InFo-TED Conceptual Model of Teacher Educators' Professional Development.	197

Chapter 21
Figure 1.	The InFo-TED Conceptual Model of Teacher Educator Professional Development (e.g., Kelchtermans et al., 2015).	216

Chapter 24
Figure 1.	Qualities of Knowledge Communities.	259

Chapter 25
Figure 1.	A Comparative Study of Four Nations in 2018–2019 (Craig et al., 2020).	274
Figure 2.	Three Data Points for Comparative Purposes.	276

Chapter 10
Table 1.	GTCS Professional Standards and Relevant Career Stage.	57

Chapter 11
Table 1.	NAPDS Nine Essentials (2021).	63
Table 2.	Blue Ribbon Report Ten Design Principles for Clinically Based Preparation.	65

Chapter 12
Table 1.	Self-Assessment Grid.	95

Chapter 15
Table 1.	National Poverty Distribution Table (2017).	121
Table 2.	Percentage of Schools in Each Quintile by Province (2017).	121

Table 3.	National Monthly Allocation for Individual Pupils (Q1–5).	122
Table 4.	Number of Learners (Ls), Educators (Es), Schools (Ss) in School Sector by Province in 2021.	122

Chapter 16

Table 1.	Reforms, Metaphors, Aberrant Attributions.	154

Chapter 17

Table 1.	Principals' Biographical Data.	165

Chapter 23

Table 1.	Visiting Scholar Demographics.	242
Table 2.	A Crosswalk of Communities of Practice and Emergent Themes in the Interviews.	244

Chapter 27

Table 1.	Emergent Themes and Subthemes.	314

ABOUT THE AUTHORS

Tatiana Baklashova is the International Relations Deputy Director of the Institute of Psychology and Education at Kazan Federal University and an Associate Professor in the Higher Education Department, Karan Federal University, Russian Republic. She is a coordinator of student teachers' practicum training and a member of the IPE KFU Academic Council.

Miriam Ben-Peretz, PhD (deceased), was a Professor Emeritus, former Head of the Department of Teacher Education, and former Dean of the School of Education at University of Haifa. In 1997, she received the Division B (Curriculum) Lifetime Achievement Award from the American Educational Research Association. In 2006, she received the Israel award for Excellence in Education Research.

Amanda Berry, PhD, is a Professor in STEM Education in the Faculty of Education at Monash University. Amanda has a distinguished international profile in science education research, particularly science teacher knowledge. Alongside her STEM education research, Amanda has a strong research interest in Self-Study of Teacher Education Practices (SSTEP).

Steven Carber, PhD, has prepared international school teachers for almost two decades, within the context of several higher-education degree programs for the international education community. He is the author of three books on international education, and has published three IB inquiry-box curriculum guides.

Marie-Anne Châteaureynaud, PhD, is a Senior Lecturer of Applied Linguistics in the Teacher Education School at the University of Bordeaux. She is involved in several European projects having to do with language teaching and LSP teaching. Her research involves sociolinguistics, language teaching, Occitan, Minority languages, multilingualism, and inclusion.

Paul F. Conway, PhD, is a Deputy Head of School at the University of Limerick, Ireland. His research interests are learning and development, teacher education, educational policy as it relates to e-learning teacher education, psychology and pedagogy of literacy and mathematics, and cognitive and sociocultural perspectives on learning. He is a joint General Editor of *Irish Educational Studies*.

Gayle A. Curtis, EdD, is a Program Manager with Asian American Studies at University of Houston and a Postdoctoral Research Associate at Texas A&M University. Her research delves into the lives of teachers, reflective practice, teacher collaboration, culture, and racialized experiences. Gayle is a member of the Portfolio Group (1998–present) and Faculty Academy (2017–present).

ABOUT THE AUTHORS

Marie-Christine Deyrich, PhD, is Professor Emerita of Applied Linguistics at the University of Bordeaux. She has been involved in several European projects involving language learning for active social inclusion. Her research deals with ethical language teaching in intercultural issues, linguistic policy, LSP learning, and teaching in higher education.

Maria Assunção Flores, PhD, works at the University of Minho, Portugal. Her research interests include teacher professionalism and identity, teacher education and professional development, curriculum, assessment and leadership. She is past Chair of the International Study Association on Teachers and Teaching and is currently coeditor of the *European Journal of Teacher Education*.

Serra Gürün is a high school senior student at ENKA Schools in Istanbul, Türkiye. As a future psychology student, she has taken part in various research studies, including one about adult ADHD with the University of Massachusetts.

Özge Hacıfazlıoğlu, PhD, is currently a visiting professor at UC Berkeley School of Education. She has served as a professor at Hasan Kalyoncu University in Turkey. She holds a doctorate in Educational Administration and pursued her postdoctorate education at Arizona State University. She has been the "outreach coordinator" on ISATT Executive Committee since 2017.

Francis Chisikwa Indoshi, PhD, is a Professor of Curriculum and Instruction. He was the Chair of the Department of Educational Communication, Technology and Curriculum Studies, School of Education, Maseno University, Kenya. He has expertise in leading major reforms in teacher education policies and the coordination of Teaching Practice component of initial teacher education.

Jennifer Jacobs, PhD, is an Associate Professor in the Elementary and Teacher Education programs at the University of South Florida. Her research is situated within the context of teacher education and focuses on teacher learning centered on equity. Central to her work is developing high-quality teacher education programs within partnerships between schools and universities.

Aydar M. Kalimullin is a Professor of the Higher Education Department and Historical Sciences Department and Head of the Institute of Psychology and Education at Kazan Federal University. He serves as the Codirector of the Volga region Center of the Russian Academy of Education. He is also Chief Executive Officer of the Annual International Forum on Teacher Education Conference.

Bilge Kalkavan, PhD, is Assistant Professor at Hasan Kalyoncu University. She completed her PhD in Applied Linguistics at Hellenic American University and holds a doctoral degree in Communication Studies at Hasan Kalyoncu University. Her research interests include interaction studies, intercultural communication, and teacher training.

Maurine Kang'ahi, PhD, is the current Chair of the Department of Educational Communication, Technology and Curriculum Studies. The department serves as the centre for pedagogical and professional training of teachers in Kenya at the School of Education, Maseno University, Kenya.

Michaelann Kelley, EdD, is Assistant Professor and Chair of the Department of Art & Design at Mount St. Joseph University. Her awards include the 2013 Stanford University Outstanding Teaching Award and 2021 Texas Art Education Association Distinguished Fellows honor. Kelley is a founding member of the Portfolio Group (1998–present) and a teacher member in the Faculty Academy (2003–2006).

Paul J. Magnuson, PhD, has worked in professional development in the United States and Switzerland for over 25 years. He also has over 20 years of experience in running summer campus. He works at Leysin American School and teaches online for Moreland University. His hobbies include languages and writing children's books.

Maria Inês Marcondes, PhD, is a full Professor at the Pontifical Catholic University of Rio de Janeiro PUC/RIO and Scientist of Our State Foundation of Rio de Janeiro State/FAPERJ and the Brazilian National Research Council/CNPq Researcher. She is Brazil's National Representative of the International Study Association on Teachers and Teaching (ISATT).

Margery A. McMahon, PhD, is Head of the School of Education at the University of Glasgow and Professor of Educational Leadership. She is currently Chair of the Scottish Council of Deans of Education (SCDE). She has been involved in teacher education, career-long professional learning, and leadership education and is the author/coauthor of a books and articles focusing on professional learning and leadership.

Maropeng Modiba, DPhil, is Emeritus professor of Education and Curriculum Studies at the University of Johannesburg. Her research focuses on two related areas, teacher education and curriculum literacy, which she captures by studying instructional practices and their significance for teachers' professional development. She is currently engaged in various research projects and writing, focusing in particular, on issues related to knowledge democracy.

Rae Newman, PhD, majors in educational leadership. She earned the doctoral distinction award for social justice impact by exploring the intersection of youth migration, identity, and international travel. Rae is an influencer, a leader, and a travel enthusiast.

Maureen Atieno Olel, PhD, is an Educationist, a DAAD Scholar and an associate professor of Educational Management, Planning and Economics of Education. She is the current Dean of the School of Education, Maseno University, Kenya. Among her research areas are efficiency and equity in education, accountability, and development issues in education.

Samuel Ouma Oyoo, PhD, is currently affiliated with Maseno University and the University of South Africa. A member of the International Study Association on Teachers and Teaching (ISATT) since 2004, he has been the ISATT National Representative for South Africa (2011 to 2017) and for Kenya (since 2019 to date).

Darlene Ciuffetelli Parker, PhD, is a Professor in the Faculty of Education and Director of Teacher Education at Brock University in Ontario, Canada. Her narrative inquiry research focuses on social justice, poverty, equity, and well-being in secondary school systems and postsecondary teacher education.

Frances Rust, PhD, is Professor Emeritus at New York University's Steinhardt School of Education where she taught between 1991 and 2007. She has directed teacher education programs at Teachers College Columbia, Manhattanville College, Hofstra University, NYU, and University of Pennsylvania. Her research interests are teacher's and teacher educators' professional learning.

Eisuke Saito, PhD, is a Lecturer for the Faculty of Education, Monash University, Australia. Eisuke has been researching school reform and teacher professional development and learning, mainly in South-East Asia, such as Vietnam, Thailand, Indonesia, and Singapore, based on the approach called 'lesson study as a learning community' or 'school as learning community.'

Kari Smith, PhD, is a Professor Emerita of Education at the Department of Teacher Education, Norwegian University of Science and Technology (NTNU). Among her research interests are teacher education, mentoring novice teachers, and assessment for and of learning. She was the Head of the Norwegian National Research School in Teacher Education (NAFOL), and a founder of the International Forum for Teacher Educator Development (InFo-TED).

Sandra Stewart, PhD, was a Research Associate in the Department of Education and Curriculum at the University of Johannesburg between 2017 and 2021. Her research focuses on teaching English as a second language, curriculum policy and teachers' professional development. She is currently involved in a literacy intervention that focuses on improving the teaching of English reading in a rural primary school.

Hanne Tack, PhD, is a Postdoctoral Researcher in the Department of Educational Studies at Ghent University, Belgium. Her research interests focus on teacher education in general, with a particular emphasis on teacher educators' professional development.

Madalina Tanase, PhD, is an Associate Professor at the University of North Florida, USA. She is originally from Romania. Her research areas are culturally responsive classroom management and pedagogy, teacher self-efficacy, and epistemological beliefs.

ABOUT THE AUTHORS

Gökçe Ünlü is a PhD student at the University of Nevada, Reno, in Education with the focus of "Equity, Diversity and Language" and is a member of ISATT as an experienced international teacher at the higher education level. Having received her BA degree in English Language Teaching at Istanbul University, Gokce completed her MSc in Education at the University of Edinburgh.

Roza A. Valeeva is a Professor and Head of the Pedagogy Department in the Institute of Psychology and Education at Kazan Federal University. She is the Chairman of the Dissertation Council in Kazan Federal University and President of the Janusz Korczak Society in Russia. She is also the Secretary General of the International Korczak Association (IKA). She is Editor in Chief of *Education and Self Development*.

Eline Vanassche, PhD, is a Professor at the University of Leuven. She is a former Marie Skłodowska-Curie Fellow at the University of East London. Her research interests includes the nature of teacher educators' professionalism and its development throughout their careers. Her more recent work seeks to understand what teacher educators "may do and not do" in complex relationships.

Ruben Vanderlinde, PhD, is a Professor in the Department of Educational Studies at Ghent University, the Coordinator of the Research Group, 'Teacher Education & Professional Development,' and is responsible for Teacher Education at Ghent University. Among his research interests are in the educational innovation, teacher induction, teacher education, and professional development.

Chunyan Yang, PhD, is an Associate Professor in the Berkeley School of Education at the University of California, Berkeley. Her research interests focus on understanding how school members interact with their living contexts to find their resilience in the face of a variety of risk factors in school settings, such as bullying, teacher-targeted violence, and mental health challenges.

Diane Yendol-Hoppey, PhD, is a Professor at the University of North Florida. Her research focuses on facilitating teacher learning, the development of school–university partnerships, enhanced job-embedded professional development, and teacher leadership. Diane has coauthored/edited 14 books, acquired over $20 million in external funding, and published over 50 articles in peer-reviewed journals.

FOREWORD

The International Study Association on Teachers and Teaching, which started the International Study Association on Teacher Thinking, celebrates/ed its 40th anniversary in 2023, the publication year of its four-volume Anniversary Yearbook. The study association became a full-blown organization not only with a biennial international conference and a regional conference in the in-between years, but with an awards program, a small grant program, and a graduate student preconference as well. Further to this, a special kind of kinship developed, which made ISATT a beloved organization in the hearts and minds of its members.

Several features distinguish the Yearbook's four volumes. These features include tributes in each book, sections outlining distinct lines of ISATT research, and reprint articles by selected authors. The four volumes also share the same frontispiece, a photo taken by Christopher Clark at the second ISATT Meeting in Tilburg, The Netherlands. Further to this, internationalism is a powerful strength streaming naturally across all four books, not as an intermittent cover story.

The titles of the four volumes are:

Volume 1: Teacher Education in the Wake of Covid-19
Volume 2: Teaching and Teacher Education in International Contexts
Volume 3: Approaches to Teaching and Teacher Education
Volume 4: Studying Teaching and Teacher Education

This volume (Volume 2), *Teaching and Teacher Education in International Contexts*, follows closely in the footsteps of *Teacher Education in the Wake of Covid-19* (Volume 1). A sincere thank you is extended to this book's section editors, Diane Yendol-Hoppey (US), Maria Assunção Flores (Portugal), Amanda Berry (Australia), and Özge Hacıfazlıoğlu (Türkiye). Thanks also goes out to Daniela Hotolean (UK) and Wendy Moran (Australia) who assembled and edited the Tributes honoring past and present ISATT members. In addition, we recognize Xiao Han (US) who coordinated the technical details of all the manuscripts and Hulya Avci (Türkiye) who prepared Volume 2's Index. Without the diligence of all these people, this volume would have been near-impossible to complete, given how short our publication window was. Lastly, we are grateful to our members who authored chapters amid significant time constraints to ensure that ISATT would have a 40th Anniversary Yearbook ready to celebrate at our 20th Biennial Conference in Bari, Italy, in 2023.

SECTION 1
TRIBUTES

TRIBUTE TO JOHN LOUGHRAN

Amanda Berry

John Loughran, PhD, was an early career researcher at Monash University when he first learned about ISATT. A colleague shared a letter at a staff meeting about a newly formed organization that was seeking members, The International Study Association on Teacher Thinking. In John's words, "I read the blurb – it really fitted with my work." The rest, as they say, is history. John Loughran's association with ISATT has been long and rich; his academic career has been closely connected with the people, the institutions, the ideas, and the values of ISATT as a community concerned to enhance the quality of teaching and raise the status of teachers and teaching through research and practice.

All of John's undergraduate and academic career was spent at Monash University. After completing a Bachelor of Science in 1978 and a Graduate Diploma in Education in 1979, John worked as a high school science teacher for a decade before completing a Master of Educational Studies in 1987. It was during this time of working as a science teacher that John began forming his ideas about the value of teachers' work and the specialized knowledge that teachers develop about their practice through experience and reflection.

John completed his doctoral degree (*Developing Reflective Practice: Learning about Teaching and Learning through Modelling*) as a part-time student in 1994, was appointed as the Foundation Chair of Curriculum and Pedagogy in 2004 and ultimately, Dean of the Faculty of Education at Monash, in 2010. His ongoing concern for better understanding and improving teacher education informed his research program on a Pedagogy of Teacher Education and led to his AERA (Division K) Excellence in Research Award in 2007. That was followed by his appointment as a Fellow of the Academy of Social Sciences in Australia (2009), then a Doctor of Letters (2011). He was appointed as a Sir John Monash Distinguished Professor at Monash University in 2016. John served the Faculty of Education and Monash University for 30 years before retiring in 2019. Besides his AERA award, John has been the recipient of numerous national and international awards for his work as a teacher and researcher, as well receiving an

Australian Council of Deans of Education (2018) Award for Outstanding Service to Education.

The main areas of John's research include Science Teachers' Pedagogical Content Knowledge; Science Teaching and Learning; Pedagogical Reasoning; Professional Learning; and, Self-study of Teaching and Teacher Education. His research is driven by a genuine interest in, and concern for, the professional development of teachers and teacher educators and his approach is based on his belief in the importance of collaboration and mentoring. John has enjoyed long-standing and fulfilling collaborations with many colleagues over the years, but two, in particular, were Professor Amanda Berry, a former PhD student of John's, and Professor Tom Russell, with whom John co-founded the journal of self-study, *Studying Teacher Education* in 2005.

For John, ISATT was always a place of opportunity and community. As a relatively small conference, John valued the opportunity to meet researchers whose work he admired, but who were often inaccessible at larger, busier conferences. Being able to meet and exchange ideas with top scholars such as Max van Manen, from whom John learned about the value of teacher produced anecdotes, and Philip Jackson, who shared the influence of his biography on his scholarship, left a lasting impression on John as a newly emerging scholar. John recalled that during an ISATT annual meeting, Chris Day publicly invited him to be part of the review board for the ISATT journal, *Teachers and Teaching Theory and Practice (TTTP)*. John felt privileged to be recognized in this forum and to be offered this exciting opportunity as a junior academic. He found the experience a powerful way to learn about how the publication process operated from the 'inside' – including how to review, how to deal with authors, as well as issues such as the importance of focusing on professional critique and productive feedback as opposed to personal criticism laced with disparaging remarks.

As well as connecting with established names, John enjoyed the opportunity to meet other early career academics at ISATT conferences, for example, Jan van Driel (Netherlands), Ruth Kane (Canada), and Christopher Clark (US), who have remained colleagues and friends throughout his career. For John, so much of the value of ISATT was in the ways it "opened up doors for people" through the structure of the sessions, which were longer than traditional conference presentations so that ideas could be examined and "played with," and the social aspects that extended beyond quick conversations between sessions, to really get to know, and learn from and with, others.

John presented two ISATT keynote addresses. The first was in Leiden, in 2003, at the invitation of Douwe Beijaard who asked John to present his work on Self-study of Teaching and Teacher Education. The significance of this invitation was not lost on John because although self-study was gaining acceptance in Australia and the USA, European colleagues were less familiar with this methodology, and this keynote gave John a platform for self-study to be recognized and discussed. John's second ISATT keynote was in Auckland, in 2015, which was based on his seminal book, *What Expert Teachers Do*.

The ISATT conference dinner was always a highlight. It was not necessarily the food, or even the venue (although there were some amazing venues!), but how people socialized and enjoyed themselves. The Dublin conference (1999) was particularly memorable – the guests were having such a great time that when the venue finally closed, the buses had already left and at least half of the guests were still there, without any transport to return to their accommodation. They had to walk miles back to their hotels. John remembered getting into his hotel at about 5 a.m. – and almost as soon as he got into bed it was time to get up and go to the conference for the next day. But, as John recalls, "That was ISATT! It was great."

TRIBUTE TO JEAN CLANDININ

Eliza Pinnegar and Cheryl J. Craig

D. Jean Clandinin is Professor Emerita and Founding Director of the Centre for Research for Teacher Education and Development, University of Alberta, Canada. Initially a teacher, counselor, and psychologist, she authored/coauthored 20 books as well as many articles and chapters. Her books include *Narrative Inquiry, Engaging in Narrative Inquiry, Engaging in Narrative Inquiry with Children and Youth, and Relational Ethics in Narrative Inquiry.* An invited volume, *Journeys in Narrative Inquiry: Selected Works of Jean Clandinin* was released as part of Routledge's World Library of Educationalists in 2019. She edited the *Handbook of Narrative Inquiry: Mapping a Methodology* in 2007 and coedited the *Handbook of Research in Teacher Education* in 2017. Clandinin's most recent coauthored book (2022) is *Narrative Inquiry: Philosophical Roots.* With Mary Lynn Hamilton, Jean Clandinin was co-Editor-in-Chief of *Teaching and Teacher Education* (2009–2015). She is a Past Vice-President of Division B (Curriculum) of the American Educational Research Association (AERA). She is the 1993 winner of AERA's Early Career Award, AERA's 2002 Division B Lifetime Achievement Award, the 1999 Canadian Education Association Whitworth Award for Educational Research, the 2015 AERA Division K (Teacher Education) Legacy Award and the 2015 International Study Association on Teachers and Teaching's (ISATT's) STAR award. The University of Alberta awarded her the 2001 Kaplan Research Achievement Award, the 2004 Killam Scholar, the 2008 Larry Beauchamp Award, the 2009 Killam Mentoring Award and the 2010 Faculty of Education, University of Alberta Graduate Teaching Award. In 2016, she received the Benjamin Cluff Jr. Award for Educational Research from Brigham Young University. She was awarded an honorary doctorate by the University of Pretoria in 2017.

Jean Clandinin's research initially unfolded at the intersection of teaching/teacher education and curriculum. Her doctoral research and subsequent articles focused on the epistemological nature of teacher knowledge. She presented on this work at the 1983 ISSAT Symposium, Tilburg University. Her 1988 and 1992 work on teacher-as-curriculum-planner/curriculum-maker (Clandinin & Connelly, 1992; Connelly &

Clandinin, 1988) inspired a world-renowned curriculum-teaching line of research. She worked with colleagues to develop narrative inquiry as a qualitative methodology used for autobiographical and field-based research purposes (Clandinin & Connelly, 2000; Connelly & Clandinin, 1990). A Narrative Research Special Interest Group soon appeared at AERA. Narrative inquiry is among the top three qualitative research methodologies in teaching and teacher education. Narrative inquiry is both a view of experience and a way of inquiring into experience. Narrative inquiry lets experience lead the way. Narrative inquiry is a relational research methodology in which participants and researchers engaged in relational ways so that publications are an experiential amalgam.

Clandinin's groundbreaking work on teacher knowledge and the contexts of teaching in her early years of career morphed in multiple directions to include youth who leave school early, early career teacher attrition, the experiences of youth and families of Aboriginal heritage, and the experiences of the professional learning of school administrators. She coauthored articles in medical education and is currently engaged in a Social Sciences and Humanities Research Council of Canada-sponsored study of the experiences of Syrian refugee families. Experience, relationality, and narrative inquiry remain the glue tying her research program together. In addition to giving keynote addresses around the world, she has maintained long-standing collaborations with colleagues in Brazil, Japan, Finland, Norway, and the United States. She is affiliated with Griffith University in Australia and Royal Roads University in Canada, and has worked at the Universities of Alberta, Calgary, and Toronto. An active ISATT member, Jean Clandinin regularly contributed to *Teachers and Teaching: Theory and Practice* (*TTTP*) and served as an associate editor from 2003 to 2010. Her *TTTP* articles focused on narrative and education (1995), teachers' stories on the professional knowledge landscape, teachers' learning spaces (2008), and sustaining teachers' stories to live by (2019). She contributed a number of editorials to *TTTP*.

The Centre for Research for Teacher Education and Development (CRTED) is an important accomplishment. The Centre is known for its weekly interdisciplinary research conversations, visiting scholars, summer institutes, and programs of research in teacher knowledge and teacher education. Guests from national and international universities spent time at the CRTED. Among those visitors were ISATT members, Christopher Clark (Michigan State University), Miriam Ben-Peretz (University of Haifa) and Stefinee Pinnegar (Brigham Young University). Other visitors included Gary Fenstermacher (University of Arizona), Virginia Richardson (University of Arizona), Nona Lyons (Brown University), Sandra Hollingsworth (Michigan State University), Ken Zeichner (University of Washington), Robert Stake (University of Illinois), Nel Noddings (Stanford University), Elliot Eisner (Stanford), Anna Richert (Mills College), and Jan Gray (Edith Cowan University). Research delegations from Japan and the University of the West Indies also visited the CRTED. Repeat visitors from Brazil, Chile, South Africa, the US, and Ireland, among other nations, visited. The Centre sponsored summer institutes (1993–2016) on themes of teacher research, collaborative research, inclusive education and peace education.

Students from around Canada and the globe (Korea, Kenya, China, Brazil, Australia) traveled to study with her. Her graduate students currently work in

Canada, Kenya, Korea, China, Australia, Brazil, and the United States. Jean also supervised international postdoctoral fellows from China, Spain, Brazil, Korea, and the U.S. Several of her doctoral students and their students are current ISATT members. The legacy of Jean Clandinin lives on in a multitude of ways.

REFERENCES

Clandinin, D. J., & Connelly, F. M. (1992). Teacher as curriculum maker. In P. Jackson (Ed.), *Handbook of research on curriculum* (pp. 363–401). Macmillan.

Clandinin, D. J., & Connelly, F. M. (2000). *Narrative inquiry: Experience and story in qualitative research.* John Wiley & Sons.

Connelly, F. M., & Clandinin, D. J. (1988). *Teachers as curriculum planners. Narratives of experience.* Teachers College Press.

Connelly, F. M., & Clandinin, D. J. (1990). Stories of experience and narrative inquiry. *Educational Researcher, 19*(5), 2–14.

TRIBUTE TO GEERT KELCHTERMANS

Maria Assunção Flores and Lily Orland-Barak

Geert Kelchtermans was born and grew up in the eastern part of Belgium close to the Dutch and German border. He studied educational sciences and philosophy at the University of Leuven between 1980 and 1985 and completed a final internship at the national office of the Dutch Yena-Plan school movement, which also became the topic of his master's degree thesis (coauthored by Ann Deketelaere). The Yena-Plan School was developed in the German city Jena by Peter Petersen in the first decades of the twentieth century; it became one of the many innovative school models of the international movement for a more child-centered education (Reformpädagogik). Finding a school model that would support the development of the full and unique personality of each child was its central concern. From the late 1950s onwards, the Yena-Plan inspired many schools and teachers in the Netherlands to fundamentally rethink and reform their practices. For Geert Kelchtermans, the study of this innovative movement formed the basis for his later work as a researcher and academic: an interest in educational innovation (and in particular its normative aspect: its ambition and claim to be an "improvement" rather than just a change); the conviction that educational research should value and incorporate teachers' beliefs and personal commitments in order to understand (and possibly improve) educational practices; the experience that narrative-biographical approaches (taking teachers' career stories seriously) constitutes a powerful venue for understanding these practices; and finally the acknowledgment that educational practices are fundamentally entrenched in the school's organization and in teachers' personal biographies. During his PhD studies, he developed the "narrative-biographical approach" which proposed an innovative theoretical and methodological framework for understanding and conceptualizing the study of teachers and teaching, and which has had a strong impact within the ISATT community. His theoretical and methodological choices, which were grounded in qualitative methodologies, were not exactly "mainstream" in his faculty. Although the work was personally and academically fascinating and rewarding, he often felt as if he was struggling in the margins. A significant critical incident in his career occurred during the ISATT conference in Guilford (UK) in 1991. Seeking critical feedback from the international research community, he submitted a paper based on his first empirical findings and was happy that it got accepted, first as a paper in the conference and later as a chapter in the conference book. He recalls that recognition as a boost for his self-confidence, as was meeting in person a number of established scholars whose work he had studied so intensely. Those were the days when the ISATT conference took place during the summer, on campus, with participants staying in student residences and enjoying all meals together, which made it easy to meet, mingle and engage in discussions in an atmosphere of collegiality and vibrant intellectual work. He also recalls returning to Leuven feeling reinvigorated and determined to continue his line of work, even if it went against much of mainstream scholarship there. He obtained his PhD in 1993, presented the final work at the ISATT conference in Göteborg, and continued to do so during his years as post-doc and later as a professor. He collaborated with Christopher Day from the very beginning in the ISATT Journal *Teachers and Teaching: Theory & Practice*, first as a member of the editorial board, and later as an executive editor. He was also a keynote speaker at the ISATT conferences in Sydney, Australia (2005) and Braga, Portugal (2011). The network of colleagues from around the world that he built up through his ISATT contacts grew steadily throughout the years and became a vital international source for critical intellectual collaboration and discussion, as well as for intense collegiality and friendship. An illustrative anecdote is how during the 1997 conference dinner, on a ship at sea outside Kiel, Sigrun Gudmundsdottir introduced him to a group of colleagues from the University of Oulu in Finland (Leena Syrjälä and Eila Estola). He writes:

> This was the start of a fruitful collaboration on narrative research which developed into a visiting professorship in Oulu for five years and still ongoing research collaborations with the new generation of educational scholars there.

That is just one example of what he says ISATT has meant to him and his work. He continues:

> Another great memory is the long drive in a van after the AERA meeting New York to Queens University in Kingston (Canada) in 2008 with a number of co-authors for the special issue of the ISATT journal on "teaching as a discipline" edited by John Loughran and Tom Russell (published in 2009). The conversations in that van included chit-chat, intense conceptual discussions, thoughtful silences as well as singing and discovering shared knowledge of 60s and 70s pop and rock classics. And exactly that intense mix of serious work and discussion, with bonding and joyful exchanges as colleagues and friends continued during the two days of intense work at Queens University on the manuscripts.

Echoes of ISATT-related contacts, ideas, exchanges, friendships, and collaborations are evident in Geert's vast publications. A further recognition of his scholarship and contribution to the ISATT community, was when he became the recipient of the Michael Huberman Award in 2017 from the AERA Lives of Teachers SIG.

Geert Kelchtermans is a true educational researcher in every sense of the word. His outstanding work is recognized internationally, particularly as a leader in the area of teachers' work and professional development, induction and the development of the narrative-biographical perspective on teachers' work and lives, with a particular focus on the emotional dimension of teaching.

Such is his rich legacy to the ISATT community, and for that the ISATT community thanks you, Geert.

TRIBUTE TO THEO WUBBELS

Luce Claessens and Tim Mainhard

When we think about teacher–student interactions, we think about Theo Wubbels. As a longtime researcher at Utrecht University in The Netherlands, Theo's work on the interpersonal perspective shaped research into teaching and teacher education but also teacher education programs. Most teachers in secondary education in the Netherlands have used the Questionnaire on Teacher–student Interactions (the QTI) developed by Theo and Hans Créton, which has been translated into many languages. With this tool teachers can, for instance, see whether students think they are friendly and good leaders.

In teacher research, Theo has put the student perspective on the map. His academic work started in 1984 with his PhD thesis focusing on classroom management problems of novice teachers. Theo taught us that simply observing teacher behavior and thinking in behavioristic terms does not suffice, it is the student perception of this behavior that matters since this perception guides students.

Looking into teacher and student perceptions is now the first choice of many researchers and educators when they study classroom processes and their relevance for teachers and students. However, this was certainly not the case when Theo became a researcher. Process-product research was mainstream and teacher thinking was not of any interest. But then again, Theo's entry into teacher research was also far from normal.

Theo's interest in teacher research began during his own time as a beginning physics teacher and later, when helping new teachers with classroom management problems. He started working as a teacher educator in a physics university department mostly consisting of physics researchers. The teacher education group wanted to become more research oriented and asked their staff to embark on research. Theo had always loved to write and volunteered immediately. Given this context, Theo's PhD was not just a personal trajectory, it sat at the heart of the interest of the teacher education group in which he was working. During this time, he collaborated with many of his colleagues, such as Hans Créton, Anne Holvast, Herman Hooymayers, and Mieke Brekelmans.

It was also during this time that a focus on teacher thinking captured researchers' attention in the Netherlands and ISATT was formed. Given the specific focus on internal cognitive processes, Theo quickly became involved. He attended the second conference in 1984 in Tilburg. Researchers like Douwe Beijaard and later Nico Verloop became his "Dutch teacher thinking pals" and together with his network within ISATT, they played a major role in the development of teacher thinking. Attending ISATT conferences was very interesting to Theo as a novice researcher. There was a feeling of togetherness and like-mindedness and it was possible for Theo to meet scholars such as Lee Shulman (USA) and Chris Clark (USA), and he started collaborating with Sigrun Gudmundsdottir (Norway) and Neville Bennett (Great Britain). Meanwhile, Berry Fraser convinced Theo that his research was in essence learning environments' research, because the teacher is an important factor in the classroom social environment. Chris Day told Theo he was doing research into teacher thinking because Theo was looking into how teachers think about themselves and their students' reactions. It was not much later that Theo became Associate Editor of the ISATT journal *Teachers and Teaching: Theory and Practice*, which celebrated its 20th anniversary in 2022.

Besides the enormous inspirational qualities of the conferences, ISATT was also a lot of fun. Theo remembers Nottingham where, after a social event involving dressing up as Robin Hood characters, they arrived back at the conference venue after closing time. Together with unnamed others, they had to climb through a window when it was pitch black to get back into their room.

Theo built a research group that accumulated over the years with many collaborative publications on the topic of interpersonal teacher behavior. The work of his group puts the interpersonal relations with students' center stage in classrooms. Without a safe and structured classroom environment and a pleasant relationship with a teacher, a student cannot gather the cognitive space for learning and get motivated.

Given Theo's own background as a physics major, this transition into the social sciences was not an easy one. Overall, it took him 20 years to feel comfortable calling himself a social scientist. During this time, he also took on several service roles. Theo chaired the Dutch association for educational research, was the Editor in Chief of the Dutch journal *Pedagogische Studiën* and was President of the European Educational Research Association.

In addition to his love for research, Theo's career was also characterized by his interest for and investment in management and administration at his home university and elsewhere. This combination of highly evolved expertise in both fields; research and management, is what made Theo an extraordinary force in the field of teacher education in the Netherlands. Already as a young teacher in secondary school he soon became deputy headmaster. When he returned to the university, he became affiliated Head of his department and eventually Head of Teacher Education at Utrecht, Vice Dean of the social sciences faculty and Admissions Dean. He shared his managerial skills with a new generation of university managers but also with students in various consultative bodies. On the day of his farewell from his department, students organized a candle lit boat ride through the canals of Utrecht as a farewell gift to him.

And, all this time, Theo Wubbels kept publishing and up to date in his field. He supervised over 40 PhD students with real commitment, not just to the project but also to the person behind the PhD student (such as us). He never really lost sight of the teacher within himself. As a supervisor, he was wise but always open to suggestions, very loyal and focused on learning, maybe even more than on the output. He created a safe environment and even though he was very busy, he was available when help was needed. This is what we call a helpful teacher who provides guidance. Theo's legacy shows that this is what students *and* teachers think is ideal.

Thank you, Theo, you did make things better. ISATT salutes your many accomplishments.

TRIBUTE TO CHRISTOPHER DAY

Maria Assunção Flores

Christopher Day is a well-known and well-respected researcher in the field of school leadership and teachers' work and lives internationally. He is Emeritus Professor of Education, at the University of Nottingham, UK and member of the Centre for Research on Educational Leadership and Management (CRELM). He is also Professor of Educational Leadership, University of Sydney, Australia, Chair Professor of Educational Leadership, Beijing Normal University, China, and Visiting Professor at the Inholland University, The Netherlands.

Christopher Day is one of the "founding fathers" of ISATT and is the longest standing active member of ISATT. He was present at the very first meeting in the early 1980s in the Netherlands with another six to eight people resulting in ISATT's formation. He served as ISATT Secretary for 13 years. For a period of 10–15 years, apart from hosting a memorable second ISATT conference at the University of Nottingham in 1984, he argued for and established the ISATT journal – *Teachers and Teaching Theory and Practice* (TTTP) and became its Editor-in-Chief, developing it from two issues annually to six. During this period, the journal also became recognized by Social Sciences Citation Index. Furthermore, during this time, he established the publication of a series of commercially produced books with Routledge edited by ISATT members. The name of ISATT was eventually changed from "International Study Association on Teacher Thinking" to its present name in 1993. As Chris Day argued, "this was significant in relation to its ability to attract members and the profile of their work collectively and one of the reasons why it does not compete with the European Association for Research on Learning and Instruction (EARLI)." As one of ISATT's longest serving member and as the founding editor-in-chief of TTTP, Christopher Day has consistently made significant contributions to ISATT events and conferences over time by giving keynote addresses and workshops for ISATT members at the biennial conferences. He has also served in leadership roles in international organizations in addition to ISATT. For example, he had a leading role at the International Council on Education for Teaching (ICET), founded in 1953, and at the European Educational Research Association (EERA).

Christopher Day is also a member of the Editorial Boards of The *British Educational Research Journal* (BERJ), *Teaching and Teacher Education* (TATE), and the *Journal of Educational Administration* (JEA). He is series editor of the book series (together with Ann Liberman) "Teacher Quality and School Development" by Routledge; and book series editor together with Judith Sachs of *Professional Learning and Development in Schools and Higher Education* by Springer.

Furthermore, he has led national, European and international research and development projects in the areas of teachers' work and lives and school leadership and collaborated in these projects with colleagues in Europe, North and South America, China, and Australasia. His abiding interests are teacher quality, school leadership, improvement and effectiveness and, within these, understanding how schools, school networks and universities may provide effective management and support for teachers' and principals' long-term professional development, wellbeing and effectiveness through research and teaching.

Christopher Day has an impressive number of books and articles published in international journals with high impact factor to his credit. His books have been published in several languages. These include *Teachers' Worlds and Work: Understanding Complexity, Building Quality* (2017); *A Decade of International Research on School Leadership* (2016); *Successful School Leadership: Lessons from the Field* (2014); *Resilient Teachers, Resilient Schools* (2014); *The International Handbook of Teacher and School Development* (2012); *New Understandings of Teachers' Work: Emotions and Educational Change* (2011); *Successful School Leadership: Linking with Learning and Achievement* (2011); *The New Lives of Teachers* (2009); *Teachers Matter* (2007); *Successful Principalship: International Perspectives* (2007); *A Passion for Teaching* (2004); *International Handbook of the Continuing Professional Development of Teachers* (2004); *Effective Leadership for School Improvement* (2003); *Theory and Practice in Action Research* (2002) (coedited); *Developing Teachers: The Challenges of Lifelong Learning* (1999).

Christopher Day is ranked 130 in the world and 20 in the UK by Research.com's citation-based ranking of the top 1000 scientists in the area of Social Sciences and Humanities, and is among only nine educational leadership researchers in the top 1000 social scientists in the world. His numerous research studies have been instrumental in improving the effectiveness of school leaders and teachers, reforming school leadership practices and organizational strategies, and impacting on educational policy in the UK and internationally.

In recognition of his international work in the field of continuing professional development for teachers, he was awarded an Honorary Doctorate from the University of Linkoping, Sweden, in 1993 and, in 2010, the Michael Huberman Award for Excellence in Research on Teachers by the American Educational Research Association. In 2009, he was awarded a D.Litt by the University of Nottingham, and in 2012, he was elected as a Fellow of the Academy of Social Sciences. He was also awarded an honorary doctorate by the Education University of Hong Kong in 2018.

Christopher Day has also an impressive reputation as a teacher and supervisor. He supervised research students working toward research degrees in the following areas: school leadership and change; teachers' work and lives; continuing professional development; leadership; teacher thinking; reflection; qualitative research; action research; biography and narrative; school development, change and improvement.

His outstanding work as an editor and author is recognized internationally, particularly his editorial book work, his international research and his publications. His work on teaching, teachers' lives, and school leadership is particularly relevant and influential internationally. He is an exemplary scholar, an outstanding academic, and a visionary leader for change. His international experience, editorships, research, publications, honors, research student supervision, and teaching clearly demonstrate the excellence of his work and his international reputation not only at the ISATT community but also beyond. Such is the legacy that Christopher Day leaves ISATT.

TRIBUTE TO JUDITH WARREN LITTLE

Rebecca Cheung

Judith Warren Little's research focuses on teachers' work and careers, the organizational and policy contexts of teaching, and teachers' professional development. In particular, she investigates the policies and resources that support or constrain teacher learning in both formal professional development and informal workplace settings. In pursuing these interests for over 40 years, she has attempted to balance attention to the daily life of schools and locally situated meanings, identities, and relationships with a broader view of the social, institutional, and policy environments in which the work of teaching resides. In recent years, she has also pursued an interest in national and international developments in the composition, quality, distribution, and preparation of the teacher workforce, and has become involved in cross-field studies of education for the professions. In 2021, she chaired the planning committee for *Covid-19 and the Teacher Workforce*, a two-day workshop of the US National Academies of Sciences, Engineering and Medicine. Throughout her distinguished career, Judith received many awards including the Frank H. Klassen Award for leadership and scholarly contributions in teacher education from the International Council on Education for Teaching (2008). She became an elected member of the National Academy of Education in 2000 and was elected as a Fellow of the American Educational Research Association in 2009.

Born in Amherst, a suburb of Buffalo, NY, Judith attended the Park School of Buffalo, a school started by a protégé of John Dewey's: Mary Hammet Lewis, who wrote *An Adventure with Children*. The world Lewis describes is the world Judith was fortunate to inhabit as a student at Park – a school that cultivated individual interests and talents while also building strong bonds of community and a sense of collective responsibility to the public good. Judith describes her experiences at the Park School of Buffalo as "a place that shaped my ideas about a good school at a young age." Later, Judith attended Brown University and then (after a move) the University of Colorado, earning a BA in English Literature and a teaching credential in secondary school English. She started her career as a substitute teacher in mountain schools near Boulder, discovering that schools were not the most professionalized of workplaces. That sobering realization inspired much of the research she has done throughout her career. Eventually, Judith earned her PhD in sociology at the University of Colorado, with a focus on ethnomethodology, sociolinguistics, and the study of workplace interaction and learning.

After several years at a small research organization in Boulder, Judith was recruited in 1983 to Far West Laboratory for Educational Research and Development in San Francisco (now WestEd) as a Senior Program Director, leading studies of teachers' work, teacher collaboration, teachers' professional development, and teacher leadership. She took a faculty position at the University of California, Berkeley, in 1987 and was named an Endowed Chair in Education Policy in 2002. In 2010, Judith was appointed as the first female Dean of the Graduate School of Education, a groundbreaking appointment after a 100-year history of male leadership.

At the encouragement of colleagues in 1993, Judith joined what was then known as the International Study Association on Teacher Thinking (ISATT) because it had evolved to embrace multidisciplinary perspectives on teachers' work and aspects of teaching beyond teacher thinking. In total, she participated in five conferences between 1993 and 2003. At the 1993 conference in Gothenburg, Sweden, she remembers being struck by the depth of intimate conversation that flowed from each session throughout the day into evening meals. In 1995, at Brock University in St. Catherines, Ontario, Judith presented the paper, *A Ground to Stand On: Paradoxes of Professional Identity and Community Within Interdisciplinary Teams*. In 1997, in Kiel, Germany, she presented *Teachers' Work Conditions and Professional Development in 'Ordinary' and 'Innovating' Secondary Schools*. For the 2001 conference in Faro, Portugal, she gave an invited address entitled, *Inside Teacher Community: Representations of Classroom Practice*. The address later became a published article in *Teachers College Record*. Finally, at the 2003 conference in Leiden, the Netherlands, she contributed to a pre-conference workshop on Qualitative Data Analysis, focusing on establishing a "transparent path of inference."

Judith reflected, "it was through ISATT that I established relationships with colleagues in the Netherlands, Belgium, Norway, Portugal, England, Australia, and elsewhere; many of these have lasted my whole career." Among those colleagues is Professor Klaas van Veen of Groningen University who shared, "Professor Judith Warren Little's perspective on teachers' work and especially how the organization of teachers' work impacts how they learn and especially how their students learn influenced me deeply." Klaas and Judith met at AERA in 1999 when he was a PhD student. After his presentation, she walked up to him, peered over her reading glasses, and asked to meet later that evening. ISATT helped them stay connected and upon graduation, he spent a year in Berkeley joining Judith's Friday research group. Of note was the way she guided students to improve. "In contrast to what I would call the Dutch style of bluntly directing, Judith asked questions. These questions helped the student self-evaluate the strong and the weak points of their work, motivating them to revise and write. I [Klaas] feel honored that I had the opportunity to meet her and learn so much from her."

Judith has many fond memories of the intellectual exchanges and friendships established through ISATT, as well as the joys of international travel. From Sweden, for example, she still has the wool cape she bought because it was reportedly the coldest summer in 50 years. At the conference in Gothenburg, Judith described the intimate design of the conference space and the sessions that allowed for both formal and informal discussion. A vigorous discussion centered on a reconsideration of Daniel Lortie's book *Schoolteacher*, which remains of particular note to this day. The connections established through ISATT also went beyond conferences, and she has sustained career-long relationships with colleagues she met at them. While no longer an active member, Judith continues to read the ISATT journal with interest.

SECTION 2
TEACHER EDUCATION REFORM

INTRODUCTION

Diane Yendol-Hoppey

> If a nation's children are not doing well in schools, if a nation's teachers don't appear to be well-prepared for their jobs, if they choose not to go into hard-to-staff schools, or if they choose not to stay in teaching, eyes turn to teacher preparation. (Aydarova, 2015, p. 10)

Because of these pressures, teacher education has been at the center of educational reform and policy mandates for decades. No matter where we are in the world, teacher education reform is recognized as a critical component of the broader educational reform terrain. As a result, attention must be given to teacher education reform if we are to improve teaching practice and student performance. To these ends, teacher educators face a multitude of reforms consisting of standards and curricular revision, policy initiatives including government-driven mandates that include the whims of politicians, financial shifts, accreditation, public perceptions, and attitudes about the purposes of education and the teaching profession, current trends in public schools and higher education, and the professions own initiatives to name a few (Wiseman, 2012).

Given the importance of context in teacher education reform, readers of this section are invited to metaphorically travel across contexts to identify similarities and differences in the tensions and outcomes related to reform from an international perspective. Over a decade ago, Wang et al. (2010) recognized that:

> Teacher education reform has become an international trend (Bates, 2008; Garm & Karlsen, 2004), which in spite of the different national contexts and traditions, shares a set of similar expectations, foci, and even policy interventions. (Loomis et al., 2008)

Across these global contexts, improving teacher education likely requires aligning efforts to comprehensively reinvent, reorganize, and revitalize our field by creating systems that allow for the preparation of excellent teachers. The chapters in this section are dedicated to exploring teacher education reform by collectively investigating the past, present, and future directions of teacher education.

The section begins with *Tensions and Paradoxes in Teaching: Implications for Teacher Education*. In this chapter, Ben-Peretz and Flores set the stage for understanding teacher education reform as they describe the tensions and paradoxes that exist in the highly varied contexts within which we work. These tensions are particularly relevant as we globally seek to prepare teachers for diverse student populations. The authors raise important questions that provide insight into the conflicting values that often emerge such as preparing teachers who will have professional autonomy and discretion versus preparing educators for externally imposed educational policy focused on achieving immediate results and success in external exams.

Recognizing these tensions and paradoxes, our global journey of teacher education reform begins in Kenya followed by visits to Scotland, the United States, and France to provide teacher educators insights into the kaleidoscope of dimensions impacting teacher education within and across contexts allowing us to identify both similarities and differences in the impacts of teacher education reform around the world. Samuel Oyoo, in his chapter, *Teacher Education Reforms in Kenya: Presenting the Past and Present, and Mapping the Future*, takes us on a journey of teacher education reform in Kenya beginning in the mid-nineteenth century where European Christian Missionaries led the establishment of teacher education programs patterned after Western Europe and Canada. Since then, the preparation of Kenya's teachers has undergone massive reforms in structure and scope. This chapter reports and analyzes the trends in teacher education reforms and identifies future reforms needed to enhance teacher education programs in order for teachers to enact the Competency-Based Curriculum sought for Kenyan schools.

Our journey continues into Scotland with McMahon et al.'s chapter, *Teacher Education Reform in Scotland*. Although part of the United Kingdom, the authors illustrate Scotland's own distinctive education and schooling system, with university-based teacher education preparing teachers through an all graduate profession. The chapter begins in 1965 with the establishment of a regulatory body for the teaching profession and traces reform through the twenty-first century where they outline the two major reform programs that seriously have impacted the teaching profession. Just as our illustration from Kenya revealed, major reform currently underway will make further changes for teacher education likely.

The nature of ongoing reform continues as we visit the teacher education context in the United States. In the chapter *Teacher Education Reform in the United States: Colliding Forces?*, Yendol-Hoppey, Jacobs, and Tanase focus primarily on the last decade of reform in the United States, and they argue that these reforms are positioned to collide with one another as well as the reforms currently ongoing in PK-12 education. These colliding forces make a systematically and intentionally designed system for change unlikely. Insights garnered from the US teacher education reform activities demonstrate the complexity of reform and focus on four main areas: (1) strengthening the clinical component of teacher education, (2) preparing educators with the tools needed for equity and social justice, (3) participating in heightened accountability demands, and (4) expanding alternative certification.

Finally, Châteaureynaud and Deyrich invite us into the French context of teacher education. Their chapter *Innovative Research Training in Higher Education for LSP Teachers: From Institutional Policy to the Development of Custom-Made Projects* helps us explore the importance of ongoing reform and what happens when teacher education reform is leaving gaps in the support for teacher preparation for most teachers of languages for specific purposes (LSP). The chapter describes how university teacher educators pivoted during the pandemic to create online professional support to create professional learning using a distance learning format. The authors describe how the innovative online training module utilized action research and resulted in the empowerment of participants. This work returns us to the work of Ben-Peretz and Flores by reflecting on the values of teacher autonomy and professional discretion as well as the role that research should be positioned to play in the work of educational reform.

REFERENCES

Aydarova, O. (2015). Glories of the soviet past or dim visions of the future: Russian teacher education as the site of historical becoming. *Anthropology and Education Quarterly, 46*(2), 147–166. https://doi.org/10.1111/aeq.12096

Bates, R. (2008). Teacher education in a global context: Towards a defensible theory of teacher education. *Journal of Education for Teaching, 34*(4), 277–293.

Garm, N., & Karlsen, G. E. (2004). Teacher education reform in Europe: The case of Norway; trends and tensions in a global perspective. *Teaching and Teacher Education, 20*(7), 731–744.

Loomis, S., Rodriguez, J., & Tillman, R. (2008). Developing into similarity: Global teacher education in the twenty-first century. *European Journal of Teacher Education, 31*(3), 233–245.

Wang, J., Odell, S. J., Klecka, C. L., Spalding, E., & Lin, E. (2010). Understanding teacher education reform. *Journal of Teacher Education, 61*(5), 395–402. https://doi.org/10.1177/0022487110384219

Wiseman, D. L. (2012). The intersection of policy, reform, and teacher education. *Journal of Teacher Education, 63*(2), 87–91. https://doi.org/10.1177/0022487111429128

TENSIONS AND PARADOXES IN TEACHING: IMPLICATIONS FOR TEACHER EDUCATION*

Miriam Ben-Peretz and Maria Assunção Flores

ABSTRACT

This chapter focuses on the tensions and paradoxes in teaching. At present time, teacher education has the obligation to prepare teachers for diverse student populations, living in a highly varied context. This situation creates several competing expectations of the meaning of teacher education, for instance, preparing for professional autonomy in a world of externally imposed educational policy. The tension between achieving immediate results and success in external exams versus the need to prepare students in an era of migration and growing multiculturalism in school contexts is addressed. It is argued that a common knowledge base is a necessary response to growing multiculturalism while simultaneously leaving space in the curriculum for multicultural aspects of the student population. These double requirements have implications for teacher education which are discussed in the last section of the chapter.

Keywords: Teaching; teacher education; policy implementation; professional autonomy; multiculturalism

---

*This chapter was originally published in full by Taylor & Francis: Ben-Peretz, M., Assunção Flores. (2018) "Tensions and paradoxes in teaching: implications for teacher education". *European Journal of Teacher Education*, Volume 41, Issue 2. https://doi.org/10.1080/02619768.2018.1431216. This version published under non-exclusive license, Emerald Publishing.

Teaching and Teacher Education in International Contexts
Advances in Research on Teaching, Volume 42, 33–38
Copyright © 2023 Emerald Publishing Limited, with the exception of Tensions and Paradoxes in Teaching: Implications for Teacher Education © Taylor & Francis.
All rights of reproduction in any form reserved
ISSN: 1479-3687/doi:10.1108/S1479-368720230000042009

Teachers' work has been affected by policy environments in many contexts in diverse ways. Several issues relating to the relationship between the societal environment and the content and process of teacher education have been chosen to be dealt with in this work. These issues make teacher education a highly complex process raising many problems and having important implications for the process itself. Issues such as the rise of a performance culture through increased accountability and imposition of standards (Sachs, 2016), the compliance of teachers with the demands of performance policies and the tyranny of audit (Lo, 2012), the decline in teacher autonomy, and an environment of distrust have been identified in many parts of the world (Sachs & Mockler, 2012). Added to these are, more recently, issues of increased diversity of student populations and school contexts owing to migration and multiculturalism. All of these have implications for teachers' work and teacher education.

Teacher professionalism is shaped by external environments, and, in times of increased accountability and regulation, different discourses of professionalism proliferate, gaining legitimacy and impact on how professionalism is understood and enacted (Sachs, 2016). Drawing attention to the "multi-faceted and complex" nature of teachers' responses to imposed change, Osborn underlines that "externally imposed requirements are mediated by the perceptions, understandings, motivation and capacity of both individual and groups of teachers in different contexts to produce particular practices and actions" (Osborn, 2006, p. 252). Thus, in different times, different responses are required (Sachs, 2016).

In this chapter, we look at current tensions and paradoxes in teaching. In the first part of the chapter, we look at the competing expectations of teachers' work related to the implementation of externally determined policy and the exercise of professional autonomy. We focus, as well, on the tension between achieving immediate results and success in external exams, versus the need to prepare students in an era of migration and growing multiculturalism in school contexts. It is argued that a common knowledge base is a necessary response to growing multiculturalism, while simultaneously leaving space in the curriculum for multicultural aspects of the student population. In the last part of this work, we discuss the implications for teacher education.

THE PARADOX OF IMPLEMENTING EXTERNAL POLICY VERSUS USING PROFESSIONAL AUTONOMY

In the next section, we analyze the paradox of implementing external policy versus using professional autonomy in the light of international research literature. Several terms seem to govern the way teachers' work is presented in the literature. Among these terms, accountability, efficiency, and effectiveness, as well as managerial professionalism play a central role. In general, trends in international research literature suggest that teachers' work has become increasingly demanding and complex over the last decades. Accountability, new forms of managerialism, and a "new vocabulary of performance" (Ball, 2003, p. 7) have dominated the education agenda worldwide. This situation has implications for schools and teachers' work within the context of greater economic competitiveness in a globalized world.

Despite externally imposed changes on schools and teachers' work, it seems that teachers respond differently to school reform and policy initiatives. Some teachers comply with them, even if sometimes disagreeing; others translate them into practice in different ways and others seem to resist and maintain their commitment and effectiveness in times of instability and pressure due to their resilience and sense of identity (Osborn, 2006; Day & Smetham, 2009; Flores, 2011, 2012; Flores et al., 2014). In the next section, we present results from a national survey carried out in Portugal that analyzes the ways in which teachers view their work in policy context.

The Teaching Profession in the Eyes of Teachers

In a nationwide survey carried out in Portugal, in which 2,702 teachers participated, it was concluded that recent policy initiatives associated with a context of austerity and economic crisis, had a deep influence on teachers. This situation led to greater control of teachers' work, to an increase of their workload and bureaucracy and to a deterioration of their working conditions including their social economic status. This study also indicated that teachers have been subject to greater public scrutiny and that the image of teaching and teachers in the media has contributed to the deterioration of the teaching profession as well as to a decrease in teachers' motivation (Flores et al., 2014).

These findings parallel those in other countries which relate to current tensions and contradictions that mark teachers' work. Looking at the opportunities and threats in teaching, among other features, Hargreaves and Fullan (2012, p. 43) noted that there was "more interactive professionalism among teachers but they also warned that it "can turn into hyperactive professionalism" as teachers are thrown into hurried meetings to devise quick-fix solutions that will lead to instantaneous gains in student achievement results" (Hargreaves & Fullan, 2012, p. 43).

In the next section, we explore the possibilities and opportunities for teacher agency and professionalism in contexts marked by accountability and performativity agendas.

Teacher Agency and Professionalism

Teacher professional agency relates to the ability of teachers to control their work within structural constraints (Quinn & Carl, 2015). Teachers' control of their work is a key capability for facilitating student learning, as well as for continuing individual and collective teacher professional development (Toom et al., 2015).

Conversely, teachers might make use of their professional space even in contexts marked by growing standardization (Oolbekkink-Marchand et al., 2017).

THE TENSION BETWEEN OBTAINING IMMEDIATE RESULTS AND PREPARING STUDENTS FOR MULTICULTURALISM IN SCHOOLS

Over the last decades, schools and teachers have been confronted with new challenges, including multiculturalism, changes in social agencies regarding family welfare, competing educational agenda, migration, and implications for teaching and learning in the digital era. Teachers' work has become more fragmented and complex and more demanding in terms of creating learning situations for an increasing number of diverse student populations (Day, 1999; Estrela, 2001; Hargreaves, 2001; Klette, 2002; Day & Sachs, 2004). At present, teachers have to work in multicultural settings often within the context of more and more outcome-oriented education systems. Thus, they found themselves in the middle of a set of tensions as identified in the context of Nordic countries: (1) "the tension between a wider cultivating and moral mission of teaching on the one hand, and a narrow instrumental mission of teaching" on the other hand; (2) "increasing autonomy versus increased control of teachers," in which the rhetoric of teachers being autonomous professionals coexists with "growing systems of control mechanisms and of external constraints and demands" (Klette, 2002, p. 267). Similarly, it is possible to identify the increasing pressure on teachers in terms of student attainment while at the same accounting for their "well-being" and citizenship (Day & Smethem, 2009). Another pressure is for teachers to collaborate (an "imposed" collaboration) accompanied by increasing forms of managerialism and accountability in their work, along with a greater focus on student and school outcomes (Flores, 2012).

Research suggests that teachers experience intense emotional ambivalence in their efforts to cope with growing diversity and multiculturalism in schools (Zembylas, 2010). On one hand, issues of social justice and poverty, and the cultural and social aspects of teaching, might suffer lack of attention (Flores & Ferreira, 2016). On the other hand, creating an ethic of discomfort offers opportunities to challenge structures of power, privilege, racism, and oppression (Zembylas, 2010).

Multiculturalism in Teacher Education

The need for issues of diversity and multicultural perspectives to be included in initial teacher education has been advocated by several scholars (Acquash & Commins, 2013; Coronel & Gómez-Hurtado, 2015). The same authors argue that opportunities for teacher learning are crucial for developing the school ability to serve the academic, linguistic and socio-cultural needs of immigrant students.

Implications for the Future of Teacher Education

Teacher education needs to respond to increasing demands of the multicultural contexts in which teachers have to work. The need to develop inclusive pedagogies and social competence in teacher education has been advocated by many scholars. It has been recommended to promote initial teacher education diversity and intercultural competence (Keane & Heinz, 2016).

Teaching about culture in teacher education is recognized as a challenging task (Ogay & Edelmann, 2016). The authors identify intercultural metaphors of culture and argue for the dynamic and complex understanding of culture and cultural diversity in education.

The need for pedagogies of praxis that move beyond (and sometimes against) the official policy definitions of inclusion is highlighted in England by Alexiadou and Essex (2016). They draw on a more critical approach to the development of future professionals and they recognize that teacher education can act as an important agency in achieving inclusion within classrooms.

In demanding and contradictory school contexts marked by performative cultures and by the need to meet the increasingly diverse expectations and backgrounds of student populations, teachers find themselves in the middle of tensions and paradoxes that are not easy to deal with. Policy environments that are more and more outcome-oriented and school contexts that call for different responses to students' needs require teachers to master knowledge and competences to handle diversity, inclusiveness, and multiculturalism but also with accountability and competitive logics.

As Sachs and Mockler (2012) argue, the "cultures of performativity" might be seen both as a threat and as an opportunity. It is argued for a "perspective of development" that conciliates the interests of various stakeholders, community, teachers, parents, and students (Sachs & Mockler, 2012). This perspective tries to balance externally imposed accountability with the development needs of teachers. Ben-Peretz (2012) discusses the effects of the external surveillance mechanisms and the logics of regulation and measurement that have extended teachers' dilemmas as professional educators and interpreters of educational policies. She argues for the need to find a balance between accountability and professional autonomy in order to adapt accountability policies to the contexts of teachers. Similarly, it is advocated that the teaching profession needs to revitalize its professionalism in face of the adversities through a more activist position, and the promotion of essential values (Lo, 2012).

There is a need to foster in teacher education both the technical and cognitive dimensions of teaching, as well as its social and cultural dimensions. It is important to include a set of competencies for "professional and ethical" teachers in light of the moral dimension of their work dealing with a rising number of immigrant students and children with learning difficulties (Tirri, 2014). Teachers are seen as ethical professionals whose education requires more than teaching and management skills (Zeichner, 2014).

In our view, a common knowledge base of teaching is a necessary response to growing multiculturalism simultaneously leaving space in the curriculum for multicultural aspects of the student population. Such an approach might structure teacher education programs that have a common core of general topics, such as teaching and learning modes, that apply to all students. This core might be accompanied by courses focusing on diverse ethnic-cultural groups, with their specific histories and traditional modes of teaching and learning. Such a global view of teacher education programs might serve the creation of some unity in processes of teaching and learning, on one hand, while expanding the world of potential diversity and learning about others, on the other hand. As human beings, we share some unifying characteristics, while celebrating as well cultural diversity. A film called "babies" (2010) showed how different cultures treat their children in the first year of life. The differences are enormous, but in the end all children learn to walk and talk.

REFERENCES

Ben-Peretz, M. (2012). Accountability vs. Teacher autonomy. An issue of balance. In C. Day (Ed.), *The routledge international handbook of teacher and school development* (pp. 57–66). Routledge.

Day, C., & Sachs, J. (2004). Professionalism, performativity and empowerment: Discourses in the politics, policies and purposes of continuing professional development. In C. Day, & J. Sachs (Eds.), *International handbook on the continuing professional development of teachers*. Open University.

Flores, M. A. (2012). Teachers' work and lives: A European perspective. In C. Day (Ed.), *The routledge international handbook of teacher and school development* (pp. 94–107). Routledge.

Flores, M. A., & Ferreira, F. I. (2016). Education and child poverty in times of austerity in Portugal: Implications for teachers and teacher education. *Journal of Education for Teaching, 42*(4), 404–416.

Sachs, J. (2016). Teacher professionalism: Why are we still talking about it?. *Teachers and Teaching: Theory and Practice, 22*(4), 413–425.

Sachs, J., & Mockler, N. (2012). Performance cultures of teaching. Threat or opportunity?. In C. Day (Ed.), *The routledge international handbook of teacher and school development* (pp. 33–43). Routledge.

Zeichner, K. (2014). The struggle for the soul of teaching and teacher education in the USA. *Journal of Education for Teaching, 40*(5), 551–568.

Zembylas, M. (2010). Teachers' emotional experiences of growing diversity and multiculturalism in schools and the prospects of an ethic of discomfort. *Teachers and Teaching: Theory and Practice, 16*(6), 703–716.

TEACHER EDUCATION REFORMS IN KENYA: THE PAST, THE PRESENT, AND MAPPING THE FUTURE

Samuel Ouma Oyoo, Maureen Atieno Olel, Maurine Kang'ahi and Francis Chisikwa Indoshi

ABSTRACT

Teacher education in Kenya was formally started in mid-nineteenth century by European Christian missionaries. The urge to establish teacher education programs at the time was to address the shortage of teachers due to the unplanned and rapid expansion of schools. The need to produce schoolteachers was also to relieve missionaries who were required to concentrate on evangelization. At their inception, teacher education programs were patterned on Western European and Canadian established teacher education models of the early nineteenth century. The education (preparation) of teachers in Kenya has over time undergone massive reforms including in structure and scope. This chapter presents both reports and analyses of the trends in the teacher education reforms to date. Also included in the chapter are recommendations/debates on more reforms/changes needed to enable teacher education programs to equip teachers for effective practice in the twenty-first century including the successful implementation of the Competency Based Curriculum in Kenyan schools.

Keywords: Teacher education; Kenya; reforms; competency based curriculum; twenty-first century skills; teacher certification

All societies in the world have always needed teachers (as the knowledgeable others) to propagate or transmit their cultures from one generation to another

(Kafu, 2011; Ssekamwa, 1969). In order to be effective in this task in formal settings, practicing teachers will necessarily have undertaken a recognized pedagogical training program and attained accredited certification. This requirement is a revelation that teacher education is indeed a key component of education. This chapter discusses teacher education developments in Kenya; the "examination of education system in Kenya from ancient times to today reveals that elaborate and deliberate practices of teacher education existed" (Kafu, 2011, p. 44) though this was in indigenous and traditional African education systems (Kenyatta, 1963). With this particular focus, the teacher education system may not have been formal in the sense of Western European education systems. However, this "informal" teacher education system produced competent teachers who sustained the African indigenous/traditional education systems (Indire & Sifuna, 1974). But since these practices of teacher education were not properly documented, the focus of this chapter will be on the formal teacher education in Kenya. It presents reports and analyses of the trends in the formal teacher education reforms from its inception to today. Also included in the chapter are recommendations/debates on other reforms/changes needed to enable teacher education programs to be able to equip teachers for effective practice in the twenty-first century including in the successful implementation of the Competency Based Curriculum already introduced to Kenyan schools up to grade 6 in 2022.

HISTORICAL DEVELOPMENT OF TEACHER EDUCATION IN KENYA

Formal teacher education preparation program was introduced in Kenya in the mid-nineteenth century by European Christian missionaries (Kafu, 2011). This program of education was patterned on the Western European and Canadian established teacher education models of the early nineteenth century. The urge to establish teacher education programs at the time was necessitated by the rapid expansion of the school system in Kenya (Indire & Sifuna, 1974), a development that called for an equally sharp increase in the supply of teachers to work in the newly established schools. In addition, there was need to produce schoolteachers to relieve missionaries who were required to concentrate on missionary/evangelization work. Since the schools established by the Christian missionaries provided primary education (Classes B and A, and Standards I–IV) schools and intermediate (Standards V–VIII) schools (Indire & Sifuna, 1974), they needed primary school teachers. The designed teacher education preparation program, conducted by the missionaries themselves, therefore catered mainly for Primary School leavers from the level of Standard[1] Three to Eight (Standard III–VIII). This shows that most of the teacher-trainees were of low academic qualifications although for that period in time, they were the most well-educated individuals (Kafu, 2011). Initially, the teachers were awarded with the Elementary Teacher Certificate. In 1948, rules for the issue teacher certification were changed. T4 certificate replaced the elementary teacher's certificate. The T4 were to teach up to standard IV; T3 replaced lower primary school teachers' certificate and were to teach up to standard VI. T2 were to teach up to Form II.[2]

An important turn in teacher education took place after the First World War (1914-1918). The increased demand for African education especially higher education was referred to as secondary school education. This demand led to establishment of secondary schools which needed teachers of higher caliber. Consequently, Makerere College in neighboring Uganda was established to train teachers of Diploma in Education qualifications in the early 1940s (Ole Katitia, 2015; Karanja, 1995). This was followed by the introduction of Kenyatta College in 1965 and Kenya Science Teachers College in 1966 to train S1 teachers, and then Kenya Technical Teachers College in 1977 to train teachers in technical subjects at Diploma level (Otiende et al., 1992). However, much earlier and meant to compliment the effort of Makerere University College, University of Nairobi College had started training graduate secondary teachers with Bachelor of Arts/Bachelor of Science (Education option) qualification in 1966. The BA/BSc (Education option) was later transformed into the Bachelor of Education (BEd) Arts/Science professional degree qualification in 1970. The preparation of graduate teachers holding the BEd qualification was expanded with the establishment of Kenyatta University College in 1972. Today all the public universities in Kenya, except Jomo Kenyatta, the Technical University of Kenya, Multimedia and the Technical University of Mombasa offer degrees in education (Maangi et al., 2013).

The teacher education preparation programs in Kenya have been to prepare teachers to meet the challenge of the shortage of teachers in the country in the pre-primary, primary and the secondary school levels. However, as now evidenced, the hosting of the preparation programs have all not been hosted at fully formal institutions. Currently there are five teacher education *programs/levels in Kenya. These reveal that the hosting of the preparation programs have not* all been at fully formal institutions.

CURRENT PROGRAMS OF TEACHER EDUCATION IN KENYA

Otunga et al. (2011) have documented the four levels of teacher education in Kenya: Early Childhood Development Education (ECDE), Primary Teacher Education, Diploma and graduate teacher education. Each of these is now discussed in some detail.

For a long period of time, training of *early childhood development teacher* has not been taken seriously. Different agencies train the ECDE teachers in different ways. Training is usually offered by the district centers for early childhood (DICECE) and Montessori. Entry qualifications for training are usually low. Kenya Certificate of Primary Education (KCPE) holders can be admitted to the proficiency course offered by the Kenya National Examination Council (KNEC). Upon completion of the proficiency course, they can be admitted for a certificate course. Equally, KCSE D+ holders can be admitted directly to the certificate program. The ECDE diploma program requires one to have a C (plain) at Kenya Certificate of Secondary Examination (KCSE) or its equivalent, a certificate course in ECDE or P1. ECDE centers are run by communities, parents, and churches. Most of the certificate holders teach at these centers. The diploma in ECDE attracts the P1 teachers because it costs less in ECDE training centers. The central government through the Teachers' Service Commission does not employ ECDE teachers but they promote the P1 teachers who acquire ECDE diploma qualifications. Various universities in Kenya including Moi, Kenyatta, Nairobi, Kabianga, Maasai Mara, Pwani, and other private universities are training ECDE teachers at degree and even postgraduate level (Namunga & Otunga, 2012).

As may already be evident, *primary teacher education* has had the longest history than the other levels. Currently, there are 21 public primary teacher training colleges and about 70 private colleges. The private colleges have played an enormous role in providing training opportunities for primary school teachers. The teacher training in primary teachers' colleges undergo a preservice training of 2 years after successful completion, they are awarded a primary teacher education certificate (Namunga & Otunga, 2012). Currently, the entry qualification to the training is C (plain) at KCSE or its equivalent and a D (plain) in mathematics and C− (minus) in English. The training colleges have a curriculum that was revised in 2004. The broad curriculum enables the teacher trainees to study ten subjects in first year and then specialize in the second year. They specialize in either Sciences or Arts. Teaching practice sessions are usually thorough and are conducted three times, once in the first year and two times in the second year (Aglazor, 2017; Republic of Kenya, 2001). Primary teacher education is also offered at diploma and degree levels. Egerton and Moi Universities have pioneered in this endeavor.

The *diploma teacher education* usually prepares teachers to teach at secondary schools. The program takes 3 years. In recent years, diploma teacher education doesn't attract many trainees, perhaps because the admission requirement is the same as for degree programs in education: a C+ (plus) at KCSE and at least a C+ (plus) in each of the two subjects of specialization. In addition, those taking sciences must have a C (plain) in mathematics, a D+ (plus) for those taking humanities and C (plain) in English for all the applicants. Currently, Kagumo offers the sciences and Kibabii offers the humanities.

Diploma teacher education for *special education teachers* is offered at the Kenya Institute of Special Education (KISE). The program targets P1certificate holders with a C (plain) at KCSE. Additionally, the Kenya Technical Teachers' College (KTTC) offers technical education at diploma level.

Regarding the *graduate teacher preparation*, this is the level at which teachers holding the Bachelor of Education as the qualification are prepared. Maangi et al. (2013) and Ole Katitia (2015) confirm that the Bachelor of Education programs are designed to train/prepare teachers for: Secondary Schools, Primary Teacher Education Colleges and Diploma Teacher Education Colleges. The program is offered in different specializations including Arts, Science, Technology, Early childhood and primary education studies, and finally guidance and counseling. The most popular Bachelor of Education specializations/programs are the BEd (Arts) and BEd (Science). The BEd course has two major components: the teaching subject content and the professional component. The subject content component is where respective prospective teachers of particular subjects are taken through advanced topics in the subjects they would be teaching in the schools and colleges, i.e., mathematics, physics, geography. The professional component includes studies in educational psychology, educational foundations areas, curriculum and instruction, issues in education management, tests and measurement or assessment issues, and common units in Environmental studies, HIV/AIDS, and special needs in education issues. Teaching practice is also compulsory and preservice teachers must obtain a pass in it before being awarded the Bachelor of Education degree certificate (Maangi et al., 2013; Ole Katitia, 2015; Otunga et al., 2011).

At each of the levels or respective teacher education programs, the curricula are such that on certification, any graduate, in the main have been able to competently handle all that comes with teaching at respective levels, be it at ECDE, primary schools, secondary schools as well as at both primary and diploma teacher education colleges. The demands of teaching in the twenty-first century as discussed immediately below are however placing new demands on the teacher and teacher education management, especially because of what it takes to successfully teach the twenty-first-century learner.

DEMANDS ON TEACHERS FOR SUCCESSFUL PRACTICE IN THE TWENTY-FIRST CENTURY

First, the teacher preparation education program needs to include content knowledge which is about the actual subject matter to be learned or taught. Teachers needs to understand and know the subjects that they teach including the knowledge of central facts, concepts, theories, and even procedures within a given field, knowledge of explanatory frameworks that organize and connect ideas, and knowledge of the rules of evidence and proof (Atieno, 2022; Shulman, 1986). In addition, prospective teachers also need to understand the nature of knowledge and inquiry in different fields. For example, how is a proof in mathematics different from an explanation in history or geography? This is because if they lack the understanding, they might misrepresent those subjects to their learners (Ball & McDiarmid, 1990).

Further, the twenty first-century teachers need to understand the person, the spirit, of every child and find a way to nurture that spirit. And they need the skills to construct and manage classroom activities efficiently, communicate well, use technology, and reflect on their practice to learn from and improve it continually. Thus, schools of education must design programs that help prospective teachers to understand deeply a wide array of things about learning, social and cultural contexts, and teaching and be able to enact these understandings in complex classrooms serving increasingly diverse students; in addition, if prospective teachers are to succeed at this task, schools of education must design programs that transform the kinds of settings in which novices learn to teach and later become teachers.

An educational program for both prospective and practicing teachers needs to develop their pedagogical content knowledge (PCK) which is how particular topics, problems or issues are organized, presented and adapted to the diverse interests and abilities of learners. PCK equips teachers on how to transform content to the learners (Atieno, 2022; Shulman, 1987). Consequently, teachers need to integrate and use knowledge in skillful ways in the classroom and not only worry about what to teach but how to teach, teachers also need to figure out what students know and believe about a topic and how the learners are likely to get new ideas from it through interacting with them and also involving them in the discussion.

In Kenyan teachers training colleges, emphasis is on child-centered and interactive pedagogic methodologies. However, these methodologies are unduly influenced by the nature and purpose of examinations administered at the end of the program. These examinations and the general assessment tools are mainly used as final judgment instruments and they often incidentally test low levels of achievement and factual cognitive domain traits. Since the pedagogics and methodologies are heavily influenced by examinations, Teacher's preparation colleges should give a greater weight to the trainees' ability to organize educational assessment. Consequently, teacher preparation colleges need to change from traditional models of teacher education is the importance of extensive and intensely supervised clinical work tightly integrated with course work that allows candidates to learn from expert practice in schools that serve diverse students. All the adjectives in the previous sentence matter: extensive clinical work, intensive supervision, expert modeling of practice, and diverse students are critical to allowing candidates to learn to practice in practice with students who call for serious teaching skills (Ole Katitia, 2015). Securing these features will take radical overhaul of the status quo. Furthermore, to be most powerful, this work needs to incorporate newly emerging pedagogies such as close analyses of learning and teaching, case methods, performance assessments, and action research that link theory and practice in ways that theorize practice and make formal learning practical.

Teacher preparation for the twenty first century needs to include the issue of clinical schools. This clinical school helps teachers transform knowledge gained through course work into skilled practice, and it expose teachers to real teaching for a long time before posted to various schools. In addition, Darling-Hammond (1996) states that teachers' preparations need to encourage the teaching of skills in using array of teaching strategies like the cooperative learning and even classroom management, and technologies as this will increase effectiveness in working with students from diverse backgrounds. In clinical school the prospective teachers will learn through observation of the learners, learn to assess learners authentically and get to understand how children learn, through this they will be able to strengthen their practice. At the clinical schools beginning teachers get the opportunity to work with senior teachers who will work as mentors, co-researchers and teacher leaders. Moreover, the prospective teachers are engaged in studying research and conducting their own inquiries through action research, cases, and even structured reflections. In Kenya, teachers are taken out for teaching practice by their respective institutions for a period of 3 weeks. This is a short period and teachers would not have interacted with the learners' very well and that at the end of the 3 weeks nothing much would have been covered by the teacher.

The twenty first-century teacher preparation should include the teaching of the special need learners in the regular classroom. Thus, it is imperative that teachers are trained to handle inclusive classrooms. In Kenyan context, the prospective teachers' curriculum has very little to offer on handling these learners and those who need to specialize in that field have to take a special course. However, dual training in general and special education may produce educators who are more willing and capable to deal with students with diverse learning needs in the same regular classes. This suggests that teachers need much deeper knowledge including for teaching of diverse learners (Darling Hammond, 2006). The current curricula in some teacher preparation institutions in Kenya already include skills in the handling of the special learners.

The twenty first-century teachers need to be familiar with the new technology and incorporate it in classroom teaching. This use of technology in learning helps the students interacts with the contents, programmed interface, the instructor, and other learners both individually and in groups (Ole Katitia, 2015). The use of technology in teaching in classroom requires the prospective teachers to have used the facilities and are familiar with the use of ICT in their classes. Indeed, the teachers need to have skills on the operating particular technologies, which includes knowledge of operating systems and computers hardware and also use standard sets of software tools such as word processors, spreadsheets, browsers, and emails.

It is of great importance also for the prospective and the practicing teachers to understand about curriculum resources and technologies to connect their students with sources of information and knowledge that allows them to explore ideas acquire and synthesize information. For example, learners can play with the computers and construct shapes and forms which change the nature of learning geometry (Darling-Hammond, 2005). In order for this to happen, teachers need to be trained to use technology. In my context, teachers are not trained on the integration of the technology and computers and hence are not able to use to integrate with their classroom teaching. For example, donors donated computers to my school and they were kept in the storeroom as there was no teacher with computer skills.

Technology can and should be used to support new social arrangements in teacher education. It may be useful for teacher preparation institutions to think of one of their responsibilities as the need to produce technically literate teaching professionals. At the core of all communities are their literacies. Accordingly, schools will have to develop specific use of technology. However, the tasks of teacher preparation should first be to recognize and include these literacies and secondly, to deepen and articulate these emerging literacies. Teachers in the early twenty-first century will need to be fluent in the school-centered uses of general productivity tools. Second, teachers will need to be fluent in the distinctive technologies that are in use in their specialized communities of practice (i.e., mathematics). We now turn to these general and distinctive technical literacies.

Furthermore, the prospective and practicing teachers need to understand what individual learners believe about themselves, what they care about, and what tasks are likely to give them enough success to encourage them to work hard to learn. The theory underpinning this concept is Vygotsky (1987) theory of social constructivism which states that learners are capable of constructing their own knowledge. Additionally, the theory of social learning states that people learn from one another. Though the theory states that people learn from each other, the education offered currently in our teacher preparation colleges, prepare people who assume they know everything and hence have no need to learn from their learners. The theory is contrary to Plato's view (Barrow, 2010) that knowledge is out there and people have to be taught to gain it. The teacher who is conversant with the learners will use student centered method to allow them to participate in their own learning. Dewey (1938) suggests that learners need to actively engage with the world to learn from it.

Teachers are supposed to learn to work collaboratively. This will enable them work, acquire, and continue to share knowledge on behalf of their students. Through this, teachers will be able to learn and understand how students learn and what various need if they are to learn effectively and they will incorporate into their teaching and curriculum construction. Additionally, the teachers have to understand how to structure interactions among learners such it enables learning to occur, and the prospective teachers need to collaborate with other teachers in their training as this will help them understand how to work with parents to learn more about their children and hence reshape supportive experiences at school and home. Although teachers are supposed to learn how to work with others and even the education stakeholders to understand their students, currently every teacher is working as an individual to attain the required mean score (Ole Katitia, 2015).

The prospective and the practicing teachers in the field need to be able to analyze and reflect on their practice to assess the effects of their teachings and see how to improve it for the benefit of the learners. In addition, teachers should continuously evaluate what students are thinking and understanding and see how to reshape their plans to take account of what they have discovered.

Currently, the practicing teachers are not reflective teachers in the sense that for them to understand their learners, they gauge them through the many continuous assessment tests they give them (Ole Katitia, 2015; Oyoo, 2013). This could be possible when teachers are prepared to be using action research as a way of solving the classroom problems. This is because action research is a reflective process that allows for inquiry and discussion as components of the "research." Often, action research is a collaborative activity among colleagues searching for solutions to everyday, real problems experienced in schools, or looking for ways to improve instruction and increase student achievement. Further, the teacher education program need to prepare teachers as classroom researchers and expert collaborators who can learn from one another is essential when the range of knowledge for teaching has grown so expansive that it cannot be mastered by any individual and when students' infinitely diverse ways of learning are recognized as requiring continual adaptations in teaching.

In sum, teachers are an important component of education whose services are important in the realization of educational goals the world over. Due to their central role in the enterprise of education, teachers require effective and sufficient preparation to be able to adequately carry out their roles and responsibilities. Otiende et al. (1992) acknowledge that trained teachers are vital for quality education. Teaching according to Ole Katitia (2015, p. 62) is an activity, a unique professional, rational, and human activity in which one creatively and imaginatively uses himself/herself and his/her knowledge to promote the learning and welfare of others hence need proper preparation. It is imperative to note that teachers are in charge of the education programs at all levels of education and their influence permeates all spheres of life. It is for this reason that they are regarded as the drivers of social, economic, and political development of society. Consequently, it is suggested that teacher education preparation programs should be carefully managed to incorporate all sociocultural, economic, and political aspects of life for the teachers to effectively serve their roles as instructional leaders in their spheres of influence. The best approach to realizing this is for teacher education program to be based on relevant research findings focused on enhancement of teacher education program.

An effective education program therefore will prepare teachers for the enormous tasks of the twenty first century. Educators need to prepare teachers with enough exposure through the clinical school and with the use of technology. This will prepare them to handle both large classes and diverse learners.

Furthermore, twenty-first century teachers need to be able to use technology and integrate it into their classroom teaching. The teachers also need to be prepared to use action research as a way of solving problems in their classroom. This is done through reflecting on what is being taught and how it can be changed for the benefit of the learners.

IMPLICATIONS OF DEMANDS ON TEACHER EDUCATION IN KENYA

The issues discussed about the demands on teachers in the twenty-first century have revealed that teacher education in Kenya needs a re-look at the current teacher education by making adjustments in line with the following suggestions (Otieno, 2016).

Design and Formulating of Policy Framework

This is a priority in administering teacher education program efficiently and effectively. Through this strategy the concepts of teacher education and teaching profession will be provided; guidelines for organizing and administering this program shall be stated; the proper structure and procedures for administering the program will be provided. This may reduce the existing politicization of and apparent confusion in the program.

Review of the Existing Structure of Teacher Education

There is urgent need to review the policies, administrative structures, recruitment of staff and students, financing of teacher education program and teacher education curriculum. This should be done to reflect modern needs in teacher education locally and globally. But for this process to succeed, there must be adequate and reliable sources of funding and good will from political establishment (the government and society).

Improvement of Information and Communication Systems in Teacher Education

To change for better the face of teacher education, program, teaching profession and schoolteachers respectively, there is need to adapt to and adopt new educational communication and technology materials. That is design, develop and use modern educational technology to prepare schoolteachers. This will improve the training and instruction of teachers and teacher-trainees. The initial costs of adapting to and adopting these systems may be high but the eventual benefits are rewarding.

Investment in Facilities and Resources for Teacher Education

There is concern that quality of teachers produced today is wanting (Kiptoon, 1996). The teachers are said to be incompetent, undisciplined and disinterested in their service. But the cause root(s) of this behavior is known to everyone in Kenya. This include the factors outlined and discussed elsewhere—that is, poor administration of teacher education, terms and conditions of service for teachers, teacher preparation program, etc. To reverse this trend in teacher education, the government must invest heavily in it and recognize this program as an essential service to the society. Therefore, those recruited in it should be accorded the same treatment as those in other essential services. This will attract and retain the best brains and committed individuals in this program and teaching profession respectively. But this means that the government must provide adequate funding generated through well performing economy, collaboration and co-operation with other stakeholders in teacher education and encouraging teacher training institutions to conduct income generating activities. These funds, if well managed, can be used to improve facilities and resources for the teacher preparation program.

Identity of Teacher Education

Today, there is confusion over what teacher education means and what it does. This confusion can be traced from the colonial period when emphasis was on pedagogy rather than on the preparation and development of schoolteachers and how the teacher education program was conducted. Therefore, there is a need to broaden the teacher education curriculum to include areas that are being demanded by the modern, technologically oriented society. This will ensure teachers are equipped with relevant competencies to manage emerging challenges in education and the society. In fact, this is the major shortcoming in the present teacher preparation program.

Further, there is need to professionalize teacher education further, to make it an exclusive rather than inclusive (stakeholding) enterprise. This will give a clear identity to this program and teaching profession. If this is buttressed by strong and attractive packages of terms and conditions of service for teachers, the identity of this program and teaching profession will not be a problem at all.

CONCLUSION

In this chapter, an attempt has been made to examine the present status of teacher education as practiced in Kenya to today. It has also addressed some of the issues that are impacting it. The influence of the latter on this program of education has been noted seriously. However, the conclusion to be drawn from the discussion is that the development and practice of teacher education in Kenya is not unique. It reflects the global practice of this program of education which means that Kenya needs to adopt collaborative and cooperative strategies with relevant/global stakeholders in teacher education and institute national concerted effort to promote the quality and image of teacher education program in Kenya.

AUTHOR'S NOTES

1. Elementary three or Grade 3 level equivalent.
2. Grade 10 equivalent.

REFERENCES

Aglazor, G. (2017). The role of teaching practices in teacher education programmes: Designing framework for best practice. *Global Journal of Educational Research, 16*, 101–110. http://dx.doi.org/10.4314/gjedr.v16i2.4

Atieno, R. O. (2022). Education students' pedagogical content knowledge: Retooling the professional development process in Kenya's schools of education. *African Journal of Teacher Education, a Journal of Spread Corporation*, 27–55.

Ball, D. L., & McDiarmid, G. W. (1990). The subject-matter preparation of teachers. In W. R. Houston, M. Haberman, & J. Sikula (Eds.), *Handbook of research on teacher education* (pp. 437–449). Macmillan

Barrow, R. (2010). *Plato, utilitarianism and education*. Routledge.

Darling-Hammond, L. (1996). What matters most: A competent teacher for every child? *Phi Delta Kappa, 78*(3), 193–201.

Darling-Hammond, L. (2006). Constructing 21st century teacher education. *Journal of Teacher Education, 57*(3), 300–314.

Darling-Hammond, L. (Ed.). (2005). *Professional development schools: Schools for developing a profession* (2nd ed.). Teachers College Press.

Dewey, J. (1938). *Experience and education*. MacMillan.

Indire, F. F., & Sifuna, D. N. (1974). *A history of the development of teacher education in Kenya*. University of Nairobi Press.
Kafu, P. A. (2011). Teacher education in Kenya: Emerging issues. *International Journal of Curriculum and Instruction, 1*(11), 43–52.
Karanja, M. R. (1995). *The perceptions of students in Moi and Kenyatta Universities and co-operating teachers of teaching practice procedures* (Unpublished M.Phil. thesis). Moi University, Kenya.
Kenyatta, J. (1963). *Facing Mount Kenya*. University of London Press.
Kiptoon. (1996). *Half-baked graduates: Challenges of Education in Kenya*. Nation Media Group.
Maangi, E. N., Benecha, A. J., Wekesa, N. W., Ongaga, E., & Orina, F. (2013). The changing trends in the development of teacher education in Kenya: The role of the Teacher's Service Commission. *Research on Humanities and Social Sciences, 3*(19), 82–85.
Namunga, N. W., & Otunga, R. N. (2012). Teacher education as a driver for sustainable development in Kenya. *International Journal of Humanities and Social Sciences, 2*(5), 228–234.
Ole Katitia, D. M. (2015). Teacher preparation program for the 21st century. Which way forward for Kenya? *Journal of Education and Practice, 6*(24), 57–63.
Otiende, J. E., Wamahiu, S. P., & Karagu, A. M. (1992). *Education and development in Kenya: A historical perspective*. Oxford University Press.
Otieno, M. A. (2016). *Assessment of teacher education in Kenya*. https://kerd.ku.ac.ke/handle/123456789/1005. Accessed on April 25, 2023 at 21:15 hrs EST.
Otunga, N. R., Odeo, I. I., & Barasa, L. P. (Eds.). (2011). *A handbook for curriculum and instruction*. Moi University Press.
Oyoo, S. O. (2013). Enhancing and sustaining teacher effectiveness as the "Trojan Horse" in successful science education in Kenya. In C. J. Craig, P. C. Meijer, & J. Broeckmans (Eds.), *From teacher thinking to teachers and teaching: The evolution of a research community* (pp. 457–477). Emerald Publishing Limited. https://doi.org/10.1108/S1479-3687 (2013)0000019025. ISSN: 1479-3687.
Republic of Kenya. (2001). *Primary teacher syllabus: Volume two*. Kenya Institute of Education.
Shulman, L. S. (1986). Those who understand: Knowledge growth in teaching. *Educational Researcher, 15*(2), 4–14.
Shulman, L. S. (1987). Knowledge and teaching: Foundations of the new reforms. *Harvard Educational Review, 57*(1), 1–22.
Ssekamwa, J. (1969). History of teacher education in East Africa. *Makererean*. Makerere University College.
Vygotsky, L. (1987). *Thinking and speech*. Plenum.

TEACHER EDUCATION REFORM IN SCOTLAND

Margery McMahon

ABSTRACT

Although part of the United Kingdom, Scotland has its own distinctive education and schooling system, with university-based teacher education preparing teachers for an all-graduate profession. Through the establishment, in 1965, of the General Teaching Council (GTC) as the regulatory body for the teaching profession in Scotland, the General Teaching Council of Scotland became one of the first teaching councils in the world. In the twenty-first century, there have been two major reform programs impacting the teaching profession: A Teaching Profession for the 21st Century *in 2001 and* Teaching Scotland's Future *in 2011. Currently, there is a major reform program underway arising from the recommendations of a further review looking at aspects of education reform and structural and functional change of key national agencies (the Scottish Qualifications Authority and Education Scotland). The reform program will have a number of implications for teacher education. These developments are explored in this chapter which situates them in the wider context of teacher education reform globally and current challenges such as recruitment downturns and retention issues, strengthening research on teacher education and the pressures of increasing accountability.*

Keywords: GTCS; MQuITE; Teaching Scotland's Future; professional standards; teacher education reform; accountability

Scotland is one of the devolved nations of the United Kingdom, with its own government located in the capital, Edinburgh, and a distinctive education and schooling system. A referendum in 2014 sought to establish full independence for Scotland from the UK government. Though unsuccessful then, pressure for a second referendum has gained additional momentum in recent years.

With a population of 5.47 million (National Records Office, 2022), the central belt of the cities of Edinburgh, Glasgow, and Stirling are the most densely populated, with rural and remote regions, including the Scottish islands and highlands, experiencing challenges in recruiting and retaining teachers and in ensuring equitable provision for all children and young people.

Teaching is a high-status profession with major reform programs in the twenty-first century seeking to ensure pay and parity with other professions and initiatives to improve teacher quality and leader development. A national research strategy for education was launched in 2017 (Scottish Government, 2017), though opportunities for funded research arising from this have been limited due to austerity measures. However, a partnership between teacher education providers and Scottish government supports a funded project on teacher education to provide evidence and data on quality in initial teacher education.

This chapter explores the impact of these reform programs for teaching and teacher education in Scotland. It begins by setting out the context and circumstances for teacher education before providing a critical overview of two major reform programs for workforce reform and teacher and leader development. The General Teaching Council of Scotland has had a central role in how teaching and teacher education has evolved, and this is then explored. The role of research as part of this evolution is considered, examining the rationale for the Measuring Quality in Initial Teacher Education project (MQuITE). Finally, the future implications for teacher education of systems-level reform relating to curriculum and national qualifications and the replacement of national agencies is examined.

TEACHER EDUCATION IN SCOTLAND: CONTEXT AND CIRCUMSTANCES

Teacher education in Scotland is university based and delivered by 11 higher education providers. Until the late 1990s, teachers were prepared in monotechnic teachers' colleges. However, a strategy to strengthen quality and rationalize provision led to the closure of the independent colleges and their mergers with local and regional universities (Humes, 2020, pp. 43–44). Since then, the number of teacher education providers in higher education has increased from 9 to 11, partly due to an effort to diversify provision and intake.

Education and schooling are overseen by the Scottish Government through its Learning Directorate and its national agency, Education Scotland, which provides support and development for schools, but also inspects them. The local authorities, of which there are 32, are the direct employers of teachers and play a central role in facilitating student placements/practicum and provision for newly qualified teachers. The Scottish Council of Deans of Education (SCDE) is the representative body for the 11 teacher education providers.

Unlike other parts of the United Kingdom and internationally, Scotland has resisted fast track approaches for teacher preparation, as well as models involving non-university providers. A qualification for teaching is acquired through either completion of a 4-year undergraduate program (and exiting with a bachelor's degree) or a 1-year postgraduate certificate or diploma. In recent years some undergraduate programs have been extended to 5 years enabling students to complete an optional Master's degree in their 5th year. Upon completion of their initial teacher education, all new teachers are guaranteed one full year of paid employment as part of the Teacher Induction Scheme (TIS), which is explored in more detail in this chapter.

In Scotland, strong emphasis is placed on *teacher education* rather than *teacher training*, seeking to avoid reductionist and technicist approaches, with teaching conceptualized as "engaged, reflective, empowered and skilled" as set out in the GTCS professional standards (GTCS, 2021, p. 4). Emphasis is also placed on school-university partnerships with the education of teachers being seen as a shared responsibility. Partnership for teacher education has been a key driver in reform initiatives that have occurred over the past 20 years, though as Beck and Adams (2020) have observed "the language deployed may bear testament to partnership being taken seriously, however, the ways in which this is operationalized do not always match expectations," and they argue that partnership is a national issue that needs a local approach' (p. 75). A consensus seeking approach, however, can slow implementation and cause tension when partners and stakeholders are challenged in commitments, particularly in times of economic constraint. This was the case in a major workforce reform program which is now explored.

A TEACHING PROFESSION FOR THE TWENTY-FIRST CENTURY

In the late 1990s, tensions between the government, employers, teachers' trade unions, and professional associations had mounted to the point of imminent industrial action. To break through the stalemate, a review of pay and conditions for the teaching profession was launched, resulting in an agreement "A Teaching Profession for the 21st Century" (Scottish Executive Education Department, 2000, 2001). This settled the dispute by introducing a number of measures to improve teachers' pay and conditions. These included an improved pay settlement, a commitment to a 35-hour working week, mandatory 35 hours of Continuing Professional Development (CPD) for all teachers and the introduction of a new teacher category, Chartered Teacher, designed to recognize and reward (i.e., remunerate) excellence in teaching. Chartered Teacher was the most controversial component of the reform package. Similar to models of accomplished teaching in other systems (i.e., Advanced Skills Teachers), the lack of a clearly defined role, at least in its initial phase of implementation, was problematic and sometimes divisive. It came to an end in 2012 (Forde & McMahon, 2018, pp. 179–184). Subsequent recommendations for the creation of a new Lead Teacher role as part of review of career pathways for teachers, remain, as yet, largely unimplemented (Boland, 2019, p. 4).

The priority attached to teachers' professional development was an important milestone for the teaching profession in Scotland. The obligation for 35 hours of CPD to be completed annually, and the need to evidence this, formalized the expectation that all teachers should continue to develop their professional practice. Defining what constituted CPD, the sites of professional learning and the need for regulation of increasingly commercialized activities resulted in an approvals framework for CPD providers and the development of courses for school leaders by some teacher education providers on Leading Professional Learning. The system continued to evolve with the *Teaching Scotland's Future* report in 2011, which is explored further in this chapter. The following section explores another important strand of teacher learning and development in Scotland, the Teacher Induction Scheme (TIS) which was introduced alongside the changes associated with *A Teaching Profession for the 21st Century*.

TEACHER INDUCTION SCHEME

Addressing concerns regarding teachers' pay and conditions of service resulted in *A Teaching Profession for the 21st Century*, a workforce modernization (Ozga, 2005) and remodeling agreement. Specific concerns relating to the "fragmented" experiences of new teachers (Hulme & Menter, 2014, p. 682) and issues of retention, led to the introduction of a new scheme to support teachers in the initial phase of their careers and through this, in the longer term strengthen teaching quality and professionalism (McMahon, 2021). Key features of the new Teacher Induction scheme included the guarantee of a full time, salaried teaching position for 1 year, post initial qualification, a reduced teaching timetable, a school-based mentor and access to professional development opportunities provided by the local education authority. Upon successful completion of their initial teacher preparation, new teachers (known in Scotland as probationary teachers or probationers) are deemed to have met the Standard for Provisional Registration, and it is only after successful completion of the induction period that they are deemed to have met the Standard for Full Registration, "the benchmark of competence required of all registered teachers in Scotland" (GTCS, 2021, p. 3).

The Teacher Induction Scheme has been in place for over 20 years, and apart from a change to the teaching load and time for professional development (from 0.7/0.3 FTE to 0.8/0.2 FTE), adapted in response to challenging economic circumstances in local education authorities in 2008 and 2009), the main components of the original scheme remain unchanged. There are however tensions with aspects of this, as Shanks (2020) has identified, including the mentor's dual role in support and assessment; the vulnerable position of induction year teachers; and the role of universities in teacher induction (pp. 160–161). There also employment challenges for new teachers beyond the induction year and challenges for more rural and remote schools in attracting and retaining teachers. Despite its central role in shaping the future of teaching and the teaching profession in Scotland, the body of research and evaluation relating to the TIS remains relatively sparse (McMahon, 2021), and as Shanks (2020) has noted, there has not been an official review or overhaul since its introduction (p. 151). *The Teaching Scotland's Future* report did, however, make several recommendations to strengthen the induction experience and program for new teachers which are now explored.

TEACHING SCOTLAND'S FUTURE

Following a review of teacher education, led by the former Chief Inspector of Schools, the *Teaching Scotland's Future* report made 50 recommendations, all accepted, in part or in full, taken forward through a national implantation board (NIB). Recommendations relating to initial teacher education included the need for more rigorous selection to teacher education programs "drawing on existing best practice and using a wider set of section criteria" (Donaldson, 2011, p. 86). The phasing out of the traditional Bachelor of Education degree was also recommended, to be replaced with degrees which combine in-depth academic study in areas beyond education with professional studies and development, involving other university departments and staff (Donaldson, 2011, p. 88). To ensure greater continuity across the early phase of initial teacher education and induction, the review recommended that "initial teacher education and induction should be planned as one overall experience' recognizing that this would require strengthened partnership to underpin joint delivery" (Donaldson, 2011, p. 89). The possibility of Master's credits, where appropriate, was also recommended (Donaldson, 2011, p. 89).

In the post qualifying stage, the report recommended that professional learning should be at Masters-level, shying away from making a Master's degree and qualification a requirement for admission to the profession. Arguably, this aspect of the report was weakly implemented, as non-higher education providers struggled to define Masters-level learning.

The *Teaching Scotland's Future* report represented a significant reform program for teacher education resulting in change and innovation in teacher preparation programs and for teachers' career-long professional learning. The recommendation for a new professional standard for "active registration" (implemented as the Standard for Career-long Professional Learning, see below) and a new "Professional Update" scheme requiring teachers to evidence every 5 years how they are maintaining and developing their professional practice, introduced a new element of teacher accountability.

There was also considerable change relating to leadership development arising from the *Teaching Scotland's Future* report. The establishment of a leadership development framework and a new leadership college were two key recommendations from TSF that were taken forward and the Scottish College for Educational Leadership existed from 2011 until 2018, until its incorporation into the national education agency, Education Scotland, in a pattern similar to the fate of the English National College of School Leadership.

In main, the TSF recommendations were adopted across the system, with little resistance, though some recommendations were less impactful than others. Subsequent reform initiatives, such as the Career Pathways report, have sought to address these to some extent. Hayward (2018) attributes the success of the TSF program of reform to several key elements:

- Scotland is a small country with a sense of shared values and the report ran with the grain of Scottish society. Its commitment to education, to high-quality professionalism and to the central role of the teacher, was consistent with attitudes to education throughout Scotland's history.
- Among teacher educators, there may have been a sense of relief that the report had taken a strong line on continued partnerships between universities, local authorities, and schools in contrast to the proliferation of routes into teacher education in England, e.g., to private organizations and to school-based training.
- The model used in the development of the report was highly inclusive, using the policy process as a means of building consensus.
- TSF left control of the profession with the profession and supported a model of accountability that sought not only to set high entry standards, but also to enhance career-long professional development, to promote high-quality leadership and to encourage a standards-based approach to professional engagement for all teachers.

(Hayward, 2018, pp. 46–47)

As Hayward notes, TSF reinforced the importance of the professional standards for system-level reform and improvement, though expresses caution too:

> The evidence emerging from the evaluation of *Teaching Scotland's Future* suggests that the Professional Standards and the model of accountability that they promote are beginning to be effective. However, the model where such confidence is shown in teachers and teacher educators as collaborative professionals is relatively rare in a world where accountability all too often has a much harder edge (Cochran-Smith et al., 2016). It has to be guarded with care (Hayward, 2018, p. 47).

The role of the General Teaching Council as the regulatory and accrediting body for teachers and for teacher education has therefore been central to the implementation of the initiatives for teacher education reform, which is now considered.

REGULATION AND ACCREDITATION: THE ROLE OF THE GENERAL TEACHING COUNCIL

Since its inception in 1965, the General Teaching Council of Scotland has had a key role in the evolution of the teaching profession in Scotland. Originally established to maintain a register of teachers eligible to teach in Scottish schools, its other responsibilities for maintaining the professional standards for teaching and the professional update scheme, accreditation of teacher education programs, and increasingly in the last 20 years, a more expansive role in teachers' professional development, positions the GTCS as a key stakeholder and partner for teacher education in Scotland.

The professional standards for teaching represent one of the distinctive elements of teacher education in Scotland in that there is a professional standard linked to each career stage, as shown in Table 1.

A key role for the GTCS is in the overseeing and ongoing development and review of the professional standards. This has developed considerably since first Standard for Initial Registration was launched in 2000 and the Standard for Full Registration in 2002 (McLennan, 2020, p. 57). This moved definition and regulation of teacher competence beyond initial "benchmarks" set out in an initial White Paper in 1999 (Matheson, 2015, p. 60). According to Matheson (2015, p. 60), "the importance of the creation of this Standard can hardly be over-estimated" primarily because it had two purposes: (1) to provide a clear and concise description of the professional qualities and capabilities teachers are expected to develop during their probation or induction year; and (2) to provide a professional standard against which reliable and consistent decisions can be made on the fitness of new teachers for full registration with GTC Scotland. Matheson (2015) goes on to say: "In defining what was expected of a teacher on completion of induction the Standard defined the essence of what it is to be a teacher, dividing the attributes into three areas: professional knowledge and understanding; professional skills and abilities; and professional values and personal commitment" (p. 60).

These three areas provide the architecture for other professional standards for teaching that have subsequently been developed. With the incorporation of the Standard for Headship, which had been developed separately in 1998, and maintained by the Scottish Government (SEOID, 1998), there is now a set of professional standards reflecting the professional continuum for teachers and key leadership roles. A shared preface and introduction for all these Standards states clearly what it means to be a teacher in Scotland today and the values underpinning teacher professionalism, as set out in the Standards: social justice, trust, respect and integrity (GTCS, 2021).

Table 1. GTCS Professional Standards and Relevant Career Stage.

Professional Standard	Incorporating	Career Stage
Standards for Registration	Standard for Provisional Registration	Initial Teacher Education
	Standard for Full Registration	Induction/Probation/Early Professional Development
Standard for Career-Long Professional Learning		Post induction
Standards for Leadership	Standard for Middle Leadership	School-level heads of department/ faculty or equivalent
	Standard for Headship	Mandatory for all new principals/head teachers from 2021

Accreditation of teacher education programs, which must be mapped to the relevant professional standard, is a primary way in which the professional standards can be embedded, though questions remain as to how teachers engage with them in an ongoing basis. Mars (2012) stresses that teacher enactment and interpretation of standards need to be seen as a dynamic, fluid, and ever-evolving construct, one that may be changeable over teachers' career stages. An OECD review of education in Scotland raised questions about "how deeply the GTCS standards have moved from the theory to the practice and become embedded in the professional culture of the Scottish educational system?" (OECD, 2015, p. 126) and noted that "... while regulatory mechanisms and architecture have been put in place, the extent to which professional standards have been adopted by the profession and become embedded within the wider system for teacher development has not been fully tested" (OECD, 2015, p. 126). The introduction of the "Professional Update" scheme, referred to above, and introduced as part *Teaching Scotland's Future* was a means to try to ensure career-long professional development and engagement with the professional standards. The need to know more about the ways in which teachers and school leaders engage with and interact with professional standards, individually and collectively, is key, though as with other key reform initiatives, research is limited (McMahon & Torrance, 2022). However, the MQuITE project has been an important research project for continuing to advance and progress teacher learning in Scotland and which is now considered in the final section of this chapter.

MEASURING QUALITY IN INITIAL TEACHER EDUCATION (MQUITE)

MQuITE was a 6-year research project, seeking to track ITE graduates over 5 years and the largest ITE study in Scotland to date, representing the views of 946 early career teachers across 1414 individual survey responses (Kennedy, Carver, & Adams, 2023, p. 2). Developmental in design and intent, the research seeks to identify markers of quality, and through data from the project, provide dynamic interpretation modified in light of progression both of students as they become teachers and the various routes into teaching that exist in Scotland (MQuITE, online). The MQuITE project involved all stakeholders in the development of a contextually appropriate means of measuring quality in initial teacher education in Scotland and engaged with both literature and practice to inform this process (ibid). Tracking data and findings from MQuITE were reported to stakeholders at an annual "self-evaluation" conference for all teacher education providers and stakeholders, made more widely available through publication in academic journals and channeled into program review and design by each of the higher education providers. The final MQuITE report, published in April 2023 found that while "the overall headline message from the MQuITE study is that the ITE system as a whole is generally healthy, and there is definitely no 'crisis'" some aspects such as greater personalisation of professional learning in the early career phase; partnership working; and mentoring require strengthening (p. 74).

CONCLUSION

Teacher education in Scotland is an ongoing project of reform and innovation, responsive to emerging circumstances and crises. This chapter has sought to capture these strategic and contingent responses. Context and scale matter, and while, comparatively, Scotland is a small education system, there are challenges of equity and quality across urban, rural and remote regions. The reform initiatives explored in this chapter reflect efforts to ensure that teachers in Scotland can respond to these challenges. The professional standards and professional update scheme provide the mechanisms for ensuring and assuring this, though, as this chapter has noted, there is a need, through evaluation and research, to know more about how teachers engage with professional standards.

The prospect of further change for teacher education is inevitable, as the outcomes of the current reform program are taken forward and teacher education providers address issues of diversity and decolonization in teaching (Arshad, 2018). As cost-of-living implications begin to be felt and issues of recruitment mount, alternatives to university-based teacher education may become more attractive to governments and decision makers. This chapter has sought to set out the strengths of teacher education in Scotland: university based, grounded in values, embedded in professional standards, increasingly research-led and self-evaluative, and responsive to change.

REFERENCES

Arshad, R. (2018). Teaching in a diverse Scotland: Increasing and retaining minority ethnic teachers in Scotland's schools Edinburgh Scottish Government. https://www.research.ed.ac.uk/portal/en/publications/teaching-in-a-diverse-scotland(f78c20b3-284f-461a-be6c-ea903305062e).html. Accessed on 09 August 2020.

Beck, A., & Adams, P. (2020). The Donaldson Report, Teacher education partnership. In R. Shanks (Ed.), *Teacher preparation in Scotland*. Emerald Publishing Limited. https://ebookcentral.proquest.com/lib/gla/detail.action?docID=6354154

Boland, M. (2019). *Independent panel on career pathways for teachers final report*. https://www.gov.scot/publications/independent-panel-career-pathways-teachers-final-report/documents/

Cochran-Smith, M., Stern, R., Sánchez, J. G., Miller, A., Keefe, E. S., Fernández, M. B., ... Baker, M. (2016). *Holding teacher preparation accountable: A review of claims and evidence*. National Education Policy Center. http://nepc.colorado.edu/files/pb_cochran-smith_teacher_prep_0.pdf

Donaldson, G. (2011). *Teaching Scotland's future: Report of a review of teacher education in Scotland*. Scottish Government. http://www.gov.scot/Resource/Doc/337626/0110852.pdf. Accessed on 07 October 2022.

Forde, C., & McMahon, M. (2018). *Teacher quality, professional learning and policy*. Palgrave MacMillan.

General Teaching Council for Scotland. (2021). *The standard for full registration Edinburgh GTCS*. https://www.gtcs.org.uk/professional-standards/professional-standards-for-teachers/

Hayward, L. (2018). Notes from a small country: Teacher education, learning innovation and accountability in Scotland. In C. Wyatt-Smith & L. Adie (Eds.), *Innovation and accountability in teacher education. Teacher education, learning innovation and accountability*. Springer. https://doi.org/10.1007/978-981-13-2026-2_3

Hulme, M., & Menter, I. (2014). New professionalism in austere times: The employment experiences of early career teachers in Scotland. *Teachers and Teaching: Theory and Practice, 20*. https://doi.org/10.1080/13540602.2014.885707

Humes, W. (2020). Reshaping teacher preparation in Scotland: Curricular, institutional and professional changes 1920–2000. In R. Shanks (Ed.), *Teacher preparation in Scotland*. Emerald Publishing Limited. ProQuest Ebook Central. https://ebookcentral.proquest.com/lib/gla/detail.action?docID=6354154

Kennedy, A., Carver, M., & Adams, P. (2023). *Measuring quality in initial teacher education: Final report*. Scottish Council of Deans of Education. https://www.mquite.scot/publications-and-presentations/

Mars, E. (2012). Professional standards, teacher careers and the enactment of professional judgement: An exploration of the discourses. Paper presented at *joint AARE and APERA conference 2012*. https://www.aare.edu.au/data/publications/2012/Mars12.pdf

Matheson, I. (2015). *Milestones and minefields—A history of GTC Scotland*. GTCS Publication.

McLennan, C. (2020). Teacher preparation post-devolution, 1999–2007. In R. Shanks (Ed.), *Teacher preparation in Scotland. Emerald studies in teacher preparation in national and global contexts* (pp. 49–61). Emerald Publishing Limited. https://doi.org/10.1108/978-1-83909-480-420201005

McMahon, M. (2021). The teacher induction scheme (TIS) in Scotland: Adoption, evolution, revolution. In J. Mena & A. Clarke (Eds.), *Teacher induction and mentoring. Palgrave studies on leadership and learning in teacher education*. Palgrave Macmillan. https://doi.org/10.1007/978-3-030-79833-8_3

McMahon, M., & Torrance, D. (2022). Standards for school leadership and principalship. In I. Menter (Ed.), *The Palgrave handbook of teacher education research*. Springer.

National Records Office Scotland. (2022). *Mid-2021 population estimates, Scotland*. https://www.nrscotland.gov.uk/statistics-and-data/statistics/statistics-by-theme/population/population-estimates/mid-year-population-estimates/mid-2021

OECD. (2015). *Improving schools in Scotland: An OECD perspective*. OECD.

Ozga, J. (2005). Modernizing the education workforce: A perspective from Scotland. *Educational Review, 57*(2), 207–219. https://doi.org/10.1080/0013191042000308378

Scottish Executive Education Department. (2001). *A teaching profession for the 21st century (agreement reached following recommendations made in the McCrone report)*. HMSO.

Scottish Executive Education Department. (2000). *A teaching profession for the 21st century: Report of the committee of inquiry into professional conditions of service for teachers (the McCrone report)*. HMSO.

Scottish Government. (2017). *A research strategy for education in Scotland*. Scottish Government. https://www.gov.scot/binaries/content/documents/govscot/publications/research-and-analysis/2017/04/research-strategy-scottish-education/documents/00512276-pdf/00512276-pdf/govscot%3Adocument/00512276.pdf

Scottish Office Education and Industry Department. (SOEID). (1998). *The standard for headship*. Edinburgh.

Shanks, R. (Ed.). (2020). *Teacher preparation in Scotland*. Emerald Publishing Limited. ProQuest Ebook Central. https://ebookcentral.proquest.com/lib/gla/detail.action?docID=6354154

TEACHER EDUCATION REFORM IN THE UNITED STATES: COLLIDING FORCES?

Diane Yendol-Hoppey, Madalina Tanase and Jennifer Jacobs

ABSTRACT

Teacher education reform in the United States has been an ongoing theme over the past 100 years, particularly since A Nation at Risk *in the 1980s, when education became increasingly politicized and less of a public good with which the American public did not tinker. These reforms have four different themes: (1) strengthening the clinical component of teacher education, (2) preparing educators with the tools needed for equity and social justice, (3) participating in heightened accountability demands, and (4) expanding alternative certification. This chapter explores these four strands of reform and concludes they are colliding forces in which the country pours time, resources, and energy. Ongoing collisions on the reform landscape produce increasingly negative consequences for teacher education, teacher recruitment, and retention and America's public schools.*

Keywords: Teacher education reform; clinical practice; equity and social justice; accountability demands; alternate certification; professional development schools; Holmes Group

Throughout the last century, teacher education reform in the United States has created challenging terrain with these reforms intensifying during the last decade. Many scholars have traced these reforms describing the shifts created across the teacher education landscape (Bales, 2015; Blanton et al., 2018; Cochran-Smith & Villegas, 2015; Cochran-Smith, Ell, et al., 2016; Wang et al., 2010; Wiseman, 2012). During this period, teacher educators have also heard from voices outside of the university-based teacher education community with increasingly harsh critiques of our efforts to improve teacher preparation and professional learning (Green, 2014; Walsh, 2006, 2013). Regardless of the perspective of these voices, the last decade of reform has primarily emphasized four main areas: (1) strengthening the clinical component of teacher education, (2) preparing educators with the tools needed for equity and social justice, (3) participating in heightened accountability demands, and (4) expanding alternative certification. Recognizing that teacher education reform is situated within the broader ecosystem of education (Goodlad, 1994), this chapter investigates these reform areas and describes how they often influence or collide with one another or the broader context of K-12 education.

Our analysis considers teacher education policy and teacher education practice as sources of reform. The first source of teacher education reform consists of the principles and policy decisions that influence the field of teacher education, as well as the laws and rules that govern the field of teacher education. Over the last century, the United States has shifted from primarily local control of education to state control with national influence resulting in principles and policies often differing by state. In many cases today, the differences found in policy across states are politically driven creating substantial differences between teacher education across the United States. The second source of teacher education reform, and often less visible to the general public, is driven by change in practice typically driven by teacher education research. In both policy and practice-based reform, the claim is that the change or reform is driven by concern for teacher and student learning. This chapter explores the four reform areas, all of which have roots in prior decades, that have increasingly characterized the teacher education policy and practice reform landscape.

REFORM THEME ONE: CLINICAL PRACTICE

Building on decades of calls for enhancing clinical practice, the last decade has brought continued attention to the importance of working in and with schools. Clinical practice refers to opportunities for teacher candidates to "work in authentic educational settings and engagement in the pedagogical work of the profession of teaching, closely integrated with educator preparation course work and supported by a formal school-university partnership" (AACTE, 2018, p. 11). This notion of clinical practice remains a significant part of the discussion of teacher education reform documents and policies moving beyond student teaching at the end of a program to aligned field experiences throughout the program (Jacobs & Burns, 2021). The reform has focused on creating programmatic coherence and establishing contexts for clinical practice such as professional development schools and teacher residencies designed to help embed clinical practice throughout teacher preparation programs.

Strengthening Clinical Practice Through Professional Development Schools

The development of school-university partnerships in the form of professional development schools (PDSs) and teacher residencies continue to evolve as contexts for clinical practice. PDSs emerged from The Holmes Group (1986) over 30 decades ago which called for PK-12 schools and universities to work together. In a collection of books, entitled *Tomorrow's Teachers, Tomorrow's Schools*, and *Tomorrow's Schools of Education*, these educators advocated for the creation of PDSs as robust school-university partnerships focused on simultaneous renewal for preservice, in-service, and university stakeholders creating exemplary contexts for clinical practice (Holmes, 1986; NAPDS, 2008). Since this time, several documents have articulated characteristics of PDSs more specifically. For example, the NCATE PDS Standards (2001) identified five standards, 21 elements, and dozens of descriptors to help evaluate the efficacy and development of particular PDSs. The standards included four stages that schools and universities could utilize to assess their progress (beginning, developing, at standard, and leading). The five PDS standards are: (1) the learning community, (2) accountability and quality assurance, (3) collaboration, (4) diversity and equity, and (5) structures, resources, and roles. In 2008, the National Association of Professional Development Schools created Nine Essentials to describe what it means to be a PDS and these Essentials were revised in 2021 (see Table 1). In combination, the elements within these documents were written to provoke teacher educators to

Table 1. NAPDS Nine Essentials (2021).

Essential 1: A Comprehensive Mission: A professional development school (PDS) is a learning community guided by a comprehensive, articulated mission that is broader than the goals of any single partner, and that aims to advance equity, antiracism, and social justice within and among schools, colleges/universities, and their respective community and professional partners.
Essential 2: Clinical Preparation. A PDS embraces the preparation of educators through clinical practice.
Essential 3: Professional Learning and Leading. A PDS is a context for continuous professional learning and leading for all participants, guided by need and a spirit and practice of inquiry.
Essential 4: Reflection and Innovation. A PDS makes a shared commitment to reflective practice, responsive innovation, and generative knowledge.
Essential 5: Research and Results. A PDS is a community that engages in collaborative research and participates in the public sharing of results in a variety of outlets.
Essential 6: Articulated Agreements. A PDS requires intentionally evolving written articulated agreement(s) that delineate the commitments, expectations, roles, and responsibilities of all involved.
Essential 7: Shared Governance Structures. A PDS is built upon shared, sustainable governance structures that promote collaboration, foster reflection, and honor and value all participants' voices.
Essential 8: Boundary-Spanning Roles. A PDS creates space for, advocates for, and supports college/university and P–12 faculty to operate in well- defined, boundary-spanning roles that transcend institutional settings.
Essential 9: Resources and Recognition. A PDS provides dedicated and shared resources and establishes traditions to recognize, enhance, celebrate, and sustain the work of partners and the partnership.

develop school-university partnership that could strengthen the role of clinical practice within preparation programs.

Strengthening Clinical Practice Through Teacher Residencies

In 2007, the National Center for Teacher Residencies helped launch more than 40 teacher residency programs to prepare diverse, talented, and effective educators. Teacher residencies are a type of school-university partnership that includes rigorous full-year classroom apprenticeship for preservice teachers with academic coursework that is closely aligned with the classroom experience (Wagoner, 2022). Residents work with an inservice mentor teacher for the entire year. Often within residencies, the pre-service teacher may commit to teach within that district for a certain number of years. Additionally, the National Education Association published the report entitled, *Teacher Residencies: Redefining Preparation Through Partnerships* (Coffman & Patterson, 2014). This report provided guiding principles for teacher residencies so that pre-service teachers are "profession-ready" upon completing their residency. These principles include designing residencies that support teacher preparation and school renewal as well as collaborative decision making between schools and universities. Important to note is that in some cases professional development schools include teacher residencies as a part of their partnership work.

Strengthening Clinical Practice Through Coherent Program Design

In addition to creating specific partnerships to support clinical practice reform, several documents and policies emerged that articulate principles and recommendations for coherent teacher education program design. These documents emphasize the intentional and systematic linkages that support professional learning connections by embedding clinical practice within teacher preparation programs. For example, in 2010, the National Council for the Accreditation of Teacher Education (NCATE) (prior to becoming CAEP) Blue Ribbon Report (NCATE, 2010) reemphasized the need to ground teacher preparation within clinical practice. Specifically, the report called for "centering" clinical practice within teacher preparation rather than the separation of coursework and clinical experiences or coursework followed by clinical practice. In order to center clinical practice, the Blue Ribbon Panel Report included 10 design principles for restructuring teacher preparation programs around clinical practice (see Table 2). The Report described how coursework should not work in isolation, but be integrated into clinical practice. Teacher preparation programs must "shift away from a norm which emphasizes academic preparation and coursework loosely linked to school-based experiences. Rather, it must move to programs that are fully grounded in clinical practice and interwoven with academic content and professional courses" (p. ii). Also in 2010, NCATE and the Teacher Education Accreditation Council (TEAC) merged to form the Council for the Accreditation of Educator Preparation (CAEP). The 2015 CAEP standards delineated that P-12 schools and colleges of education "share responsibility for continuous

Table 2. Blue Ribbon Report Ten Design Principles for Clinically Based Preparation.

(1) Student learning is the focus.
(2) Clinical preparation is integrated throughout every facet of teacher education in a dynamic way.
(3) A candidate's progress and the elements of a preparation program are continuously judged on the basis of data.
(4) Programs prepare teachers who are expert in content and how to teach it and are also innovators, collaborators and problem solvers.
(5) Candidates learn in an interactive professional community.
(6) Clinical educators and coaches are rigorously selected and prepared and drawn from both higher education and the P-12 sector.
(7) Specific sites are designated and funded to support embedded clinical preparation
(8) Technology applications foster high-impact preparation.
(9) A powerful R&D agenda and systematic gathering and use of data supports continuous improvement in teacher preparation.
(10) Strategic partnerships are imperative for powerful clinical preparation. (NCATE, 2010, pp. 5–6)

improvement of candidate preparation" (p. 1). Specifically, Standard 2: Clinical Partnerships and Practice included three components around partnerships, clinical educators, and clinical experiences. For partnerships, there should be the co-construction of mutually beneficial partnerships between universities, PK-12 schools/districts, and community organizations to collaboratively develop expectations for teacher candidate selection, preparation, and credentialing. A second component around clinical educators is once again about collaboration but on the selection, preparation, support, evaluation, and retention of clinical educators. Under the clinical experience component, there are five essential characteristics of (1) depth, (2) breadth, (3) diversity, (4) coherence, and (5) duration.

Continuing to emphasize the role of clinical practice in teacher education, in 2018 the American Association of Colleges for Teacher Education (AACTE) brought together a Clinical Practice Commission that released *A Pivot Toward Clinical Practice, Its Lexicon, and the Renewal of Educator Preparation* (2018). This report centered on developing a framework and lexicon for clinical practice citing the "haphazard" implementation of the Blue Ribbon Report principles and struggle for teacher preparation programs for actualizing the call. The AACTE Clinical Practice Commission Report included 10 proclamations designed to strengthen the ability of teacher preparation programs to understand and implement clinical practice in their programs. The *Central Proclamation* spoke to clinical practice as the foundation of teacher preparation with clinical experiences occurring throughout a teacher preparation program and coupling those clinical experiences to methods' coursework. The report also offered a *Partnership Proclamation* which called for mutually beneficial clinical partnerships that focused on collaboratively seeking positive outcomes for K-12 students, preservice teachers, and in-service teachers.

In sum, several themes cut across the policies and documents. One of the main recommendations is that clinical practice needs to be a joint venture between schools and universities. This collaboration should result in a mutually beneficial partnership where clinical practice is not framed solely around preservice teacher learning, but an opportunity to impact the learning of in-service teachers, and most importantly the learning of PK-12 students. Partnerships for clinical practice also need to involve joint decision making and collaboration around expectations and curriculum. School-based partners need to have a voice in teacher preparation. Zeichner (2010) described the need to rethink the relationship between schools and universities. Clinical practice can serve to create a third space. Within this third space, expertise and knowledge from both universities and schools are positioned as valuable (Beck, 2020; Martin et al., 2011; Zeichner, 2010). Therefore, there are not just opportunities for theory to practice connections in clinical practice, but practice to theory connections. In these documents, clinical practice is not afterthought of teacher preparation that occurs after coursework is complete, but a central focus.

Clinical Practice as a Colliding Reform

Although the need for improved clinical practice within teacher education has received a great deal of attention, the reform has faced multiple issues making it a colliding reform. First, a disconnect related to clinical practice emerged in relation to alternative certification made possible through federal and state policy shifts. While teacher preparation organizations and accreditation bodies have called for heightening the clinical component for university teacher preparation, educational policy such as the *No Child Left Behind Act* (NCLB, 2001) opened the door for alternative routes for teacher preparation that compete with university teacher preparation. As these alternative routes rapidly expand, they draw candidates away from university-based teacher preparation. The coupling of less enrollment and heightened costs associated with the clinical component of teacher education has made university-based teacher preparation increasingly expensive, positioning colleges of education at risk in the United States.

The influence of alternative certification has also created difficulty identifying qualified mentor teachers for teacher candidates as it becomes increasingly difficult to find career teachers to serve as mentors who have been pedagogically prepared. Unfortunately, as university teacher education programs worked toward creating quality clinical practice, NCLB provided entry to teaching by passing a subject matter test. The mismatch creates tangible differences in mentor teachers' pedagogical preparation resulting in a decreasing pool of teachers prepared to mentor the next generation of teachers. Another collision related to clinical reform is the impact of No Child Left Behind (NCLB) which also resulted in high stakes testing that created a narrowing of the PK-12 curriculum. As university teacher preparation programs sought to strengthen clinical practice by aligning curriculum and building partnerships, PK-12 schools became increasingly scripted, presenting additional complexity for partnerships related to building coherence by linking coursework and field work.

Finally, while professional development schools and teacher residencies have continued presence in policy documents as contexts for high-quality clinical preparation and organizations such as the National Association of Professional Development Schools and the National Center for Teacher Residencies continue to thrive, the research literature related to these reforms has become increasingly scarce (Yendol-Hoppey & Garin, 2022). For example, dissertations focused on PDSs have rapidly declined since 2000 and a similar trend is evident in the *Journal of Teacher Education*, a leading publication in our field. Between 1992 and 2007, the journal published over 20 articles related to PDSs and Teacher Residencies while after 2010 the articles specifically related to these areas were nearly non-existent. In combination, this evidence illustrates the complexity of clinical education reform in the United States and the disconnects that exist between policy, practice, and research in the United States.

REFORM THEME TWO: EQUITY, DIVERSITY, AND SOCIAL JUSTICE

In US public schools, 80% of the elementary and secondary public school teachers are female of European ancestry (75%), while the student population looks more diverse than ever with 50% of all public school students being students of color (National Center for Educational Statistics, n.d.). Black teachers are chronically underrepresented in US public schools with only 20% of the workforce represented by teachers of color (White et al., 2019). This discrepancy exacerbates classroom management and instructional issues, pushing many novice teachers to leave the field. Consequently, teacher turnover is 50% greater in US Title 1 schools than in non-Title 1 schools (Carver-Thomas & Darling-Hammond, 2017). In addition, when teachers lack the knowledge, skills, and dispositions to use culturally relevant pedagogy in their classrooms, the achievement gap between students of color and their white peers increases (Bell et al., 2022). To address these challenges, teacher educators have recognized that it is imperative to prepare teacher candidates to serve a diverse student body (Wiseman, 2012). Equally important, teacher education programs recognize the need to diversify the teacher candidate population, by recruiting and preparing teachers of color. Recognizing the importance of addressing the stark discrepancy that exists between the US teacher and student population, teacher educators have been instrumental in leading reform related to equity and social justice.

Teacher Educators Committed to Strengthening Equity, Social Justice, and Diversity

The commitment of US teacher educators to equity, diversity, and social justice is evidenced in a variety of ways. First, in an effort to prepare all teachers for diverse contexts, many teacher education programs have undertaken course revisions which focused on equity and social justice issues. These were meant to increase the white teacher candidates' understanding of multicultural issues

(Wiseman, 2012) and to help teacher candidates develop a social justice mind-set (Rojas & Liou, 2017) so they confront educational inequities (Cochran-Smith, Stern, et al., 2016; Mills & Ballantyne, 2016). Such revisions are noticeable in both coursework and the field experiences. The courses that teacher candidates enroll in prepare them to implement equitable teaching practices and become activists in their classrooms and schools (Freire, 2018), through the use of Culturally Responsive Pedagogy (Banks, 2007; Ladson-Billings, 2009) and Culturally Responsive Classroom Management (Ullucci, 2009; Weinstein et al., 2004). Additionally, efforts are made to strategically place teacher candidates in the field, so they can shadow and observe culturally responsive mentor teachers, who engage with the communities to which their students belong, and who are thus "committed to learning and growing with candidates" (Wiseman, 2012).

Secondly, reforms related to equity, diversity, and social justices have caused many teacher education programs to increase focus on recruiting minority teachers, due to the evidence that teachers of color are beneficial to learning outcomes for all students and for students of color in particular (Carter Andrews, Castro, et al., 2019; Gershenson et al., 2017). Researchers (Kohli et al., 2022; Villegas & Davis, 2007) argued that the recruitment, admissions, and retention processes of diverse candidates have been racialized (Carter Andrews, Brown, et al., 2019; Sleeter et al., 2014) and historically conducted without intentionally recruiting diverse teacher candidates. A shift in recruiting is necessary to disrupt racialized gatekeeping mechanisms (Kohli et al., 2022). Recently, some teacher education programs have enacted a number of practices to address this recruitment reform area such as providing teaching experiences for local high school students during the academic year and in the summer (Sutcher et al., 2019), or by working with districts on "grow-your-own" programs (Carver-Thomas & Darling-Hammond, 2017; Gist, 2017).

Curriculum and pedagogy reforms are also in progress. Gist (2017) argued that although teacher education programs are tasked with preparing teachers who can effectively serve increasingly racially diverse students, they are not always designed to serve their increasingly racially diverse teacher candidates. Retaining diverse teacher candidates needs to be done intentionally. This can be accomplished by designing courses that focus on curriculum and pedagogies that are responsive to the needs of racially diverse communities, and which support them to understand the assets of communities of color (Yosso, 2005). Moreover, this can be accomplished by expecting faculty to have the curricular and pedagogical expertise necessary to foster teacher candidates' racial literacy (Kohli et al., 2022), as well as by paying attention to structural, institutional, and environmental factors that keep, and push teachers of color out of the profession (Carter Andrews, Castro, et al., 2019). Equally significant to preparing teachers of color to serve students of color in important ways, teacher education programs need to prepare them "to navigate or confront the hostile racial climate of schools" (Kohli, 2019, p. 43). Absent this preparation, teachers are at risk of being pushed out of a predominantly White profession.

Current reform has also included policies to strengthen workforce diversity which are geared toward initiatives to reduce "revolving door" patterns of teacher turnover and thus focus on retention of teachers of color who work in hard-to-staff public schools (Ingersoll et al., 2017). But as advocates push for teacher diversity in public schools, the organization and governance of public schools have been restructured in dramatic ways due to broader political currents and policies, which have serious implications for all teachers and teacher subgroups (White et al., 2019). These efforts, conducted with the purpose to enable teacher education programs to respond to the needs of diverse students and teacher candidates, have been spurred by reform and policy endeavors in teacher preparation at local, state, and national levels (Wiseman, 2012).

Accreditation Focused on Equity, Social Justice, and Diversity

While our US teacher education community has often taken leadership in advocating for rigorous reform related to equity, social justice, and diversity, our US accreditation policies have also highlighted the important need for change in social justice, equity, and diversity. For example, the National Council for Accreditation of Teacher Education (hereon NCATE) Blue Ribbon Panel (2010) identified the need for teacher preparation programs to increase their rigor and diversity for admission by balancing GPA requirements against other factors, including characteristics of effective educators (i.e., leadership, commitment, persistence, etc.). This will ultimately serve to improve the candidate pool and attract diverse candidates. In addition, the Panel recommended that teacher candidates be provided with opportunities to work in hard-to-staff schools, by placing interns and residents in high-needs schools, and providing them with a paid mentored internship. Another recommendation included providing incentives to support programs that produce more effective teachers for high-needs schools and in needed disciplines.

Legislation Related to Equity, Social Justice, and Diversity

Simultaneous to these initiatives designed by the profession and professional organizations to support advancement related to social justice, diversity and equity, reform in the last decade has also been impacted by legislation. For example, the American Recovery and Reinvestment Act (ARRA) with Race to the Top (RttT) (2012) provided provisions to address equity, diversity and social justice goals through education. The legislation established an approach to alleviating poverty by providing health care for children and families, ensuring early childhood education, redesigning schools, and upgrading teaching. The proposed $6 billion annual budget was to be invested in the teaching profession through preparing teacher candidates who will teach in high-need fields and communities, improved teacher education, stronger mentoring for beginning teachers, professional development and collaboration time, and career ladder programs to reward expert teachers and to share teaching expertise (Darling-Hammond et al., 2010). Primarily focused on PK-12 education, RttT identified the improvement of teacher quality as one of the most pressing educational issues, stressing the significance of placing well qualified teachers in high-need schools (Crowe, 2010).

Following RttT, the Every Student Succeeds Act (ESSA) (2015) also claimed to focus on equity, social justice, and diversity. Replacing the "Elementary and Secondary Education Act" (ESEA) and putting an end to the NCLB, this new national law sought to provide equitable access to education for all students. In contrast with the heavily centralized tendency of NCLB, ESSA deferred to the states and local authorities the responsibility to design school interventions and supports for low-performing schools (Egalite et al., 2017). But while ESSA required states to develop and implement improvement plans, the federal government could not mandate how states should intervene to turn around their lowest performing schools, leaving each state and their local districts to determine the needs of these schools and to figure out ways in which funding will be distributed to provide equitable access to education for all students.

Today, the United States faces an unprecedented teacher shortage, resulting in key positions going unfilled, the granting of emergency certifications, or teachers teaching out of their certification area. These shortages disproportionately impact students of color: in schools with the highest percentage of students of color, there are three times more uncertified teachers than in schools where the percentage of students of color is the lowest; for example, only 1 in 5 teachers are people of color, compared to more than half of public school students (The White House, 2021). The Build Back Better Agenda (Government, 2021) proposes an investment in teacher preparation at Historically Black Colleges and Universities, Tribal Colleges and Universities, and Minority-Serving Institutions. These investments are targeted at improving the quality of education for all students by preparing new teachers, increasing retention rates, and growing the number of teachers of color.

Equity, Social Justice, and Diversity as a Colliding Reform

Our federal interest in advancing educational equity has consistently appeared as a part of US teacher education, accreditation, and legislative reform efforts. However, these efforts have not necessarily been well aligned with state approaches and at times created collisions and barriers with other reforms. For example, over a decade ago, Darling-Hammond (2010) feared that RttT might not bring the desired changes of improving teacher quality, producing significant advancements in achievement in international competitions, closing the achievement gap, and reducing the inequality in access to school resources. Early on researchers pointed out that students of color, low-income, and low-performing students continued to be disproportionately taught by less qualified teachers (Darling-Hammond & Bransford, 2005; Jerald, 2002; Lankford et al., 2002). As the RttT legislation was designed to strengthen the profession, the market policies resulted in weaker preparation of teachers who teach in high needs areas. As the ease of access to licensure via alternative certification is predicated on cheaper, less rigorous preparation as well as access to licensure for Black prospective teachers, creating a flow of unprepared and inexperienced teachers into communities of color results (White et al., 2019). Thus, in spite of a reform that triggered many changes in the culture of teacher education programs (e.g., coursework, fieldwork, accreditation, accountability, and recruitment of more teacher candidates of color), the educational inequity continued (The Learning Policy Institute, 2018). As such, RttT has not ensured that all students are entitled to equitable funding and to equally well-qualified teachers.

The outcomes of the Every Student Succeeds Act (ESSA) (2015) also did not result in tangible changes in equity. While ESSA created local movement of decision making to states and districts the results have not equalized learning opportunities by providing equitable funding across schools. For example, novice teachers continue to be clustered in higher poverty and higher minority schools within districts nationally (Knight, 2019). Left to make the decision by themselves, districts generally allocate in general more funding to their higher poverty schools by lowering class sizes rather than having more experienced teachers in those schools. In addition, many districts provide less funding per student for teacher salaries in schools with the highest percentage of low-income students and students of color, while other districts have equal to or more experienced teachers in their highest need schools (Knight, 2019).

Most recently, the *American Rescue Plan – Build Back Better* (2021) Agenda has tried to create greater alignment and support for equity in educational opportunity. The plan seeks to address the deep educational inequities that have long existed in the United States through its proposed investment in students and teachers by revitalizing our education system so that students have the opportunities to learn and prepare for successful jobs. To ensure that every student, including those from underserved and under-resourced communities, can learn and thrive, the President's discretionary budget provided an additional $20 billion in funding for Title I schools (The Department of Education, 2022). These investments target inequity in funding between under-resourced and wealthier school districts given that a $23 billion annual funding gap exists between white and nonwhite districts, and gaps between high- and low-poverty districts as well (The White House, 2021). The use of this funding is likely to differ from state to state depending on the state's commitment to preparing skilled teachers who can provide stronger preparation for, access to, and success in rigorous coursework for students. In states where equity, diversity, and social justice are recognized as areas of need, the budget seems to respond to the long-standing inequities in education. However, political differences in state approaches to education will likely impact whether this funding will produce the expected outcomes.

REFORM THEME THREE: ACCOUNTABILITY

Although it is unclear the extent to which any components of accountability initiatives have enhanced teacher quality and student learning, or helped meet workforce demands, accountability has seriously contributed to rising rates of attrition resulting in the teacher shortage, a narrowed curriculum, and the deprofessionalization as well as demoralization of the profession (Achinstein &

Ogawa, 2006). Important to note is that these calls for increased accountability began decades ago from those inside of the profession (Cochran-Smith, 2001; Darling-Hammond, 2006; Goodlad, 1991; National Council for Accreditation of Teacher Education, 2010) and have strengthened in the last decade by critics from outside of the profession (Walsh, 2006).

Today in the United States, an unprecedented cacophony of voices are pressing teacher educators to improve teaching quality. These voices echo the other highest achieving nations that have engaged in reform by overhauling teacher education (Darling-Hammond et al., 2010, p. 2). However, the approach by which these groups believe teacher quality will improve are strikingly different. Many from outside of the profession characterize teaching as mechanistic and view educators as transmitters of standardized content knowledge (Mirra & Morrell, 2011) while teacher educators typically point to the increasing complexity of the profession and a deepening research base that contributes to understanding that complexity (Cochran-Smith, 2003). As a result, when addressing areas of accountability and market reform, striking differences of opinion emerge that reflect these differing understandings of teaching and learning. Our analysis identified three prominent accountability related reform efforts that are influencing our field: the influence of high stakes testing in some states to measure quality of teacher education, competition between accreditation bodies, and the introduction of performance assessment tools such as EdTPA.

The Influence of High Stakes Testing and VAM on Teacher Education

The introduction of Value-Added Models (VAM) connected to high stakes testing has likely been one of the most controversial teacher education reforms of the last decade. This approach, fueled by emerging data systems that linked teachers and students at the individual level, has been used to judge teacher and teacher education program effectiveness. The process uses student multiple choice test scores and VAM as a core part of summative teacher performance ratings (Bastian et al., 2018). Strom (2016) describes this movement toward high stakes as emerging from neoliberal logic that emphasizes individualism, privatization, and competition drawing on "a wave of corporate education policy reforms aiming at accountability, productivity, and efficiency" (Strom, p. 321). The assumption is that external data and accountability systems will lead to positive change in teaching, learning, and teacher preparation that would result in higher K-12 student test scores (Ingram et al., 2004).

A brief review of US education policy illustrates the ongoing shifts related to high stakes testing in the last decade that led to the use of VAM for rating teacher preparation programs. After a decade of high stakes testing in US Public Schools, in 2011, the federal government incentivized all states through federal *Race to the Top (RttT)* funds to enhance accountability in teacher education by encouraging the use of value-added measures of student outcomes as a part of external assessments of teacher preparation programs (Crowe, 2010; U.S. Department of Education, 2011). This expanded the use of VAM in many states beyond teacher evaluation and merit pay, tenure, or continuing teaching contracts that were tied to student performance to include the evaluation of teacher preparation programs in some states. This high stakes teacher education evaluation, although influenced by the federal government, emerged differently from state to state and program to program (National Research Council, 2010). To provide an example of the influence of VAM, Louisiana, Florida, Tennessee, Texas, and North Carolina conducted state-mandated assessments of individual Teacher Preparation Programs (TPP) based on the performance of teacher education program graduates' impact on K-12 students' learning (Lincove et al., 2014). These states established new standards of teacher preparation program accountability that included such elements as K-12 student standardized test performance during the first 3 years following a teacher's certification, pass rates on state certification exams, feedback from school administrators, and the quality of field supervision (Lincove et al., 2014). In many cases, the programs were provided an evaluation ranking with the scores made public. Lincove et al. (2014) noted that "Despite questions about validity and reliability, the use of value-added estimation methods has moved beyond academic research into state accountability systems for teachers, schools, and teacher preparation programs" (p. 24). Although accountability requirements continue in many states, VAM has become increasingly controversial with its utility challenged (Bastian et al., 2018; Lincove et al., 2014) and many lawsuits were filed (Sawchuck, 2015).

Recognizing the complexity of evaluating teacher performance, in 2016, the federal government revisited and revised the policies of RttT resulting in Every Student Succeeds Act (ESSA). In response to the challenges, ESSA retracted the federal government's previous control over states' teacher evaluation systems and teacher education program evaluation to return more local control. In some cases, this has allowed the decoupling of high stakes tests from the evaluation of teacher preparation programs but in many cases, the coupling remains. To date, the state policymakers' choice of controversial high stakes teacher evaluation and teacher education program evaluation approaches has placed the teaching profession in many US states under siege with experienced and novice teachers leaving the profession in record numbers and under enrolled teacher education programs that are threatening the pipeline (Sutcher et al., 2019). In the United States, increasing differences are emerging between states related to how to assess the quality of teacher preparation causing movement of professionals not only out of the profession but sometimes to different states raising questions such as why is teacher preparation evaluated so differently from state to state?

Competition Between Accrediting Bodies

Although extensive pressure on teacher education is exercised by the federal and state governments in the United States, also overseeing teacher education are accrediting bodies. This effort is made even more complex given that accreditation differs by state. The teacher preparation accreditation landscape is tumultuous as accrediting organizations merge and emerge without establishing a shared teacher education professional accountability system. The last decade there has brought a tug-a-war between accreditation organizations. For decades,

National Council for Accreditation of Teacher Education (NCATE) was the most influential accrediting body for teacher education programs producing guiding documents to improve the profession such as the NCATE Blue Ribbon Report which called for turning teacher education programs "upside down" in order to build a system of excellent programs (NCATE, 2010). However, in 2014, NCATE and the Teacher Education Accreditation Council (TEAC) merged into a single organization hoping to create a more rigorous and shared bar for teacher preparation accountability. The result was the creation of the Council for the Accreditation of Educator Preparation (CAEP). CAEP sought to bring together a united professional accrediting body and be the only US educator preparation program accreditor. The goal was to raise the bar for quality educator preparation and create one voice about what that standard looks like and how it should be implemented (Sawchuck, 2010). However, the organization struggled with building confidence as their standards and guidelines changed continuously over the first few years (Sawchuck, 2015; Will, 2019). In response to dissatisfaction, the *Association for Advancing Quality in Educator Preparation* (AAQEP) emerged as an alternative teacher education program approval organization. AAQEP's approach (2018) focused on student success related to quality educator preparation, improvement and innovation, and collaborative partnerships with teacher preparation faculty, administrators, and state officials.

Although these national accrediting bodies continue to fight for a stage on the teacher education accreditation landscape, many states prefer their own systems of program approval giving little attention to any national accreditation. For example, in Florida, the state does not require a national accreditation and has not shown interest in a relationship with CAEP or AAQEP. However, in New York, CAEP accreditation remains a key component of the state's ESSA proposal with detailed description of the actions the State will take to improve preparation programs. The shifting and debated landscape of accreditation makes it difficult to demonstrate to policymakers and our public a collective professional commitment and responsibility to a shared knowledge base.

edTPA as a Shared Performance Evaluation Tool

Designed to serve as the same type of career-entry assessment used in other professional fields, the edTPA was launched to establish performance expectations for beginning teachers across the nation. According to the American Association of Colleges of Teacher Education (AACTE), the edTPA has been used by more than 600 teacher preparation programs across at least 40 states as a performance-based assessment and support system designed to measure the skills and knowledge that all teachers need (Chirichella, 2022). Although once again a state decision, the goal was to adopt a commonly administered tool across teacher education institutions that could reliably score teaching performance. The use of the edTPA was initially a teacher education response to the emerging emphasis on the systematic collection of evidence to inform decisions about how teacher preparation can best be improved (Crowe, 2010). The edTPA was developed by American Association of Colleges of Teacher Education (AACTE) and the Stanford Center for Assessment, Learning, and Equity as a standardized assessment to measure teacher candidate ability to plan, instruct, and assess student learning (SCALE, 2013). According to Kissau et al. (2019), the "assessment requires teacher candidates, during the student teaching internship, to provide convincing evidence of their ability to teach using best practices that have a positive impact on their K-12 students" (p. 102) with passing makes them eligible for certification.

Even though the edTPA was designed by a respected university team of educators in partnership with our leading teacher education organization, over time much critique has emerged related to its use for evaluating teacher candidates. For example, Sato (2014) highlighted a variety of tensions associated with the edTPA such as (1) outsourcing of the scoring process from higher education to a corporate entity that has the business infrastructure to build an electronic platform, (2) marginalizing the value of personalized relationships that are developed between the teacher candidate, supervisor and mentor teacher, (3) standardizing the process of teacher preparation, (4) lacking a shared core body of knowledge and skills that teachers ought to know and be able to do, and (5) reflecting particular kinds of pedagogy that are valued over others. Although the tool has been used in a variety of contexts, Blanton et al. (2018) have demonstrated that the introduction of edTPA as a teacher education candidate assessment tool creates numerous tensions including reifying the general-special education divide by narrowing the curricular function.

Accountability Resulting in Colliding Reforms

As indicated, teacher education accountability reform remains contested. The federal and state governments continue to place pressure on teacher preparation programs to show evidence of program quality. However, differences exist by states creating varied approaches to measuring teacher education programs and the quality of teacher candidates. This often creates results in a lack of alignment between states regarding what teacher candidates learn within their programs. Similarly, we continue to experience colliding expectations regarding accreditation in the presence of multiple accrediting organizations and differences in each states' approach to teacher preparation program credentialing. Finally, the use of edTPA which was initially designed and developed by teacher preparation professionals has now collided with critique from within the very same community. Upon widespread adoption by a variety of states and the hiring of Pearson, a for-profit corporation, to facilitate test distribution university teacher educators' opinions regarding the utility of the tool increasingly collide leaving the US teacher education community once again without a shared tool to measure minimum performance of our graduates. Reform is compromised by colliding legislation, accreditation, and performance assessment opinions.

REFORM THEME FOUR: ALTERNATIVE CERTIFICATION AS A MARKET-BASED INITIATIVE

Given the teacher shortage that has been created by a combination of these reforms, alternative certification has become a market-based initiative to expand the pool of "eligible" teachers. According to Redding (2022), one of the most substantial reforms in the last decade has been the continuing expansion of alternative certification pathways (Fraser & Lefty, 2018). In response to a shortage of qualified teachers as well as the critiques of the teacher workforce, many states have deregulated entry to the profession by promoting alternative certification. Alternative certification programs in the United States provide candidates the opportunity to begin teaching prior to completing all certification requirements and in some states without obtaining a bachelor's degree in teaching. Today, approximately 20% of the teachers in the United States have been alternatively prepared (National Research Council, 2010) and many districts report that 70% of their first year teachers are products of some form of alternative preparation.

Some of these alternative programs are provided through an Institute of Higher Education while many are non-IHE alternative certification programs that are offered by for-profit or nonprofit organizations as well as within school districts. According to Yin and Partelow (2020), alternative certification programs provide individuals who already have a bachelor's degree with an alternative pathway to certification and licensure while they are teaching. Alternative certification programs can be run by a postsecondary institution but can also be run by organizations that are not associated with a postsecondary institution. The length of time, coursework, and training for these alternative certification programs vary widely depending on state laws for teacher licensure and programs' design. Examples of alternative certification include districts growing their own programs such as "Teach for America" and "Troops to Teacher" with each program targeting their own market of prospective educators. Based on RttT legislation that defined highly qualified teachers as those who had subject matter knowledge, the Teach for America (TFA) Program expanded to 35 regions recruiting students, often from Ivy League schools, to teach in high needs schools without an education degree or any clinical experiences, but learning on the job (Donaldson & Johnson, 2011). Given that alternative certification is a market-based initiative, many of these pathways are designed by social entrepreneurs who are interested in utilizing choice and competition to incite change (Zeichner, 2016).

Scholars have consistently noted the importance of examining the nuances of state-level alternative certification policies, given that each state's policy context is unique (Grossman & McDonald, 2008; Nadler & Peterson, 2009). As noted by Grossman and McDonald (2008), "'Alternative' in Florida looks very different from 'alternative' in New York, given state regulations" (p. 195). According to many scholars, alternative certification policies have allowed for the expansion of preparation programs with low recruitment standards, resulting in lower academic standards of incoming teachers (Constantine et al., 2009; Fraser & Lefty, 2018; Redding, 2022). In a recent report (2020), Yin and Partelow (2020) state:

> Alternative teacher certification programs that are run outside of institutions of higher education (IHE) are an especially varied group that have enjoyed steady growth in enrollment in the past decade. Unfortunately, analysis from this report has found that a majority of students in the non-IHE alternative certification sector are enrolled in programs run by for-profit organizations, the largest of which operates fully online. (p. 1)

As we continue to advance pathways to teaching, US reforms might consider Bowling and Ball's (2018) question, "Is alternative certification a solution or an alternative problem?"

Alternative Certification as a Colliding Reform

Alternative certification as a market reform offers the United States access to more teachers during a time when teachers are scarce. However, the approach presents important concerns when the initiative collides with many other reforms that emphasize the importance of creating a more highly qualified and diversified workforce and seems to skirt the standards expected for traditional teacher preparation. As more teachers enter the field with alternative licensure, the need for ongoing professional learning support will become increasingly critical. However, in many states or districts, there is little incentive for practicing teachers to continue their professional learning as graduate education receives little relative compensation or recognition. Without a systematic and intentional plan to continue teacher learning once they enter the classroom, the expectation that teachers will be prepared to meet the educational needs of an increasingly diverse student body is unlikely.

CONCLUSION

The landscape of the last decade of teacher education reform has been rocky. Reforms have focused on alternative certification, accountability, accreditation, the edTPA, value added modeling, addressing equity and diversity, creating program coherence that includes enhancing clinical practice. Individually, these are challenging. Collectively, they have dominated the US education landscape and taken aim at teacher preparation. These reforms in the United States are particularly tricky given the substantial differences created by the state control that characterizes the US education context. This variation creates an educational landscape of teacher education reform that in many ways collides with other reforms making change difficult to enact, complex to study, and rapidly shifting.

There are a variety of documents/policies that all call for an increased focus on clinical practice; particularly related to schools and universities working together in partnership to design and prepare teachers. These documents also call for regular opportunities throughout a program for teacher candidates to engage in clinical practice within partnership schools. However, while this has been called for since the Holmes Report – actualizing these calls has been challenging. This seems to be the case because even in the AACTE 2018 Commission Report the calls were quite similar. Additionally, these calls have not been actualized within the research literature. While there is research on clinical practice, there is a lack of literature compared to other areas of teacher education. This could be due to the fact that those engaging in clinical practice are not teacher educator researchers but teacher educator practitioners. Also, the work of actualizing clinical practice is highly complex and involves a great deal of time with building relationships, structures, and practices in collaboration with school districts. This work is often not valued by universities within tenure and promotion processes, etc. Also, while teacher education organizations and accreditation call for clinical practice and partnerships between teacher preparation programs and qualified school and university-based teacher educators, much of the US education policy did not align with those goals. Instead, policy reforms have promoted alternative routes that do not necessarily include clinical practice. These education policy shifts increased the focus on teacher preparation program evaluation while opening up alternative routes with less scrutiny. Additionally, while these reports include what should be done around clinical practice, they do not necessarily talk about how to actualize these recommendations.

In regard to social justice, equity, and diversity, a potential alignment of legislation and teacher educator concern has not created needed change. The decentralization of ESSA, which provided states and districts the opportunity to allocate funding themselves, did not bring about the desired outcome, as there are stark differences between districts within the same state in funding allocation, still resulting on more districts providing less funding per student for teacher salaries in schools with the highest percentage of low-income students and student of color. Similar differences are striking across states making the nature of education very different depending on what state, community, and neighborhood one lives and teaches in. In spite of the ambitious goal of The American Rescue Plan to address educational inequities that have long existed in the United States, it is too early to measure its impact. Given the many and often conflicting reforms impacting teacher quality, an aligned educational landscape is essential if the United States is to strengthen teacher preparation.

Although calls for accountability have been present from within the educator ranks for decades, many inside and outside education have lost patience waiting for teacher educators in the United States to assume the responsibility of improved K-12 learning by creating high quality educator preparation. As a result, others outside the profession have assumed control. Although there appears to be a shared interest in assuring that a well-qualified teacher is found in every classroom, evidence suggests there is less of a shared understanding of how to craft and implement teacher education reform. The reform approaches continue to vary tremendously due to differing views about the vastly complex endeavor we call teaching and learning. Teacher educators in the United States have been forced to "feed the dragon of reform" by continuing to pour time, resources, and energy into a situation that is constantly shifting and self-perpetuating, with reforms colliding. The reform landscape is characterized by collisions that have had increasingly negative consequences for teacher education, teacher recruitment, and retention and our schools.

REFERENCES

Achinstein, B., & Ogawa, R. (2006). (In)fidelity: What the resistance of new teachers reveals about professional principles and prescriptive educational policies. *Harvard Educational Review, 76*(1), 30–63.

American Association of Colleges for Teacher Education. (2018). *A pivot toward clinical practice, its lexicon, and the renewal of educator preparation: A report of the AACTE clinical practice commission.* Author.

American Association of Colleges for Teacher Education (AACTE). (2022, August 22). *EDTPA.* https://aacte.org/faq/edtpa/

American Recovery and Reinvestment Act, Public Law 111-5, 111th Congress, February 17, 2009.

Association for Advancing Quality in Educator Preparation. (2020). *Guide to AAQEP accreditation.* Author.

Bales, B. L. (2015). Restructuring teacher education in the United States: Finding the tipping point. *Athens Journal of Education, 2*(4), 297–312.

Banks, J. A. (2007). *Educating citizens in a multicultural society* (2nd ed.). Teachers College Press.

Bastian, K. C., Patterson, K. M., & Pan, Y. (2018). Evaluating teacher preparation programs with teacher evaluation ratings: Implications for program accountability and improvement. *Journal of Teacher Education, 69*(5), 429–447.

Beck, J. S. (2020). Investigating the third space: A new agenda for teacher education research. *Journal of Teacher Education, 71*(4), 379–391.

Bell, N., Soslau, E., & Wilson, C. (2022). The student teaching equity project: Exploring teacher candidates' knowledge, skills, and beliefs. *Journal of Teacher Education, 73*(1), 23–36. http://dx.doi.org/10.1177/00224871211039849

Blanton, L. P., Pugach, M. C., & Boveda, M. (2018). Interrogating the intersections between general and special education in the history of teacher education reform. *Journal of Teacher Education, 69*(4), 354–366.

Bowling, A. M., & Ball, A. L. (2018). Alternative certification: A solution or an alternative problem? *Journal of Agricultural Education, 59*(2), 109–122.

Carter Andrews, D. J., Brown, T., Castillo, B. M., Jackson, D., & Vellanki, V. (2019). Beyond damage-centered teacher-education: Humanizing pedagogy for teacher educators and preservice teachers. *Teachers College Record, 121*(4).

Carter Andrews, D. J., Castro, E., Cho, C. L., Petchauer, E., Richmond, G., & Floden, R. (2019). Changing the narrative on diversifying the teaching workforce: A look at historical and contemporary factors that inform recruitment and retention of teachers of color. *Journal of Teacher Education, 70*(1), 6–12. http://dx.doi.org/10.1177/0022487118812418

Carver-Thomas, D., & Darling-Hammond, L. (2017). *Teacher turnover: Why it matters and what we can do about it.* Learning Policy Institute.

Chirichella, C. (May 10, 2022). *Annual administrative report on EDTPA data shows continued growth and support for the first nationally available assessment of teacher candidates.* American Association of Colleges for Teacher Education (AACTE). https://aacte.org/2016/10/annual-administrative-report-on-edtpa-data-shows-continued-growth-and-support-for-the-first-nationally-available-assessment-of-teacher-candidates/

Cochran-Smith, M. (2001). Reforming teacher education: Competing agendas. *Journal of Teacher Education, 52*(4), 263–265.

Cochran-Smith, M. (2003). The unforgiving complexity of teaching: Avoiding simplicity in the age of accountability. *Journal of Teacher Education, 54*(1), 3–5.

Cochran-Smith, M., Ell, F., Grudnoff, L., Haigh, M., Hill, M., & Ludlow, L. (2016). Initial teacher education: What does it take to put equity at the center? *Teaching and Teacher Education, 57,* 567–578.

Cochran-Smith, M., Stern, R., Sánchez, J. G., Miller, A., Keefe, E. S., Fernández, M. B., Change, W. C., Cummings Carney, M., Buton, S., & Baker, M. (2016). *Holding teacher preparation accountable: A review of claims and evidence*. National Education Policy Center.

Cochran-Smith, M., & Villegas, A. M. (2015). Framing teacher preparation research: An overview of the field, part 1. *Journal of Teacher Education, 66*(1), 7–20.

Coffman, A. N., & Patterson, R. (2014). *Teacher residencies: Redefining preparation through partnerships*. National Education Association.

Constantine, J., Player, D., Silva, T., Hallgren, K., Grider, M., & Deke, J. (2009). *An evaluation of teachers trained through different routes to certification (Final report NCEE 2009-4043)*. National Center for Education Evaluation and Regional Assistance.

Crowe, E. (2010). *Measuring what matters: A stronger model for teacher education accountability*. Center for American Progress. http://www.american-progress.org/issues/2010/07/pdf/teacher_accountability.pdf

Darling-Hammond, L. (2006). Assessing teacher education: The usefulness of multiple measures for assessing program outcomes. *Journal of Teacher Education, 57*(2), 120–138.

Darling-Hammond, L. (2010). Teacher education and the American future. *Journal of Teacher Education, 61*(1–2), 35–47. http://dx.doi.org/10.1177/0022487109348024

Darling-Hammond, L., & Bransford, J. (Eds.). (2005). *Preparing teachers for a changing world: What teachers should learn and be able to do*. Jossey-Bass.

Darling-Hammond, L., Wei, R. C., & Andree, A. (2010). *How high achieving countries develop great teachers*. Stanford Center for Opportunity Policy in Education. (Research Brief 1–8).

Donaldson, M. L., & Johnson, S. M. (2011). Teach for America teachers: How long do they teach? Why do they leave? *Phi Delta Kappan, 93*(2), 47–51.

Egalite, A. J., Fusarelli, L. D., & Fusarelli, B. C. (2017). Will decentralization affect educational inequity? The every student succeeds act. *Educational Administration Quarterly, 53*(5), 757–781. https://doi.org/10.1177/0013161X17735869.

Every Student Succeeds Act (ESSA). (2015). 114 U.S.C. § 1177.

Fraser, J. W., & Lefty, L. (2018). *Teaching teachers: Changing paths and enduring debates*. Johns Hopkins University Press.

Freire, P. (2018). *Pedagogy of the oppressed* (M. Ramos, Trans.) (50th anniversary ed.). Bloomsbury Academic.

Gershenson, S., Hart, C., Lindsay, C., & Papageorge, N. (2017). *The long-run impacts of same-race teachers* (Discussion Paper Series). IZA Institute of Labor Economics. http://ftp.iza.org/dp10630.pdf

Gist, C. D. (2017). Culturally responsive pedagogy for teachers of color. *The New Educator, 13*(3), 288–303.

Goodlad, J. I. (1991). Why we need a complete redesign of teacher education. *Educational Leadership, 49*(3), 4–6.

Goodlad, J. I. (1994). *Educational renewal: Better teachers, better schools*. Jossey-Bass Inc.

Green, E. (2014). *Building a better teacher: How teaching works (and how to teach it to everyone)*. WW Norton & Company.

Grossman, P., & McDonald, M. (2008). Back to the future: Directions for research in teaching and teacher education. *American Educational Research Journal, 45*(1), 184–205. https://doi.org/10.3102/0002831207312906

Ingersoll, R., May, H., & Collins, G. (2017). *Minority teacher recruitment, employment, and retention: 1987 to 2013*. Learning Policy Institute.

Ingram, D., Louis, K. S., & Schroeder, R. G. (2004). Accountability policies and teacher decision making: Barriers to the use of data to improve practice. *Teachers College Record, 106*(6), 1258–1287.

Jacobs, J., & Burns, R. W. (2021). *(Re)designing programs: A vision for equity-centered, clinically based teacher preparation*. IAP.

Jerald, C. D. (2002). *All talk, no action: Putting an end to out-of-field teaching*. Education Trust.

Kissau, S., Hart, L. C., & Algozzine, B. (2019). Investigating the impact of edTPA professional development on classroom practice and student teaching experience. *Journal of Teacher Education, 70*(2), 102–115.

Knight, D. S. (2019). Are school districts allocating resources equitably? The every student succeeds act, teacher experience gaps, and equitable resource allocation. *Educational Policy*, *33*(4), 615–649. https://doi.org/10.1177/0895904817719523

Kohli, R. (2019). Lessons for teacher education: The role of critical professional development in teacher of color retention. *Journal of Teacher Education*, *70*(1), 39–50. http://dx.doi.org/10.1177/0022487118767645

Kohli, R., Dover, A. G., Mazyck Jayakumar, U., Lee, D., Henning, N., Comeaux, E., Nevarez, A., Hipolito, E., Carreno Cortez, A., & Vizcarra, M. (2022). Towards a healthy racial climate: Systemically centering the well-being of teacher candidates of color. *Journal of Teacher Education*, *73*(1), 52–65.

Ladson-Billings, G. (2009). *The dreamkeepers: Successful teachers of African American children*. Jossey-Bass.

Lankford, H., Loeb, S., & Wyckoff, J. (2002). Teacher sorting and the plight of urban schools: A descriptive analysis. *Educational Evaluation and Policy Analysis*, *24*(1), 37–62.

Lincove, J. A., Osborne, C., Dillon, A., & Mills, N. (2014). The politics and statistics of value-added modeling for accountability of teacher preparation programs. *Journal of Teacher Education*, *65*(1), 24–38.

Martin, S. D., Snow, J. L., & Franklin Torrez, C. A. (2011). Navigating the terrain of third space: Tensions with/in relationships in school-university partnerships. *Journal of Teacher Education*, *62*(3), 299–311.

Mills, C., & Ballantyne, J. (2016). Social justice and teacher education: A systematic review of empirical work in the field. *Journal of Teacher Education*, *67*, 4263–4276.

Mirra, N., & Morrell, E. (2011). Teachers as civic agents: Toward a critical democratic theory of urban teacher development. *Journal of Teacher Education*, *62*(4), 408–420.

Nadler, D., & Peterson, P. E. (2009). What happens when states have genuine alternative certification? *Education Next*, *9*(1).

National Association for Professional Development Schools. (2008). *What it means to be a professional development school*. The Executive Council and Board of Directors from the National Association for Professional Development Schools. NAPDS.

National Center for Education Statistics (NCES) home page, part of the U.S. Department of Education National Center for Education Statistics (NCES) Home Page, a part of the U.S. Department of Education. (n.d.). https://nces.ed.gov/

National Council for Accreditation of Teacher Education. (November 2010). *Transforming teacher education through clinical practice: A national strategy to prepare effective teachers*. Blue Ribbon Panel on Clinical Preparation and Partnerships for Improved Student Learning.

National Council for Accreditation of Teacher Education. (2001). *Standards for professional development schools*. Author.

National Research Council. (2010). *Preparing teachers: Building evidence for sound policy*. National Academies Press.

No Child Left Behind Act of 2001 (NCLB) (2001) Pub. L. No. 107-110, 115 Stat. 1425.

Redding, C. (2022). Changing the composition of beginning teachers: The role of state alternative certification policies. *Educational Policy*, *36*(7), 1791–1820. https://doi.org/10.1177/08959048211015612

Rojas, L., & Liou, D. D. (2017). Social justice teaching through the sympathetic touch of caring and high expectations for students of color. *Journal of Teacher Education*, *68*(1), 28–40. https://doi.org/10.1177/0022487116676314

Sato, M. (2014). What is the underlying conception of teaching of the edTPA? *Journal of Teacher Education*, *65*(5), 421–434.

Sawchuk, S. (2010). Merger lies ahead for accrediting bodies of teacher preparation. *Education Week*, *30*(10), 6.

Sawchuk, S. (2015, March 5). Teacher education group asserts 'crisis of confidence' in accreditor [Blog]. *Education Week*. http://blogs.edweek.org/edweek/teacherbeat/2015/03/teacher_college_group_asserts_.html

Sleeter, C. E., La Vonne, I. N., & Kumashiro, K. K. (Eds.). (2014). *Diversifying the teacher workforce: Preparing and retaining highly effective teachers*. Routledge. https://doi.org/10.4324/9781315818320

Stanford Center for Assessment, Learning and Equity. (2013). *edTPA field test: Summary report*. Author.

Strom, K. (2016). Teaching-assemblages: Negotiating learning and practice in the first year of teaching. In *Expanding curriculum theory* (pp. 135–157). Routledge.

Sutcher, L., Darling-Hammond, L., & Carver-Thomas, D. (2019). Understanding teacher shortages: An analysis of teacher supply and demand in the United States. *Education Policy Analysis Archives*, *27*(35).

The Department of Education. (2022). *Education for the disadvantaged fiscal year 2022 budget request*. https://www2.ed.gov/about/overview/budget/budget22/justifications/a-ed.pdf

The Holmes Group. (1986). *Tomorrow's teachers: A report of the Holmes group*. The Holmes Group.

The Learning Policy Institute. (2018). https://learningpolicyinstitute.org/product/understanding-teacher-shortages-interactive?gclid=EAIaIQobChMIlZbktfGP8AIVg-DICh10CQyXEAAYAiAAEgJgV_D_BwE

The United States Government. (December 3, 2021). *The build back better framework*. The White House. https://www.whitehouse.gov/build-back-better/

The White House. (2021). *Fact sheet: How the Biden-Harris administration is advancing educational equity*. https://www.whitehouse.gov/briefing-room/statements-releases/2021/07/23/fact-sheet-how-the-biden-harris-administration-is-advancing-educational-equity/

Ullucci, K. (2009). "This has to be family": Humanizing classroom management in urban schools. *Journal of Classroom Interaction*, *44*, 13–28.

U.S. Department of Education. (2011, September). *Our future, our teachers: The Obama administration's plan for teacher education reform and improvement*. Author. http://www.ed.gov/sites/default/files/our-future-our-teachers.pdf

Villegas, A. M., & Davis, D. E. (2007). Approaches to diversifying the teaching force: Attending to issues of recruitment, preparation, and retention. *Teacher Education Quarterly*, *34*(4), 137–147.

van Wagoner, C. (2022, March 15). National Center for Teacher Residencies. NCTR. https://nctresidencies.org/

Walsh, K. (2006). *Teacher education: Coming up empty. Fwd: Arresting insights in education*. Volume 3, Number 1. Thomas B. Fordham Foundation & Institute.

Walsh, K. (2013). 21st-century teacher education: Ed schools don't give teachers the tools they need. *Education Next*, *13*(3), 18–25.

Wang, J., Odell, S. J., Klecka, C. L., Spalding, E., & Lin, E. (2010). Understanding teacher education reform. *Journal of Teacher Education*, *61*(5), 395–402.

Weinstein, C., Curran, M., & Tomlinson-Clarke, S. (2004). Toward a conception of culturally responsive classroom management. *Journal of Teacher Education*, *55*, 25–38.

White, T., Woodward, B., Graham, D. V., Milner, H. R., & Howard, T. C. (2019). Education policy and black teachers: Perspectives on race, policy, and teacher diversity. *Journal of Teacher Education*, *71*(4), 449–463. https://doi.org/10.1177/0022487119879895

Will, M. (2019, July 24). Teacher-preparation programs again have a choice of accreditors. But should they? *Education Week*. http://www.edweek.org/ew/articles/2019/07/24/teacher-preparation-programs-again-have-a-choice-of.htm

Wiseman, D. L. (2012). The intersection of policy, reform, and teacher education. *Journal of Teacher Education*, *63*(2), 87–91.

Yendol-Hoppey, D., & Garin, E. (in press). *The past is prologue: A trend and content analysis of professional development school dissertation research*. School University Partnerships.

Yin, J., & Partelow, L. (2020). *An overview of the alternative teacher certification sector outside of higher education*. Center for American Progress.

Yosso, T. (2005). Whose culture has capital? A critical race theory discussion of community cultural wealth. *Race, Ethnicity and Education*, *8*(1), 69–91.

Zeichner, K. (2010). Rethinking the connections between campus courses and field experiences in college-and university-based teacher education. *Journal of Teacher Education*, *61*(1–2), 89–99.

Zeichner, K. (2016). Advancing social justice and democracy in teacher education: Teacher preparation 1.0, 2.0, and 3.0. *Kappa Delta Pi Record*, *52*(4), 150–155.

INNOVATIVE RESEARCH TRAINING IN HIGHER EDUCATION FOR LSP TEACHERS: FROM INSTITUTIONAL POLICY TO THE DEVELOPMENT OF CUSTOM-MADE PROJECTS

M.A. Châteaureynaud and M.C. Deyrich

ABSTRACT

In the context of higher education and further education, scientific research plays a major role in the development and quality of teaching and careers (research active teachers). However, this opportunity is denied to most teachers of languages for specific purposes *(LSP) who find themselves teaching their subject without any prior training in a specialized field with which they are not familiar. To compensate for the lack of specific training for these teachers, a training experiment including a component devoted to an initiation to scientific research was conducted (TRAILs, 2021). The arrival of the pandemic forced us to change the project to a distance learning format shortly before its implementation, which was planned for a summer session at the university. We describe the innovative online training module for developing a research career that focused on action research and empowerment of participants.*

Keywords: LSP (Language for Specific Purposes) teachers; social justice; research training; professional development; empowerment; non-specialist English teacher

Our research is based on an experiment carried out within the framework of a European project (TRAILs, 2021), which was aimed at creating a tailor-made training for teachers of *languages for specific purposes* (LSP) in higher education.

This training was intended to compensate for the lack of specific training for these teachers, who most often are forced to teach their subject in an unfamiliar field of specialization (Châteaureynaud & John, 2022, in press). This situation discriminates even more against them in terms of their career prospects, since very few engage in research and most of them are blocked from professional development and career prospects. From a personal point of view, their skills, creativity, and experience appear not to be valued. It should also be considered from an academic point of view, that this severs the development of their knowledge and, in the long run, the influence of their university. Paradoxically, the question of their real training needs is not a priority, despite the emphasis placed on the notion of lifelong learning.

In the absence of institutional reforms likely to provide proposals or even solutions to counteract what we believe to be a form of social injustice, collaboration on a European scale has made it possible, within the framework of the TRAILs project (explanation follows), to better situate the training needs and place a specific focus on the opportunities offered in research work and in the interest of belonging to a research community for personal development.

This study is rooted in socio-constructivist theoretical foundations (Vygotsky, 1986) which enable us to anchor our approach to training in a dialogical conception of preparation that is empowering, emancipating and open to the community of researchers in the field in addition to being autonomy enhancing and self-learning (Debon, 2003; Eneau, 2016). This orientation toward autonomy, which guarantees harmonious career progression, seems to us to need to be put into perspective with the notion of self-efficacy (Bandura, 1977) and pedagogy for social justice (Freire, 2005), as well as with the institutional reforms that could play a driving role.

CONTEXTUALIZATION: HIGHER EDUCATION TEACHER EDUCATION AT EUROPEAN LEVEL

In the first part of this chapter, we will look at the history and context of this situation, and briefly discuss the European context and reforms, to gain a better understanding of the situation.

Reforms, Research, and Quality in the European Higher Education Area

The issue of quality in higher education has been particularly high on the agenda, especially since the early 2000s, when the prospect of a "European Higher Education Area" promoted through the Bologna Process the widespread dissemination of quality issues in education. To facilitate the development of a "quality culture," the European Association for Quality Assurance in Higher Education published in 2005 a first version of the European Standards and Guidelines for Quality Assurance (ENQA, 2015). The focus is placed on challenges in terms of social cohesion and the economy, and on the common understanding of quality assurance for learning and teaching across borders and among all stakeholders. In this framework document, a position is taken on an explicit linkage between the expected quality of teaching and the competencies of teachers, while delegating responsibility to institutions. Among the measures advocated for this purpose is an emphasis on the recognition of the importance of the teaching act and the need for professional development:

Such an environment

- sets up and follows clear, transparent, and fair processes for staff recruitment and conditions of employment that recognize the importance of teaching.
- offers opportunities for and promotes the professional development of teaching staff.
- encourages scholarly activity to strengthen the link between education and research.
- encourages innovation in teaching methods and the use of new technologies (p. 13).

Compliance with the guidelines has followed recommendations in most member countries (e.g., Cardoso et al., 2015) in order to ensure the quality of the teaching faculty in higher education institutions. This has morphed, over time, into the provision of training for teachers employed in higher education.

Teacher Training in Higher Education Teacher Education: Insights into the Institutional Scene in a Context of Reform

The benefits of teacher training in higher education have been researched and investigated (Darling-Hammond, 2017; Postareff et al., 2007) and teacher-researcher training is generally included in the university's terms of reference as a policy instrument (Kirsten, 2020).

At the member state level, universities are beginning to become aware of the training needs to teach in higher institution. In France, in 2017, a decree required institutions to offer training (sometimes very brief) for new lecturers. For example,

> A policy of support and training for teacher-researchers and teachers has been implemented, which makes it possible to support them in their professional career, in their teaching activity (particularly in relation to the steps to improve training), in the case of reorientation of their research, or in support of their investment in other missions. (MEN, 2017)

Newly recruited teacher-researchers must thus receive training prior to assuming their official duties. Efforts have been made in this direction. In the case of the University of Bordeaux, 30 hours of training are provided. In higher education teaching at the University of Bordeaux, the importance of the pedagogical development of teacher-researchers is stressed. If the institution does not include training needs in higher education, it focuses on initial training for the time being. Inservice training remains to be built.

In Spain, this is being put in place and the LOSU (Ley Orgánica Para el Sistema Universitario) also provides initial training for teacher researchers (Silio, 2022 El país)

> Los nuevos profesores de universidad recibirán un curso inicial para aprender a enseñar (New university teachers will receive an initial course to learn how to teach.)
>
> La ley que prepara el departamento de Subirats obligará a los docentes ayudantes doctor a pasar por un programa de metodologías. El ministro recuerda que leer la tesis no convierte al investigador en un buen maestro. (The law being prepared enables teaching assistants to go through a methodology programme. The minister reminds us that reading a thesis does not make a researcher a good teacher.)

Indeed, some universities were already offering training, but it was not compulsory. Thus, European universities are becoming aware of the need to train newly recruited teacher-researchers; however, this preparation, which is often minimal, concerns novice teacher-researchers.

For teachers who work in universities without research university status, there is no research training offered. When training is available, it is very limited in terms of time and content. The training offered is inadequately developed and often limited to pedagogical advice, which loses sight of the multiple needs of teachers in higher education, especially in specialized language instruction at the university level:

> Although there is growing evidence that teacher education is a key element in promoting the quality of higher education, many teacher preparation programs are short-term training efforts within a policy-based 'social market' perspective, which emphasize training in pedagogical skills and the development of the teaching profession. (Astaíza-Martínez et al., 2021, p. 187)

The issue of the quality of teaching and research and the need for high level training for professional development and quality teaching, are often lost sight of.

TEACHING IN THE FIELD OF LSP

The Context of Teaching Languages to Nonspecialists at University

While job offers targeting language for specific purposes (LSP) teachers are proliferating, many among those vacancies tend not to be filled, due to a mismatch between the profiles of the jobseekers and the skills which are needed. The demand for skilled foreign language teachers in higher education exceeds the supply. This is explained by the expectations of universities and wider society: the foreign language sector is seen as an asset and a springboard to ensure a sufficiently high level of proficiency in one or more foreign languages to compete successfully in the present labor market (Anesa & Deyrich, 2022).

The Issue of Training Needs

In a period of teacher shortage, there is a tendency to massively recruit people of good will, qualified or not in the field of teaching, without really caring about the required skills. France is unfortunately experiencing this on a large scale at present for all levels of education. The university has not escaped this logic over the years, especially in the field of LSP where the need for teaching is great. Thus, they hire teachers who have a command of the language to be taught but who originally had no competence in the field of specialized languages and their teaching.

The most typical case is that of English language teaching, where it is institutionally assured that mastery of general English is sufficient to teach ESP, without prior training. The debate has been opened on many occasions. For example, Faure (2014, p. 9) addresses the question of the knowledge required to teach the following:

How much does a teacher of medical English need to know about medicine?
How should he/she go about designing a course in medical English?
How can he/she manage video and role-play activities?

The author explains that the impact of lack of training can be very damaging, even dangerous: teachers of English are very often sent to university hospitals without any prior training and have to cope with difficulties that could have been avoided if enough time, thought, and material had previously been devoted to them.

In contrast, in the field of ESP/LSP teaching research, the discourse is very different. Dudley-Evans (1997, p. 61) does not seem to consider teacher training is necessary, as their command of the language allows them to improvise:

- LSP teachers need to have the skills and sense of adventure of the jazz musician improvising around a melody or a chord sequence.
- Following this line of reasoning, one could consider that LSP/ESP teachers do not need to be trained.

Specific Issues to Be Addressed for LSP Teaching

Research in the field shows that the need for training is particularly acute for this group of teachers who face many problems in carrying out their duties. The following reasons can be given for this.

The question of the specific identity of the LSP teacher was raised as a point of tension by Anesa and Deyrich (2022). It was also questioned in terms of its practicability by Taillefer (2013) who took stock of the roles expected of these LSP/ESP teachers, among them: teacher, course designer, materials provider, collaborator (with subject specialists), researcher and evaluator of courses, materials and student learning; as well as advisor on content and language integrated learning (CLIL) programs in English-medium university teaching contexts. These excessive expectations were mentioned by Basturkmen (2014, p. 19), who concluded that it is only possible if training is provided:

LSP teachers therefore generally face an array of work needs, all of which require knowledge and skills and presumably some form of teacher education.

Needless to say, LSP teachers' roles are quite challenging. LSP teachers need to be experts not only in specific language teaching, but also in acquiring specific knowledge, providing materials, designing syllabuses, collaborating with subject area specialists, researching, and evaluating the course and the students.

SPECIFIC DIFFICULTIES TO OVERCOME

The language teacher who now accepts a position to lecture at a university as an LSP teacher certainly does not imagine the complexity of the context, specifically because of the following two reasons: (1) specific student population and (2) excessive program expectations.

Specific Student Population

The aim is not to teach students who are no longer adolescents but not yet experienced adults, who are engaged in various specialties while they are non-specialists in languages, and who do not yet know what their professional activity will be exactly.

Excessive Program Expectations

All of this unfolds in a landscape of economic globalization, competition between universities in the midst of budgetary restrictions and against a backdrop of ambitious European language policies (Poteaux, 2015).

These two complexities of context produce barriers to career progression and engagement in research, which is problematic for several reasons, notably because of critical gender factors that negatively influence career progressions (Crisan, 2022; Khan & Siriwardhane, 2021). Studies of LSP teaching agree with the finding that LSP educators are a predominantly female population whose careers rarely evolve. Many of them teach at university without any specific training to encourage them to develop their research careers.

Three additional points need to be added. The first is the precariousness of academic research careers, with a growing portion of these teachers being employed as temporary workers (OECD, 2021). Second, there is a lack of self-efficacy with the LSP teachers feeling excluded from opportunities that would help them progress. In short, they are often left behind where research and research productivity are concerned. Third, there is a lack of a self-image of one's professionalism and abilities (Bao & Feng, 2022) and the idea of possessing a professional identity needs to be reinforced (Suarez & McGrath, 2022).

LSP TEACHERS' NEEDS AND THE IMPORTANCE OF TRAINING IN RESEARCH

LSP teachers have numerous training needs. The study carried out before the experimentation within the framework of the TRAILs project highlighted the fact that the training of language for specific purposes teachers in higher education is infrequent and poorly developed. This project has helped to identify the specific needs of this group (Bocanegra Valle & Basturkmen, 2019), such as vocabulary which is work-related, specialized knowledge, and specific LSP teaching skills.

These needs, as Woodrow (2018, p. 29) reminds us, should then be "translated into course objectives and teaching aims through a series of steps." This has also been attained in the TRAILs project with the development of the LSP teacher school. Furthermore, the provision of training in research methodology in LSP teaching and learning in European higher education institutions is insufficient in relation to the identified needs of LSP teachers. The reality of the field, the needs of the teachers and of the institution are rarely considered. This is particularly disturbing with respect to the help to be given in the field of research, an essential element for the development of their careers but also for their universities, which experience difficulties in recruiting teacher-researchers conducting research in relation to their fields of specialization.

Regarding personal development, lifelong learning, and and social justice, research training in those areas also seems necessary.

The issues for teachers working in higher education have clearly identified "the research component of the professorial task [as] highly valued" (Deschenaux, 2013) and of strategic importance to their careers.

LSP teaching often requires teachers to become researchers as well as teachers (Basturkmen, 2014). Still, this type of study is often marginalized, and the topic completely ignored, yet many teachers train themselves and bring added value to their universities because research is vital for institutions in terms of visibility and prestige.

METHOD: A CUSTOMIZED RESEARCH MODULE

Within the framework of the TRAILs project, an analysis of the needs of European specialized language teachers was thus carried out. TRAILs was a 30-month (2018–2021) project titled *LSP Teacher Training Summer School (TRAILs)* that was co-funded by the Erasmus+ program of the European Union (Re: 2018-1-FR01-KA203-048085). The project addresses the issue of teacher education and skills development to promote high quality and innovative teaching in the field of Language for Specific Purposes (LSP).

A lack of initial and in-service training was identified, and this lack was even more glaring when it came to training in research and professional development for these teachers (Châteaureynaud & John, under press). We therefore proposed a specific training module on February 22, 2021 to address these needs.

Research Module Design

Throughout the module, the idea of giving teachers confidence seemed central to us, as Bao and Feng (2022) point out when they assert that "doing research is not beyond my reach" Moreover, the importance of self-efficacy, a concept developed by Bandura (1977), is at the heart of professional development processes.

Another characteristic of our study should be noted. We were not able to carry out this training in person as initially planned. Due to the pandemic, this training was carried out online, under very constrained conditions, but which also allowed us to analyze this teaching modality under pandemic conditions.

Research Skills Development: A Project-Based Approach

We designed this research module with an eye to the type of audience: many teachers who are not necessarily researchers. We wanted to help them discover LSP research in relation to their teaching, to help them design a personal research project by considering the networks of associations, the journals in which to publish, and the main methodological principles.

The objective was to help participants consider how the field of research can relate to their teaching and contribute to the development of a personal research project based on their own needs that they can develop autonomously their own and within a career development perspective. LSP research trends and opportunities were explored and discussed, as a steppingstone to discussions about research questions. Theoretical and practical guidance was provided to assist in the selection process of relevant and interesting research topics and questions in the field of LSP. We then raised the question of the research possibilities offered according to the fields of observation and the methodological options for developing a research plan and considering its publication. Designing the development of the participants' own career paths was our final focus. Reflection was centered on personal development by considering personal assets and needs and the opportunities for development and collaboration that are both available and promising.

Learning Outcomes

The teacher-researcher training has been designed in three main steps:

(1) LSP Research Trends and Opportunities

They help to understand the current trends in LSP research and to understand and become familiar with different types of feature and research papers, and know and recognize journals. They then choose a relevant research topic and develop a research plan or proposal.

(2) LSP Research Methods

They are reminded of the different methodologies used in LSP research (quantitative and qualitative research methods) and different digital tools useful for data analysis. Additionally, we ask them to reflect on the questions they had and to formulate hypotheses. After that, they consider a methodology to verify the hypotheses put forward. After pooling of ideas and discussion, each participant formulates research questions for a personally relevant research topic.

(3) Formal Professional Development Opportunities

Finally, in the last part of the training, the participants worked on the overall development of their careers. The final part of the module focused on the overall development of their career, with an identification of the different areas concerned and a self-assessment of their situation in order to have a clear vision of the areas to be developed (Self-assessment grid).

This part of the module enables them to understand the importance of being active in unstructured and structured activities (either as a delegate, speaker, or panel member) for one's own professional development, find and select opportunities in addition to digital and formal and informal lifelong professional development (i.e., teacher education courses, conferences, MOOCs, etc., related to LSP teaching).

Above all, the LSP educators should be able to define their own LSP teaching strengths and weaknesses and choose adequate opportunities for further development. Accordingly, in order to design and/or continue the development of their own career paths, they need to apply the gained knowledge to start and/or develop innovative and collaborative LSP teaching practices as well as create and present their own short-term and long-term professional development plans.

An Innovating Training Module: Self-Training Through Research

The innovative points of our research aim to contribute to the empowerment of the participants whether it is the initiation to research and specifically to action research or the self-assessment grid of their situation. In short, everything is meant for awareness development and thus for them to initiate actions in their own careers and for their own professional development.

The aim is appropriation and implementation of their own learning capacity, in line with Eneau (2016) who considers that research on self-education and self-directed learning has contributed to the conceptual field of adult education. In that field, the notions of autonomy and emancipation are sometimes mistaken for their original meaning, despite different research paths and modes of interpretation. This should lead researchers to the "use of terms like empowerment, capacitation and capabilities, which renew issues for self-education and self-directed learning, if not more generally for adult education."

For Debon (2003), self-education leads to empowerment. The exercise of this power refers to the capacity of the person to self-create through actions carried out by reflecting on self in one's learning process through integrating goals, projects and strategies.

Self-learning also refers to a form of socialization and includes resource people. It is important to consider that those who self-train are human resources that generate value: "the new knowledge, relationships to knowledge and power, and mediations that are established are necessary for the knowledge economy and can be transferred to other activities."

The mandatory use of technological means has made it possible to offer more services and materials.

Action Research: Taking the Plunge

The example we have chosen has to do with action research, which allows participants to use their own professional context to develop research themes.

The problem is observed in a specific context, which fuels the need for professional development (Martell, 2014, p. 4). For practitioners, action research "offers important insider knowledge that is often missing from other types of educational research." This viewpoint is shared by Burns and Westmacott (2018, p. 15) who examined the ways to move from teaching to research in the article, *Reflections on a New Action Research Program for University EFL Teachers.*

The starting point in any research project is to formulate a question, which is an explicit query about a problem or issue that can be questioned, examined, and analyzed, and that will lead to useful new information. However, guidance is needed for the teacher to take the plunge, so that the individual understands the merits of the research process.

What follows is an activity that aims to enable trainees to facilitate empowerment and self-reliance.

The task they had to do began with choosing a relevant research topic and developing a research plan or proposal.

Fig. 1 provides an overview of the research approach that the LSP teacher can use to prepare a specific teaching-learning program to take account of the situation.

(1) The starting point is the observation of a problem in a specific situation, identified either through observation or experience.
(2) A question then arises which is likely to guide the research.
(3) Before proposing a solution, the researcher takes a step back and relates the question to theoretical contributions (T) likely to help him/her to better understand the implications of the question that was posed.
(4) Based on this theory, statements or hypotheses (H) will be proposed (i.e., "Listening to vocal music has a negative effect on learning a word list.").

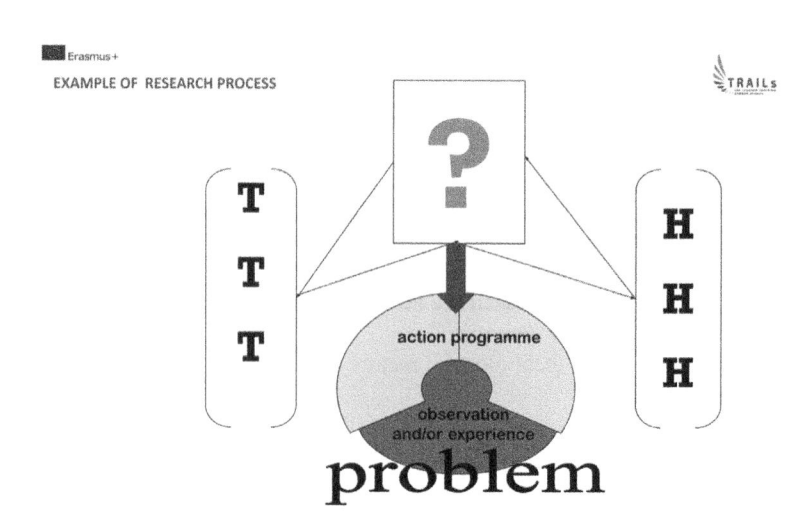

Fig. 1. Research Process Outlined in the TRAILS Erasmus+ Grant Award.
Source: Used with permission.

From these hypotheses, predictions about specific events are derived (i.e., "People who study a word list while listening to vocal music will remember fewer words on a later memory test than people who study a word list in silence."). These predictions can then be tested with a suitable experiment. Depending on the outcomes of the experiment, the theory on which the hypotheses and predictions were based will be supported or not or may need to be modified and then subjected to further testing.

In sum, the research approach with which we experimented in this training essentially aimed at providing a framework from which the trainees could experience a process that would allow them to start from their own personal interests and observations and, in turn, use their experiences as a valuable source of questions. Here is where the impetus – the dare to engage in research, to take the plunge – occurs! The many questions that the training generated led to the observation that successful research often raises new queries, even while it answers old ones. This process of empowerment proved to be rewarding and, in most cases, led to progress on the LSP teachers' proposed research plans.

The Self-Assessment Grid: From Teaching to Research and Back (Again)
Our approach is part of a dynamic self-positioning process [create a mind map (Fig. 2)] for each participant, which allows him/her to evaluate for him/herself which areas will be useful. We then engage in a coaching process based on the completed maps and comments and questions that arise.

The objective is to help participants consider how the field of research can relate to their teaching and contribute to the development of a personal research project based on their own needs and within a career development perspective. It seemed interesting to offer them a self-positioning grid so that they could situate themselves and see what they could improve in research for their institutional career. The following possibilities presented themselves when LSP research was related to LSP teaching:

(1) Development of a personal research project based on a career pathway perspective
(2) LSP research trends and opportunities
(3) LSP research publications
(4) Theoretical and practical guidance
(5) Design of participants' own career development

Then we asked them to comment on these various areas and, using Table 1 (sample). The mind map above served as basis to define which fields they considered as essential: academic position, researchers' associations research development, technical skills, opportunities, valorization, and/or project management. They had to decide which areas they felt they needed to develop as a priority to progress in their research and careers: they were asked to rate their own situation in each of the areas from 1 to 5 in order to better perceive in which

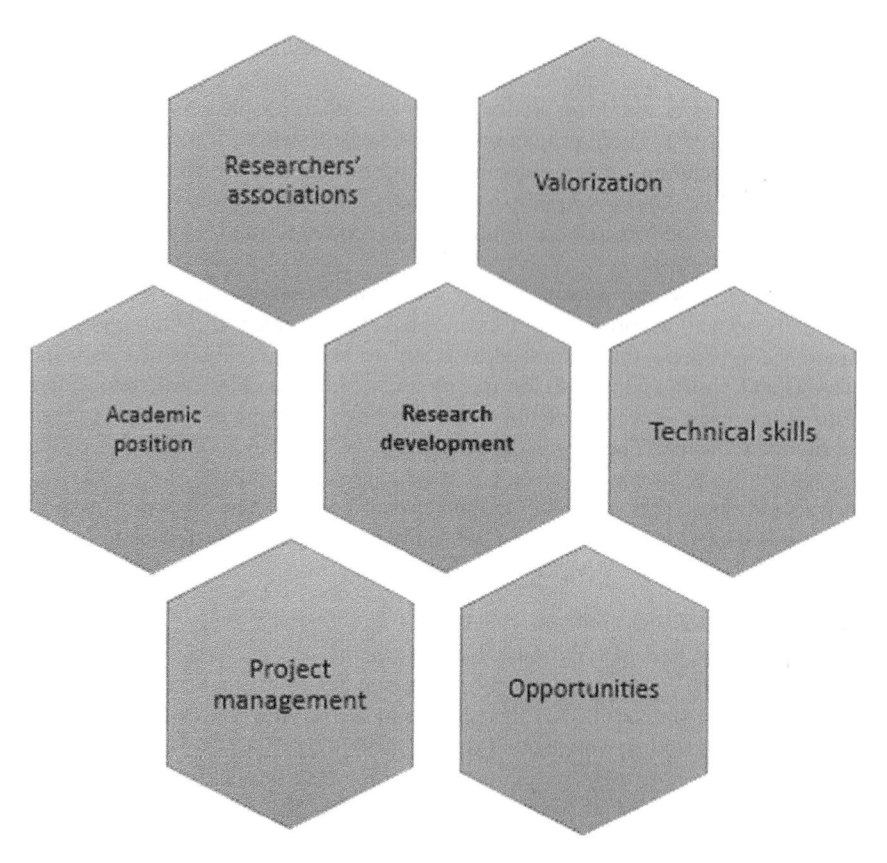

Fig. 2. Mind Map Commented on Collectively.

area they should move forward. This awareness was aimed at enabling them to design a personal project with the challenges and benefits of such development clearly in mind.

This grid takes up the fields highlighted on the mind map and allows students to rate their own situation on a scale of 1 to 5 in each field. They do it on their own then share with the group.

Although this module was designed for face-to-face training, we had to run the course remotely during the pandemic. The participants expressed their satisfaction many times afterward despite the difficulties experienced in the fluidity of exchanges and the spontaneity of videoconferencing.

DISCUSSION

The self-assessment research grid is an innovation – a reform – since this reflective work on their own career had never been proposed to these teachers. First, the

Table 1. Self-Assessment Grid.

Self assessment scale	Academic position	Researchers' associations	Valorization	Project management	Technical skills	Opportunities
	Doctoral studies graduation	Network Advices Community	Publication CV Site referencing (ORCID)	Communication human resources management interculturality	software data processing bibliography	Calls for projects Calls for proposals in congresses Job positions Researchers' mobility
1						
2						
3						
4						
5						

mind map with self-positioning is an innovative task that allowed the participants to situate themselves, to identify areas for development specifically for their own professional development. We used the discussion space to keep track of their questions and feedback on the module. Two, the data we recorded form the basis of this study, which shows the value of including all categories of teachers in a research process by helping them to identify areas for development and objectives themselves. In doing so, they were given more agency and power over their own career development, both intellectual and academic. Third, tracing the participants' and teachers' activities in the recordings helped to develop the reflection and knowledge of the evolution of professional gestures linked to the pandemic. Fourth, there was a lot of positive feedback and questions asked. These had to do with career development, the viability of certain research projects, and the importance of resource persons.

This training allowed LSP teachers to pivot into research-oriented tasks, to better understand the different mechanisms of how research works and to self-assess their needs. The feedback was positive because they had never had access to such a proposal, which had to be adapted to the coronavirus circumstances, and which probably did not allow as many exchanges as those envisaged in the planned face-to-face training.

CONCLUSION

In the pursuit of greater social justice, professional recognition, and research capacity, we decided to propose the experiment discussed in this article. The training needs of specialized language (LSP) teachers were explored during the

TRAILs Project and the results led to the proposal of training modules to develop this field. In the training that took place at a distance due to the pandemic, an innovative tool for the inclusion of non-research teaching staff in the research was designed and proposed. The feedback from the participants led to both a positive evaluation and to avenues for improvement that we will develop to enable this category of teachers to have real prospects in higher education.

REFERENCES

Anesa, P., & Deyrich, M. C. (2022). Responding to LSP teacher needs: Evolving challenges and new paradigms. In M. A. Châteaureynaud & P. John (Eds.), *LSP teacher training summer school the trails project*. Peter Lang.

Astaíza-Martínez, A. F., Mazorco-Salas, J. E., & Castillo-Bohórquez, M. I. (2021). Teacher-researcher training in higher education: A systems thinking approach. *Systemic Practice and Action Research, 34*(2), 187–201.

Bandura, A. (1977). Self-efficacy: Toward a unifying theory of behavioral change. *Psychological Review, 84*(2), 191–215. https://doi.org/10.1037/0033-295X.84.2.191

Bao, J., & Feng, D. W. (2022). "Doing research is not beyond my reach": The reconstruction of college English teachers' professional identities through a domestic visiting program. *Teaching and Teacher Education, 112*, 103648. https://doi.org/10.1016/j.tate.2022.103648

Basturkmen, H. (2014). LSP teacher education: Review of literature and suggestions for the research agenda. *Ibérica: Revista de la Asociacion Europea de Lenguas para Fines Específicos*, (28), 17–34.

Bocanegra Valle, A. M., & Basturkmen, H. (2019). Investigating the teacher education needs of experienced ESP teachers in Spanish universities. *Ibérica*, (38), 127–150.

Burns, A., & Westmacott, A. (2018). Teacher to researcher: Reflections on a new action research program for University EFL teachers. *Profile Issues in Teachers' Professional Development, 20*(1), 15–23. https://doi.org/10.15446/profile.v20n1.66236

Cardoso, S., Tavares, O., & Sin, C. (2015). The quality of teaching staff: Higher education institutions' compliance with the European Standards and guidelines for quality assurance—The case of Portugal. *Educational Assessment, Evaluation and Accountability, 27*(3), 205–222.

Châteaureynaud, M. A., & John, P. (Eds.). (2022). *LSP teacher training summer school the trails project*. Peter Lang.

Crisan, E. L. (2022). Academics career success: The impact of organizational context and individual variables. *Rajagiri Management Journal, 16*(2), 90–104. https://doi.org/10.1108/RAMJ-11-2020-0065

Darling-Hammond, L. (2017). Teacher education around the world: What can we learn from international practice? *European Journal of Teacher Education, 40*(3), 291–309. https://doi.org/10.1080/02619768.2017.1315399

Debon, C. (2003). L'autoformation, avec ou contre l'enseignement supérieur? *Distances et Savoirs, 1*, 435–439. https://doi.org/10.3166/ds.1.435-439

Deschenaux, F. (2013). Les enjeux de l'enseignement pour les professeurs d'université au Québec. *Recherches en éducation*, (17). https://doi.org/10.4000/ree.7968

Dudley-Evans, T. (1997). Five questions for LSP teacher training. In R. Howard & G. Brown (Eds.), *Teacher education for languages for specific purposes*. Multilingual Matters.

Eneau, J. (2016). Autoformation, autonomisation et émancipation: De quelques problématiques de recherche en formation d'adultes. *Recherches & Éducations, 16*, 21–38. https://doi.org/10.4000/rechercheseducations.2489

European Association for Quality Assurance in Higher Education (ENQA). (2015). *Standards and guidelines for quality assurance in the European Higher Education Area (ESG)*. ENQA.

Faure, P. (2014). Enjeux d'une professionnalisation de la formation des enseignants de langue (s) de spécialité: Exemples de l'anglais et du français de la médecine. *Recherche et pratiques pédagogiques en langues de spécialité. Cahiers de l'Apliut, 33*(1), 50–65.

Freire, P. (2005). *Teachers as cultural workers: Letters to those who dare teach* (1st ed.). Routledge. https://doi.org/10.4324/9780429496974

Khan, T., & Siriwardhane, P. (2021). Barriers to career progression in the higher education sector: Perceptions of Australian academics. *Sustainability, 13*(11), 6255.

Kirsten, N. (2020). A research review of teachers' professional development as a policy instrument. *Educational Research Review*, 100366. https://doi.org/10.1016/j.edurev.2020.100366

Martell, C. C. (2014). *Action research as empowering professional development: Examining a district-based teacher research course. Online Submission.* ERIC.

MEN. (2017). Décret n° 2017-854 du 9 mai 2017. https://www.legifrance.gouv.fr/jorf/id/JORFTEXT000034632129/

OECD. (2021). *Reducing the precarity of academic research careers.* In *OECD Science, Technology and Industry Policy Papers, n° 113*, Éditions OCDE. https://doi.org/10.1787/0f8bd468-en

Postareff, L., Lindblom-Ylänne, S., & Nevgi, A. (2007). The effect of pedagogical training on teaching in higher education. *Teaching and Teacher Education, 23*(5), 557–571.

Poteaux, N. (2015). L'émergence du secteur LANSAD: Évolution et circonvolutions. *Recherche et pratiques pédagogiques en langues de spécialité. Cahiers de l'Apliut, 34*(1), 27–45.

Silio, E. (2022). Los nuevos profesores de universidad recibirán un curso para aprender a enseñar. *El País*. https://elpais.com/educacion/universidad/2022-02-23/los-nuevos-profesores-de-universidad-recibiran-un-cursillo-para-aprender-a-ensenar.html#?prm=copy_link

Suarez, V., & McGrath, J. (2022). Teacher professional identity: How to develop and support it in times of change. In *Documents de travail de l'OCDE sur l'éducation, n° 267*, Éditions OECD. https://doi.org/10.1787/b19f5af7-en

Taillefer, G. (2013). CLIL in higher education: The (perfect?) crossroads of ESP and didactic reflection. *ASp. la revue du GERAS*, (63), 31–53.

Vygotsky, L. S. (1986). *Thought and language.* MIT Press.

Woodrow, L. (2018). *Introducing course design in English for specific purposes* (Vol. 184). Routledge.

SECTION 3

SCHOOL REFORM SECTION

INTRODUCTION

Maria Assunção Flores

Concerns about student achievement in national and international assessments and the need to raise the standards of teaching and to improve the quality of pupil learning have led governments to pursue a number of reforms. While there are differences in content, context, and pace of reform, along with different historical, political, and cultural backgrounds, the process of changing policies and practices entails complex and multilayered challenges. These are associated with issues of power and control over what counts in education (and why) but also with the focus, process, and nature of school reform and its outcomes. Day (2002, p. 679), for instance, identifies five common factors in reforms in different contexts: (1) the change of the conditions under which students learn in order to accelerate improvements and raise standards of achievement, (2) the need to address implicit worries concerning a perceived fragmentation of personal and social values, (3) the challenge of teachers' existing practices, (4) increased workload, and (5) lack of attention to teachers' identities.

Analysts state that, in general, the "social market model" dominates the educational field in which an outcome-led conception of teaching has become prevalent. The increased managerialism in education and the emphasis on efficiency and effectiveness have contributed to the marketization of education and to a greater focus on performativity in which teachers' work is judged against an instrumental perspective, in many cases according to a set of standards (Flores, 2012). This is, in general, related to a simplistic and narrow view of quality which points to "a linear relationship between policy and educational outcomes without accounting for school culture, resources and communities" (Mayer, 2014, p. 471). Cochran-Smith (2021, p. 415) identifies the emergence of teacher quality as a global concept and she argues that "despite the global nature of teacher quality, what this concept means and how reforms are designed and implemented in particular countries vary considerably."

Different stakeholders hold different expectations and interests in relation to school reform seen as a process of changing educational policy and practice in order to obtain given outcomes. In addition, some stakeholders have more power than others in defining the direction and the focus of the reform as well as how it is going to be put into practice. Existing literature points to a number of challenges, namely managing dilemmas and conflicting expectations, balancing conflicting goals and managing tensions of implementation (Flores & Derrington, 2017). Cheng (2020, p. 87) discusses a set of fundamental dilemmas in education reforms: (1) *orientation dilemmas* (between globalization and localization); (2) *paradigm dilemmas* (between the first, second, and third waves of change since the 1980s, including the effective education movement, the quality education movement, and the world-class education movement); (3) *financial dilemmas* (between public interest and privatization), (4) *resources dilemmas* (between parallel initiatives), (5) *knowledge dilemmas* (in planning and implementation at different levels); (6) *political dilemmas* (between multiple stakeholders), and (7) *functional dilemmas* (between school-based management and central platform in education reforms). The author identifies tensions associated with the direction, support, and execution of the reforms, for instance the need to manage the diverse needs and conflicting expectations of multiple stakeholders and argues that "Without understanding and managing these multiple dilemmas and related tensions appropriately, many education reforms with good intentions may finally fail in implementation" (p. 88).

Research has demonstrated the need to pay attention to the meaning (and sense-making) of the stakeholders involved in the implementation of a given policy, their values, and emotions as well as the social interactions and the contexts in which such change is going to be put into operation (Spillane et al., 2002). Literature has drawn attention to the importance of teachers' perceptions and the complexity of the social dimension in policy implementation (Fullan, 2001). While teachers play a pivotal role in putting a given policy into practice, school reform also has implications for other stakeholders, particularly students, principals, and school communities.

The four chapters in this section illustrate four reforming contexts that, in one way or another, point to the tensions, side-effects and paradoxes of mandated policy initiatives. The overarching themes include issues of voice and diversity but also clearly show how the stakeholders experience school reform in context and how they look at its intended and unintended outcomes.

The first contribution, "Listening as a Basis of Reforming Schools in Asia: From Hostility to Trust," by Eisuke Saito, from Australia, focuses on how lesson study for learning communities (LSLC) can be used as a strategy to counteract the negative sentiments associated with education systems based on competitive high-stakes examinations and to foster relationships for mutual learning and well-being. The chapter begins with the contextualization of what is described as a sense of alienation and hostility in competitive systems. The author then focuses on the conceptualization of LSLC which started in 1990 in Japan. The need to fight against student disengagement and to promote a culture of listening constitutes the basis of LSLC which Saito describes as a systematic approach of school reform aimed at reforming daily practices based on collaborative learning for mutual consultation, enhancing collegiality and professional capacities through mutual observation and reflection by the teachers beyond the subject boundaries, and engaging parents and local people in the learning process. The author argues that listening is a basis and premise of learning and asserts that LSLC fosters the listening relationships between the teacher and students, between the students and between the teachers.

In the second chapter, "School Reform in South Africa and the Struggle for Social Mobility," Maropeng Modiba and Sandra Stewart examine how schooling in South Africa represents a history of gains and losses for sections of the society rather than societal betterment on the whole. The authors state that the colonial, missionary, and apartheid political systems made schooling a weak instrument for mobility for the majority within society. School reform in the post-apartheid context, they argue, continues to crystallize socioeconomic inequalities although it has provided greater access to formal education. Looking at the new funding system and equity rhetoric that is employed to justify education access to different types of schools, Modiba and Stewart conclude that school reform fails to compensate for the adverse effects of apartheid education being largely reproductive rather than socially transformative.

In the third chapter in this section, ""Data is [G]od": The Influence of Cumulative Policy Reforms on Teachers' Knowledge in an Urban Middle School in the United States," Cheryl J. Craig shows how mandated changes impacted the work of a department chair in a T. P. Yaeger Middle School in the United States. The author uses narrative inquiry to look at a teacher's experience of systematic policy-related reforms in the school from a longitudinal perspective. In particular, attention is given to the pay-for-performance reform and how it has affected the teacher's career which eventually came to an end.

The final chapter included in this school reform section, "Principals' Views in a Context of Reform: The Case of School Curriculum Policy in Portugal," by Maria Assunção Flores, looks at how school leaders see recent policy initiatives focusing on school curriculum. The author draws on data from a 3-year wider research project to discuss the key features of the new policy. In general, a critical view emerged from the findings which also point to the lack of adequacy of the conditions existing in schools to put the policy into operation, namely issues of bureaucratic control, the policy's lack of clarity and teachers' resistance to change. Overall, the regulatory and centralized orientation stands in sharp contrast to the very essence of the policies that call for local, contextualized, and innovative solutions. Flores looks at the implications of the findings for policy and practice within a centralized and bureaucratic education system in which a logic of control and standardized management of education still dominates.

The chapters in this section address the specific features of school reform in four different international contexts but they also point to overarching themes and global challenges. The political dilemmas around the interests and concerns of multiple stakeholders and their competing demands and conflicting expectations (Cheng, 2020) are evident, in one way or another, in all of the chapters but especially in Portugal and USA. This is visible, respectively, in school leaders' overall skepticism and resistance to a mandated school curriculum policy and in teachers' negative experiences of systematic change that has affected their careers in an indelible manner. The functional dilemmas focusing on issues of autonomy and external control (Cheng, 2020) are also illustrated. Such dilemmas are linked to the prescriptive and normative dimension of policy-related reforms and to the lack of involvement of the stakeholders. The chapter from Portugal clearly points to such tensions illustrated by the imposed policy and its intent to grant schools more autonomy to manage the curriculum within a centralized and bureaucratic education system. The voice of the stakeholders and the diversity of the educational contexts are also two emerging themes arising from the chapters that need to be considered in school reform. As such, it is important not only to unpack the ultimate goals and outcomes of the reforms but also their processes of implementation considering the mediating factors such as school leadership and culture as well as the role of the stakeholders and the local dynamics. The chapter from Asia, for instance, shows how lesson study for learning community (LSLC) is used as a strategy to counteract the negative effects of education systems based on competitive high-stakes examinations by promoting listening as a basis and premise of learning. In turn, the contribution from South Africa unpacks the intent and reality of the reform which is seen as reproductive rather than socially transformative. Overall, the four chapters explore the purposes and the effects of school reforms in specific contexts but also collectively raise questions about the complex, multiple and dynamic layers inherent in their development, in particular the perceptions and experiences of those who are directly affected by them.

REFERENCES

Cheng, Y. C. (2020). Education reform phenomenon: A typology of multiple dilemmas. In G. Fan & T. S. Popkewitz (Eds.), *Handbook of education policy studies: Values, governance, globalization, and methodology* (Vol. 1, pp. 85–110). Springer.

Cochran-Smith, M. (2021). Exploring teacher quality: International perspectives. *European Journal of Teacher Education, 44*(3), 415–428.

Day, C. (2002). School reform and transitions in teacher professionalism and identity. *International Journal of Educational Research, 37*, 677–692.

Flores, M. A. (2012). Teachers' work and lives: A European perspective. In C. Day (Ed.), *The routledge international handbook of teacher and school development* (pp. 94–107). Routledge.

Flores, M. A., & Derrington, M. L. (2017). School principals' views of teacher evaluation policy: Lessons learned from two empirical studies. *International Journal of Leadership in Education, 20*(4), 416–431.

Fullan, M. (2001). *The new meaning of educational change* (3rd ed.). Routledge Falmer.

Mayer, D. (2014). Forty years of teacher education in Australia: 1974-2014. *Journal of Education for Teaching, 40*(5), 461–473.

Spillane, J. P., Reiser, B. J., & Reimer, T. (2002). Policy implementation and cognition: Reframing and refocusing implementation research. *Review of Educational Research, 72*(3), 387–431.

LISTENING AS A BASIS OF REFORMING SCHOOLS IN ASIA: FROM HOSTILITY TO TRUST

Eisuke Saito

ABSTRACT

In many Asian countries, education systems are competitive based on high-stakes examinations. Additionally, due to the traditional one-way teaching styles, classroom practices can be highly authoritarian. The issue in such education systems is the alienation of students. They do not learn about themselves; rather, they work toward and/or get distracted by securing their positions according to the standards set by other people and institutions. Many students are thus disengaged from learning and share one common reason for their disengagement: their sense of loss about the meaning of learning is unheeded and they have no opportunity to voice their opinions. Consequently, various sentiments are prevalent, even extremely negative ones, almost equivalent to mutual hostilities. This chapter conceptually discusses the importance of listening in school reform, with special reference to the cases initiated by Manabu Sato and his fellow school leaders, such as Toshiaki Ose and Masaaki Sato. Their approach is known as school as a learning community (SLC) or lesson study for learning community (LSLC); the latter is used herein. LSLC is now widely practiced in various countries in Asia, including China, Taiwan, Korea, Indonesia, Vietnam, and Thailand. LSLC aims to overcome the negative sentiments described above and establish communal relationships for mutual learning and well-being. To achieve this, teachers in the schools running LSLC always start listening to each other. This chapter discusses how listening transforms hostilities into trust.

Keywords: Listening; school reform; Asia; lesson study for learning community (LSLC); one-listening; the listened-to

In many Asian countries, educational systems are highly competitive due to high-stakes examinations (Ashadi & Rice, 2016; Chen & Kuan, 2021; Kumar & Chowdhury, 2021; Shin & Cho, 2020; Teng et al., 2021; Wong et al., 2021; Zhang, 2021). One core problem in such systems is the students' sense of alienation – a learner not being able to "affirm himself but denies himself, does not feel content but unhappy, does not develop freely his physical and mental energy but mortifies is body and ruins his mind" (Lave & McDermott, 2002, p. 36). Such a sense of alienation can turn into hostility against everyone in the school if the degree of alienation increases (Sabic-El-Rayess, 2021; Saito, 2022). Not only do student learn with such emotions, but there is also a risk of teachers experiencing similar emotions. Relationships with students, other colleagues, and authorities or management can be the sources of teacher vulnerability (Kelchtermans, 1996).

Such alienation and hostility stem from a very weak development of relationships between the stakeholders, for one fundamental reason: lack of listening. This severe lack can be between students and teachers, students and students, and teachers and teachers. Thus, a vicious circle exists, where a lack of listening results in insufficient development of relationships among the stakeholders; subsequently, insufficient relational development would cause alienation among the stakeholders, which may exacerbate the degree of hostility against others. Although a school is a place for learning regarding cognitive, social, and ethical senses (Cazden, 2001; Inagaki & Sato, 1996; Sato, 2012a), human beings cannot sufficiently learn due to the aforementioned environment. In other words, it is critical to reform schools to enable the members – the students and teachers – to listen to each other. However, listening itself has not been sufficiently focused on as a necessary condition for reform in previous studies.

To break this vicious circle, there has been an attempt of school reform under an approach called "lesson study for learning community (LSLC)" or "school as learning community (SLC)" and hereafter LSLC is used. This chapter aims to discuss listening relationships in LSLC. To achieve this goal, this chapter is divided into the following sections: introduction to LSLC; discussion about listening in LSLC; and detailed concluding remarks.

LSLC

LSLC started to be practiced at the end of 1990s in Japan, where serious problems occurred in many schools regarding disengagement with, and doubts about the meaning of, learning, as demonstrated by the students (Kariya, 2001; Sato, 2000, 2001) in the forms of chitchats, or even threats of violence against other peers or teachers. This is partly due to the blow-up of the bubble economy and its consequent default in Japan at that time (Saito & Takasawa, 2018), thus shattering the societal belief which told that better academic scores would enable the student to get into highly ranking schools, lead them to admission to a prestigious university, and eventually into respected jobs with good incomes (Sato, 2001). However, the economic shock and collapse of the societal belief negatively impacted the motivation to study of many students (Kariya, 2001; Sato, 2000, 2001).

Instead of emphasizing possible futures without guarantee, which forces students to bear the burden to survive in competitive high-stakes examinations, LSLC underlines the need for students to experience the pleasure of learning (Sato, 1999) through appreciating the process and satisfying the intrinsic desire for learning itself. It requires authenticity and collaboration in the process of learning. This is based on the high-quality tasks reflecting the uniqueness of disciplines of the subjects (Saito & Fatemi, 2022; Sato, 1996) and close consultations with peers through help-seeking (Saito & Fatemi, 2022; Saito, Takahashi, et al., 2020; Sato, 2012a; Webb, 2013).

For this aim, listening is a significant concept in LSLC. It involves pondering the meaning of representations, like texts, remarks, images, or any other forms of expressions, and not just physically hearing a noise. This deeper contemplation would be a basis to raise the voice to others about what they do not understand in those representations, and to respond to those voices. Thus, listening is a basis and a premise of learning. It is a series of dialogues with disciplines, others, and selves (Cazden, 2001; Inagaki & Sato, 1996; Sato, 1999), which necessarily involves caring (Noddings, 2013). In these ways, listening relationships are considered as an underpinning anchor for practicing LSLC, as discussed in detail in the next section.

The aforementioned philosophy about listening deeply reflects a notion of democracy, namely, "associated ways of living" (Dewey, 1916). LSLC is also a systematic approach of school reform, to pursue: (1) reforming daily practices based on collaborative learning for mutual consultation; (2) enhancing collegiality and professional capacities through mutual observation and reflection by the teachers beyond the subject boundaries, and (3) engaging parents and local people in the learning process. The vision of reform presented to the three schools contained three central goals: assuring learning opportunities for (1) every child, (2) every teacher, and (3) as many parents and local community members as possible.

For this, the teachers engaged in LSLC need to be expert as it requires extensive professional learning and development. Thus, it is emphasized letting teachers observe and reflect on each other's lessons. During a school year, each school offered about 80–100 opportunities for teachers to observe their colleagues and reflect on various practices. To provide teachers with time for such frequent and intensive collaboration, the school leaders reviewed, restructured, and reduced their daily administrative chores. To facilitate better learning opportunities for the children, the reforms also called for the introduction of collaborative activities in each lesson.

LCLS was advocated by Manabu Sato, who was then a professor of the University of Tokyo. Since the end of 1990s, its practice began in a few pilot schools in collaboration with school leaders like Toshiaki Ose and Masaaki Sato (Ose & Sato, 2003; Sato, 2003; Sato & Sato, 2003). Then, it gained popularity among the teachers and school leaders, who understood the limits of conventional, one-way teaching practices or authoritarian ways of school management within a decade (Sato, 2012a). Since then, the LSLC has been internationally practiced in many other countries, for example, China (Sato, 2022), Taiwan (Huang, 2019), Korea (Shin & Son, 2019), Indonesia (Saito, Khong, et al., 2020;

Suratno et al., 2019), Vietnam (Saito, 2021; Saito & Khong, 2017), and Thailand (Luanrit et al., 2022; Sato, 2022). In these countries, the education systems are likely to be very hierarchical and competitive under authoritarian political regimes, where only one way of listening is forced upon the people. There is no dialogue in such contexts and their school or classroom lives function as oppressive means to alienate students, teachers, and even parents from the real purpose and meaning of learning, as discussed earlier. The rapid and intense support for LSLC meant that the teachers, students, and parents wish to reform their schools and create a space where they can appreciate the joy and pleasure of learning together through mutual listening.

LISTENING IN LSLC

Teachers and Students

In LSLC, the listening relationships between the teacher and students are underlined. In many Asian countries, the relationships between the teacher and students tend to be hierarchical (Bjork, 2005; Saito & Atencio, 2013; Sato, 2012a; Suwinyattichaiporn et al., 2019). In such a classroom or school, monologues given by the teachers dominate the process of interactions between the teacher and students, and listening to students by the teacher is unlikely (Sato, 2012a). Here, listening refers to the premise of learning and care as discussed earlier. LSLC aims to promote their learning by changing their relationships to more listening oriented.

The teacher in Japan tends to be considered as someone who speaks about the content to teach or ask questions to the students to see whether they can answer correctly (Sato, 2012a). This expectation is largely applicable to other Asian countries as well (Saito & Atencio, 2013; Saito et al., 2008). This mode of pedagogical practice establishes micropolitical relationships in the classrooms, where the teacher puts themselves in the position of authority to rule the space, and the students are supposed to either take notes of the lecture or compete among themselves to be recognized by the teacher and other peers. This nature of relationships is exceedingly individualistic with no space for collaboration (Sato, 2012a).

In LSLC, the nature of the work by the teacher would be largely transformed. Here, they are expected to change their identity from speaker to listener (Saito & Atencio, 2013) – that is, someone capable of identifying who would experience difficulties and who would need to, but cannot in reality, seek help from others (Webb, 2013). The teacher would encourage and provide opportunities for those students to connect themselves with other peers by proactively asking questions and collaborating with them (Saito et al., 2015). In this sense, the teacher is expected to be a facilitator of learning for the students, rather than a speaker to deliver the content one-sidedly, under LSLC.

By engaging themselves with the transformation of their identities, the teachers are expected to change the underpinning values in classrooms and schools – from competition to learning. Previously, the teacher's work involved successively calling on the students with correct answers, which made the students competitive for the teacher's attention and praise (Saito et al., 2008). The notions behind this were that the class must be conducted smoothly and that it would be sufficient if some leading students could correctly answer – and if some others could not, they were likely to be dismissed or considered as responsible for their failure in understanding the content (Flores et al., 2015; Saito et al., 2008; Sanders & Munford, 2016; Strati et al., 2017).

In contrast, in LSLC, each student is valued, and their struggle or misconception is considered as a starting point of learning. Such struggles are the sources of collaborative learning based on help-seeking (Webb, 2013) and the students are encouraged to say to their peers, "Can you help me?" (Sato, 2012a). This would diverge the process of learning from student to student and group to group, based on the same, shared the contents or tasks. This reflects the perspectives held by the advocates and practitioners on the curriculum, curriculum of history, or experience of learning (Sato, 1996) or "emergent curriculum" (Saito & Fatemi, 2022). It is different from the idea of unified form of curriculum, where only the teacher has the right to design or operate and is based on the notion to consider the students in a class as a whole, rather than individuals (Inagaki & Sato, 1996).

Students and Students

Thereafter, in LSLC, the listening relationships between the students are also aimed to be transformed. In many Asian countries, the nature of competitive systems (Ashadi & Rice, 2016; Chen & Kuan, 2021; Kumar & Chowdhury, 2021; Shin & Cho, 2020; Wong et al., 2021; Zhang, 2021) is likely to influence the student relationships too (Ashadi & Rice, 2016; Charoenkul, 2018; Chiam, 2009; Lee, 2009; Saito et al., 2008; Tong et al., 2018). In LSLC, this competitive nature of their relationships would be transformed into collaborative ones based on mutual listening (Hakkarainen et al., 2013; Roschelle & Teasley, 1995). This emphasis on mutual listening was due to abundant monologues of the teachers, textbooks, or the students with high achievements in Asian classrooms (Saito & Atencio, 2013; Saito et al., 2008; Sato, 1999), which force the students to follow correct and standardized answers rather than questioning them or sharing different ways of thinking in the dialogues, which are necessary elements for learning.

Indeed, the students are forcibly exposed to competitive relationships in various ways in Asian schools. One of the most obvious competitions is standardized scholastic achievements. As Foucault (1995) argued, the students are always concerned about their ranking, and they try not to model those who are considered as failures. This sense of competition or over-consciousness about ranking would not necessarily be limited to the cognitive achievements. It would escalate to the degree of more violent and aggressive micro-political relationships, for example, bullying, that is victimizing some students by collective power (Chan & Wong, 2015; Yoneyama & Naito, 2003). Then, those who are marginalized or victimized suffer greatly. If their suffering turns violence toward themselves, it may result in self-destructive behaviors like suicidal attempts or psychological issues like depressions (Murshid, 2017; Pengpid & Peltzer, 2019; Sittichai & Smith, 2015). If their anger is expressed externally, they demonstrate hostilities against others (Sabic-El-Rayess, 2021; Saito, 2022). These competitive climates in the classrooms and schools come from a hardship to share their concerns and questions, which can be taken as weaknesses.

In LSLC, therefore, it is aimed to transform this relationship into a more listening one. Here, first is the listening for care. This stance of listening would suggest the counterpart who seeks help or request, "I am here for you." That is, those who are asked for help, or one-caring, would be and remain conversation with those who seek help, or the cared-for (Noddings, 2013). After having such conversations for numerous times, the students start to trust each other. In LSLC, the groups or pairs are not organized by achievements, rather randomly and groups are changed on a regular basis to let the students work with everyone else. Such efforts eventually let some students with anger in their nature, due to their complex life-histories, eventually trust others (Saito et al., 2015; Sato, 2012b).

Then, listening is a premise for learning too. As discussed above, the students are expected to share what they are perplexed about or exchange different observations or ideas. Accumulation of such smaller experiences of successful learning would lead the students to have richer development – zone of proximal development (Vygotsky, 1978). For this, trust on others and themselves about ability and relationship to share anything is required. It also suggests that the tasks must have the inspiringly challenging nature to the degree that the students need to consult with others (Saito & Fatemi, 2022; Saito, Takahashi, et al., 2020). Through the interactions, the students would listen to each other about their approach toward the tasks in front of them and learn how more knowledgeable, skillful, or informed peers would handle the tasks (Hakkarainen et al., 2013; Saito & Atencio, 2014; Saito & Fatemi, 2022; Saito, Takahashi, et al., 2020; Webb, 2013).

By engaging themselves with such change in the student-student relationships, they are changing the values in the classrooms or schools too. They shift from the hierarchically competitive ones (Chinh et al., 2014; Jung & Hasan, 2015; Lathapipat, 2016; Ng, 2014; Rolleston & Krutikova, 2014) to more like *educational polyphony*, where everyone is respected and valued as an individual with their own voice, and not alienated or marginalized in a given educational organization (Saito, 2022). In the hierarchically competitive setup, the most important would be to identify who has the power, which would lead the students to divide themselves between the leads and accompaniments in their classrooms or schools. Here, those who are in the lower positions under a certain hierarchy would never have any opportunities to be listened, since they are not considered important enough. Almost always those who have power are listened to.

However, in LSLC, everyone is valued whatever their backgrounds are so that their voices should be listened. Rather, it is an important norm for those who attend someone raising their voices – however small and soft the voices are, because those with such small and soft voices are likely to be highly vulnerable too – to carefully listen (Sato, 2012a, 2012b). In so doing, another norm is to consider a gap as a resource (Saito & Atencio, 2014; Saito & Fatemi, 2022). A gap can be about anything, the degree of comprehension about the content or opinions about phenomena in the classrooms or the outside world. It is critical to share the understanding that the students can deepen understanding about the issue itself and themselves through exchanges of ideas, knowledge, or skills, which would start from the awareness of the gap. In other words, without a gap, the students cannot learn meaningfully through collaborative dialogues and the gap must be positively appreciated and utlised, and everyone with difference from each other must be appreciated too.

Teachers and Teachers

In LSLC, collegial relationships between the teachers would also be transformed. In many Asian schools, collegial relationships between the teachers tends to be fragmented – indifferent to each other in many cases, otherwise even competitive or hostile. Such relationships would be revealed most in the occasions of joint observations of and reflections on the practices. They would insist and force their ideas upon, or bash those who open their practices for public observations, to show their power and capacities: for example, in Vietnam (Saito et al., 2008), where it can be applicable to the university levels (Le et al., 2018; Nguyen & Pham, 2020), or in Japan (Inagaki & Sato, 1996; Sato, 2003). Even not to this degree, nuanced conversations between mentors and mentees may generate the sense of negativity as shown in a study from Singapore (Kim & Silver, 2016). Furthermore, the teachers can be highly isolated from each other and indifferent to learn from each other, thus making the knowledge or know-how their hidden properties, as observed in Indonesia (Rahman, 2022). Such climates inevitably make the teachers apprehensive to open their practices to other fellows and it is difficult to expect that they would learn together from joint observations of and reflections on practices.

This type of relationship is targeted to be transformed into more mutually listening and learning in LSLC. In LSLC, joint observations of and reflections on the practices are regularly conducted beyond the boundaries of subjects but based on each year group, for their professional learning and development (Sato, 2012a). Through practicing these activities regularly, around 80–100 times per year as a total number of the school, the teachers would acquire pedagogical content knowledge as reflective practitioners over the time, as observed in Japan (Kitada, 2019; Sato, 2003, 2012a, 2022). Likewise, in Vietnam, the teachers learned from each other about the student learning with reference to the video clips they produced by editing the recordings (Saito, 2021). Such change occurs when they realize that their practices would be at the edge – obstacles or confinements in their practices, which need to be overcome and for this the teachers themselves need to change (Saito & Khong, 2017). In other words, such obstacles are likely to be the realities of the lack of learning in the students and their constrained voices would reach the teachers; the teachers would listen to such voices for the first time.

Such changes in relationships between the teachers would represent a transition from Balkanization to publicness. Balkanization is a state where the teachers are highly individualized and have no sense of professional ties with other colleagues (Hargreaves, 1994). This notion originated from the realities of the schools in the Western, developed countries but it is largely applicable to those in

Asian countries too (Inagaki & Sato, 1996; Ng, 2011; Rahman, 2022; Saito et al., 2008). This would be partly because of the bureaucratic nature of school organizations with hierarchical orders, which forces the teachers to compete among themselves, rather than professional autonomy for and based on mutual learning (Saito & Atencio, 2013; Saito et al., 2008). In such organizations, the momentum to listen to each other for learning is unlikely. Rather, the teachers tend to hide their practices from the peers and are apprehensive to listen to others' comments. In such practices, the teachers are unlikely to listen to the voices of the students too (Saito & Atencio, 2013; Saito et al., 2008).

In LSLC, the teacher relationships are expected to be transformed into more public ones. Individualization and fragmentation in the Balkanised schools would be addressed to unite and communalize the teachers; to openly learn from, about, and with colleagues about practices mutually. In the process of enhancing publicness in the schools, the key is to promote mutual listening among the teachers. For this purpose, as in the case between the students, it is critical for the teachers to feel secure and safe in professional conversations, for example, joint observations and reflections. Thus, it is important for the teachers to pay attention to how students learn, not how the teachers should teach (Sato, 2012a). The conflicts among the teachers (Saito et al., 2008) tend to be due to the attention of the observing teachers regarding how the teachers have taught without much evidence. In LSLC, teachers exchange their reflections with reference to the observed facts about the students as evidence (Kitada, 2019; Saito, 2021; Sato, 2012a).

CONCLUDING REMARKS

This chapter has discussed the listening relationships in LSLC between (1) teacher and students, (2) student and student, and (3) teacher and teacher. For the teacher-students relationship, the teacher is expected to change their professional identity from a speaker to a listener who facilitates student learning. This shifts the values of the classroom/school from competition to learning. Regarding relationships among students, they need to change their competitive relationship, which does not allow students to seek help because it would imply showing weaknesses. They should nurture listening relationships for mutual care and learning – changing the value from hierarchical competition, which marginalizes and alienates those who cannot rank high, to educational polyphony, where everyone is respected and cared for. As for relationships among teachers, fragmented relationships – indifferent, competitive, or even hostile – would be targeted for them to mutually listen for their professional learning. This change would also imply a shift in values within the teachers from Balkanization to publicness – a community for open dialogues and learning by listening to each other.

Listening, therefore, constitutes learning in three ways. First, if a person who listens is called one-listening and a person who is listened to as the listened-to just as Noddings (2013) refers to one-caring and the cared-for, by listening, the one-listening tries to understand the messages in speech or any form of representation given by the listened-to. Thus, it is a cognitive activity. Second, by listening, the one-listening tries to build trust with the listened-to – improving social relationships. Third, one-listening would listen to their own voices in themselves – they themselves become the listened-to, which is an ethical activity. Thus, LSLC enables everyone in the school, students and teachers, to become one-listening and listened-to.

LSLC positively transformed numerous schools with problems of delinquencies (Saito et al., 2015; Sato, 2012a, 2012b). In such schools, people are becoming either one-listening or the listened-to. The voices throughout such schools comes from those in power, saying, "you are there for me." In the LSLC reform, efforts are made for everyone to become the listened-to. If the wounds of the past are healed, eventually, they would be willing to become one-listening for others, by paying forward (Saito et al., 2015), to tell, "I am here for you." This will transform hostilities into trust, and this is what LSLC aims to create in every school where it is practiced.

AUTHOR'S NOTES

The author received financial support for this research from the School of Education, Society and Culture, Faculty of Education, Monash University [Grant Number: ECS Research Grant 2022]

REFERENCES

Ashadi, A., & Rice, S. (2016). High stakes testing and teacher access to professional opportunities: Lessons from Indonesia. *Journal of Education Policy, 31*(6), 727–741. https://doi.org/10.1080/02680939.2016.1193901

Bjork, C. (2005). *Indonesian education: Teachers, schools, and central bureaucracy*. Routledge.

Cazden, C. B. (2001). *Classroom discourse: The language of teaching and learning* (2nd ed.). Heinemann.

Chan, H. C., & Wong, D. S. W. (2015). Traditional school bullying and cyberbullying in Chinese societies: Prevalence and a review of the whole-school intervention approach. *Aggression and Violent Behavior, 23*, 98–108. https://doi.org/10.1016/j.avb.2015.05.010

Charoenkul, N. (2018). Shadow education in Thailand: Thai and international perspectives. In G. W. Fry (Ed.), *Education in Thailand: An old elephant in search of a New Mahout* (pp. 627–650). Springer. https://doi.org/10.1007/978-981-10-7857-6_25

Chen, I. C., & Kuan, P. Y. (2021, January 29). The heterogeneous effects of participation in shadow education on mental health of high school students in Taiwan. *International Journal of Environmental Research and Public Health, 18*(3). https://doi.org/10.3390/ijerph18031222

Chiam, C. L. (2009). Knowledge sharing in Singapore's public post-secondary educational institutions. *BiblioAsia, 5*(1), 4–9.

Chinh, N. D., Linh, L. T., Quynh, T. H., & Ha, N. T. (2014). Inequality of access to English language learning in primary education in Vietnam. In H. Zhang, P. W. K. Chan, & C. Boyle (Eds.), *Equality in education: Fairness and inclusion* (pp. 139–153). Sense Publishers. https://doi.org/10.1007/978-94-6209-692-9_11

Dewey, J. (1916). *Democracy and education: An introduction to the philosophy of education*. Macmillan.

Flores, N., Kleyn, T., & Menken, K. (2015). Looking holistically in a climate of partiality: Identities of students labeled long-term English language learners. *Journal of Language, Identity and Education, 14*(2), 113–132. https://doi.org/10.1080/15348458.2015.1019787

Foucault, M. (1995). *Discipline and punish: The birth of the prison* (2nd Vintage Books ed.). Vintage Books.

Hakkarainen, K., Paavola, S., Kangas, K., & Seitamaa-Hakkarainen, P. (2013). Sociocultural perspectives on collaborative learning: Toward collaborative knowledge creation. In C. E. Hmelo-Silver (Ed.), *The international handbook of collaborative learning* (pp. 57–73).

Hargreaves, A. (1994). *Changing teachers, changing times*. Teachers College Press.
Huang, Y. (2019). The challenge of school as learning community in Taiwan: Late start and rapid spread. In A. Tsukui & M. Murase (Eds.), *Lesson study and schools as learning communities* (pp. 59–73). Routledge.
Inagaki, T., & Sato, M. (1996). *Jugyo kenkyu nyumon (Introduction to lesson study)*. Iwanami.
Jung, H., & Hasan, A. (2015). The impact of early childhood education on early achievement gaps in Indonesia. *Journal of Development Effectiveness*, 8(2), 216–233. https://doi.org/10.1080/19439342.2015.1088054
Kariya, T. (2001). *Kaisoka nihon to kyoiku kiki [Stratified Japan and educational crisis]*. Yushindo.
Kelchtermans, G. (1996). Teacher vulnerability: Understanding its moral and political roots. *Cambridge Journal of Education*, 26(3), 307–323. https://doi.org/10.1080/0305764960260302
Kim, Y., & Silver, R. E. (2016). Provoking reflective thinking in post observation conversations. *Journal of Teacher Education*, 67(3), 203–219. https://doi.org/10.1177/0022487116637120
Kitada, Y. (2019). School-wide lesson study across subject areas: Creating school-based professional learning communities in Japanese secondary schools. In A. Tsukui & M. Murase (Eds.), *Lesson study and schools as learning communities* (pp. 29–44). Routledge.
Kumar, I., & Chowdhury, I. R. (2021). Shadow education in India: Participation and socioeconomic determinants. *Journal of South Asian Development*, 16(2), 244–272. https://doi.org/10.1177/09731741211032472
Lathapipat, D. (2016). Inequality in education and wages. In P. Phongpaichit & C. Baker (Eds.), *Unequal Thailand* (pp. 43–54). NUS Press. https://doi.org/10.2307/j.ctv1xxzt4.9
Lave, J., & McDermott, R. (2002). Estranged labor learning. *Outlines. Critical Practice Studies*, 4(1), 19–48. https://tidsskrift.dk/outlines/article/view/5143
Lee, Y.-J. (2009). Not if but when pedagogy collides with culture in Singapore. *Pedagogies: An International Journal*, 5(1), 17–26. https://doi.org/10.1080/15544800903406274
Le, H., Janssen, J., & Wubbels, T. (2018). Collaborative learning practices: Teacher and student perceived obstacles to effective student collaboration. *Cambridge Journal of Education*, 48(1), 103-122. https://doi.org/10.1080/0305764X.2016.1259389
Luanrit, T., Saito, E., & Saejea, V. (2022). School leadership to prevent collateral damage: A case study of a Thai principal during the COVID-19 pandemic. In S. Chitpin & R. E. White (Eds.), *Leading under pressure* (pp. 121–144). Emerald. https://doi.org/10.1108/978-1-80117-358-220221008
Murshid, N. S. (2017). Bullying victimization and mental health outcomes of adolescents in Myanmar, Pakistan, and Sri Lanka. *Children and Youth Services Review*, 76, 163–169. https://doi.org/10.1016/j.childyouth.2017.03.003
Ng, S. W. (2011). Managing teacher balkanization in times of implementing change. *International Journal of Educational Management*, 25(7), 654–670. https://doi.org/10.1108/09513541111172072
Ng, I. (2014). Education and social mobility. In *Inequality in Singapore* (pp. 25–49). Co-Published with Institute of Policy Studies, National University of Singapore. https://doi.org/10.1142/9789814623841_0003
Nguyen, P. V., & Pham, H. T. (2020). Academics' perceptions of challenges of a peer observation of teaching pilot in a Confucian nation: The Vietnamese experience. *International Journal for Academic Development*, 1–15. https://doi.org/10.1080/1360144x.2020.1827260
Noddings, N. (2013). *Caring: A relational approach to ehics and moral education*. University of California Press.
Ose, T., & Sato, M. (2003). *Gakko wo kaeru [Reforming the school]*. Shogakkan.
Pengpid, S., & Peltzer, K. (2019). Bullying victimization and externalizing and internalizing symptoms among in-school adolescents from five ASEAN countries. *Children and Youth Services Review*, 106. https://doi.org/10.1016/j.childyouth.2019.104473
Rahman, A. (2022). Investigating school conditions for teachers' professional learning and development in Indonesia. *Teacher Development*, 26(2), 240–262. https://doi.org/10.1080/13664530.2022.2034662

Rolleston, C., & Krutikova, S. (2014). Equalising opportunity? School quality and home disadvantage in Vietnam. *Oxford Review of Education*, *40*(1), 112–131. https://doi.org/10.1080/03054985.2013.875261

Roschelle, J., & Teasley, S. D. (1995). The construction of shared knowledge in collaborative problem solving. In C. O'Malley (Ed.), *Computer supported collaborative learning* (pp. 69–97). Springer Berlin Heidelberg. https://doi.org/10.1007/978-3-642-85098-1_5

Sabic-El-Rayess, A. (2021). How do people radicalize? *International Journal of Educational Development*, *87*. https://doi.org/10.1016/j.ijedudev.2021.102499

Saito, E. (2021). The evolution of joint teacher observations and reflections as sites of heteroglossia and heteroopia: An actor–network theoretical discussion. *Reflective Practice*, *22*(5), 682–696. https://doi.org/10.1080/14623943.2021.1964946

Saito, E. (2022). Educational polyphony for a contemplative under tragic tension: Implications from the early life of Smerdyakov in the Brothers Karamazov. *Journal of Beliefs and Values*, *43*(3), 364–374. https://doi.org/10.1080/13617672.2021.1982559

Saito, E., & Atencio, M. (2013). A conceptual discussion of lesson study from a micro-political perspective: Implications for teacher development and pupil learning. *Teaching and Teacher Education*, *31*, 87–95. https://doi.org/10.1016/j.tate.2013.01.001

Saito, E., & Atencio, M. (2014). Conceptualising teacher practice and pupil group learning through developmental stages and integration factors. *Policy Futures in Education*, *12*(4), 558–571. https://doi.org/10.2304/pfie.2014.12.4.558

Saito, E., & Fatemi, G. (2022). Enabling students to become co-makers of emergent curricula through authentic and collaborative learning. *Management in Education*. https://doi.org/10.1177/08920206221123177

Saito, E., & Khong, T. D. H. (2017). Not just for special occasions: Supporting the professional learning of teachers through critical reflection with audio-visual information. *Reflective Practice*, *18*(6), 837–851. https://doi.org/10.1080/14623943.2017.1361921

Saito, E., Khong, T. D. H., Sumikawa, Y., Watanabe, M., Hidayat, A., & Tinoca, L. (2020). Comparative institutional analysis of participation in collaborative learning. *Cogent Education*, *7*(1). https://doi.org/10.1080/2331186x.2020.1779556

Saito, E., Takahashi, R., Wintachai, J., & Anunthavorasakul, A. (2020). Issues in introducing collaborative learning in South East Asia: A critical discussion. *Management in Education*, *35*(4), 167–173. https://doi.org/10.1177/0892020620932367

Saito, E., & Takasawa, N. (2018). Going against peril: Neo-liberal threats and school reform in Japan. In M. J. Nakkura & A. J. Schneider-Muñoz (Eds.), *Adolescent psychology in today's world: Global perspectives on risks, relationships, and development* (Vol. 2, pp. 153–174). Praeger.

Saito, E., Tsukui, A., & Tanaka, Y. (2008). Problems on primary school-based in-service training in Vietnam: A case study of Bac Giang province. *International Journal of Educational Development*, *28*(1), 89–103. https://doi.org/10.1016/j.ijedudev.2007.08.001

Saito, E., Watanabe, M., Gillies, R., Someya, I., Nagashima, T., Sato, M., & Murase, M. (2015). School reform for positive behaviour support through collaborative learning: Utilizing lesson study for a learning community. *Cambridge Journal of Education*, *45*(4), 489–518. https://doi.org/10.1080/0305764x.2014.988684

Sanders, J., & Munford, R. (2016). Fostering a sense of belonging at school—Five orientations to practice that assist vulnerable youth to create a positive student identity. *School Psychology International*, *37*(2), 155–171. https://doi.org/10.1177/0143034315614688

Sato, M. (1996). *Karikyuramu no hihyo: Kokyosei no saikochiku he [Critique of the curriculum: Reconstrucing the publicness]*. Seori Shobo.

Sato, M. (1999). *Manabi no kairaku—daiarogu he [Pleasure of learning: Towards dialogue]*. Seori Shobo.

Sato, M. (2000). *Manabi Kara Toso Suru Kodomo Tachi [Children escaping from learning]*. Iwanami.

Sato, M. (2001). *Gakuryoku wo toinaosu: Manabi no karikyuramu he [Re-questioning scholastic achievements: Towards curriculum for learning]*. Iwanami.

Sato, M. (2003). *Kyoshitachi no chosen [Challenges taken up by the teachers]*. Shogakkan.

Sato, M. (2012a). *Gakko kaikaku no testugaku [Philosophy for school reform]*. University of Tokyo Press.

Sato, M. (2012b). *Gakko kenbunroku [School visit records]*. Shogakkan.
Sato, M. (2022). *Manabi no kyodotai no sozo [Creating school for learning community]*. Shogakkan.
Sato, M., & Sato, M. (2003). *Koritsu chugakko no chosen [Challenge taken up by a neighbourhood lower secondary school]*. Gyosei.
Shin, D., & Cho, E. (2020). The National English ability test in Korea and its legitimising discourses. *Journal of Multilingual and Multicultural Development*, *42*(6), 537–550. https://doi.org/10.1080/01434632.2020.1745818
Shin, J., & Son, W. (2019). School reform practices through building learning community in Korea. In A. Tsukui & M. Murase (Eds.), *Lesson study and schools as learning communities* (pp. 45–58). Routledge.
Sittichai, R., & Smith, P. K. (2015). Bullying in South-East Asian countries: A review. *Aggression and Violent Behavior*, *23*, 22–35. https://doi.org/10.1016/j.avb.2015.06.002
Strati, A. D., Schmidt, J. A., & Maier, K. S. (2017). Perceived challenge, teacher support, and teacher obstruction as predictors of student engagement. *Journal of Educational Psychology*, *109*(1), 131–147. https://doi.org/10.1037/edu0000108
Suratno, T., Joharmawan, R., Chotimah, H., & Takasawa, N. (2019). Harbinger of lesson study for learning community in Indonesia. In A. Tsukui & M. Murase (Eds.), *Lesson study and schools as learning communities* (pp. 74–89). Routledge.
Suwinyattichaiporn, T., Johnson, Z. D., & Fontana, J. (2019). Investigating the influence of student–Teacher Facebook interaction in Thailand. *Asian Journal of Communication*, *29*(5), 391–404. https://doi.org/10.1080/01292986.2019.1651882
Teng, S. S., Abu Bakar, M., & Layne, H. (2021). Education reforms within neoliberal paradigms: A comparative look at the Singaporean and Finnish education systems. *Asia Pacific Journal of Education*, *40*(4), 458–471. https://doi.org/10.1080/02188791.2020.1838884
Tong, L., Reynolds, K., Lee, E., & Liu, Y. (2018). School relational climate, social identity, and student well-being: New evidence from China on student depression and stress levels. *School Mental Health*, *11*(3), 509–521. https://doi.org/10.1007/s12310-018-9293-0
Vygotsky, L. S. (1978). *Mind in society: The development of higher psychological processes* (V. M. Cole, John-Steiner, S. Scribner, & E. Souberman, Trans.). Harvard University Press.
Webb, N. M. (2013). Information processing approaches to collaborative learning. In C. E. Hmelo-Silver, C. A. Chinn, C. K. K. Chan, & A. O'Donnell (Eds.), *The international handbook of collaborative learning* (pp. 19–40). Routledge.
Wong, H. M., Kwek, D., & Tan, K. (2021). Changing assessments and the examination culture in Singapore: A review and analysis of Singapore's assessment policies. *Asia Pacific Journal of Education*, *40*(4), 433–457. https://doi.org/10.1080/02188791.2020.1838886
Yoneyama, S., & Naito, A. (2003). Problems with the paradigm: The school as a factor in understanding bullying (with special reference to Japan). *British Journal of Sociology of Education*, *24*(3), 315–330. https://doi.org/10.1080/01425690301894
Zhang, J. (2021). A moderated mediation analysis of the relationship between a high-stakes English test and test takers' extracurricular English learning activities. *Language Testing in Asia*, *11*(1). https://doi.org/10.1186/s40468-021-00120-x

SCHOOL REFORM IN SOUTH AFRICA: A STRUGGLE FOR MOBILITY

Maropeng Modiba and Sandra Stewart

ABSTRACT

Schooling in South Africa represents a history of gains and losses for sections of the society. The colonial, missionary, and apartheid political systems made schooling a weak instrument for mobility for the majority within society. Post-apartheid, although school reform has provided greater access to formal education, it continues to crystallize socioeconomic inequalities. A relatively small number of the previously disadvantaged receive education that facilitates economic and social mobility. The authors examine the new funding system and equity rhetoric that is employed to justify education access to different types of schools and argue that coupling the rhetoric of social transformation with the funding system for schools and thus class, continues the unequal historical education provision. School reform fails to compensate for the adverse effects of apartheid education and is largely reproductive rather than socially transformative. The conclusion is that unless South Africa overcomes the appeasing semantic trap in its policies, historical trends that make the constitutional ideal of equal rights unrealizable are likely to be entrenched.

Keywords: South Africa; school reform; semantic trap; funding; equity; social transformation

INTRODUCTION: BACKGROUND AND CONTEXT TO SCHOOL REFORM

In South Africa, past and current attempts at reforming schooling present no significant differences (Castells, 1997). From the colonial and missionary era in the nineteenth century to the present post-apartheid period, material advantage is used to varying degrees to determine and justify the provision of differentiated education (Alexander, 2000, 2005). For a number of years following the occupation of the country, no earnest consideration was given to equal rights between the colonists and indigenous people. There is a level on which, for example, the colonial and missionary policies operated with what others (Kane-Berman, 1978) described as a kind of altruism, but also other levels on which there was the blatant ideology of white domination (Hunter, 2019; Kallaway, 1984). The impact of colonial and apartheid policies can thus not be fully grasped without referring to landmarks that stand out in the history of education provision and showing how they were significant in the process of school reform.

First, in the nineteenth century, education was provided mainly by the British colonial authorities in free schools that prioritized teaching the *Bible*, reading and how to write. Later, missionary schools such as Lovedale, continued to offer education that resembled what was offered in the mother country (Duncan, 2009). With industrial expansion after the First World War and the scientific restructuring of the economy that resulted from the expansion of gold mining, manufacturing industries and migration from rural areas to towns, it became important to secure the position of Whites and reserve jobs for them. The recommendations of the Phelphs-Stokes Commission of 1922 urged the adoption of a differentiated schooling system and teacher training course (Davis, 1976). The process was finalized with the recommendation of the Inter-departmental Committee of 1935–1936 that raised concerns about the alleged missionary aim of Europeanizing indigenous people in open free schools. To create a separate system, the committee emphasized the development of "the education of the Native" as regards the control and financing of education and medium of instruction to ensure that indigenous people were equipped with "socially desirable knowledge and skills" (Report, U.G 1935/36, p. 90) and were not compromising jobs reserved for Whites.

When the Nationalist Party won the election in 1948, it used its Calvinistic Christian National Education (CNE) model to separate schools on the basis of race (Horrell, 1968; Malherbe, 1977). A hierarchical four-tiered education system was formalized with the Bantu Education Act of 1953. Educational funding became race-based. Whites received the greatest share of funding, R1, 211 per learner; and incrementally the amounts were R771 for Indians; R498 for Coloureds (term used for mixed race people in SA) and R146 for Blacks (Dass & Rinquest, 2017, p. 143). Consequently, all other schools (Model B) were poorly resourced while the White (Model C) schools were better resourced. The distribution resulted in unequal schooling/teaching and learning and after graduation, economic and social mobility.

In 1994, Apartheid education was rejected, and schooling was reformed, at least rhetorically (Cross, 1986; Vally et al., 2010). The Bill of Rights of the Constitution and Act 108 of 1996 specifically underscores issues of diversity and points out that learners must be afforded equal rights and responsibilities.

SCHOOL REFORM POST-APARTHEID

In 1996, driven by a commitment to equity and redress, the four separate education departments were unified into one education system. The National Education Policy Act 27 of 1996 together with the National Norms and Standards for School Funding (NNSSF) of 1998 amended in 2006 legislated that schools must be equitably funded. The South African Schools Act 84 of 1996 (SASA) was amended in 2003 to further provide a statutory base for a pro-poor funding model that would break down economic barriers that underpinned inequities in the provision of education and "... ensure the learner's right to basic education is realised" (Adams, 2020, p. 72). The amendment also provided school communities with the autonomy to appoint their own school governing bodies (SGBs) to be responsible for governance and key decision making. It (SASA) created two types of SGBs; Sections 20 and 21.

SGBs in public schools fall under either Section 20 or Section 21. The latter are allowed to raise funds and are financially self-managed, while Section 20 schools receive funds largely from government and their finances are centrally managed by their respective provincial education departments. This two-tiered SGB structure resulted in Section 20 SGBs having limited power over their funding and being restricted in both management and mandate while Section 21 SGBs have greater control of their funds and school fees (see Sayed et al., 2020, p. 3). Motala and Carel (2019 cited in Sayed et al., 2020, p. 4) argue that "the key funding characteristic of post-apartheid education expenditure was that it was norm-based primarily on the number of learners in a school, with built-in equity measures for distributing resources and capital expenditure ... the poverty of the provinces was an overall factor in tax revenue disbursement across provinces." Sayed et al. (2020, p. 4) describe the system as underpinned by "a neo-liberal prescription of user charges in education on one hand ... and a parent as consumer of education approach."

The South African Schools Act was again amended in 2005 to establish a system that classifies schools into five groups or quintiles based on the relative wealth of a school's surrounding community. All South African state/public schools (approximately 25,000) were ranked into five quintiles, primarily for the allocation of funding from the state based on the literacy rate and levels of unemployment in the community in which a school is located. Schools in poorest communities were categorized as Quintile 1 while in the wealthiest communities, schools were classified as Quintile 5 (Department of Education, 2008).

The recommended allocation per learner for each quintile is determined by the national Department of Basic Education (DBE) based on the poverty levels of the school community and other infrastructural factors. Initially (in 1996), the "determination of these poverty rankings was based on income levels, dependency ratios and literacy rates in the surrounding community" (see Sayed et al., 2020, p. 3).

Quintile 1, 2, and 3 schools are poorer, have more government funding, and are not allowed to charge fees (Ally & McLaren, 2016b). They also receive additional funding for safety, nutrition programs and classroom construction.

The schools can supplement income only with voluntary contributions or donations (Adams, 2020; Dass & Rinquest, 2017, pp. 85, 147) to pay for learning support materials (LSMs) such as library books, non-LSM materials (telephones, paper copiers, hardware tools, cleaning equipment), consumable items of an educational nature(stationery for learners), consumable items of a non-educational nature (stationery for office use, cleaning materials), services relating to repairs and maintenance (building repair work) and other services (TV licenses, internet service providers) (see Makhafola, 2022).

Quintile 4 and 5 are the "least poor" and are mainly in previously advantaged white communities. The schools receive less funding but can charge fees and/or attract private contributions that allow them to compensate for the reduced subsidy. They are allowed to complement their staff by employing more well-qualified teachers and keep their pupil-teacher ratio lower. The quintiles thus include affluent schools that are well-resourced and usually privately well-funded to "supplement the resources provided by the state in order to improve the quality of education provided by the school to all learners..." (Republic of South Africa (RSA), 1996, p. 24 as cited in Sayed et al., 2020, p. 3). However, they are subject to a fee reduction or exemption policy and equalization of expenditure that is based on strict rules regarding income to allow access to children from poorer homes who reside in communities in which these fee-charging schools are located. But, in a video of the Legal Resources Centre (LRC), called "Some children are more equal than others: Education in South Africa (February 16, 2015)," a parent complains that it is very difficult to get their children into good schools. They are told there is "no space ... the school is full." What is not said is that 66% of positions are reserved for middle class children. They continue that "fee [-paying] schools never turn away a white child ... and the department of education doesn't help." For one interviewee, education in these schools is like a see-saw where there must be a balance between the number of white and black children so that the white fee-paying children do not leave.

The initial thinking was that each quintile would comprise 20% of learners. However, the policy "has resulted in an increase in learners who do not pay school fees, from just 3% in 2006 to 65% in 2014" (StatsSA, 2021). As it is evident from Table 1, it is large, rural populations such as the Free State (85%), KZN (83%), and the Eastern Cape (96%) that have the majority of learners in Q1–3 schools. In Limpopo, (77%) of learners are in Q1–3 schools—Q1 (28.2%), Q2 (24.6%), and Q3 (24.2%)—rather than 60%; while only 23% of learners are in Q4 and Q5 schools instead of 40%. Wealthier, predominantly urban provinces, such as Gauteng (48%) and the Western Cape (56%) have more learners in Q4 and Q5 schools.

The National Poverty table for 2017 indicates that the policy revisions implemented in 1997 (cf. Table 3) seem to have contributed to an increase in Q1–3 schools. Table 2 indicates the percentages of schools that were not charging fees in 2017.

The funding model was revised in 2006 to further equalize funding. However, from Table 3, it is evident that the funding allocation for Quintile 1–3 schools has remained fairly static and has not kept up with an average rate of inflation of

Table 1. National Poverty Distribution Table (2017).

Provinces	Quintiles				
	1	2	3	4	5
Eastern Cape (EC)	27.3%	24.7%	19.6%	17.0%	11.4%
Free State (FS)	20.5%	20.9%	22.4%	20.8%	15.4%
Gauteng Province (GP)	14.1%	14.7%	17.9%	21.9%	31.4%
Kwa Zulu Natal (KZN)	22.1%	23.2%	20.2%	18.7%	15.8%
Limpopo Province (LP)	28.2%	24.6%	24.2%	14.9%	8.0%
Mpumalanga Province (MP)	23.1%	24.1%	21.5%	17.7%	13.5%
Northern Cape (NC)	21.5%	19.3%	20.7%	21.4%	17.1%
Northwest (NW)	25.6%	22.3%	20.8%	17.6%	13.7%
Western Cape (WC)	8.6%	13.3%	18.4%	28.0%	31.7%
South Africa (National)	20.0%	20.0%	20.0%	20.0%	20.0%

Source: Adapted from Department of Basic Education (2017) and Van Dyk and White (2019).

Table 2. Percentage of Schools in Each Quintile by Province (2017).

Provinces	Q1	Q2	Q3	No-fees (Q1–3)	Q4	Q5	Fees (Q4–5)
Eastern Cape (EC)	36%	29%	31%	96%	2%	2%	4%
Free State (FS)	49%	17%	19%	85%	7%	8%	15%
Gauteng Province (GP)	15%	12%	25%	52%	18%	30%	48%
Kwa Zulu Natal (KZN)	32%	30%	20%	83%	10%	8%	18%
Limpopo Province (LP)	40%	42%	16%	98%	1%	2%	2%
Mpumulanga Province (MP)	31%	27%	21%	79%	12%	9%	21%
Northern Cape (NC)	37%	18%	19%	74%	11%	15%	26%
North-West (NW)	36%	21%	34%	91%	8%	1%	9%
Western Cape (WC)	19%	11%	13%	44%	23%	34%	56%

Source: Adapted from Sayed et al. (2020, p. 8).

5.3% per annum (1997–2022). If the R1 177 allocation of 1997 grew at the average rate of inflation of 5.3% per annum over the same period (1997–2022) the 2022 allocation should equate to R4 280. However, the actual growth in the allocation over the same period only grew at the rate of 1.07% per annum. So, while it appears that funding has increased over the 25 years (1997–2022), it has not grown in line with inflation (see Government Gazette 44254, Government Notice 192 of March 2021 in Makhafola, 2022, p. 2).

Across all nine provinces the learner-to-teacher ratio is higher for teachers in government-only paid schools (34:1) while for schools where there is additional payment from the School Governing Body (SGB), the ratio is 31:1 (see Department of Basic Education, 2021).

The high learner dropout rates in public schools are often attributed to overcrowded classrooms and inadequate resources. As Table 4 indicates, teachers paid solely by the government are faced with a higher number of learners in classes. The

Table 3. National Monthly Allocation for Individual Pupils (Q1–5).

Quintiles	1997	2021	2022	2023
1, 2, and 3	R1177	R1466	R1536	R1610
4	R590	R735	R770	R807
5	R204	R254	R266	R279

Source: Adapted from Isaacs (2020) and Makhafola (2022).

Table 4. Number of Learners (Ls), Educators (Es), Schools (Ss) in School Sector by Province in 2021.

Province	Public Learners	Public Educators	Public Schools	Independent Learners	Independent Educators	Independent Schools	National Ls	Total Es	% Ss
EC	1,772,877	58,824	5,109	75,176	3,874	232	13.8	14.0	21.5
FS	706,269	22,686	990	20,044	1,181	81	5.4	5.3	4.3
GT	2,227,733	72,162	2,067	337,079	19,796	874	19.1	20.6	11.8
KZN	2,831,417	92,232	5,801	62,541	4,427	221	21.6	21.6	24.2
LP	1,723,583	50,021	3,675	75,547	3,561	180	13.4	12.0	15.5
MP	1,101,224	34,837	1,654	33,665	2,126	131	8.5	8.3	7.2
NC	298,253	9,984	545	6,313	502	40	2.3	2.3	2.3
NW	848,086	26,796	1,450	24,515	1,452	89	6.5	6.3	6.2
WC	1,196,715	37,508	1,449	67,812	5,154	306	9.4	9.5	7.0
National	12,706,157	405,050	22,740	703,092	42,073	2,154	100.0	100.0	100.0

Source: Adapted from Department of Basic Education (2021, p. 1).

drop-out rate tripled from 230,000 to 750,000 in May 2021 (Spaull & Daniels, 2021, p. 2). This decline was highest in public schools nationally; 30.6% in the Foundation Phase (Grades 1–3), 24.6% in the Intermediate Phase (Grades 4–6), 23.8% in the Senior Phase (Grades 7–9) and 32.7% in the Further Education and Training Phase (Grades 10–12).

Spaull (2019, p. 4) asserts that the "stubbornness of inequality and its patterns of persistence ... the color of ... skin, the province where ... born and the wealth of ... parents" highlights the complex multi-faceted nature of the quintile system in South Africa. Perhaps it is for these reasons that De Clercq (2020) as well is concerned about why the many educational reforms in South Africa have not significantly transformed the educational system and performance. She sees the question as tied to the role of education in mitigating socio-economic inequalities and argues that many authors focus on "the nature and form of educational inequalities in different areas of the system since 1994 ... [but] rarely engage explicitly with educational theories ... to explain better the causes of these persistent inequalities and poor efficiencies in the education system" (De Clercq, 2020, p. 3).

De Clerq (2020) prefers a post-structuralist approach that considers the history, values, aspirations, and traditions that have influenced and shaped structure, agency, and power relations within a context. For her, a post-structuralist position provides a better lens to understand "the impact of education reforms on poor and persistent education inequalities … the influence of unequal socio-economic and educational structures and agencies on the nature and evolution of the education system [and] … why socio-economic and education reforms" (De Clercq, 2020, p. 10) were insufficient to redress such inequalities within a context of shifting/unequal power relations and contestation (see De Clercq, 2010).

A post-structural analysis acknowledges that education is a contested terrain and stakeholders need to challenge and pressurize the government/education department to introduce reforms that are largely class-based. However, such challenges and pressure are impossible without policy studies that also focus on peculiarities and conditions of people acting within a context. In the case of school reform, these aspects would be about the capacity of people to provide for themselves and, therefore, the material conditions in which school reform occurred/is occurring. To attempt to bifurcate these aspects, as De Clercq explains, prevents what Lather (2010) has described as policy research that is inextricably linked to policymaking, likely to disrupt taken-for-granted assumptions, ensures better understanding of policy and its impact and makes research transformative rather than reproductive. This notion of policy research takes seriously the view that even though researchers may be explicitly working from or informed by a particular theory in their work, their work has to be grounded in a reality that they are immersed in and is being studied. Context enables an analysis and assessment of the processes of policy making and implementation as integral parts of the policy and therefore, values the policymaking process/implementation on the basis of which the adopted theory should be problematized.

According to Denzin and Lincoln (2011) too, applying a critical lens through research can create empowering qualitative research, which expands, contracts, grows, and questions itself within the theory and practice examined. Such a lens dissuades researchers from being mere appliers of theory and become theorists who deconstruct and reconstruct knowledge in ways that are meaningful and empowering in a context. More importantly, the lens helps researchers to reflect on taken-for-granted positions. However, this would not involve a simple process of studying policymaking and/or implementation but a complex gaze on the policy text and its making or implementation based on the researcher's theoretical stance and a consideration of the broader contextual circumstances in which the policy was formulated and used. Policy consideration cannot be decontextualized. Local and other trends have to be taken into account before conclusions are drawn on its value. In short, policy analysis should clarify humanly promoted issues embedded in it, negotiated, often power-related and therefore contestable. As research, such an analysis will help researchers rethink policy related issues in ways that facilitate understanding of the particularities of lived realities and aspirations within a context. For example, focusing on research studies in

Chicago, San Francisco, and Atlanta after the Civil War in the United States of America (USA), Peterson (1985) found that because urban public schools existed within a politically pluralistic society, the growth in numbers of other stakeholders such as trade unions, immigrant groups and the working class allowed them to exercise greater political power and decision-making in what school reforms happened. Archival data used in his research revealed the solid support of these stakeholders for issues such as common schooling, free compulsory education, school financing, and the modernization of the curriculum. In Labaree's (1997) view as well, the competing views of citizens, taxpayers, and consumers of education as a public or private good have been at the center of conflicts in US education over the years. For him, the views represent an understanding of education as representing three educational goals namely (1) democratic equality in which the role of schools is to prepare citizens for society, (2) social efficiency in which the training of workers is the focus (1 & 2 public good), and (3) social mobility in which schools prepare individuals to compete for socio-economic positions (private good). These competing views have, in Labaree's opinion, resulted in an education system that has been weakened by a focus on social mobility, status, and credentials (private good) rather than the acquisition of knowledge (public good). Therefore, in the context of South Africa, where school reforms seem to be compounded by the poverty gap, they (reforms) cannot be understood without considering the people they are meant for, their living conditions and context for which the reforms were conceptualized and being implemented.

South Africa's school reforms and features related to, for example, race, education, employment level, and class are discussed next to provide a more nuanced understanding of school reform as both a concept and response to lived experiences of communities.

THE QUINTILE SYSTEM POLICY AND SCHOOL REFORM IN SOUTH AFRICA

Adams (2020, p. 85) argues that, while "the quintile funding system has had a major impact on reducing apartheid-inherited inequalities by providing learners with economic access to basic education in public schools ... the quintile funding system cannot on its own, achieve the aim of establishing an equal level of education across the country." The model cannot guarantee equitable provision. While free access to a basic education is legislated and available to all learners, this does not ensure the redress and equity intended especially in the Q1–3 poorest most under-resourced schools that are mainly in previously discriminated against black communities. This is the case for a number of reasons.

The bifurcation of schooling into two divisions of poor and wealthy schools has "facilitated access to very differently resourced schools for different socio-economic groups" and resulted in a system where "the poor, mainly Black population is schooled in under-resourced and dysfunctional schools, largely in former township schools (about 80%), while the wealthy have access to semi-private public schools (e-Model C schools) that primarily serve the White population and the new Black elite" (Sayed et al., 2020, p. 5). The separation has also created a movement of learners from poorer areas who can now attend former Model C (white) schools known as "commuter" schools. Wealthier parents are abandoning Q1–3 schools and Black learners are "racial hopping" (Chisholm, 2004) from the townships to schools attended mainly by children from middle class and wealthier families in formerly Whites only areas/suburbs. According to Hunter (2019, p. 106), "those who study at formerly white schools, whether by traveling to or living in an affluent suburb, are most likely to pass the matriculation exam at the advanced level required to access higher education institutions (certificate, diploma, or bachelor level). They are also more likely to pass 'gateway' subjects such as pure maths rather than maths literacy."

Ally and McLaren (2016a, 2016b) have expressed serious concerns about the funding system based on quintiles. In the authors' view, it has a "lopsided effect" on educational provision within the provinces. Sayed et al. (2020, pp. 4–5) attributes three reasons for the disjuncture between the intention, effect, and outcome of this system and why equity and redress have not been realized. First, the failure of post-apartheid transformation is due to policies that are based on notions of equity and redress that have left the historically accrued privileges of wealthier schools unaffected. As a result, they continue to perpetuate inequality (see Motala, 2009; Sayed & Motala, 2012). Second, provinces vary greatly in their socio-economic status, poverty and employment levels and the federal system of provinces that has been created is unequal financially. This makes the autonomy they enjoy over school operation ineffective. Third, the quintile funding system is based on a "weak quintile modeling system and a less than robust equitable share formula" (Sayed et al., 2020, p. 9).

The calculation of the poverty levels of schools based on census data provides what Chutgar and Kanjee (2009, p. 18) refer to as "province-specific-poverty targeting criteria" that should result in poorer schools receiving sufficient funds from the state to transform their schooling. However, since learners do not always attend schools in their geographical areas but may commute to better resourced Q4 and Q5 schools, this means some Q1–3 will be underfunded as they are paid per learner while the Q4 and Q5 schools are unaffected and remain "well-resourced and advantaged" (Van Dyk & White, 2019, p. S3) because their better organized SGBs provide "societal, material ... [and] organizational advantages." Furthermore, the schools in more affluent communities, tend to have better physical facilities, additional financial resources, and are thus not adversely affected by the inflow of children from outside communities. Van Dyke and White (2019, p. S1) have highlighted the urgency for "equitable funding of public schools to reduce the disparities in education inherited by the post-apartheid government." While the introduction of the quintile funding system should have made improvements to teaching and learning in impoverished schools (Q1–3), the authors argue that many challenges still exist in the implementation and calculation of this funding; particularly with regard to distributional equity (see also Motala, 2006).

Veriava (2007, p. 188) has also highlighted the "inaccurate, overstated quintile rankings of many poor schools ... [resulting] in inaccurate ranking results, low state allocations and insufficient resource allocation." Motala and Sayed (2009, p. 4) too, comment that access to wealth and not only headcount has significant implications for meaningful educational provision and learners' social mobility. Therefore, the inaccurate poverty determination in some poorer schools and less funding, caused by the movement into nearby highly ranked Q4 schools, disadvantages Q1–3 areas due to geographic location. Motala and Sayed (2009) argue that because parents look at the quality of education when enrolling their children in a school, to promote just educational provision, the economic status of the school community should be considered in a more nuanced way that also captures the movement of learners that attend schools in "wealthier" areas outside their local community.

SCHOOL REFORM AND IMPLICATIONS FOR LEARNERS' SOCIAL MOBILITY

A recent report from Amnesty International (2020, p. 1) highlights the "stark inequalities and chronic underperformance ... the child's experience of education still very much depends on where they are born, how wealthy they are, and the color of their skin ... children in the top 200 schools achieve more distinctions in Mathematics than children in the next 6600 schools combined." Despite every child having access to education, democratic South Africa has not effectively tackled the quality of educational experience and outcomes remain unequal. The government has widened educational access but continues to miss its targets regarding meaningful educational provision. Fleisch (2018) also explains how the poverty gap plus poor schooling ultimately results in poor life chances for such children.

In 2018, according to the Department of Education's own statistics, out of 23,471 schools, 20,071 (85.5%) had no laboratories, 18,019 (76.8%) had no libraries, and 16,897 (72%) had no internet (Amnesty International, 2020, p. 3). Other barriers to effective learning included a lack of sufficient transport forcing mainly rural children/children from lower-income groups to walk long distances to school. For example, in Kwa-Zulu Natal, more than 201,000 pupils walk more than an hour each way and 659,000 walk for between 30 and 60 minutes each way. This has implications for regular school attendance and safe and successful schooling.

Internationally, while 5–7 years of schooling would be considered sufficient to provide basic literacy this is not happening in South Africa. The high illiteracy rate continues to reflect the poor-quality education provision for the majority that has been worsened by the quintile system.

CONCLUSION

As argued at the beginning of this chapter, school reform in South Africa targeted mainly Black schools but the funding system as school reform, is still largely racially focused and does not look critically at the notion of access and participation that is promoted by the quintile system. The reform underplays the impact and intricacies of the apartheid discriminatory policies. Simply focusing on the number of children for whom there is access to a school without reflecting on the conditions under which they have to learn reflects a semantic entrapment or logic that largely tries perhaps to appease taxpayers whose children are in Q4 and Q5 schools. De Clercq's promotion of a post-structuralist analysis helped us clarify the impact of the reluctance or failure to deal with the material conditions in Q1–3 schools. These are conditions that are rooted in the political, structural and schooling history of the country. As suggested by Lather (2010) and Denzin and Lincoln (2011), foregrounding context has enabled us to go beyond the policy discourse/rhetoric and quantitative detail mainly provided in the literature and develop a more robust and multifaceted approach to understanding the conceptualization and implementation of the quintile-based funding system as main school reform in South Africa. We trust were able to highlight how more factors influence the outcomes of the funding levels of, in particular, Q1–Q3 schools, such as restrictions as regards donations, the commuting of non-resident children into communities where Q4 and Q5 schools are located and the effect on the per learner funding. A more nuanced, richer, and complex concept of disadvantage that shifts (1) focus from simple deprivation in determining funding and (2) the restrictions that quintiles 1, 2, and 3 schools face in raising funds is needed if South Africa is to realize its constitutional ideal of, among others, equal education for everyone.

REFERENCES

Adams, G. (2020). *The impact of the quintile funding system in reducing apartheid-inherited inequalities in education.* Thesis (LLM), Stellenbosch University.

Alexander, N. (2000). *English unassailable but unattainable: The dilemma of language policy in South African education.* PRAESA Occasional Papers No. 3.

Alexander, N. (2005). Language, class and power in post-apartheid South Africa. Paper presented at *the Harold Wolpe Memorial Trust Open Dialogue Event*, Cape Town, 27 October 2005. T.H. Barry Theatre, Iziko Museum.

Allly, N., & McLaren, D. (2016a). Education funding formula needs to be fixed. GROUNDUP part two in the series: Towards equality in school funding. Opinion | South Africa. https://www.groundup.org.za/article/education-funding-formula-needs-be-fixed/

Ally, N., & McLaren, D. (2016b, November 12). Fees are an issue in school too, not just university. *Project Rise*. https://projectrise.news24.com/fees-issue-school-not-just-university/

Amnesty International. (2020). *Broken and unequal: The state of education in South Africa.* https://www.amnesty.org/en/latest/news/2020/02/south-africa-broken-and-unequal-education-perpetuating-poverty-and-inequality/

Castells, M. (1997). *The power of identity, the information age: Economy, society and culture* (Vol. I). Blackwell.

Chisholm, L. (Ed.). (2004). *Changing class: Education and social change in post-apartheid South Africa.* HSRC Press.

Chutgar, A., & Kanjee, A. (2009). School money funding flaws. *HSRC Review, 7*(4), 18–19.
Cross, M. (1986). A historical review of education in South Africa: Towards an assessment. *Comparative Education, 22*(3), 185–200.
Dass, S., & Rinquest, A. (2017). School fees. Section 27. In F. Veriava, A. Thoms, & T. S. Hodgson (Eds.), *Basic education rights handbook: Education rights in South Africa*. http://section27.org.za/wp-content/uploads/2017/02/CHapter-7.pdf
Davis, R. H. (1976). Charles T. Loram and the American model for African education in South Africa. *African Studies Review, 19*(2), 87–99.
De Clercq, F. (2010). Meta-analysis of South African education policy studies: How have we fared so far and what needs to be expanded? *Journal of Education, 49*, 91–112.
De Clercq, F. (2020). The persistence of South African educational inequalities: The need for understanding and relying on analytical frameworks. *Education as Change, 24*(1), 2–22.
Denzin, N. K., & Lincoln, S. (Eds.). (2011). *The SAGE handbook of qualitative research*. SAGE Publishing.
Department of Basic Education. (2021). *School Realities 2021*. EMIS Publication. https.//www.education.gov.za
Department of Basic Education, Republic of South Africa. (2017). Poverty ranking of schools (Quintiles) [PowerPoint presentation]. https://view.officeapps.live.com/op/view.aspx?src=http%3A%2F%2Fpmg-assets.s3-website-eu-west1.amazonaws.com%2F171129Quintiles.pptx
Department of Education. (2008, October 8). *South African Schools Act: National norms and standards for school funding*. Amendment No. 1087. Pretoria. www.gov.za/sites/default/files/gcis_document/201409/314961087.pdf
Duncan, G. (2009). Coercive agency in mission education at Lovedale Missionary Institution. *Hervormde Teologiese Studies, 60*. https://doi.org/10.4102/hts.v60i3.614
Fleisch, B. (2018). *The education triple cocktail: System-wide instructional reform in South Africa*. Juta.
Horrell, M. (1968). *Bantu Education to 1968*. South African Institute of Race Relation (SAIRR).
Hunter, M. (2019). *Race for education: Gender, white tone, and schooling in South Africa*. International African Library. Cambridge University Press.
Isaacs, B. (2020). How the quintile system for schools works. *The Cape Argus*. Opinion. https://www.iol.co.za/capeargus/opinion/how-the-quintile-system-for-schools-works-8bab7f23-f23d-431e-816a-883bb00fe90b
Kallaway, P. (1984). *Education and apartheid—The education of black south Africans*. Ravan Press.
Kane-Berman, J. (1978). *Soweto Black Revolt, White reaction* (pp. 103–108). Ravan Press.
Labaree, D. F. (1997). Public goods, private goods: The American struggle over educational goals. *American Educational Research Journal, 3*(1), 39–81.
Lather, P. (2010). *Engaging (social) science: Policy from the side of the messy*. Peter Lang.
Legal Resources Centre (LRC). (2015, February 16). Some children are more equal than others: Education in South Africa. https://www.youtube.com/watch?v=hiEUu-Is0Ao
Makhafola, K. (2022). *Focus: Funding of South African public schools explained*. http://www.accountacy.sa.org.za
Malherbe, E. G. (1977). *Education in South Africa—Volume II (1923–1975)*. Juta.
Motala, S. (2006). Education resourcing in post-apartheid South Africa: The impact of finance equity reforms in public schooling. *Perspectives in Education, 24*(2), 79–93.
Motala, S. (2009). Privatising public schooling in post-apartheid South Africa—Equity considerations. *Compare: A Journal of Comparative and International Education, 39*(2), 185–202.
Motala, S., & Carel, D. (2019). Educational funding and equity in South African schools. In N. Spaull & J. D. Jansen (Eds.), *South African schooling: The enigma of inequality—A study of the present situation and future possibilities*. Springer. http://doi.org/10.1007/978-3-030-18811-5_4. https://www.researchgate.net/publication/337033802_Educational_Funding_and_Equity_in_South_African_Schools
Motala, S., & Sayed, Y. (2009). "No Fee" schools in South Africa. https://www.semanticscholar.org/paper/%27No-fee%27-schools-in-South-Africa-Motala-Sayed/ede038b42728c44e10dcbfcaeda2ca17231ecb0f
Peterson, P. E. (1985). *The politics of school reform*. The University of Chicago Press. Digitalized by The Internet Archive in 2013. http:///archive.org/details/politicsofschoolreform

Report of the inter-departmental committee on native education. U.G. (1935/6). passim.

Sayed, Y., & Motala, S. (2012). Equity and "no fee" schools in South Africa: Challenges and prospects. *Social Policy and Administration, 46*(6), 672–687. https://doi.org/10.1111/j.1467-9515.2012.00862.x

Sayed, Y., Motala, S., Carel, D., & Ahmed, R. (2020). School governance and funding policy in South Africa: Towards social justice and equity in education policy. *South African Journal of Education, 40*(4), 1–12. Art#2045. http://doi.org/10.15700/saje.v40n4a2045

Spaull, N. (2019, January 19). *Priorities for education reform in South Africa: Input document for treasury's economic colloquium*. A report to President Rhamaposa and Minister Mboweni. University of Stellenbosch. https://nicspaull.files.wordpress.com/2019/01/v2-spaull-priorities-for-educ-reform-treasury-19-jan-2019.pdf

Spaull, N., Daniels, R. C., Ardington, C., Branson, N., Breet, E., Bridgman, G., Brophy, T., Burger, R., Casale, D., English, R., Espi, G., Hill, R., Hunt, X., Ingle, K., Kerr, A., Kika, J., Kerr, A., Kika-Mistry, J., ... Wittenberg, M. (2021). *NIDS-CRAM wave 5 synthesis report*. https://cramsurvey.org/wp-content/uploads/2021/07/1.-Spaull-N.-Daniels-R.-C-et-al.-2021-NIDS-CRAM-Wave-5-Synthesis-Report.pdf

StatsSA. (2021). *Department: Statistics South Africa*. STATISTICAL RELEASE P0141 Consumer Price Index December 2021. www.statssa.gov.za/publications/P0141/P0141December2021.pdf

Vally, S., Motala, E., & Ramadiro, B. (2010). Education rights, education policies, and inequality in South Africa. In S. Macrine, P. McLaren, & D. Hill (Eds.), *Revolutionizing pedagogy. Marxism and education* (pp. 41–63). Palgrave Macmillan. https://doi.org/10.1057/9780230104709_3

Van Dyk, H., & White, C. J. (2019). Theory and practice of the quintile ranking of schools in South Africa: A financial management aspect. *South African Journal of Education, 39*(1), S1–S9. https://doi.org/10.15700/saje.v39ns1a1820

Veriava, F. (2007). The amended legal framework for school fees and school funding: A boon or a barrier? *South African Journal of Education, 32*(2), 215–226. https://doi.org/10.1080/19962126.2007.11864915

"DATA IS [G]OD": THE INFLUENCE OF CUMULATIVE POLICY REFORMS ON TEACHERS' KNOWLEDGE IN AN URBAN MIDDLE SCHOOL IN THE UNITED STATES[*]

Cheryl J. Craig

ABSTRACT

This narrative inquiry centers on teachers' longitudinal experiences of policy-related reforms systematically introduced to T. P. Yaeger Middle School, a campus located in the fourth largest, second most diverse city in America. The embedded research study, with roots tracing back to 1997, uses five interpretive tools to capture six mandated changes in the form of a story serial. Special research attention is afforded pay-for-performance, the sixth reform in the series. The deeply lived consequence of receiving bonuses for his teaching performance prompted Daryl Wilson, Yaeger's long-term literacy department chair, to proclaim "data is [G]od." Wilson's emergent, inventive metaphor aptly portrays the perplexing conditions under which his career ended, and how my long-term research project likewise concluded.

Keywords: School reform; teacher knowledge; contexts of teaching; teaching metaphors; narrative inquiry; accountability; data

---

[*]This chapter is reprinted from *Teaching and Teacher Education*, 93, July, Cheryl J. Craig, "Data is [G]od": The influence of cumulative policy reforms on teachers' knowledge in an urban middle school in the United States, Copyright (2020), with permission from Elsevier.

Teaching and Teacher Education in International Contexts
Advances in Research on Teaching, Volume 42, 131–159
Copyright © 2023 Emerald Publishing Limited, with the exception of "Data is [G]od": The influence of cumulative policy reforms on teachers' knowledge in an urban middle school in the United States © Elsevier
All rights of reproduction in any form reserved
ISSN: 1479-3687/doi:10.1108/S1479-368720230000042017

> This is what we have come to...
> There is no other way to explain it...
> Data is [G]od ....

The above statement uttered by Daryl Wilson, the literacy department chair at T. P. Yaeger Middle School, metaphorically captures the sense he made of payment-for-performance, the sixth of six consecutive policy reforms introduced to T. P. Yaeger Middle School over a 20-year period. Policy-related reforms (e.g., Darling-Hammond, 2010; Lewis & Young, 2013; Wiseman, 2013, pp. 303–322), such as professional learning communities or performance pay, originate with school districts, state agencies, and/or federal governments and become funneled in a conduit-like manner (Craig, 2002) down to schools and teachers. In Daryl's case, the reforms were initiated by one of the largest school districts in America, a state education agency and the national department of education. Teacher implementation of such change efforts is non-negotiable. Consistent with the meaning of a conduit, educational demands funnel freely down the pipeline to teachers but rarely flow up it. The overarching intent of policy-related reforms is to improve student performance through prescribing teachers' practices. Policy-makers believe good teaching comes from the techniques and formulas they dictate for teachers to use, not from "the identity and integrity" of teachers themselves (Palmer, 1998, p. 10). It follows, then, that their policy impositions privilege the teacher-as-implementer image and run counter to the teacher-as-curriculum-maker (Clandinin & Connelly, 1992; Craig & Ross, 2008), despite neither image being exclusive. Over the course of Daryl's employment at Yaeger, six waves of reform were introduced to his 90+ year old campus, all having to do with one form of standardization or another. This narrative inquiry examining the influence of context on teachers' knowing, doing and being documents the cumulative impact of the policy-driven changes leading to Daryl's proclamation that "this is what we have come to ...."

This chapter begins with my theoretical framework and is followed by a description of narrative inquiry and its subsidiary parts. After that, six narratives generated by Daryl Wilson, Laura Curtis and Anna Dean, along with contributions from their anonymous colleagues, are presented in a story serial format. The story serial concludes with the sixth narrative where Daryl maintains "data is [G]od." This latter tale brings the Yaeger story continuum to a close – not because it was the end per se, but because of the "choice" Daryl made as a senior teacher in a constrained employment situation. Concurrently, my ongoing teacher knowledge-reforming schools project at Yaeger ended.

THEORETICAL FRAMEWORK

Experience

According to John Dewey (1938), experience is the raison d'être for education. If it were not for experience, education would not exist (Clandinin & Connelly, 2000). The human flow of experience can be educative or non-educative depending on how events unfurl within the past-present-future continuum of time. Educative experiences advance growth whereas miseducative experiences arrest growth (Dewey, 1938). As Eisner (1982) once observed, "learning can diminish the mind as well as expand it" (p. 13). In other words, all that education has been, is, or will be depends on experience and its three simultaneously interacting qualities: temporality (past-present-future), sociality (interactions between and among people) and place (context). It follows, then, that teachers in classrooms and school contexts, who have "larger experience and riper wisdom" than the students they teach, are tasked with how "life should come to child[ren]" (Dewey, 1897, p. 79). As minded professionals (Dewey, 1938), they historically have overseen how youth's educational experiences unfold.

Knowledge

What people (teachers and students alike) know depends on the life experiences to which they have been privy and the extent to which they have been able to make sense of them through processes of reflection. Teacher knowledge has broadly been divided into two knower and known relationships (Dewey & Bentley, 1949; Fenstermacher, 1994): knowledge for teaching (formal knowledge) and teacher knowledge (practical knowledge). Knowledge for teaching is what those representing the state and/or the academy declare teachers should know and do; teacher knowledge is what teachers glean from their own experiences and hold, express and enact in their own terms (Clandinin, 1986; Connelly & Clandinin, 1985). What Connelly and Clandinin (2005) define as teachers' personal practical knowledge is a kind of knowing "... in the [teacher]'s present mind and body, and in the [teacher]'s future plans and actions ... It is seen and found in ... practice ..." (p. 25). This research is practical knowledge research because it focuses on teachers' ongoing school reform experiences from the teacher perspective.

Nevertheless, formal knowledge has a role to play in this work because the sense teachers make of the directives showering down of them is necessarily filtered through their experiential knowledge forged in context. What teachers formally know is unavoidably reliant on the personal practical knowledge that they have refined over time. This is because knowledge, in the Deweyan sense, "arise[s] from experience and return[s] to experience for validation" (Clandinin & Rosiek, 2006, p. 39). In essence, policy and research imperatives have no other way to enter teachers' minds than through teachers' personal experiences of them and no other way to enter teachers' bodies than through teachers' minds and embodied actions (Craig et al., 2018).

Story

The vehicle through which teacher knowledge becomes known is story. Story is created "at the junction where self and world meet" (Penwarden, 2019). According to Christensen (2016), story opens up individuals' lives and "let's the world in" (p. 21); it gives "shape to 'chaos'" (Shapiro, 2016, p. 195). The individual s the link to "universality" (Strayed, 2016, p. 214) with story capturing universality "through the singular" (Christensen, 2016, p. 21). Ultimately, stories touch us where we live – in our bodies (Richardson, 1994).

Not only are individuals' narratives explored through story, so, too are "the social narratives of which we are part, the landscape on which [educators] live" also interrogated (Clandinin & Connelly, 2000, p. 65). To Kerby (Kerby, 1991), "much of self-narration is a matter of becoming conscious of the narratives we already live with and in—for example ... in the sociopolitical area" (p. 6). Hence, our "narratives articulate not just isolated acts but whole sequences of events or episodes, thereby placing particular events within a framing context..." (Kerby, 1991, p. 3).

Metaphor

Narrative and metaphor – which some (Arkhipenka & Lupasco, 2019) consider two-sides of the same coin – facilitate our understanding of how people frame challenges (Schon, 1993). In this work, Daryl Wilson used the metaphor, "data is [G]od," for example, as a heuristic to communicate how educational policies became lived and known in his middle school context. In short, his personally crafted metaphor was a "code word" that opened up his "compressed narrative" (Hanne, 2015; Ritchie, 2010). It produced "flashes of connection" (Egan, 2017) for him between two unlikely sources: research data and the deity of [G]od. It also connected the teacher's experiences with those trying to enter into and understand his worldview. To Gadamer (1960/1985, p. 458), "every word breaks forth from a center [and] causes the whole of the language ... to resonate and the ... worldview that underlines it to appear ... each word carries with it the unsaid..." (p. 458). These metaphorical words can be "stock-plots" – stock metaphors – culled from the vast human inventory prior to activities or events happening or they can be inventive metaphors that organically surface in the midst of human action (Craig, 2018a). Daryl's "data is [G]od" metaphor is of the emergent, non-stock plot type as it naturally appeared in his living and telling, and re-living and re-telling, of his narratives of experience to me. Other emergent, inventive metaphors were crafted by Laura Curtis ("butterfly under a pin"), Anna Dean ("learning to teach in the eye of a storm") and anonymous others (i.e., "hidden in clear view"), who laid the evidence trail to Daryl's "data is [G]od" commentary, as readers will soon see.

RESEARCH METHOD

Narrative Inquiry

Narrative inquiry is a vein of personal experience research that is said to reach back to the origins of the species (Maran, 2016, p. 13). White (1980, p. 5) claims it reflects the nature of humanity itself. According to Clandinin et al. (2016), narrative inquiry is based on the proposition that stories lived and told by an individual [or individuals] are embedded within cultural, social, institutional, familial, political and linguistic narratives. It represents the phenomenon but also constitutes a methodology for its study (p. 1). Narrative inquirers stay within the narrative realm and "linger amid complex layers of intertwined and interwoven stories" (Clandinin et al., 2016, p. 20). This is because ... stories are lived and told, not separate from each person's living and telling in time, place and relationship ... [they] are not ... text[s] to be separated from the living and telling to be analyzed and dissected (Clandinin et al., 2016, p. 20).

Research Tools

The three original interpretive tools of narrative inquiry (Connelly & Clandinin, 1990) – broadening, burrowing, and storying and restorying – are employed in this investigation. Broadening captures "the social, cultural and institutional narratives in which individuals' experiences [are] constituted, shaped, expressed and enacted" (Clandinin & Rosiek, 2006, p. 420). Burrowing involves "div[ing] deep[ly]" into experience and "spend[ing] a long-time floundering" (Palmer, 2018, p. 92) to decipher embedded meanings of complex intertwined and interwoven stories lived and told and re-lived and re-told in context over the continuum of time. Meanwhile, storying and restorying, narrative inquiry's third analytical tool, shows changes that occur in how experiences became storied over the long haul. Where this chapter is concerned, a 20-year time sequence covers a sweep of six standardized school reforms with the final story, "data is [G]od," receiving special interpretative attention because it previously has not been unpacked.

A fourth device, fictionalization (Caine et al., 2017; Clandinin et al., 2006), is a more recent tool that has been added to narrative inquiry's research repertoire. It allows for the shifting of personal details to safeguard participants' identities. Fictionalization is needed in published works like this one because protecting the literacy teachers and their contributions from each other is an additional concern. Taken together, generalized information about the state, a fake name for the school, pseudonyms for the teachers, subtle altering of identities, and generic references to others who were involved provide an increased level of protection for the central research participants, although there is no guarantee of anonymity.

Serial interpretation (Schwab, 1983), this inquiry's fifth research tool, is used to cull deeper understandings of the research phenomenon, which in this case is teachers' perceptions of policy-based school reforms. According to Schwab, serial interpretation allows researchers to "look across" (Clandinin et al., 2018, p. 131) and "think across" (Craig, 2009) longitudinal data in ways that add heft to understandings accumulated over time. Serial interpretation has been previously employed by Craig (2018a), Craig et al. (2018), and (Craig et al., under review). These works formed models of how serial interpretation could unfold in this inquiry.

Research Representation

As narrative inquirers, we work hard to find representational forms that resonate with the meanings and emotions of our research participants' narratives of experience.)Caine et al. (2013) explain that "representation ... necessitates our living with unfitting stor[ies] rather than ... attempt[ing] to tame, sanitize, or analyze. As narrative inquirers, we attend to difficult stories and experiences, we stay with them; we dwell alongside participants ... to retell them" (p. 581). Hence, the long-term research in this article does not appear as a single story.

Instead, it is a story serial comprised of six sequential reforms introduced to one middle school campus over two decades. This makes sense because a serial:

> ...starts out as a story but it does not reach a conclusion; it is a chorus of interconnected stories. Each episode is a skillful mix of problems that are solved and problems that arise. And even if the actor[s] continually push the message that things will get better, the [reader] discovers there is a certain balance between what gets better and what gets worse. (Czarniawka, 1997, p. 107)

As foreshadowed, a story serial is kaleidoscopic – "changing, flowing, crashing [in] an infinity of patterns" (Ayers, 1992, p. 155). This is because school reform – and school contexts – for that matter – involve "a skein of myriad threads" that are "infinitely susceptible to circumstances and ... highly liable to unexpected change" (Schwab, 1970, p. 3).

Truth Claims

In narrative inquiry research, truth is not formulaic like it is in quantitative research studies. It is not historical either, despite neither narrative inquiry nor historical research "hav[ing] ... control groups" (Zuboff, 2019, p. 54). Because narrative inquirers use stories to study the narrative sense people make of their lives as lived, they focus on narrative truths with "discernable ... patterns" (Lopez, 1989, p. 69) rather than historical facts lined up in chronological order. They arrive at trustworthy "findings"; their takeaway points are "apprehensible to others" (Palmer, 2018, p. 98). To Palmer, if stories are told too literally or formulaically, their patterns look less "like the wind in the grass and more like stakes hammered into the ground" (p. 98). Despite themes in narrative inquiries being cross-walked and verified by three or more sources, readers organically realize that the answers for their own and others' situations are the stories themselves (Clandinin & Connelly, 1996; MacIntyre, 1981; Sacks, 2017), not what researchers tack on or hammer in at the end.

Introduction to the Research Context

Located on the perimeter of one of the wealthiest neighborhoods in America, T. P. Yaeger Middle School, a grand campus in the Grecian architectural design, was built with an underground swimming pool in the "roaring '20s." Its early attendance roster read like "who's who in America." Among its early principals was an individual favoring racial segregation. Later in time, the federal government forced the southern states to desegregate public school children. This shift forever changed education in the South and in the entire US, for that matter. The introduction of students of color to T.P. Yaeger's "plain vanilla wrapper" landscape (one participant's term), resulted in White flight to the suburbs, White retreat to private schools and Hispanics being substituted for English speaking Whites in the desegregation process (McAdams, 2000). After the racial and cultural mixing of youths attending Yaeger, a gifted-and-talented program was introduced to the school to retain what remained of Yaeger's zoned White population. "The brightest and best" students of color (one principal's words) from other campuses then competed to attend Yaeger, which was recognized for "setting the pace" in one of the largest school districts in the US. By the 2000s, community and state leaders made T. P. Yaeger an urban charter school within its large school district. This move enabled Yaeger to hire and fire teachers at will while remaining in the district's constellation of campuses. This development, among others, fit the political stances of many families in the wealthy neighborhood and helped catapult the district superintendent and his chief of staff to leading roles in the federal department of education. With Texans occupying the country's prime leadership positions (including the presidency), the high stakes accountability system birthed in the Lone Star State (Texas) became the national No Child Left Behind Act (2002) and has continued to hold sway since then through bipartisan support of the "Every Student Succeeds Act" (ESSA) (ESSA, 2015). The narratives featured in this article animate what happening to teachers and peripherally to students as these performativity policies took hold.

Introduction to the Research Participants and the Researcher

The narratives of teachers in the literacy department, particularly stories told by Daryl Wilson, Laura Curtis, and Anna Dean, among others, are foregrounded in this work. Daryl was born and educated in the Deep South and moved to Texas to continue his teaching career. Laura was born and raised in Texas, alongside her twin, who is also an educator; and Anna, like Laura, was Texan and received her teacher certification at a local community college. All three are White, which is representative of the district's dominant teacher population. Other teachers and assistant principals, most inside the department but some outside of it as well, served as supporting research participants. Among these informants were several administrators and teachers of color. Daryl Wilson was on the T. P. Yaeger research scene for the entire 20 years of the study; Laura Curtis was a part of the Yaeger faculty for 16 years; and Anna Dean, a beginning teacher, was at T. P. Yaeger for 6 years near the middle of the 20-year continuum. Daryl participated in all six standardized reforms, Laura was involved in five and Anna was a part of three. Their voices and emotions, along with the words and feelings of their fellow teachers, contribute to the story serial I will soon present.

I began to conduct my narrative inquiries at Yaeger shortly after I moved to the southern US from western Canada where I received all my education. I had conducted major field-based studies in the Canadian educational system, but T. P. Yaeger Middle School was my first research site in the US and my first experience of American schooling. I entered the Yaeger school landscape in 1997 at the invitation of Brianna Larson, its much-loved, now-deceased principal who was the last Yaeger leader to remain on the campus for more than 10 years. Yaeger then became a lead school in a major reform movement for five years (1997–2003) and received smaller pockets of funding for approximately seven additional years (2004–2011). After that, I continued studying teachers' experiences of school reform on the campus with on-and-off support from university-based projects (2012–2017). While I have conducted studies in many other schools since my association with Yaeger began, none of my other field-based endeavors has lasted as long as the research relationships I established at Yaeger.

From the outset, it is important that I acknowledge my lag in writing this final episode of teachers' experiences of T. P. Yaeger's reforming school context. To be honest, the lapse occurred not because I did not have a manuscript to write, but because I was scared to publish the views and feelings I intuited from the teachers and what I witnessed first-hand myself. This is because the sixth of the six reforms, the one that elicited Daryl Wilson's "data is [G]od" metaphor, pulled me up short (Dyson & Smith, 2019) and filled me with fear. For many years, I have known that I need to be awake to the stories I tell and to "watch for the stories I am told" (King, 2003, p. 10). As shared elsewhere, I have no interest in "hot stories" (Lamott, 2018) that instrumentalize teachers (Muchmore, 2002) to grab readers' attention. Two writers who helped me to manage my impending sense of dread were Ward (2016) and Waldman (2016). Ward encouraged me to "write toward whatever hurts... Don't write toward what is easy..." (p. 262). Waldman similarly opined: "If you are not uncomfortable and scared while you are writing [about particular topics], you are not writing close enough to the bone" (Waldman, 2016, p. 230). I have taken both writers' advice to heart. I now invite readers to accompany me in this narrative inquiry of the experiences of mandated reforms introduced to T. P. Yaeger Middle School over a 20-year period approached from the teacher perspective.

Teacher Stories of School Reform at T. P. Yaeger Middle School

Six teacher-generated narratives of school reform will now be featured in the form of a story serial. The reforms are: (1) standardized teaching methods (models of teaching) (1997–2000), (2) standardized teacher communities (professional learning communities) (2002–2006), (3) standardized teaching practices (readers' and writers' workshop) (2007–2009), (4) standardized teacher evaluation (school district digitized format) (2009–2012), (5) standardized workbooks (testing company-produced) (2013–2015), and (6) standardized pay-for-performance (value-added measures) (2015–2017).

Reform 1: Standardized Teaching Methods (Models of Teaching) (1997–2000)

When I initially entered T. P. Yaeger Middle School, a state-mandated reform involving models of teaching, the first change effort in this story serial, was being introduced. Its theory of action was anchored in the irrefutable belief that "how teaching is conducted impacts how students learn." Hence, a division of the state education agency required Yaeger's teachers to use specific models of teaching for instruction and to implement the models "cleanly, not creatively" as the agency's representative explained (Craig, 2001, p. 301). The teachers would learn which model they would demonstrate/be assessed on when the state-hired consultant walked into their classrooms.

The models of teaching reform planted seeds of discontent among Yaeger's teachers because Brianna Larson, their principal, had explicitly hired them for their creativity. Soon, the literacy teachers began to interact with one another using what I call "monkey language." Daryl Wilson, the literacy department chair, termed the reform "monkey see, monkey do"; novice teacher, Bob Henderson, likened it to "monkey business"; their senior colleague, Charles Wright, viewed it as "a monkey on one's back"; and Howard Woodstock, Yaeger's only African American male teacher (at the time), declared that they had been dressed up in "monkey suits" to have "monkey wrenches" thrown at them. The passage below, which I have infused with their monkey metaphors, captures some of the teachers' major concerns:

Charles: There is this mirroring thing (*"monkey see, monkey do?"*) that is not collaborative. It means doing what the expert does. It does not give individuals credit for their own smarts... (*"a monkey on one's back?" "monkey wrenches?"*)

Daryl: It is scare tactics (*"a monkey on one's back?" "monkey wrenches?"*).

Charles: I resent having to play this game (*"monkey business?"*). People cannot be worked with like they (*wear "monkey suits?"*), and their knowledge and experiences are interchangeable parts (*eliciting "monkey see, monkey do?" behaviors?*)

As a researcher, I slowly came to see that something larger was hidden behind the teachers' pervasive use of the word, monkey. The term, monkey, seemed to be a code-word for something else. When I explicitly asked Daryl Wilson to explain the monkey talk, he told me that if I wanted to understand the implemented models of teaching reform at T. P. Yaeger from the literacy teachers' perspective that I should read *The Monkey's Paw*, a short story by J. Jacobs in the Grade 8 reading anthology with which they all were familiar. Upon my reading of the story, I learned that a wizened monkey's paw, a talisman carried back to Britain from one of its colonies, had once been "an ordinary paw" but had had "a spell ... put on it ... to teach people the lesson that those who interfere with their fates do so at their own peril."

My unpacking of the monkey's paw story helped me to see that the teachers used monkey talk to creatively rebel. Also, their use of the emergent, novel metaphor, the monkey's paw, from which the monkey terms were spawned, embodied their individual and shared knowledge in their community of knowing (Craig, 1995a, 1995b, 2007; Curtis et al., 2013). The teachers' increasing knowledge, forged through their flesh-and-blood in-school experiences, led them to concur that "...[school reform] is 'the monkey's paw.' It appears as if it is a gift, but it really is not a gift. It holds many ironies for teachers" (Craig, 2001, p. 301).

When the models of teaching reform – the "monkey's paw" approach to teacher change – ended, 25 of Yaeger's 85 teachers lost their positions because long-term employment contracts no longer existed as the campus had become an in-district charter school. Shortly after that, T. P. Yaeger's long-term principal, Brianna Larson, retired from the profession, declaring she had "spent too many years on the short end of the stick" (personal communication). She did not like the way the consultant treated her nor what happened after-the-fact to Yaeger's faculty. She intimately learned the irony of school reform that Daryl and his colleagues had foreshadowed in deep and personal ways. In "monkey's paw" fashion, what came to T. P. Yaeger Middle School in the guise of a gift was not a gift because an unprecedented number of teachers lost their jobs, and everyone's autonomy was jeopardized, Brianna Larson's included.

Reform 2: Standardized Teacher Communities (Professional Learning Communities) (2002–2006)

Professional learning communities (PLCs) was the next policy-related reform in the story serial that – this time around – arrived through the school district pipeline. The following excerpt captures how the large urban school system rolled out the reform: "[The] district has ... implement[ed] professional learning communities [PLCs] ... and give[n] administrators the tools needed to create PLCs throughout the district" (School District, 2007, pp. 1–28). From the beginning, the school district's focus privileged principals' versions of teacher community not the natural versions of teacher knowledge communities that existed among teachers before their administrators imposed the PLC intervention on them. Because T. P. Yaeger Middle School had been assigned a new principal to replace Brianna Larson, he was especially eager to fulfill the district's request as he was on a one-term contract and his continuing employment depended on it.

The literacy department teachers had already been experimenting with the workshop method of teaching reading and writing, which revolved around mini-lessons, response journals, student conferences, peer editing, and embedded mechanics of language instruction. However, the new principal was impatient with the speed at which the workshop approach was spreading in the department. He therefore hired a staff developer from the east coast to bring the reform to scale in what he termed the literacy teachers' PLC. Novice teacher, Anna Dean, explained that "the principal may have been using [the staff developer] to weed people out who were not fitting his version of PLCs. Not that he did not think the consultant had a lot to offer, which she did..." (Craig, 2012a, p. 95). As for experienced teacher, Laura Curtis, she described what happened with the reform this way:

Laura: The principal was in his PLC groove and he wanted us to be a *workshop school* (emphasis in original). Whatever we would be school-wide and PLC-related.
Cheryl: Was that ever discussed with everybody?
Laura: Actually, it would not have been a problem, probably, it was the way it was done by forcing people ... I think a lot of people would not have been disturbed by what is basically an idea.
Cheryl: So, you would have been okay with it, but it was the forcing that was the problem?
Laura: It was the forcing. He wanted us all as a PLC on the same page on the same day. Because kids, particularly in the gifted-and-talented classes and in the regular program, are just not on the same page nor do they need to be. It has just been hard, very, very hard. (Craig, 2012a, p. 95)

When the PLC reform was taken to scale, each literacy teacher was visited between 20 and 50 times with six to eight people observing them instruct their students. Among the group were the staff developer, the school administrators, visitors to the school and a sprinkling of fellow literacy teachers. Each carried a clipboard where they commented positively and negatively on the quality of the teaching they witnessed. The staff developer also would interrupt the teaching-learning process and tell the demonstration teacher on-the-spot how to improve his or her practice. Laura felt badly for her colleagues, and how they were diminished in front of their students. She declared that the problem "was the... microscopic way that they came in and zeroed in on you with one child. And the children [particularly those who were English-as-a-second-language learners and possibly offspring of undocumented workers] were very nervous..." (Craig, 2012a, p. 96). She continued:

> The staff developer had a way of putting [us] on the spot saying, "Why do you do this?" "Why do your kids need that?" And everything was an instant demand... I've got to answer this person ... because the individual wants an answer now—and if I do not give the right answer, then the person will get mad at me in front of my principal, peers, and children and say ugly things to me. (Craig, 2012a. p. 96)

Another teacher agreed, saying "the bottom line was that they were not paying attention to what [teachers] already knew and could do well, you know, our knowledge and sensibilities. There was no respect for that, no trust in that at all" (Craig, 2012a, p. 96).

Not surprisingly, agendas collided, and tensions came to a head. A major confrontation between the teachers and the staff developer occurred on a Saturday professional development day. The conflict festered in the weeks that followed until the principal stepped in and made the teachers sign loyalty oaths. If they agreed to teach workshop in the manner directed by the staff developer, they could remain in their positions at Yaeger. However, if they did not concur, they would automatically be transferred to another middle school in the district. Here is how Laura Curtis storied her cumulative experience of the PLC reform:

> Laura: We gained a lot, but we have lost a lot, too. I became unhappy when I realized it [the particular reform] was being forced on us and I began to feel like a butterfly under a pin. A lot of us were feeling that way...
> Cheryl: A butterfly under a pin?
> Laura: Yes, I was very uncomfortable with the demeanors of our staff developer and our principal. It was making me feel not in charge of my own teaching when throughout my career I have felt in charge. (Craig, 2012a, p. 90)

In the end, four of the 14 literacy teachers left Yaeger (some forced; others conscientious objectors), five teachers left the mathematics department (the next department in which the PLC reform would be implemented) and the literacy assistant principal, who was Latina, quit education altogether because she "felt used" (her words) in the plan the principal and staff developer had concocted. Another unexpected person to exit the school was the principal: He was promoted to a superintendent position in the school district.

Reform 3: Standardized Teaching Practices (Readers' and Writers' Workshop) (2007–2009)

By the time the school district mandated standardized teaching practices, the third serial reform in question, Daryl Wilson and I had identified a pattern or a rhythm to how school reform imperatives unfurl. Daryl called the rise and fall of school reform efforts "a saga." I spoke of clashes that occurred, which resulted in people vacating their positions or being forced out of them or being advanced to higher ones. Below is an excerpt from our conversation at the time:

Daryl: I know it's a saga...
Cheryl: It seems to be... I try and make sense of one clash and, low and behold, another one happens...
Daryl: You'll never be done... We'll see what happens when the consultant is gone... I don't know what will happen. I can't even begin to imagine... (Craig, 2012b, p. 2).

Neither Daryl nor the new principal nor anyone else at Yaeger knew that the consultant would not be leaving. Despite the new principal appointed to T. P. Yaeger and her wanting the policy-related reform handled differently, she had no choice in the matter. The previous principal had struck a contract with the staff developer; the long-term contract could not be broken without significant financial penalty.

Apparently, the new principal met the staff developer at the airport, told her about her "kinder, gentler" approach (the principal's contrasting description) and warned the professional developer that she was not to perturb her teachers. Hence, the staff developer and the teachers managed to work together "guardedly" despite the fact "the relationship had broken down" and "no trust remained." (Craig, 2012b, p. 14) However, after a reasonably long period of calm, another "major incident" erupted, in Daryl Wilson's words. The staff developer, perhaps incited by one or two others, learned of something going on in the literacy department completely outside her margins. The seventh grade teachers, some who were returning, were preparing their students for the high stakes state-administered exams using readers' and writers' workshop as their "shell." What they were doing to workshop was blasphemous, from the staff developer's standpoint.

The controversy centered around a new teacher, a male who came to Yaeger a year after the old principal left, a teacher whose terminal degree made him more qualified in literacy, gifted education, teacher development, and leadership than the staff developer or any other member of the administrative team. According to Daryl, Laura, Anna, and others, the roots of the "head-on collision" (Craig, 2012b, p. 14) traced to the basic tenets of workshop. The new teacher was vexed by how the staff developer had "handcuffed" (Daryl's word) the Yaeger teachers to her version of workshop (Craig, 2012b, p. 14) at the exclusion of their own or others' versions. When this teacher riled against the standardization the staff developer had imposed on the department, she went ballistic. She declared that he was not doing workshop, and that he was hired as a literacy teacher to teach workshop. He retorted that "what he was hired to do, and who he was hired by, was not the staff developer's business." He added that "a professional boundary had been crossed and cautioned that he would actively do something about it, if the conversation continued" (Craig, 2012b, p. 15).

In the midst of this "crisis," Daryl Wilson and some other literacy colleagues appealed to their new female principal for support. On this occasion, the principal sided with the teachers. Yaeger's neophyte principal knew that "paying a [staff developer] to contribute to a group's dysfunction was too much" (Craig, 2014, p. 16). Unfortunately, her support came too late. Hence, the third installment of the story serial ended with three literacy teachers exiting the department and the staff developer not returning because her contract had ended. Also, Yaeger's new principal was appointed to a superintendent position a few months into the following year and the literacy assistant principal retired after serving as the interim principal for a half-year. And what, readers may ask, happened to the teacher "dropped in the grease" who found himself in the center of the ongoing controversy? He became director of literacy in a nearby school district.

Reform 4: Standardized Teacher Evaluation (New School District Approach) (2009–2012)

The fourth standardized reform in this story serial involved the district's mandated method of teacher evaluation, an approach related to state and federal regulations and to the increasing influence of value-added research (e.g., Sanders, 2000; Sanders & Horn, 1994) throughout the nation, research directly linking individual teacher performance with student test scores. This reform specifically affected Anna Dean who, as a novice teacher, had survived the second and third standardized reform efforts. By virtue of those two previous experiences, Anna had already personally concluded that "where the school/school district was concerned ... smart teachers [were] neither tolerated nor appreciated." As a teaching professional, she had learned "that teachers should [not] have something forced down their throats ... Not allowing for teacher ownership is very degrading" (Craig, 2013, p. 26).

As can be seen, Anna Dean was forthright about her flesh-and-blood experience of learning to teach in the "eye of a storm" (Craig, 2013, p. 25). In the "eye of the storm," she was acutely aware of the friction between the district's past two policy-related reforms and Yaeger's literacy teachers who sought to retain their professional autonomy and to contribute to decisions affecting how they taught. Concurrently, Anna was proud of what she personally had learned about teaching literacy using the workshop approach to instruction. As a beginning teacher, she had "figure[ed] out that the 'what' and 'how' are the teaching points [of the workshop method] ... and that connections [between the two] are the 'why'" (Craig, 2014, p. 97) About the same time, a senior teacher – unbeknownst to Anna – praised her, saying she should be named "teacher-of-the-universe," given all that she had come through amid the department's discord (Craig, 2014, p. 97). Soon thereafter, Anna proudly announced that she had finally "nailed workshop." It seems "the stories she was attempting to live and tell about her use of the readers' and writers' workshop method were now resonating with the stories her peers and assessor were giving back to her." There was "a synergy… between what she was hearing about her teaching practice and what she had personally come to know about herself as a teacher" (Craig, 2014, p. 97)

But Anna's growth was about to go unrecognized and unrewarded. In her fifth year of teaching, the new principal appointed to T. P. Yaeger came from a private school in another state and did not understand public school finance. As a result, Yaeger, which had always enjoyed a financial surplus due to the generosity of its neighborhood parents, was nearly bankrupt. Further to this, the principal was frequently absent because he privately consulted on the side. The assistant principals – all being new except one who had one-year of experience – were going "stir crazy." Not surprisingly, things at Yaeger were falling through the cracks, especially where student discipline was concerned.

It was in Anna Dean's sixth year, however, that her personal teaching situation went awry. In the backdrop, a plethora of changes conspired together: (1) the appointment of a new superintendent to her school district, (2) the naming of yet another new principal to her school (her third one), (3) the prior exit of five of Yaeger's six assistant principals, (4) the entry of anew literacy assistant principal, (5) changes to the racial-socio-economic makeup of the campus's student population, and (6) additions to, and tightening of, district policies and procedures. While all of the above affected Anna and her context of teaching, only three will be elaborated: (1) the new superintendent, (2) the change of the racial-socioeconomic backgrounds of students, and (3) the intensification of district policies and procedures being funneled into the school.

The new superintendent, who was already highly controversial, had led other prominent urban districts elsewhere in the nation. Rather than accepting the urban school district's teachers as "highly qualified" according to the No Child Left Behind policy, he outright challenged their expertise. Word on the street (i.e., PhD classes) was that the article, *No more valentines* (Donaldson, 2010), had become his rationale for training all district administrators to be hypercritical of teachers so that teachers' teaching assessments could be aligned with student scores. A second major turn was that there was now a quota – a purported total number of teacher evaluation points available to each campus. Where evaluation was concerned, one teacher's win came at another teacher's loss (Craig, 2018b). A teacher in Yaeger's foreign language department who participated in another study – one of Brianna Larson's "gems" (Larson's turn of phrase) – confirmed this point. Ashley Thomas recalled how a Yaeger assistant principal gave her "1's and 2's (out of 5) on everything," saying that Ashley "was going to retire anyhow…" and that "[her] assessment probably would not matter to [her]." But it was extremely important to Ashley who resented the "victimization" accompanying the "value-added quota game" (Craig, 2018b, pp. 20–21).

Novice teachers like Anna Dean and senior teachers like Ashley Thomas were especially vulnerable to ill-treatment as principals and assistant principals manipulated classroom observation assessments to match students' high stakes test scores, with their foci as administrators constantly changing because they too were moving in-and-out of Yaeger in "flavor-of-the-year" (an early teacher's expression) progression. The end result was that there simply were too few points to go around (i.e., quota) – especially in a school like Yaeger, which historically attracted excellent faculty. These serious constraints emanating from the policy arena had far-reaching consequences, as readers will soon learn.

As for the backgrounds of Yaeger's students, they had significantly changed as well. The district's redrawing of its boundaries, along with the approval of moving more minority (students)-to-majority (mostly White) schools, forever altered the campus's racial-socioeconomic composition. For the first time in its near-century existence, T. P. Yaeger Middle School received federal funding for high poverty students, funds that would help finance the school's high profile programs, which had been seriously jeopardized by the former principal's alleged fiscal mismanagement. Also, the minority students were admitted without the kind of preparation that Yaeger's existing faculty would have needed to ensure the incoming students' academic success.

But the biggest change for Anna was the piling on of accountability measures at both the local and state levels to satisfy federal regulations. The first shift the teachers experienced was how accountability requirements were not just a part of literacy meetings: they now consumed entire agendas. The days of debating alternative pedagogical approaches to teaching readers' and writers' workshop were over as new managerial oversight took hold. Department meetings, previously chaired by Daryl Wilson, were now controlled by the new literacy assistant principal who came from an elementary school, had no administrative experience, and majored in a subject area other than adolescent reading and writing. Under his leadership, items on meeting agendas focused on making the literacy teachers more auditable (Clarke & Moore, 2013; Connell, 2009; Mockler, 2012) and on increasing their standardization of student learning.

When the literacy assistant principal introduced teacher evaluation, agenda item 3 (Fig. 1), to the literacy department, major differences of opinion were aired. Despite district policy stating that most of Yaeger's 14 literacy teachers (Anna included) would automatically be on a relaxed evaluation schedule, the new assistant principal informed them that everyone would be subjected to full evaluations. What he did not explain was that they were required to repeat the long form process not because they needed it, but because he was new to his administrative post. What he also did not disclose was that their teaching performances would be closely tied to their students' high stakes test scores. What he further did not mention is that the edict he was implementing came directly from the chief superintendent's office.

The new assistant principal proceeded to judge the quality of the teachers' performances using the Professional Development Assessment System (PDAS), which has eight domains ranging from successful student participation to compliance with policies and operating procedures to the improvement of all students' academic performances. In sum, none of Yaeger's literacy teachers retained their "exceeds expectations" (5/5) ratings for any of the domains of their evaluations, according to Daryl. In their individual feedback, a teacher who expressed concerns about teachers not being treated like professionals received a score 27 points lower than her previous one, Daryl Wilson received a rating 20 points less than his past evaluation, and Anna Dean's score was 32 points lower

1. Benchmark assessments (in preparation for high stakes achievement testing)

2. Literacy circle books (who was in charge of purchases and where books could be purchased)

3. Mid-year instruction review (materials needed for annual teacher evaluations)

4. Individual appointments with the assistant principal (what would be discussed in post-evaluation conferences)

5. Teachers' rater and verification update (a list of the literacy teachers who were able to rate and verify the quality of students' writing products and those who had not completed their half-day of mandatory training)

6. LPAC [Language Proficiency Assessment Committee] meeting (committee reviewing students moving from ESL classes to regular classroom instruction)

7. Department sharing (two teachers announced they have seriously ill parents; a third teacher shared that the previous literacy assistant principal had successfully initiated a T. P. Yaeger support group for 30 immigrant parents)

Fig. 1. Literacy Meeting Agenda and Truncated Notes-to-File (Craig, 2014).

than what she had been awarded the previous year by Yaeger's past assistant principal. In fact, Anna went from 5s (exceeds expectations) to 3s (average) in all categories. Domain VII (Compliance with Policies, Operating Procedures and Requirements) was the section where all the teachers received the most problematic feedback. What Anna Dean found most reprehensible about her beginning teacher evaluation was that she "was docked for not setting the discipline policy for the school" – "as if that is my responsibility" (Craig, 2014, p. 107). Upon resigning from Yaeger and becoming a teacher attrition statistic, Anna had the following to say:

> In my sixth year at Yaeger, I was a cluster leader, taught 93 students every day ... and the number of high needs students had increased from 120 to 160 at my grade level [due to the past principal allowing more minority-to-majority transfers to generate more federal revenue]. The students were tough ... with significant educational problems ... [arrests for drug trafficking—a first for the campus—had been made; gang activity was also being closely monitored]. The special education teachers were totally overwhelmed and a whole new slate of assistant principals had been named. It was a very, very difficult year ... Cumulatively, it was too much for a veteran, much less a new teacher ... I decided to seek other alternatives .... The time had come to leave .... (Craig, 2014, p. 107)

The year Anna quit teaching, one ESL teacher, two special education teachers and the assistant principal left Yaeger as well.

Reform 5: Standardized Workbooks (Testing Company-Produced Materials) (2013–2015)

If the "monkey's paw" metaphor distinguished the first installment of the story serial, "butterfly under a pin" signified the second one, "a saga" characterized the third, and "learning to teach in the eye of the storm" formed the idea-seed for the fourth installment, then "hidden in clear view" would be the trigger word for the serial's fifth story, standardized workbooks. Also, in contrast to the four policy-related reforms presented thus far, "hidden in clear view" – as well as "data is [G]od," the sixth standardized reform – are shorter in length than the previous four episodes of the story serial.

I begin this fourth installment in the series by reaching back to something Laura Curtis said in her "butterfly under a pin" narrative. This was when the principal at the time required the Yaeger teachers to sign oaths to pledge their loyalty to the staff developer's version of readers' and writers' workshop. I repeat Laura's words here:

> We were all so intimidated about losing our jobs. You know, we had seen it happen before [with the charter...] And so, we saw people being fired... Do you remember [Laura recites a string of literacy teachers who no longer teach at Yaeger]? These were all teachers trained in **workshop**. An investment was made in them ... Getting rid of them just didn't make sense ... You know, we still have **book sets** with all of those teachers' names on them [Laura repeated the list of literacy teachers]... The kids loved those teachers. They were successful teachers... jewels we didn't need removed from our crown. (Craig, 2012b, pp. 97–98, bold-faced print added)

In the aforementioned passage, Laura Curtis praised her former colleagues for their contributions and mourned their totally avoidable losses in an urban district that paradoxically suffers from serious teacher shortages and an absence of faculty highly qualified to teach their subject areas. What Laura also communicated is that those employing the workshop teaching approach at T. P. Yaeger Middle School used sets of novels and non-fiction books as their primary texts, not reading anthologies and accompanying workbooks as previously was the case in the *Monkey's Paw* segment of this story serial, when a more conventional method to teach reading was employed. Hence, when the school district demanded that each school choose between two mandated workbooks, both of which were published by companies distributing test preparation materials and tests, the Yaeger teachers went along with the decree, despite them teaching the mechanics of language differently. They dutifully arranged for every teacher to attend the publishers' book showcase. The teachers then voted on hidden ballots and, to their surprise, the company to which they felt "the most animosity" was the one selected to be Yaeger's favored workbook publisher. The school's choice was then communicated in a timely fashion to the school district.

However, something bewildering to the teachers, the literacy department chair and their new principal occurred. The school district announced that the competing workbook sets would be ordered for Yaeger, not the workbooks the literacy teachers had democratically chosen. One teacher interpreted this development "as par for the course...." Another said that "there is always this semblance of teacher consultation, but in the end, everything in the school district is a forgone conclusion made from above." A third chimed in, declaring it all "a waste of teachers' valuable time."

How Yaeger ended up with the competing workbook publisher is a question begging to be asked. Did the district determine after-the-fact that all middle schools with gifted-and-talented populations should use the same workbook? Was a researcher with an Institute of Educational Studies (IES) grant needing comparison groups for a funded research project? Were the workbook vendors promised advanced shares of the market and shifting Yaeger from one vendor to the other a way to equalize percentages? Was the district concerned about lawsuits from voiced-up parents and wanting its top campuses to use the workbook flaunting a highly ranked university's name? Unfortunately, the underlying reason is not known. What the teachers were told was that $75,000 (1,500 students × $50 per expendable workbook) per year for a purported six years ($450,000) would be committed to purchasing single-use-only student workbooks for a school steeped in workshop teaching and purchasing novel sets and nonfiction books instead of anthologies and workbooks for instructional purposes. Using novels and nonfiction texts as vehicles, the Yaeger literacy teachers regularly taught integrated grammar, comprehension, and style mini-lessons, which were followed by students conferring with their peers and teacher.

I do not want to leave the impression that the mandatory workbooks were never touched at Yaeger. They were. Many teachers field-tested them and found they worked "reasonably well" (Daryl Wilson's assessment), but not better than the mini-lessons and conferring integrated into particular novel and nonfiction book studies. A second way the teachers tried to employ the workbooks was as homework assignments. Once again, challenges arose. Members of Yaeger's student body and some influential parents complained profusely about how heavy the workbooks were and how they excessively weighed down students' backpacks.

The question then arose: What should the Yaeger teachers do with the compulsory workbooks, given they were not being used daily and that their classrooms were already smaller-than-usual, given the historical period in which their school was built? This is when the teachers set their theory of action, "hidden in clear view," in motion. What happened was that the teachers found creative ways to hide the workbooks while keeping them in open sight. Some classrooms had pillows that could easily be removed from the front of the workbooks; other classrooms had novel sets at the front of bookshelves with the workbooks easily accessible behind them. A further classroom had a large chest where the consumable material was stored, while still another had a fabric screen strategically placed in front of 95 workbooks. At one point, I inquired whether the new literacy assistant principal and the new principal knew what was going on with the workbooks in the teachers' classrooms. The response was that "Yaeger is a workshop school" and "not encountering significant challenges with students' literacy scores." Therefore, the teachers could continue hiding the workbooks as long as the workbooks would be easily accessible if a school district inspection were to occur. In short, the standardized workbook reform, which may still be continuing due to contract extensions, was an innocuous "wink-wink" affair all the way round – with central leadership's wastage of the public purse being the only significant casualty.

Reform 6: Standardized Pay-for-Performance (Value-Added Measures) (2015–2017)

We now come to pay-for-performance, the sixth standardized reform installment, which became problematic in Reform 4 (Standardized Teacher Assessment) and increasingly affected teachers in previously unimaginable ways. With the standardized workbook reform, its narrative beginnings reached back to an explanation Laura Curtis shared about her "butterfly under a pin" experience. For the sixth policy-related reform, texts excerpted from Anna Dean's Reform 4 leaving story (Craig, 2014) set the context for the effects of the standardized pay-per-performance reform and ultimately its fueling of Daryl Wilson's "this is what we have come to..." remark, which effectively brought his career to an end.

In Anna's published narrative, the maximum annual value-added bonus available to any teacher in the school district was $7,000. But issues with the reform had been reported before Anna resigned, as the evidence below indicates:

> ...stories [had] spread quickly about teachers with poor evaluations from other campuses who [had been] relieved of their teaching duties. Their students were subsequently divided and taught by colleagues. Those no longer teaching apparently received the maximum pay-for-performance ($7,000 each), thanks to peers carrying their loads. (Craig, 2014, p. 19)

Also, a narrative about science teachers' bonuses was included in Anna's leaving story. One middle school teacher's bonus rose from $200 to $5,000 to $7,000 by virtue of the learners assigned to her "by the luck of the draw" (Craig, 2014, p. 20). Meanwhile, at T. P. Yaeger, another problem endemic to the value-added approach surfaced. One of the school's stellar mathematics teachers received a $5,000 award while the music teacher whose orchestra won the state championship received $500 due to his content area not being as "valued" in the formula as the Science-Technology-Engineering-Mathematics (STEM) disciplines and other core subject matters (Craig, 2014, p. 100).

For Daryl and members of his department, eligibility for the highest level of value-added bonuses was not a problem. After all, literacy was a tested core content area. However, the amount the teachers received was dependent on the teens assigned to their classes and the degree to which those students' achievement test scores increased. This automatically meant that teacher bonuses fluctuated from year-to-year. Comparing one year's bonus to another year's bonus was like comparing apples to oranges: different students = different test scores = different bonuses. The same holds true when comparing one teacher's bonus to that of another teacher in the same or different schools and in the same or different years.

Before the following school year began, Yaeger's new principal reviewed the pay-for-performance allocations paid to teachers on her campus. She noted that some teacher bonuses, while still substantial, had fluctuated. Based on this questionable evidence (i.e., different years = different students = different test scores = different bonus dollar values), she removed Daryl Wilson from his position as literacy department chair. She did the same thing with at least one other literacy teacher who was a grade-level leader and a supporting research participant. When this decision was made, Yaeger's faculty was dumbfounded. Excellence in teaching, which for nearly a century had successfully scaffolded the learning of thousands of Yaeger students, no longer felt empowering to them as teachers. Instead, their lived experiences, once translated into behavioral data, were being used – in a macabre turn of events – to diminish their efforts and identities (Zuboff, 2019, p. 53).

The logic behind publicly shaming highly reputable teachers by demoting them from leadership positions was fuzzy. Did the neophyte administrator not understand the underlying principles of value-added modeling? Did someone in the district or perhaps a private consulting firm knowingly conduct a secondary analysis, including other data points not communicated to Daryl and his colleagues? (i.e., number of years at school, number of years in career, teacher preparation method, salary, etc.) Was the decrease in bonus pay a ruse for something else (i.e., age discrimination)? Or did the principal, a newcomer to a leadership position, imagine she could more easily establish authority with malleable induction year teachers heading the department? The answer to these questions also will be never known. But we do know this – again from Reform 4 – that 80% of the teachers in the large, urban, diverse school district had five or less years of experience and that 50% of the administrators also had five or less years of experience. In short, the level of teacher and principal expertise in the school district – and increasingly at T. P. Yaeger – was extremely "thin" where both teacher and administrator experience was concerned. The following sentence warrants repetition here: "The annual replacement of ... the ... teaching [and principal] force, mostly by newcomers ... is an inadequate approach to meeting societal demands." The case I argued in 2014 is even more applicable today.

When Daryl Wilson shared his principal's decision with me, he lamented – with more than a hint of irony in his voice – that "this is what we have come to... there is no other way to explain it... data is [G]od ...." As I listened to his heartbreaking tale, I could not help but think that his words not only pertained to the sixth of the six policy-related reforms, but also to the cumulative reform effort – the story serial – that had played out over the two decades in which we had worked closely together. I could see where teachers' humanity and their right to have input into their professional lives had been stripped away by managerial and neoliberal policies privileging the measuring and interpreting of "behavioral data" (Zuboff, 2019, p. 53) over what is important in education and what matters to teachers. The "data as holy grail group," Daryl's pet phrase for those spearheading "the movements," championed calculation and strategy over educative relationships and humane living. Daryl ended by saying the most frightening thing that any research participant has ever disclosed to me in my long-term research career: "There is nowhere to go from here...." On that note, his career ended. And, with that, the sixth story of reform, the story serial and my embedded research project at Yaeger concluded.

Research Themes

So, what can be learned from this story serial of six policy-related reforms introduced over two decades to T. P. Yaeger Middle School from a teacher perspective? First, the sequence of narratives conveyed, as Ayers foreshadowed, "a chorus of interconnected stories" that were "infinitely susceptible to circumstances and highly liable to... change." Also, "crashing" most certainly occurred within, between and across the teachers' lived narratives with the stories being "intertwined" and "interwoven" regardless of the specificities of the change efforts and the particular teachers involved. These phenomena were especially noticeable as new administrators entered T. P. Yaeger, but also when the experienced male literacy teacher ignited a new chapter of the ongoing readers' and writers' workshop saga and responded in a manner akin to the conscientious objectors who exited the campus the year before. Also, no one was immune to the underbelly of the "difficult stories" that were shared. Novice teacher, Anna Dean, managed to keep her head above water for the second and third policy-related reforms, but was "sunk" (Anna's assessment) by the fourth reform in the story serial, coincidently when she recognized that she had fully grasped how to teach workshop. Laura Curtis made it through the first, second, third, and fourth reforms while having the life of her work sucked out of her like a "butterfly under a pin." Daryl Wilson remarkably weathered all of the policy-related changes but, in an unanticipated turn-of-event, had his literacy leadership role revoked – before the next academic year began – by yet another neophyte or new-to-school principal, the ninth of nine principals in his Yaeger career. It is safe to say that all four teachers – the unnamed male, Anna Dean, Laura Curtis, and Daryl Wilson – as well as Ashley Thomas from my other Yaeger study, felt "victimized" (Ashley's term) at one point or another by (1) standardization policies denying them their "own smarts" ("money's paw") and (2) botched implementation efforts masterminded by leaders ill-equipped for the tasks at hand. Mostly, readers gain a birds-eye view of the chaotic state of America's urban schools as teachers and principals (and superintendents!) are constantly hired/fired/moved/advanced in desperate attempts to "fix" intractable problems.

Underpinning all the stories was the pervasive belief that social engineering can resolve complex human issues inherent to the field of education. Keen insights were gleaned as to why novice and experienced teachers become frustrated and rapidly quit their profession of choice. Also, the multitude of ways that the sociopolitical environment weighed heavily on T. P. Yaeger's milieu were exposed. Readers witness – in a first-hand way – ongoing managerial and neoliberal attempts to resolve urban school challenges. Policymakers repeatedly intervened in teachers' and children's lives with little consideration for the residue their previous policies had left in their lifeworlds. Jean Anyon (1977) likened this blind spot to a screen door: taming (i.e., via dictates), sanitizing (i.e., via standardization), and analyzing (i.e., via high stakes tests; value-added modeling) the air on the school side of the screen, while the air on the screen's society side is inundated with never-ending problems wafting into schools – with poverty, inequity, hunger, violence, addiction, overwork, absentee parents, homelessness, and child safety being the most pernicious ones. Researchers like Anyon and Berliner (2002) suggest that policymakers need to attend to the influence of poverty on the society side of the screen door before blaming schools, teachers and administrators for social problems not of their making.

It is also crystal clear that mass standardization does not work, probably because it does not fit the country's democratic roots and the individualism cherished by American citizens. Dewey (1897) nailed the underlying issue with policy-related reforms in his pedagogical creed in the 1800s: "... reforms which rest simply upon... enactment of law, or... threatening of certain penalties, or upon changes in mechanical or outward arrangements, are transitory and futile." Policymakers' ongoing failures, however, did not deter them from forcefully favoring the teacher as curriculum implementer image at the expense of the teachers' preferred image of teacher as curriculum maker. Those in charge seemed blissfully unaware that their policy dictates could only be realized in schools like Yaeger when they become assimilated into teachers' practical knowledge and have life breathed into their inert characters through teachers' enactment of the teacher as curriculum maker image.

Additionally, the balance between "what gets better" and "what gets worse" became increasingly disproportionate and even more intimately linked to how teachers and principals relate/do not relate to one another, given the bonuses (or lack thereof) that principals received for student test scores achieved through teachers' teaching efforts. This arrangement interfered with and imperiled principal's abilities to nurture teachers' professionalism and to lead collaboratively (Hargreaves & O'Connor, 2018). In the six sequential stories, what became better was one principal who listened to the teachers at a critical juncture in "the saga" and another pair of administrators who turned a blind eye to the "hidden in clear view" workbooks. What became worse was that teaching methods were progressively determined by experts to be ultracritical of teachers ("monkey's paw," "butterfly under a pin"), teachers' relationships with their peers were increasingly placed under administrators' thumbs (PLCs, "butterfly under a pin"), student workbooks were selected outside of school contexts ("hidden in clear view"), teachers' evaluations were conducted by leaders lacking in subject matter knowledge ("eye of the storm") and teacher quality/pay-for-performance was determined by computer-generated data that was clearly "organized" and "filtered," but unfortunately not interpreted by administrators with "the [prerequisite] understandings and expertise to [make it] actionable" in defensible ways ("eye of the storm," "data is [G]od") (Marsh, 2012, p. 3).

In a nutshell, anything available to be instrumentalized, as Muchmore put it, was instrumentalized during the period of time when Yaeger's six reforms took hold. The continuous hammering of standardized stakes in the ground was the overarching theme of the story serial. Rarely did wind ripple in Yaeger's metaphorical grass as Palmer earlier discussed. The saddest part was the institutionalized surveillance that accompanied the many attempts at standardization. In the latter reforms, the teachers' human experiences became performative data surveilled by others with "decision making rights" (Zuboff, 2019, p. 90). Concurrently, those who surveilled were, in turn, surveilled by others, who likewise judged their performances. This mass auditing system continued up-and-down the line with no one escaping scrutiny.

Even the research community and certain lines of inquiry were implicated in the mix. In the background of the six reforms, the theoretical influences of the effective schools movement (models of teaching) (Levine & Lazotte, 1990), increasing teacher professionalism (professional learning communities, readers' and writers' workshop) (Vescio et al., 2008) and new managerialism (Burham, 1941; Chandler, 1977; Ferlie, 2017) (standardized teacher evaluation, standardized workbooks) were evident. These strands of literature gave way to neoliberal strategies (value-added modeling) where the value of student learning and teacher instruction (and principals' and superintendents' worth) was assessed via competitive market principles (Rizvi & Lingvard, 2010). At times, some leadership and evaluation research appeared co-opted and used in ways contrary to the authors' intents. At other times, statistical procedures discovered and applied in an untarnished theoretical world created havoc in teachers' practical lives when adopted and implemented as policy. Over the 20-year continuum, the movement was clearly in the direction of performance evaluation and away from teacher- and school-based approaches to change.

A further topic spanning the reforms was the complementary nature of narratives and metaphors in capturing teachers' knowing in context. The narratives and metaphors helped "things hang together" and gave "coherence" to what was going on (Berger, 2010, 2011, p. 275). Each hand-sculpted metaphor involved two seemingly contradictory ideas that "disturb[ed] a whole network of meaning [through] aberrant attribution" (Ricoeur, 2003, p. 23). In many ways, the metaphors were "the gloved hand that touch[ed] lightly but true" (Lane, 1988, p. 6) on the teachers' policy-related school reform experiences. Table 1 features the sources of the metaphors, their original attributions and their aberrant attributions.

The first four metaphors elicited by the Yaeger teachers have already been addressed in other works. As for the fifth metaphor, it caused no harm. In the story serial, it simply was comic relief that came with a stiff price tag. It illuminated one of the "thousands of ingenious ways in which commands on what and how to teach can, will and must be modified or circumvented..." by teachers (Schwab, 1983, p. 245).

But the metaphor, "data is [G]od," was completely different. With "data is [G]od," replicable, humanly produced, mostly mundane, "big" information was deemed comparable to a higher power – the holy father [mother] | son [daughter] | spirit, the three-in-one – to whom millions worldwide reverently bow down. When Daryl voiced this emergent, inventive metaphor, my mind immediately placed his metaphor alongside a poem written by Jorge Luis Borges (Borges, 1960/1985), an Argentine poet regarded as "a planet unto himself," an artist who "resist [s] categorization" and is "endlessly re-readable" (Parini, 1999, p. 1).

Table 1. Reforms, Metaphors, Aberrant Attributions.

Reform	Source of Metaphor	Aberrant Attribution 1	Aberrant Attribution 2
Policy Reform 1	Historical Fiction	Monkey's paw talisman under a spell tests fate of humans	School experiencing policy-related reforms tests fate of teachers
Policy Reform 2	Biology	Butterfly stretched from pillar-to-post by pins	Teacher stretched from pillar-to-post by policy-related school reform
Policy Reform 3	Meteorology	Learning to teach in the "eye of the storm"	Learning to teach at the epicenter of school reform
Policy Reform 4	Literacy	Saga/never ending, cliff-hanging story	Saga/never ending, cliff-hanging reform
Policy Reform 5	Religion	Hidden blessings/visible phenomena	Hidden books/visible phenomena
Policy Reform 6	Computing	Measured, collected, reported, transmissible, storable, computerized, "big" information	Experienced, embodied, creator, intercessor, sustainer, transcendent being

Borges wisely penned: "God moves the player, he in turn, the piece./But what god beyond God begins the round/of dust and time and sleep and agonies?" I could not help but connect the managerial and neoliberal educational policies with Daryl's "[G]od," administrators at all levels with the players, and the pieces being Yaeger's teachers/leaders, all of whom were constantly moved around on a metaphorical chessboard. Implicated in the strategic maneuvers are public school students whose futures are being manipulated "to restore confidence in markets and companies that make them function." (OECD, 2013) Borges also offers even deeper insights into Daryl's ominous metaphor. The poet, like Daryl Wilson, directs attention to the existential and the unfathomable; that is, how is it that we as human beings have been given life? How are we placed in time? And who/what initiates our agonies, sorrows and despairs? Ultimately, both Borges and Daryl challenge us to consider what lies "beyond the name" that "has no name." What sits behind accountability, performativity and standardization? Also, what might we call the ceding of our fates to programmers' algorithms that could abscond with our futures, especially since their outputs are "not neutral" (Zuboff, 2019, p. 132) and hence subject to misunderstandings, misapplications, misappropriations and/or maligned logic? And what about young teachers and administrators who have been "cut off from forms of knowledge that cannot be reduced to data or adequately represented in print?" (Bowers, 2016, pp. 71–72). These questions are the most profound ones that Borges and Daryl metaphorically cajole us to consider. Humankind largely knows where it has been – at least in the recent past. But where are we going? Will the fascination with and worshipping of big data get us to where we aspire? If not, how can humanity get off the data-driven, evidence-based, hamster wheel? In more local terms, what ultimately will series-upon-series of less-than-successful policy-driven reforms lead to? And, at the end of the day, will humans freely know each other and themselves?

Summary Statements
To end, I leave the previous discussion of large "meaning of life" questions and return to the small world living of this research study in T. P. Yaeger Middle School's literacy department. Seven years ago, I was in Daryl Wilson's classroom when his eighth grade students studied *To Kill a Mockingbird*. To this day, photos of shadow boxes his students created as a workshop activity remain etched in my mind and filed on my computer. In a follow-up mini-lesson, Daryl and his students dug deeply into how relationships in Harper Lee's novel communicated the inequities of racialized America at that point in time. In the novel, Atticus, the main character, famously tells his daughter, Scout: "You never really understand a person until you consider things from his point of view… until you climb into his skin and walk around in it" (Lee, 1960, p. 30). Over a period of 20 years, I climbed into the skins of several Yaeger teachers whose colors, ages, preparations, genders, sexual orientations, countries of origin, among many other identifiers, differed from my own. Walking alongside Daryl, Anna, Laura, and many others (i.e., unnamed teacher, Ashley Thomas), I experienced an insider view of their knowledge and the sense they made of six policy-related reforms introduced to T. P. Yaeger Middle School over two decades. The story serial I subsequently created graphically animated how each story told by the teachers folded into the next one, with all of their storied accounts winding both backward and forward to reveal narrative threads already visible *and* yet to come. The implied generativity of narrative and narrative inquiry caused me to read and re read the serial's six stories and to repeatedly circle back to Daryl's "no way to go from here" comment.

His concluding statement, which when I first heard it, had death written all over it. However, the finality embedded in Daryl's parting words did not seem to fit the life-giving qualities of narrative inquiry as a mode of research investigation. For nearly two years, I mused over this tension. Then, I re-read T. S. Eliot, a favorite poet of both Daryl and me. As I re-visited the poem, *Little Gidden*, my eyes traveled not to the renowned (and probably over-used) final stanza – but to an earlier line that jumped off the page at me: "What we call the beginning is often the end. And to make an end is to make a beginning." I believe Daryl, Anna, Laura, the unnamed teacher and many others at T. P. Yaeger, including deceased Brianna Larson, would feel comforted to know that their efforts at educating Yaeger's urban youth were not in vain. I know that I – walking in their skins as well as my own – found consolation in T. S. Eliot's words. I now know the end about which Daryl Wilson spoke clears a space where new beginnings – locally, nationally, and internationally – can spring forth.

AFTERWORD

In November 2019 (when this chapter was in revision), the State of Texas took over the school district to which T. P. Yaeger Middle School belongs. The state appointed a superintendent and board of managers to run the district, citing that it had failed, in Governor Greg Abbott's words, to "deliver the best possible education to every Texas child" (McCord, 2019, November 7).

AUTHOR'S NOTES

The early years of this research study were made possible through funding awarded to T. P. Yaeger Middle School by the local office of a major national reform movement. After that, small university grants from the University of Houston supported the work. Most recently, my Houston Endowment Endowed Chair of Urban Education funds have supported this study. This chapter was scheduled to be presented in the form of a paper at the American Educational Research Meeting in San Francisco, CA, April 17–21, 2020. Despite the conference being canceled, AERA authenticated an earlier version of this manuscript as an accepted AERA presentation/paper.

Appendix A. Supplementary data. Supplementary data to this article can be found online at: https://doi.org/10.1016/j.tate.2020.103027.

REFERENCES

Anyon, J. (1977). *Trying to fix an urban school without fixing the neighborhood in which it is embedded is like trying to clean the air on one side of a screen door* (Audiotaped interview). State University of.

Arkhipenka, V., & Lupasco, S. (2019). Narrative and metaphor as two sides of the same coin: The case for using both in research and teacher development. In M. Hanne & H. Kaal (Eds.), *Narrative and metaphor in education: Look both ways* (pp. 221–232). Routledge.

Ayers, W. (1992). In W. Ayers & W. Schubert (Eds.), *In the country of the blind: Telling our stories. Teacher lore: Learning from our own experience* (pp. 154–158). Longman.

Berliner, D. (2002). Comment: Educational research: The hardest science of all. *Educational Researcher, 31*(8), 18–20.

Borges, J. L. (1960/1985). God moves the player. In *Dreamtigers*. University of Texas Press.

Bowers, C. (2016). *Digital detachment: How computer culture undermines democracy*. Routledge.

Burham, J. (1941). *The managerial revolution: What is happening in the world*. John Day Company, Inc.

Caine, V., Estefan, A., & Clandinin, D. J. (2013). A return to methodological commitment: Reflections on narrative inquiry. *Scandinavian Journal of Educational Research, 57*(6), 574–586.

Caine, V., Murphy, M. S., Estefan, A., Clandinin, D. J., Steeves, P., & Huber, J. (2017). Exploring the purposes of fictionalization in narrative inquiry. *Qualitative Inquiry, 23*(3), 215–221.

Chandler, A., Jr. (1977). *The invisible hand: The managerial revolution in American business*. Belknap Press.

Christensen, K. (2016). In M. Maran (Ed.), *Why we write about ourselves* (pp. 9–21). Kate Christensen.

Clandinin, D. J. (1986). *Classroom practice: Teacher images in action*. Taylor & Francis.

Clandinin, D. J., Caine, V., & Lessard, S. (2018). *The relational ethics of narrative inquiry*. Routledge.

Clandinin, D. J., Caine, V., Lessard, S., & Huber, J. (2016). *Engaging in narrative inquiries with children and youth*. Routledge.

Clandinin, D. J., & Connelly, M. (1992). Teacher as curriculum maker. In P. Jackson (Ed.), *Handbook of research on curriculum* (pp. 363–401). Macmillan.

Clandinin, D. J., & Connelly, F. M. (1996). Teachers' professional knowledge landscapes: Teacher stories-stories of teachers-school stories-stories of school. *Educational Researcher, 25*(3), 2-14.

Clandinin, D. J., & Connelly, F. M. (2000). *Narrative inquiry: Experience and story in qualitative research*. Jossey Bass Publishing.

Clandinin, D. J., Huber, J., Huber, M., Murphy, M. S., Orr, A. M., Pearce, M., et al. (2006). *Composing diverse identities: Narrative inquiries into the interwoven lives of children and teachers*. Routledge.

Clandinin, D. J., & Rosiek, J. (2006). Borders, tensions and borderlands in narrative inquiry. In D. J. Clandinin (Ed.), *Handbook of narrative inquiry: Mapping a methodology* (pp. 35–76). Sage.

Clarke, M., & Moore, A. (2013). Professional standards, teacher identities and an ethics of singularity. *Cambridge Journal of Education, 43*(4), 487–500.

Connell, R. (2009). Good teachers on dangerous ground: Towards a new view of teacher quality and professionalism. *Critical Studies in Education, 50*(3), 213–229.

Connelly, F. M., & Clandinin, D. J. (1985). Personal practical knowledge and the modes of knowing: Relevance for teaching and learning. *Learning and teaching the ways of knowing, 84*, 174–198.

Connelly, F. M., & Clandinin, D. J. (1990). Stories of experience and narrative inquiry. *Educational Researcher, 19*(5), 2–14.

Connelly, F. M., & Clandinin, D. J. (2005). Narrative inquiry. In J. Green, G. Camilli, & P. Elmore (Eds.), *Complementary methods for research in education* (3rd ed., pp. 477–488). American Educational Research Association.

Craig, C. (1995a). Knowledge communities: A way of making sense of how beginning teachers come to know. *Curriculum Inquiry, 25*(2), 151–172.

Craig, C. (1995b). Safe places in the professional knowledge landscapes. In D. J. Clandinin & F. M. Connelly (Eds.), *Teachers' professional knowledge landscapes* (pp. 137–141). Teachers College Press.

Craig, C. (2001). The relationships between and among teachers' narrative knowledge, communities of knowing, and school reform: A case of "The Monkey's Paw". *Curriculum Inquiry, 31*(3), 303–331.

Craig, C. (2002). A meta-level analysis of the conduit in lives lived and stories told. *Teachers and Teaching: Theory and Practice, 8*(2), 197–221.

Craig, C. (2007). Illuminating qualities of knowledge communities in a portfolio-illuminating qualities of knowledge communities in a portfolio-making context. *Teachers and Teaching: Theory and Practice*, 617–636.

Craig, C. (2009). Research in the midst of organized school reform: Tensions in teacher community. *American Educational Research Journal, 46*(2), 598–619.

Craig, C. (2012a). "Butterfly under a pin": An emergent teacher image amid mandated curriculum reform. *The Journal of Educational Research, 105*(2), 90–101.

Craig, C. (2012b). Tensions in teacher development and community: Variations on a recurring school reform theme. *Teachers College Record, 114*(2), 1–28.

Craig, C. (2013). Coming to know in the "eye of the storm": A beginning teacher's introduction to different versions of teacher community. *Teaching and Teacher Education, 29*, 25–38.

Craig, C. (2014). From stories of staying to stories of leaving: A U.S. beginning teacher's experience. *Journal of Curriculum Studies, 46*, 81–115.

Craig, C. (2018a). Metaphors of knowing, doing and being: Capturing experience in teaching and teacher education. *Teaching and Teacher Education, 69*, 300–311.

Craig, C. (2018b). From starting stories to leaving stories: The experiences of an urban English as a second language teacher. *Research Papers in Education*, 1–17.

Craig, C., & Ross, V. (2008). Cultivating the image of teachers as curriculum makers. In F. M. Connelly, F. He, & J. Phillion (Eds.), *The Sage handbook of curriculum and instruction* (pp. 282–305). Sage.

Craig, C., You, J., Zou, Y., Verma, R., Stokes, D., Evans, P., & Curtis, G. (2018). The embodied nature of narrative knowledge: A cross-study analysis of embodied knowledge in teaching, learning, and life. *Teaching and Teacher Education, 71*, 329–340.

Curtis, G., Reid, D., Kelley, M., Martindell, P. T., & Craig, C. (2013). Braided lives: Multiple ways of knowing, flowing in and out of knowledge communities. *Studying Teacher Education*, *9*(2), 175–186.

Czarniawka, B. (1997). *Narrating the organization: Dramas of institutional identity*. University of Chicago.

Darling-Hammond, L. (2010). Teacher education and the American future. *Journal of Teacher Education*, *61*(1e2), 35–47.

Dewey, J. (1897, January 16). My pedagogical creed. *The School Journal*, *54*(3), 77–80.

Dewey, J. (1938). *Experience and education*. Macmillan.

Dewey, J., & Bentley, A. (1949). Knowing and the known. In *The later works of John Dewey* (Vol. 16). Beacon Press.

Donaldson, M. L. (2010). No more valentines. *Educational Leadership*, *67*(8), 54–58.

Dyson, C., & Smith, C. (2019). Four seasons of composing stories to live by: Teaching, learning and research strategies in teacher education. In M. Hanne & H. Kaal (Eds.), *Narrative and metaphor in education: Look both ways*. Routledge.

Egan, K. (2017). Honoring the role of narrative and metaphor in education. In M. Hanne & H. Kaal (Eds.), *Narrative and metaphor in education: Look both ways* (pp. 21–31). Routledge.

Eisner, E. (1982). *Cognition and curriculum: A basis for deciding what to teach*. Longman Publishing Group.

ESSA. (2015). *Every Student Succeeds Act of 2015*. Pub. L. No. 114-95? 114 Stat. 1177.

Fenstermacher, G. D. (1994). The knower and the known: The nature of knowledge in research on teaching. In L. Darling-Hammond (Ed.), *Review of research in education* (Vol. 20, p. 56). American Educational Research Association.

Ferlie, E. (2017, March). The new public management and public management studies. *Business Policy and Strategy*. https://oxfordre.com/business/view/10.1093/acrefore/9780190224851.001.0001/acrefore-9780190224851-e-129

Gadamer, H. G. (1960/1989). *Truth and method*. Continuum.

Hanne, M. (2015). An introduction to the 'Warring with words' conference. In M. Hanne, W. D. Crano, & J. S. Mio (Eds.), *Warring with words* (pp. 1–15). Psychology Press.

Hargreaves, A., & O'Connor, M. T. (2018). *Leading collaborative professionalism*. Center for Strategic Education. Seminar Series #274, April.

Kerby, A. (1991). *Narrative and the self*. Indiana University Press.

King, T. (2003). *The truth about stories*. Anansi Press.

Lamott, A. (2018). *Almost everything: Notes on hope*. Riverhead Books.

Lane, B. (1988). *Landscapes of the sacred: Geography and narrative in American spirituality*. Paulist Press.

Lee, H. (1960). *To kill a mockingbird*. Warner Books.

Levine, D., & Lazotte, L. (1990). *Unusually effective schools: Review and analysis of research and practice*. The National Center for Effective Schools Research and Development.

Lewis, W., & Young, T. (2013). The politics of accountability: Teacher education policy. *Educational Policy*, *27*(2), 190–216.

Lopez, B. (1989). *Crossing open ground*. Vintage.

MacIntyre, A. (1981). *After virtue: A study in moral theology*. University of Notre Dame Press.

Maran, M. (2016). Introduction. In M. Maran (Ed.), *Why we write about ourselves* (pp. 9–21). Plume.

Marsh, J. A. (2012). Interventions promoting educators' use of data: Research insights and gaps. *Teachers College Record*, *114*(11), 1–48.

McAdams, D. (2000). Fighting to save our urban schools … and winning: Lessons from Houston. *Teachers College Record*.

McCord, C. (2019, November 7). *State of Texas plans to take over district after years of serious or persistent deficiencies*. https://www.bizjournals.com/houston/news/2019/11/07/state-of-texas-plans-to-take-over-district-after.html

Mockler, N. (2012). Teacher professional learning in a neoliberal age: Audit, professionalism and identity. *Australian Journal of Teacher Education*, *38*(10).

Muchmore, J. (2002). Methods and ethics in a life history study of teacher thinking. *Qualitative Report*, *7*(4), 1–18.

OECD. (2013). How's life? https://www.oecd-ilibrary.org/economics/how-s-life-2013
Palmer, P. J. (1998). *The courage to teach: Exploring the inner landscape of a teacher's life*. Jossey-Bass.
Palmer, P. (2018). *On the brink of everything: Grace, gravity and getting old*. Berrett-Koehler Publishers.
Parini, J. (1999, May 31). Borges in another métier. *The Nation*. https://www.thenation.com/article/borges-another-metier
Penwarden, S. (2019). Weaving threads into a basket: Facilitating counsellor identity creation through metaphors and narratives. In M. Hanne & H. Kaal (Eds.), *Narrative and metaphor in education: Look both ways* (pp. 249–262). Routledge.
Richardson, L. (1994). Writing: A methodology. In Y. Lincoln & N. Denzin (Eds.), *Qualitative research: Tying knots* (pp. 379–396). Altamira Press.
Ricoeur, P. (2003). *The rule of metaphor: The creation of meaning in language*. Psychology Press.
Ritchie, L. (2010). 'Everybody goes down': Metaphors, stories and simulations in conversations. *Meaning and Symbol, 25*(3), 123–143.
Rizvi, F., & Lingvard, B. (2010). *Globalizing education policy*. Routledge.
Sacks, O. (2017). *The river of consciousness*. Albert A. Knopf.
Sanders, W. (2000). Value-added assessment from student achievement data: Opportunities and hurdles. *Journal of Personnel Evaluation in Education, 14*(4), 329–339.
Sanders, W., & Horn, S. (1994). The Tennessee value-added assessment system (TVAAS): Mixed-model methodology in educational assessment. *Journal of Personnel Evaluation in Education, 8*(3), 299–311.
Schon, D. (1993). Generative metaphor: A perspective on problem-setting in social policy. In A. Ortony (Ed.), *Metaphor and thought* (pp. 137–163). Cambridge University Press.
School District. (2007). *State of the schools: 2006 annual report*. School District.
Schwab, J. (1970). *The practical: A language for curriculum*. National Education Association.
Schwab, J. (1983). The practical 4: Something for curriculum professors to do. *Curriculum Inquiry, 13*(3), 239–265.
Shapiro, D. (2016). Dani Shapiro. In M. Maran (Ed.), *Why we write about ourselves* (pp. 167–177). Plume.
Strayed, C. (2016). Cheryl Strayed. In M. Maran (Ed.), *Why we write about ourselves* (pp. 205–214). Plume.
Vescio, V., Ross, D., & Adams, A. (2008). A review of research on the impact of professional learning communities on teaching practice and student learning. *Teaching and Teacher Education, 24*(1), 80–91.
Waldman, A. (2016). Ayelet Waldman. In M. Maran (Ed.), *Why we write about ourselves* (pp. 215–230). Plume. Ayelet Waldman.
Ward, J. (2016). Jesmyn Ward. In M. Maran (Ed.), *Why we write about ourselves* (pp. 231–242). Plume. Jesmyn Ward.
White, H. (1980). The value of narrativity in the representation of reality. *Critical Inquiry, 7*(1), 5–27.
Wiseman, A. (2013). Policy responses to PISA in comparative perspective. In *PISA, power, and policy: The emergence of global educational governance*.
Zuboff, S. (2019). *The age of surveillance capitalism: The fight for a human future at the new frontier of power*. Public Affairs.

PRINCIPALS' VIEWS IN A CONTEXT OF REFORM: THE CASE OF SCHOOL CURRICULUM POLICY IN PORTUGAL

Maria Assunção Flores

ABSTRACT

This chapter reports on findings from a wider research project undertaken in Portugal. It focuses on the views of school principals with respect to (new) policy on the school curriculum. School principals have to balance conflicting goals and to manage tensions of implementation, particularly in a context of intense school reform. As policy gatekeepers and interpreters, school leaders have a pivotal role to play in how policies are framed, managed, and discussed in the context of their schools. Data presented in this text are drawn from a wider 3-year study. Findings point to the existence of contradictory elements in the principals' accounts. In general, they are critical of the new curriculum policy and question the adequacy of the conditions currently existing in schools to put it into operation. Overall, the regulatory and centralized orientation stands in sharp contrast to the very essence of the policies that call for local, contextualized, and innovative solutions. Such findings need to be analyzed within a centralized and bureaucratic education system in which a logic of control and standardized management of education still dominates.

Keywords: School reform; curriculum; school principals; autonomy; control; policy implementation

Raising educational standards has been the driving force for reforms around the globe even though different understandings of quality can be found to justify the goals and rationale of given policies. House and McQuillan (2005) draw attention to the complexity of school reform and the need to consider technological, political, and cultural perspectives in order to fully comprehend it. Specific issues to be considered include innovation, interests and values, power and authority, meanings and values, conflict and negotiation as well as legitimacy and autonomy, to name but a few. This is particularly important when it comes to school curriculum policies. The complex and multidimensional nature of policy development and its "implementation in practice" call for the consideration of multiple variables, factors, agents, and contexts ranging from the macro to the meso and micro levels of curriculum decision making. As Timperley and Robinson (1997) argue, implementing a new policy is problematic. This is because, among other features, policy is mediated by the actors in context, specifically by the perceptions and experiences of principals and teachers. The process of implementing a policy is, therefore, complex as it entails changing (or at least challenging) existing ways of operating but also those beliefs and perspectives that are embedded in given practices. Fullan (2001, p. 71) draws attention to the dynamics of change stating that "intrinsic dilemmas in the change process, coupled with the intractability of some factors and the uniqueness of individual settings, make successful change a highly complex and subtle process." As "policies are not implemented as strictly intended" issues of compliance, mediation, and resistance have to be considered (Hoyle & Wallace, 2009, p. 210), particularly in contexts of intense school reform.

Drawing upon policy characteristics that Fullan (2001, 2007) identifies as affecting policy implementation, Tuytens and Devos (2010), in their study conducted in Belgium, conclude that the structure provided by a principal is of central importance to teachers' perceptions of the practicality of a given policy as is the level of trust that teachers have in their principal. The same study also illustrates that vision is one of the key aspects influencing teachers' perceptions of policy as it affects two essential policy characteristics: need and practicality.

Day et al. (2000) also argue that leaders have to resolve the various tensions involved in school reform, such as those between maintaining and developing practices or individuals and between externally imposed and internal drivers of change. In the process of putting a new policy into practice, school principals have to balance conflicting goals, to minimize the potentially negative side effects and to manage tensions of implementation (Flores & Derrington, 2017). As policy gatekeepers and interpreters, school leaders have a pivotal role in how policies are framed, managed and discussed in the context of their school. While policymakers debate the merits of their mandates, principals hold the key to successful implementation at the local level in this complex and dynamic process (Retallick & Fink, 2002). This chapter reports on findings from a wider research project, taking into account the views of school principals with regard to (new) policy on the school curriculum.

THE POLICY CONTEXT

The last decade has seen a huge number of reforms focusing, in particular, on school curriculum, inclusion and assessment. Decree-Law n.º 139/2012, 5th July, which was in place for 6 years, established the key principles for the organization and management of curricula and assessment of knowledge and abilities of students in elementary and secondary education. 2017 saw publication of the Student's Profile by the End of Compulsory Schooling (12 years), known as PASEO (Portuguese acronym)—which identifies the set of principles, values, and competencies for curriculum development. In the following year, two key policy documents were issued: Curriculum Autonomy and Flexibility (Decree-Law n.º 55, 6th July) and Inclusive Education (Decree-Law n.º 54, 6th July), the former stipulating a set of principles and guidelines according to which schools are granted greater autonomy (25%) to manage the school curriculum, which will be developed locally to meet the PASEO. Teachers are seen as curriculum agents and measures advocated include "contextualized flexibility," valorization of collaborative and interdisciplinarity work, emphasis on formative assessment, and diversification of assessment methods. National high-stakes exams in year 4 and 6 were abolished in 2016 and replaced by written tests (low-stakes exams) completed at national level (years 2, 5, and 8) but without any kind of impact on students' grades. The aim of such tests is to provide schools with feedback on how well students (and schools) are doing. In turn, Decree-Law n.º 54 focuses on Inclusive Education and is based on the notion that all students have learning potential, as long as they receive appropriate support. This is achieved through a multilevel approach which includes universal measures, targeting all students in order "to promote participation and improved learning" (Decree-Law 54/2018, Art. 8); selective measures, aimed to fill the need for learning supports not addressed by the universal measures; and the establishment of additional measures "to respond to intense and persistent communication, interaction, cognitive or learning difficulties that require specialized resources of support to learning and inclusion" (Decree-Law 54/2018, Art. 10). Issues of diversity, inclusion, flexibility, and autonomy are associated with the new policy context. The legislative text has granted schools and teachers more freedom to manage and implement the school curriculum. Such an approach involves reforming schools in terms of their organization, curricula and pedagogy, thus requiring school principals to play a pivotal role. This needs to be understood within the context of a centralized and bureaucratic education system in which the dominant culture considers schools as implementers of top-down policy initiatives and teachers as doers or curriculum executors.

Schools are also granted the (albeit not compulsory) opportunity to develop "innovation plans" in order to benefit from higher levels of autonomy (over 25%) to provide curricular and pedagogical responses aimed at fostering students' success and inclusion (Portaria n.º 181/2019, 11th June). This legislative text (including the changes introduced by Portaria n.º 306/2021, 17th December) defines "the terms and conditions according to which schools, in the context of autonomy and curriculum flexibility, may establish [curricular] control of over 25% of the basic curriculum matrices of educational programs offered in elementary and secondary schooling, in order to develop innovation plans." The idea is for schools to provide a diversity of contextualized organizational, curricular, and pedagogical responses to meet the needs of students and promote their success and inclusion.

METHODS

This chapter reports on findings from a wider 3-year study funded by the Portuguese Foundation for Science and Technology (PTDC/CED-EDG/28570/2017) entitled "Investigating the impact of school leadership on students' outcomes" (Flores, 2022). It focuses on principals' views on recent curriculum policy initiatives and the ways in which they have been put into place in their schools. In this chapter data are drawn from the first phase of the research project which included 25 exploratory interviews with principals in the northern region of Portugal. The interviews were conducted in schools and lasted between 32 and 140 minutes (33 hours of audio recording in total). The interviews were transcribed verbatim.

The research project was carried out according to international educational research ethics, namely data confidentiality, informed consent, voluntary participation, and the use of data collected only for research purposes. The project was approved by the Ethics Committee for Research in Social and Human Sciences at the University of Minho (CEICSH 009/2020) and permission for conducting the study in schools was granted by the Ministry of Education (Ref.[a] 0555900002).

As for the participants, most of them are male with ages ranging from 45 to 68 years old. In general, they are experienced principals (with an average 14 years of experience) (see Table 1). They have served as school principals in their current school for several years (between 6 and 25 years). The participants have also had a lengthy experience as teachers (between 21 and 44 years) and have high qualifications, with 52% holding a master's degree, 1 a PhD and the rest holding a *Licenciatura* degree (a 4–5-year degree to become a teacher, prior to the implementation of the Bologna process).

Data analysis was undertaken according to two phases: a vertical analysis (Miles & Huberman, 1994) according to which each of the respondents' accounts was analyzed separately. A second phase was then carried out according to a comparative or horizontal analysis (cross-case analysis) (Miles & Huberman, 1994). In this phase, the method of "constant comparative analysis" (Glaser & Strauss, 1967) was used to look for common similarities as well as differences.

FINDINGS

This section presents the main findings arising from the school principals' accounts according to emerging issues. The aim is to illustrate their views on recent policies regarding school curriculum. The following themes will be explored: (1) caught between flexibility and centralized bureaucratic control; (2) real or illusory autonomy; (3) mediating policy in context; (4) the challenge of changing ways of operating: teachers' resistance, and (5) controlled or autonomous innovation.

Table 1. Principals' Biographical Data.

	Gender	Age	Experience as Principal	Experience as Principal in the Current School	Experience as a Teacher	Qualification
P1	Male	61	15	15	37	Masters' degree
P2	Male	63	10	10	39	Masters' degree
P3	Male	68	17	17	25	Masters' degree
P4	Male	62	11	11	44	Masters' degree
P5	Male	59	13	9	38	Masters' degree
P6	Female	53	10	10	30	Masters' degree
P7	Male	52	12	10	30	*Licenciatura*
P8	Male	49	12	12	25	*Licenciatura*
P9	Female	58	6	6	34	Masters' degree
P10	Male	51	11	11	28	Masters' degree
P11	Male	53	19	19	26	*Licenciatura*
P12	Male	62	30	19	44	*Licenciatura*
P13	Male	47	19	12	25	*Licenciatura*
P14	Male	57	25	25	32	*Licenciatura*
P15	Male	60	13	13	40	*Licenciatura*
P16	Female	54	7	7	30	*Licenciatura*
P17	Female	47	7	7	25	Masters' degree
P18	Female	53	18	18	30	Masters' degree
P19	Female	63	15	15	40	*Licenciatura*
P20	Male	56	24	24	32	Masters' degree
P21	Female	45	7	7	21	Masters' degree
P22	Male	60	12	7	37	Masters' degree
P23	Female	58	10	10	32	*Licenciatura*
P24	Female	52	6	6	30	PhD
P25	Male	52	14	7	26	*Licenciatura*

Caught Between Flexibility and Centralized Bureaucratic Control

In general, school principals participating in the study are skeptical about the new policy and they highlight the contradictory nature of the "compulsory" autonomy and flexibility within a centralized education system. The mandatory nature of the reform and the bureaucratic and administrative issues are subject to criticisms on the part of the participating school principals. In particular, they stress the lack of clarity of the policy and implications for its implementation in schools.

> I feel that in relation to the new policy, although we have the guidelines from the Ministry of Education, some of them are not totally clear. I feel that some schools are confused and lost. (P2)

> Schools are forced to implement autonomy and curriculum flexibility. You feel that you have to do something about it. But I have to say, no thank you. (...) In this school we know what we want to do. (P11)

The persistent bureaucratic control, established through online platforms, is identified as the main obstacle for enacting the policy, in terms of more contextualized organizational, curricular and pedagogical responses, for instance. Issues of flexibility, diversity, and differentiation are difficult to consolidate with the prevailing rigid and uniform structures that lead to school cultures marked by the traditional bureaucratic centralism (Flores et al., 2022). Schools have no choice but to implement the new policy; yet principals question the real innovation and change occurring in schools.

> I have to respond to the Central Administration. Yet, I am critical and, whenever I have the opportunity, I give my opinion because I think schools should be given more autonomy. The thing is that schools are given autonomy but then they are asked to fill in an online platform to describe how they are using flexibility, how many hours in terms of flexibility, etc. This is nonsense. (P9)

> There is a need to have flexibility in two ways, or even more ways. I mean, new strategies, new experiences, etc. (...) And what do you know? All the schools are implementing it because they have no choice, but it terms of curriculum innovation, it is zero! (P20)

Real or Illusory Autonomy?

Although the policy document focuses on autonomy and curriculum flexibility, principals are critical of its contradictory nature. Some stated that the new policy did not represent anything new and they spoke of false or illusory autonomy. While some school principals admit that they have some kind of curricular autonomy, most of them claim that the lack of financial autonomy undermines the development of curriculum innovation in practice.

> This is a false autonomy. There is no point in giving autonomy to schools when, for instance, there is no financial autonomy (...) There is no point in being flexible and having new subjects if, at the end of the day, I cannot hire anyone. Such autonomy exists on paper but it is not real. (P13)

> If you look at it, you will see that there is no autonomy at all. I mean, it is the same old autonomy, you know. At the end of the day the autonomy belongs to the Ministry of Education. The school can even devise projects and the Ministry may give permission to implement them, but the power to make decisions lies in the Ministry of Education. (P14)

As this last quote illustrates, the centralized tradition of the Portuguese education system is emphasized once more along with issues of the (lack of) power to make decisions. School principals state that it is up to the Ministry of Education to decide and they would welcome wider autonomy not only in pedagogical terms but also with regard to organizational and curricular aspects. Their accounts point to a superficial model that does not translate into a real change in the decision-making process and in curricular practices. Others spoke of a fashion that will end sooner or later as other previous policy initiatives have done so.

> I think that the recent policies have made teachers, school principals and schools move away from what is really important. At present, some aspects that are valued are not essential. The most important thing is for students to have good results and get into university and choose their job. When the fashion about autonomy and flexibility has passed or has shifted away from the media and policy agendas, this model will fall. I am not saying that inclusion and flexibility are not important. But this is a model that focuses on administrative and bureaucratic questions; it is about compliance and seeing whether it complies with the inspection guidelines. (P14)

> We have very limited autonomy. Everybody can have a say about what is going on in schools, except those who work in the school. You cannot have illusions about having autonomy because it is not real, unless you are talking about pedagogical autonomy. What I would like to have is real autonomy, by which I mean the power to make decisions. (P21)

Mediating Policy in Context

Although the vast majority of the participating school principals are critical of the policy and the conditions for its enactment in practice, some of them recognize its importance in terms of changing curriculum and pedagogy. They welcome interdisciplinary and collaborative work as well as flexibility and contextualized guidance for the school curriculum. Despite this, they acknowledge the huge amount of administrative work they have to do in the context of such a policy and they stress, once again, the level of control exercised through online platforms. The impetus of mandatory policies for challenging and changing existing curricular practices in schools is advocated by some school principals although they also claim that a logic of replication tends to persist due to the amount of work that schools have to do and the lack of time to engage in a more inquiry-oriented perspective.

> The curriculum is put into practice and it is interdisciplinary. I think the policies are important for schools to rethink and learn (...) But it is unbelievable the amount of information and requests in such a short period of time. I think autonomy and curriculum flexibility are important. It is a pity that we are overwhelmed with the platforms and there is no time left for inquiry. I think that sometimes it is necessary to have some external legislative change that says to us "okay, now you are going to do this and that", although there have been too many changes over the years. My feeling is that we have a lot to do and you can start replicating practices. Such external challenges make schools look at the curriculum in a different way. (P16)

> I feel the policy documents are important to develop a more competency-based orientation to teaching. (P18)

The school principals acknowledge the complexity and the gradual nature of "implementing the policy" and they emphasize the key role of leadership in such a process. If school leadership does not adhere to the policy initiatives, change is not likely to occur. Some principals spoke of their role in mediating the policy and in interpreting it for the benefit of students' learning and achievement.

> This school had a positive reaction as we have two or three leadership people in the departments who are strong and this makes things much easier. The problem is when leadership itself is an obstacle. (P1)
>
> We have been making a more profound and flexible interpretation of the documents. This course of action has been successful and you see that in students' outcomes. (P5)
>
> You need to go step by step as this is a gradual process. You have to avoid tensions and everybody has to be willing to change. We are just at the beginning in terms of curriculum flexibility. (...) It is a slow process. (P23)

The Challenge of Changing Ways of Operating: Teachers' Resistance

Some principals are positive about the school curriculum policy but they question the conditions for its implementation. They refer to its inadequacy for existing school contexts, particularly when it comes to teachers' negative reactions regarding the issue of autonomy.

> In my view, the policies are well designed but they are not adequate for current times. Teachers find it difficult to have autonomy; they are afraid of it. They have been trained to comply with the syllabus... (P24)
>
> The principals highlight teachers' passivity which they associate with their lack of career prospects but also to issues of their beliefs and resistance to change. The ageing of the teaching workforce is also identified along with the demands and extra work that the "autonomy and curriculum flexibility policy" entails.
>
> In five years, the majority of teachers at this school will be 60 years old. Of course they are more experienced teachers but they are not willing to change their practice. Flexibility means more work. There is no doubt that it can bring great things but for this to happen teachers have to be available. (P22)
>
> Teachers are disappointed with their career and working conditions. They become more passive. A process of change is hard. When we say that we would like to make an innovation, the word is seen as a monster. I believe and try to emphasize that "a change is an opportunity"; in Education the following day is always an opportunity, but people have to be open-minded. (P21)

Controlled or Autonomous Innovation?

The school principals are, in general, skeptical regarding the possibility of submitting an "Innovation Plan" in order for their schools to be granted over 25% flexibility to manage the school curriculum. Although schools are not obliged to submit an "Innovation Plan," the participants emphasize the bureaucratic aspect and the logic of control inherent in the policy initiative. They question the concept of "innovation" underpinning it, which they consider to be rather instrumental and regulatory within a series of centrally identified criteria. Their views point to a form of controlled innovation. They illustrate well the paradoxes of innovation, especially the designation of the policy initiative itself but also aspects linked to its implementation which is incompatible with a bottom-up and autonomous perspective (Flores et al., in press).

> I haven't submitted an innovation plan. You need to question what innovation means in this context. The Ministry of Education has come to my school several times to ask "what do you need in your school"? I have given them some ideas, some of which are indeed quite complex. Anyway, I think every school principal knows what his/her school needs. I don't feel like accepting innovation plans and getting into trouble, being controlled and, in the end, it might not be considered innovation. (P8)
>
> I don't need an Innovation Plan. Innovating for what purpose? (P3)

Overall, the school principals are critical of the policy initiative as it is seen as "yet another bureaucratic initiative that does not lead to improving teaching and learning." They question the relevance and effectiveness of "innovation plans" and the policy's timing. Teachers' resistance, the wide array of projects that already exist in schools and the lack of time are also mentioned in the principals' accounts. They stress that there are "too many changes at the same time" and that "there is already a lot going on" in their schools. As they reiterate in the interviews, such an initiative requires the involvement of the stakeholders, especially teachers: "I feel that we do not have any of the right conditions. You need teachers' involvement and motivation. To move beyond their comfort zones, teachers have to be motivated (spending less time in schools, removing obstacles in career progression, etc.)"; "The timing was not as good as it could have been. People were exhausted." On the other hand, the participants highlight that they do not need a top-down initiative to make decisions about what they think is best for their schools:

> Are you joking? I don't need an Innovation Plan. I don't need it; in fact, I have never felt that I needed one over the last 25 years. My job is to avoid anyone jeopardizing what has been done. I don't follow initiatives that are only a fashion... (P21)

Only a minority of principals identified with the initiative, which they relate to issues of improvement, the image of the school and the promotion of educational success. They state that the "Innovation Plans" make sense as they constitute an important initiative to change organizational and pedagogical matters in the schools; to improve students' learning and promote school success; to enhance students' motivation and prevent them from leaving the school prematurely. Other positive aspects include the "semestrialization" (dividing the academic year into two semesters rather than into three terms), assessment, a contextualized response to specific challenges and situations, alternative curricula to meet the specific needs of groups of students. Overall, they underline the importance of the initiative and the desire for more autonomy as well as articulating the policy with existing projects in the school: "The Innovation Plan was submitted as a result of the involvement of our school cluster in the Pilot Project of Pedagogical Innovation, in which innovative pedagogical practices were developed. Those practices allowed us to respond to the needs of our students and to improve the quality of our educational offer."; "To provide training solutions for a group of students who were at risk of retention and/or dropping out of school."

Only a minority of the school principals respond positively to the initiative with most of the participants being critical of it, in particular due to the regulatory intervention by the government in the name of innovation. In addition, they identify a more fluid and inorganic innovation that is dynamic and context-dependent with regard to issues of flexibility and empowerment (Flores et al., in press).

CONCLUSION

The existing legal framework on "autonomy and curriculum flexibility" in Portugal points to the possibility for schools to manage their curriculum and to develop initiatives to promote students' achievement, and to meet their specific characteristics and learning needs (Decree-Law n.º 55/2018, 6th July; Decree-Law n.º 54/2018, 6th July). While recent policies in Portugal point to a more inclusive and flexible curriculum approach, teachers' agency as curriculum managers and decision-makers is far from being fully realized. As Maguire et al. (2015) argue, "different 'types' of policies call[ed]-up different forms of enactments." As such, the ways in which the actors in context view the policies are key in how they are put into practice. Overall, the regulatory and centralized orientation stands in sharp contrast to the very essence of the policies that call for local, contextualized and innovative solutions. Such a situation needs to be analyzed within a centralized and bureaucratic education system in which a logic of control and standardized management of education still dominates. For instance, the Decree-Law nº 75/2008 introduces the figure of the school principal who is seen as "the face" and the "first responsible" for the school. The same legislative text entails the view of leadership as mere implementation, defining the "authority of the principal" as a way to "locally execute policy initiatives issued by the central government."

The present study clearly points to the existence of contradictory elements in the principals' accounts. In general, they are critical of the new curriculum policy and they question the adequacy of the conditions currently existing in schools to put it into operation. Only a minority adhere to the policy, which they attribute to its rationale, especially the possibility for interdisciplinary work, increased autonomy for schools and teachers, and the opportunity to change classroom practices. Although some principals identified with policies favoring flexibility and interdisciplinarity, they remained critical about its implementation. This is particularly critical as school principals play a key role in mobilizing for change both subjectively and objectively, and in adhering to educational and curriculum policies (Pereira et al., 2021). Most of them agree that implementation of the new policy does not respond to the real problems and concerns of schools. Among other concerns, they mention issues of bureaucratic control, the policy's lack of clarity and teachers' resistance to change. Drawing on data from a survey conducted with 130 (out of 226) schools participating in the pilot of the new curriculum policy, before its widening to all the schools in the country in 2018/2019, Cosme and Trindade (2019) found that teachers' resistance to change and the lack of adequate conditions to put the policies into practice were two major constraints identified in its implementation (Cosme & Trindade, 2019).

Similarly, also drawing upon empirical data, Pereira et al. (2021) identified the artificial and mitigated nature of schools' autonomy since it is ultimately the Ministry of Education that ends up making the decisions; temporary measures are changed sooner or later; and the initiative's lack of novelty given that schools had already adopted such practices. The same authors conclude that such critical views were associated with the divide between local and central administration, with the former being grounded in reality and marked by concrete actions and resistance, while the latter policy-making environment is abstract and entirely focused on decisions.

In addition, principals question the relevance and effectiveness of "innovation plans" which they relate to a logic of control. Issues at the forefront of the respondents' accounts include the bureaucratic and regulatory aspect, teachers' resistance to change, inadequate timing of the proposal and the number of projects going on in schools. The reasons put forward are associated with a skeptical perspective in regard to the proposed concept of "innovation plan." This is in line with previous work focusing on the Pilot Project for Pedagogical Innovation which was "framed and coordinated by central State-actors' agendas and instruments... by fixing a priori the domains and the limits for innovative/ autonomous initiatives on curriculum and school organization" (Carvalho et al., 2021, p. 11).

In a study conducted in the United Kingdom, Knight (2020) discusses the tensions of innovation based on teachers' experiences in a school undergoing reform. The author highlights three tensions arising in such a context, namely regarding autonomy (following the model vs. taking ownership), to innovation (internal vs. external accountability) and to collaboration (personal freedom vs. collegiality). In the Portuguese context, similar tensions were also experienced by the principals. They stress the mandatory nature of the "autonomy and curriculum flexibility" policy and the bureaucratic control exercised through online platforms, which they contrast to the need for bottom-up, contextualized and autonomous responses. Their accounts illustrate their role in managing tensions around externally imposed and internal drivers of change (Day et al., 2000) and the need to pay attention not only to the technological perspective of school reform but also to its political, and cultural dimensions (House & McQuillan, 2005). This is especially relevant when what is at stake are tensions between centralized decision making and issues of autonomy and flexibility; taking ownership versus executing locally top-down directives; imposed versus autonomous innovation. In a nutshell, it is about issues of power and control in curriculum decision making, managing conflicting beliefs and practices; negotiating meaning and making sense of policy in context.

AUTHOR'S NOTES

This work was funded by National Funds through the Portuguese Foundation for Science and Technology within the context of the project "Investigating the effects of school leadership on students' outcomes" (PTDC/CED-EDG/28570/2017).

REFERENCES

Carvalho, L., Costa, E., & Almeida, M. (2021). Recontextualization of improvement-oriented policies in Portugal: The case of the pilot project for pedagogical innovation (2016–2019). *International Journal of Educational Research, 110*, 1–13. https://doi.org/10.1016/j.ijer.2021.101865

Cosme, A., & Trindade, R. (2019). O projeto de autonomia e flexibilidade curricular: Que desafios curriculares e pedagógicos? *Revista de Estudos Curriculares, n° 10*(2), 22–38.

Day, C., Harris, A., Hadfield, M., Tolley, H., & Bereford, J. (2000). *Leading schools in times of change*. Open University Press.

Decree-Law n.º 139/2012, 5th July. Diário da República n.º 129/2012, Série I de 2012-07-05, 3476–3491. https://data.dre.pt/eli/dec-lei/139/2012/07/05/p/dre/pt/html

Decree-Law n.º 54/2018. Diário da República no. 129/2018, Série I de 2018-07-06, 2918–2928. https://data.dre.pt/eli/dec-lei/54/2018/07/06/p/dre/pt/html

Decree-Law n.º 55/2018. Diário da República no. 129/2018, Série I de 2018-07-06, 2928–2943. https://data.dre.pt/eli/dec-lei/55/2018/07/06/p/dre/pt/html

Decree-Law n.º 75/2008, 22nd April. Diário da República n.º 79/2008, Série I de 2008-04-22, 2341–2356. https://dre.pt/dre/legislacao-consolidada/decreto-lei/2008-34457775

Flores, M. A. (Ed.). (2022). *Investigando os efeitos das lideranças escolares nos resultados dos alunos*. De Facto Editores.

Flores, M. A., & Derrington, M. L. (2017). School principals' views of teacher evaluation policy: Lessons learned from two empirical studies. *International Journal of Leadership in Education, 20*(4), 416–431.

Flores, M. A., Ferreira, F. I., & Machado, E. A. (2022). Conclusões. In M. A. Flores (Coord.), *Investigando os efeitos das lideranças escolares nos resultados dos alunos* (pp. 137–146). De Facto Editores. ISBN: 978-989-9013-07-0.

Flores, M. A., Machado, E. A., & Fernandes, E. L. (in press). Inovação controlada ou autónoma? A visão dos diretores sobre os Planos de Inovação. *Revista Portuguesa de Investigação Educacional*.

Fullan, M. (2001). *Leading in a culture of change*. Jossey-Bass.

Fullan, M. (2007). *The new meaning of educational change*. Teachers College Press.

Glaser, B. G., & Strauss, A. L. (1967). *The discovery of grounded theory: Strategies for qualitative research*. Aldine.

House, E., & McQuillan, P. (2005). Three perspectives on school reform. In A. Lieberman (Ed.), *The roots of educational change*. Springer.

Hoyle, E., & Wallace, M. (2009). Leadership for professional practice. In S. Gewirtz, P. Mahony, I. Hextall, & A. Cribb (Eds.), *Changing teacher professionalism. International trends, challenges and ways forward* (pp. 204–214). Routledge.

Knight, R. (2020). The tensions of innovation: Experiences of teachers during a whole school pedagogical shift. *Research Papers in Education, 35*(2), 205–227.

Maguire, M., Braun, A., & Ball, S. (2015). "Where you stand depends on where you sit": The social construction of policy enactments in the (English) secondary school. *Discourse: Studies in the Cultural Politics of Education, 36*(4), 485–499.

Miles, M., & Huberman, A. M. (1994). *Qualitative data analysis* (2nd ed.). SAGE Publications.

Pereira, D., Flores, M. A., & Machado, E. A. (2021). Autonomia e flexibilidade curricular na perspetiva dos diretores: Entre o ceticismo e a adesão. *Indagatio Didactica, 13*(2).

Portaria n.º 181/2019. Diário da República no. 111/2019, Série I de 2019-06-11, 2954–2957. https://data.dre.pt/eli/port/181/2019/06/11/p/dre/pt/html

Portaria n.º 306/2021, 17th December. Diário da República n.º 243/2021, Série I de 2021-12-17. páginas, 216–223. https://data.dre.pt/eli/port/306/2021/12/17/p/dre/pt/html

Retallick, J., & Fink, D. (2002). Framing leadership: Contributions and impediments to educational change. *International Journal of Leadership in Education, 5*(2), 91–104.

Timperley, H. S., & Robinson, V. M. J. (1997). The problem of policy implementation: The case of performance appraisal. *School Leadership & Management, 17*, 333–346.

Tuytens, M., & Devos, G. (2010). The influence of school leadership on teachers' perception of teacher evaluation policy. *Educational Studies, 36*(5), 521–536.

SECTION 4

PREPARING TEACHER EDUCATORS (InFo-TED) SECTION

INTRODUCTION

Amanda Berry

A longstanding issue in educational research and practice is that although teacher educators are acknowledged as "key players" in educational systems for their impact on the quality of teaching and learning in schools (European Commission, 2013; Vanassche et al., 2015), their professional status, including the unique nature of their work and learning, has been largely neglected in research and professional development initiatives (White & Berry, 2022). Partly, this is because teacher educators have only relatively recently been acknowledged as a separate occupational group with a unique and specialized knowledge base (Swennen et al., 2010) and partly also, because researchers and policymakers have focused their attention on the structures of teacher education and on relationships between teacher education programs and student achievement in schools, rather than on the role of teacher educators themselves (White & Berry, 2022). However, over the past two decades, this situation has begun to change, with a growing recognition that the work of teacher educators is diverse, complex, and specialized; involves supporting teachers throughout their professional careers, and "requires the cooperation of a wide range of actors" (European Commission, 2013, p. 7). Recognition of a "range of actors" involved in the education of teachers has also helped to shed light on the recurring question of who a teacher educator is, noting it involves different roles to support different stages of learning to teach. Studies continue to further tease out this question, given that being a teacher educator has been identified as a "hidden profession" (Livingston, 2014, p. 218), an "accidental career" (Mayer et al., 2011), and involves "a precarious process" (Berry & Forgasz, 2016; White & Berry, 2022).

The work of InFo-TED, the International Forum for Teacher Educator Development, has as its explicit purpose, the exchange of research, policy, and practice related to teacher educators' knowledge, professional learning, and ongoing development. InFo-TED represents a unique international group, comprised of teacher education scholars and practitioners, that aims to build and strengthen, in a sustainable way, the work and professional development of teacher educators, globally. This section focuses on the work of InFo-TED. The three articles that comprise this section have been written by InFo-TED members and document their international work and ambitions since the beginnings of InFo-TED when a group of experienced teacher educators with a shared interest in the professional knowledge involved in the work of educating teachers, came together at the Annual meeting of the American Educational Research Association (AERA) in 2012, in San Francisco. From this informal beginning, the group built their shared platform, connected by a shared fundamental premise that "the work of educating teachers requires knowledge, skills, and beliefs that are qualitatively different from those developed as an experienced classroom teacher" (Vanassche et al., 2015, p. 344). Now, more than a decade later, InFo-TED is an established international teacher educator network that aims to serve as a forum and community of practice for building a research-based understanding of teacher educators' work, learning and development.

In the first chapter, "Looking Back and Looking Forward at InFo-TED – Reflecting on Purpose, Progress, and Challenges," Kari Smith (Norwegian University of Science and Technology) and Ruben Vanderlinde (Ghent University) describe the emergence and growth of InFo-TED, as two founding members of this group. They highlight the importance of bringing international attention to the significance of teacher educators' work and the necessity for providing organized and coordinated opportunities for teacher educators' professional learning and development. They employ the metaphor of the "black box" throughout their chapter to portray the multiple mysteries of who does the work of educating teachers, teacher educator praxis, and how teacher educators learn and professionally develop. Smith and Vanderlinde recount their own career trajectories into teacher education, why they became involved with InFo-TED, their experiences, and how they see the future of InFo-TED.

In the second chapter, "InFo-TED, North America: Addressing a Problem of Practice," Frances Rust (University of Pennsylvania) and Diane Yendol-Hoppey (University of North Florida) describe the development of the North American chapter of InFo-TED (InFo-TED, NA) that emerged in 2015 with US and Canadian teacher educators, to consider ways to shape a North American initiative around teacher educators' professional learning. With a focus on teacher learning, teacher leadership, and educational reform, members of InFo-TED, NA, have engaged in a series of activities to build a contextually relevant InFo-TED community. Rust and Yendol-Hoppey describe an impressive research program, including a collective member activity to document "What does a day in the life of a teacher educator look and sound like?" Their goal was to capture the *work* of teacher educators, including the range of variations, and "what kind of whole the pieces comprise" and to share this work in ways that open up spaces for ongoing dialogue, reflection and analysis that build improved public understandings and appreciation of teacher educators' work as architects of education.

The third chapter is a re-print of a previously published work authored by several founding members of the InFo-TED group. This chapter, entitled "InFo-TED: Bringing Policy, Research, and Practice Together around Teacher Educator Development," by Eline Vanassche, Frances Rust, Paul Conway, Kari

Smith, Hanne Tack and Ruben Vanderlinde, presents and elaborates the rationale for the InFo-TED initiative, describes the underpinning conceptual framework, and provides examples of case studies from three different countries, to illustrate how teacher educators' professional development is organized and developed. They describe how the conceptual model that was collaboratively developed by InFo-TED members, makes a case for a "practice-based" approach to professional learning, that is, situated within teacher educators' own lived practices (Kelchtermans et al., 2018). The chapter authors explain the conceptual model as serving several important purposes: as a tool to map the professional development of teacher educators, to provide a common language for teacher educators in different countries and contexts to frame, describe and share their professional knowledge, and as stimulus to generate further discussion and elaboration of the professional learning and development of teacher educators.

In summary, this section provides an important overview and deep dive into issues that are both long-standing and yet still contemporary about the work, knowledge and learning of teacher educators, through the lens of InFo-TED. It is remarkable just how much this group has achieved in a relatively short time. It is testament to the strength of their impact that this volume of ISATT's 40th Anniversary Yearbook devotes a whole section to their work.

REFERENCES

Berry, A., & Forgasz, R. (2016). Becoming ourselves as teacher educators: Trespassing, transgression and transformation. In J. Williams & M. Hayler (Eds.), *Professional learning through transitions and transformations* (pp. 95–106). Springer.

European Commission. (2013). Supporting teacher educators: Teaching the teacher. http://ec.europa.eu/education/policy/school/doc/support-teacher-educators_en.pdf

Kelchtermans, G., Smith, K., & Vanderlinde, R. (2018). Towards an 'international forum for teacher educator development': An agenda for research and action. *European Journal of Teacher Education, 41*(1), 120–134. doi:10.1080/02619768.2017.1372743

Livingston, K. (2014). Teacher educators: Hidden professionals? *European Journal of Education, 49*(2), 218–232.

Mayer, D., Mitchell, J., Santoro, N., & White, S. (2011). Teacher educators and 'accidental' careers in academe: An Australian perspective. *Journal of Education for Teaching, 37*(3), 247–260. https://doi.org/10.1080/02607476.2011.588011

Swennen, A., Jones, K., & Volman, M. (2010). Teacher educators: Their identities, sub-identities and implications for professional development. *Professional Development in Education, 36*(1–2), 131–148.

Vanassche, E., Rust, F., Conway, P. F., Smith, K., Tack, H., & Vanderlinde, R. (2015). InFo-TED: Bringing policy, research, and practice together around teacher educator development. In *International teacher education: Promising pedagogies (Part C)* (pp. 341–364). Emerald Publishing Limited.

White, S., & Berry, A. (2022). School-based teacher educators: Understanding their identity, role, and professional learning needs as dual professionals. In I. Mentor (Ed.), *Palgrave handbook of teacher education research*. Palgrave Macmillan. https://doi.org/10.1007/978-3-030-59533-3_11-1

LOOKING BACK AND LOOKING FORWARD AT InFo-TED—REFLECTING ON PURPOSE, PROGRESS, AND CHALLENGES

Kari Smith and Ruben Vanderlinde

ABSTRACT

This chapter traces the development of InFo-TED, the International Forum for Teacher Educators' Development, which originated with four European teacher educators in 2013. Given that the role of teacher educators is largely missing in the description of the enactment of teacher education, this work focused attention solely on teacher educators and their professional development, as well on how its membership kept InFo-TED growing and expanding internationally. Two contrasting narratives of teacher educator are included to show the diversity in their preparation and roles. The chapter ends with generic features of teacher educators' work and a discussion of what factors are more nationally, institutionally, and not to be overlooked, personally dependent. Erasmus funding and dissemination were discussed, all with the intent of understanding how to act locally, but impact globally.

Keywords: International Forum for Teacher Educators' Development; InFo-TED; teacher educator professional development; Erasmus funding; local actions; global impact

InFo-TED is the International Forum for Teacher Educators' Development which was started in 2013 by four experienced teacher educators, Mieke Lunenberg from the Netherlands, Jean Murray from England, Kari Smith from Norway, and Ruben Vanderlinde from Belgium. When meeting at international conferences we shared a frustration over working in a profession which was vaguely defined, under-researched, and its praxis was mainly the practice of the individual. We worked in a profession which could well be called a "hidden profession" (Livingstone, 2014), or a Black Box, which is a system for which we can only observe the inputs and outputs, but not the internal workings (Card, 2017). The input, the students, were educated inside the black box of teacher education, and the output was qualified teachers. The input and the output were clearly observable; however, less was known about what had taken place during the process, and what work had been done by those who educated the teachers, the teacher educators. Not only was the profession's praxis unclear, but there was also a vague understanding of who were involved in the praxis. To put it differently: Who are the teacher educators and what constitutes their identity? The European Commission broadly defines teacher educators as all those "who actively facilitate the (formal) learning of student teachers and teachers" (European Commission, 2013, p. 8). In InFo-TED we use the term, "teacher educator" as an overarching concept, "... a generic and inclusive term, encompassing all types of people who are professionally involved and responsible for initial and on-going education of teachers" (Kelchtermans et al., 2018, p. 121).

The black box of the praxis of teacher educators becomes even blacker when the vague definition of teacher educators is added. The career trajectory into teacher education has changed since Murray and Male's (2005) study on challenges met by novice teacher educators in their first years of teaching teachers. In their study, the subjects mainly came with a background in school teaching and were often head-hunted into teacher education. Berry (2007), in her self-study of her own career shift, presents tensions she felt as a novice teacher educator coming from school teaching, and the many challenges she experienced defining her new role. However, today, teacher educators are more a mixed group, some enter teacher education with a PhD in education or in other disciplines without experience from school, whereas others might not have a doctorate, and have been head-hunted from primary and secondary school (Murray & Male, 2005). However, this latter group typically feel pressured to engage in doctoral work to be able to meet institutional and national requirements for teacher educators and for academic promotion (Smith et al., 2020). Other teacher educators enter the field with both teaching experience and a doctorate, perhaps a desired combination (Tack et al., 2017; Ulvik & Smith, 2018). There are even teacher educators who have been recruited from outside of education (i.e., social work, companies, etc.).

In the last decade, an increasing understanding of the work of teacher educators and who they are, is emerging, especially since teacher educators themselves have started to open the black box in their own research. Smith (2011) discusses the diverse roles of teacher educators, being a role model in teaching about teaching, administrator, and researcher. Sometimes these roles are in conflict with each other. For example, the "expert" teacher does not always align with the role of administrator, which is often dictated, and at times overtaken, by external factors. Following Smith's (2011) work, in 2014, Lunenberg et al. presented an overview of the roles of teacher educators as they had found in the literature. They described six roles: (1) teacher of teachers, (2) researcher, (3) coach, (4) curriculum developer, (5) broker, and (6) gatekeeper. Whereas the two first roles, teacher of teachers and researcher are often discussed in the literature (Smith & Flores, 2019; Tack & Vanderlinde, 2014) the other roles are less explicit, however, not less relevant. Cochran-Smith et al. (2018) refer to teacher educators as reformers and "... argue that within the broad phenomenon of teacher educators themselves working as agents of teacher education reform, there are multiple competing approaches that involve different institutional actors and are based on markedly different assumptions, values, and strategies" (p. 572). Teacher educators themselves should not only be subjects of reform but also be owners and shapers of reforms that impact their profession.

Another line of research opens the black box as regards the professional development of teacher educators. Here InFo-TED itself has been active in examining the professional development needs of teacher educators (Czerniawski et al., 2017; Guberman et al., 2021) pointing at the need to develop their research competence, and at the same time to find ways to balance the institutional pressures of research and publication with their ongoing efforts to improve their own teaching practice. Moreover, protected time for collaboration with colleagues in their own institutions and beyond has been found to be highly valued as a means to support teacher educators' professional development; "working collaboratively within such designated time slots will help teacher educators to create their own distinct and coherent professional identity (rather than through policy makers' enforced reforms) and further develop their profession" (Czerniawski et al., 2017, p. 138). Tack and Vanderlinde (2019) explore the affective aspects of professional development of teacher educators, and they conclude that when teacher educators are satisfied with their work conditions and the way they are treated, their experienced work pressure, and development opportunities are perceived as manageable and positive.

The aforementioned backdrop explains the current relevance of the work of InFo-TED, an international forum placing teacher educators and their professional development in focus, and the enthusiasm and commitment of its members keeps InFo-TED going. In the rest of this chapter, two InFo-TED founders will talk about their own career trajectories into teacher education, why they became involved with InFo-TED, their experiences, and how they see the future of InFo-TED.

HOW AND WHY DID YOU BECOME A TEACHER EDUCATOR?

Kari-Norway

I read a recent paper by Richter et al. (2021) in which they report on a large-scale study on motives for becoming teacher educators. They identified four main reasons: career aspirations, social contribution, escaping routines, and coincidence as the main motifs for becoming a teacher educator. When looking at my own career trajectory, I think I can identify with two of Richter et al.'s reasons, starting with the last one, coincidence. I really enjoyed my initial teacher education and experienced meeting great teacher educators, and those who taught

English teaching methodology were all previous schoolteachers. They were updated on research from that time; however, they were not involved with research themselves. Their primary expertise was teaching (Murray & Male, 2005). After a couple of years teaching in primary and secondary schools, I was asked by my former teacher educators to host student teachers in my classes, and thus, I became a school-based teacher educator. I enjoyed school teaching and was happy to share my classroom and my experience with teachers to be. I also felt I learned a lot from the student teachers. Little by little, I became hungry for further academic knowledge and started on my master's degree at the same time as I was holding a full job teaching in school. At this time, I could say that Richter et al.'s (2021) first motif for becoming a teacher educator, career aspirations, started to play a role, yet I was unaware of it at that time. I started my second degree mainly out of curiosity, more than out of career aspirations. But when working on my master's degree, I had to engage in research, and that really caught my interest. I was given tools to seek answers to the many questions I had asked myself as a teacher, mainly about assessment and how I could develop as a teacher. Then, toward the end of my master's program, I was approached by the teacher education institution where I was educated, to teach English teaching methodology for secondary school, so I was in a way "head hunted" (Murray & Male, 2005). I happily agreed but did not want to give up school teaching which I so thoroughly enjoyed. I had a combined position for nearly 10 years and found it worthwhile as I earned credibility among my teacher education students. However, I walked around with a bad conscious, feeling as though I was not doing a good enough job in either place, as I constantly rushed from school to college and vice versa. So, when I was asked to take on the position as Head of the Teacher Education Department, I quit school teaching, to my great regret. Now, career aspirations took over from the coincidence motif, and I engaged, as the Head of Teacher Education Department, in my doctorate studies. I am afraid to say that social contribution was not a reason for me to become a teacher educator. Neither was it an escape route from school. I really enjoyed school teaching, and it has to a large extent formed me as a teacher educator.

Ruben-Belgium (Flanders)

Compared with Kari, I had a totally different background and career trajectory before becoming a teacher educator. My career entry into the profession was from research, and not from teaching in the schools. After studying Educational Sciences at university, I immediately began my career as an in-service educator. I worked in several institutions and organizations, such as a center for in-service teacher training. During my first years as an educator, I was also highly involved in educational policy making, and I worked, for instance, as a staff member of the Flemish Interuniversity Council where I followed all teacher education discussions. But as a young professional, I felt the need to have a deeper and more thorough understanding of education. So, I switched from educational practice to academia. At the university, I developed a typical research career from research assistant, to postdoctoral researcher, to tenure-track professor, and associate professor. Within this research career, teacher education and professional development were always at the heart of my research interest, which is clearly illustrated in my founding of the research group "Teacher Education & Professional Development" (www.lopo.ugent.be) at Ghent University. After my PhD, I also started to teach at the university with one assignment in the Master of Educational Science degree program, on one hand, and the Teacher Education program on the other hand. From the beginning, I clearly felt that teaching in those two program areas was so different that I needed to rethink my whole teaching activities. In my teacher education context, the work of Murray and Male (2005) and the work of Loughran (2006) have been influential to my teacher educator practice. The whole idea of being a second-order teacher, of modeling, and of explicating practice had a major impact on me; and still shapes my identity as a teacher at the university, meaning that different aspects of my teaching identity are foregrounded or backgrounded when I teach in the Master of Educational Science program, or when I teach in the Teacher Education program. Against this backdrop, Boyd (2014) provides a framework for modeling based on the literature that also helps to inform and develop my work as a teacher educator. Boyd defines four levels of modeling: (1) implicit modeling using congruent teaching that models strategies and values, (2) explicit modeling of critical reflection on practice, (3) building from explicit modeling the teacher educator relates their practical wisdom to public knowledge, and (4) building from explicit modeling the teacher educator encourages reconstruction by student teachers. This framework has been helpful for me as it gives insight in the complexity of modeling, making it possible to implement different ways of modeling while I am teaching.

In addition to my teaching as teacher of teachers, I am also heavily involved in teacher education policy, at the faculty, the university, and within the Flemish region. Mine is probably not the most typical career path for a teacher educator, but I believe that teacher educators should voice their messages more strongly in public debates about the future of education. Again, these policy responsibilities have an impact on my teacher educator practice, especially in my strong belief to educate the next generation of teachers with strong and informed views about teaching.

Both my career trajectory and Kari's, illustrate how different career stories of teacher educators can be. Within InFo-TED, and more specifically within the organization of our Summer Academies (described later in this chapter), we also try to bring these different career trajectories to the foreground by drawing on our own storylines (Oolbekkink et al., 2021). Storyline methodology fits in a narrative research tradition in which the importance of personal stories is emphasized; and in InFo-TED, we use this methodology with teacher educators to literally draw their own professional story, to have dialogues with each other on these stories, and the link theory and research with these stories or career trajectories. Oolbekkink et al. (2021), for instance, illustrates two storylines of teacher educators.

HOW AND WHY DID THE IDEA OF INFO-TED DEVELOP?

Kari

Personally, I had felt a need to further develop as a teacher educator without really knowing how to go about it by myself, besides reading and critically studying my own values and practice. When meeting colleagues at international conferences, and especially at the International Study Association on Teachers and Teaching (ISATT) conference in 2013 in Ghent, it became clear that some of us shared the same feelings, that there was an aspiration to establish a European open learning dialogue about teacher educators and their work. The optimism for a stronger focus on teacher educators by policy makers was ignited following the European Commission's report (2013) *Supporting Teacher Educators for Better Learning Outcomes*, and the EU Presidency conference, *Integration, Innovation and Improvement—The Professional Identity of Teacher Educators* in Dublin, in February 2013 where I had the honor of being a keynote speaker discussing the issue of teacher educators being a profession, or not. However, we did not see a serious follow up from European and national politicians. I became aware that the profession itself, we, the teacher educators, had to be active in opening the black box, and that we would create a stronger voice by working collaboratively. The four founding members of InFo-TED shared their personal narratives about their professional learning through InFo-TED (Lunenberg et al., 2016). We also collected the few national initiatives for teacher educators' professional developments in our respective countries, to learn from each other and to develop a European framework for how to further promote professional learning (Lunenberg et al., 2016). We could say that we wanted to create a forum for collaboration and sharing of experiences of teacher educators and started to look for colleagues who would like to join us. At this time, the only resource we had at our disposal was our personal enthusiasm, which I claim is still the main force driving InFo-TED.

Ruben

As founding members, we were meeting each other at conferences (ISATT, 2013 in Ghent and the American Educational Research Association (AERA) 2013 in San Francisco) and we started to develop our idea—as Kari explained—of establishing a European dimension in thinking about teacher educators' professional development. At that time, I was also responsible for a professional development initiative at my own university to support teacher educators' professional learning (Tack, 2017). Although this professional development initiative was highly important, I also recognized that professional development for teacher educators is mostly organized on an "ad hoc" basis (Berry, 2016). Indeed, our professional development initiative was organized as a single initiative without a long-term engagement. I felt that as a community of teacher educators we needed to collaborate more strongly to put a more organized approach to teacher educators' professional development on the agenda. And, not only on the agenda of our own universities, but also on the agenda of our different national contexts.

From the very beginning, we shared the idea that InFo-TED could act here as a lever to move from "ad hoc" initiatives to more structural initiatives embedded in our different cultures and structures. But this embeddedness in our different cultures and structures, also immediately emphasized that we needed to develop a common language to understand each other when talking about teacher educators' professional development. As such (see also later), one of the first things we did as InFo-TED, was to develop a conceptual model to understand what we mean when speaking about teacher educators and professional development for this group.

WHAT IS THE FOCUS OF INFO-TED?

Kari and Ruben

The overall focus of InFo-TED has always been to understand and promote the work of teacher educators in Europe and beyond. We wanted to explore what are generic features of teacher educators' work and what factors are more nationally, institutionally, and not least, personally dependent. We wanted to learn about the differences between teacher educators' work and needs, and a major motivation was to learn from each other. We often discussed how to act locally, but impact globally. We aspired to disseminate the value and the needs of the profession beyond our universities and conferences. At the start of InFo-TED, we did not really understand how huge the task was. We began to realize the size of the challenge when, in one of the first meetings of InFo-TED in Amsterdam, we decided to develop a comprehensive, yet not exhaustive model for teacher educators' responsibilities and development needs. After long and intense discussions, spending hours drawing numerous versions of possible models, the InFo-TED model for teacher educators' professional development was created, and with ongoing minor revisions, this has been the heart of our work since then. Our model conceptualizes teacher educators' professional practices, taking those practices as its starting points. We contrast our approach with previous work on the development of professional standards, arguing that the latter approach risks over-looking the complexity of teacher educators' professional work. The first publication of the model was in a joint book chapter (Vanassche et al., 2015), which has reprinted in this section of the Yearbook. This model is still the main message of InFo-TED and it has been widely disseminated internationally. Another, more recent focus of InFo-TED's work has been to learn more about the professional learning needs for teacher educators internationally as well as in our respective countries.

HOW DID INFO-TED GROW?

Kari and Ruben

As already mentioned, we talked about InFo-TED at conferences and in our own networks, and more and more teacher educators became interested, especially since the focus was on teacher educators and our work, and not teacher education in terms of structures and organization. The InFo-TED Forum members numbered approximately 15 after one year and formed a kind of convenience group. We wanted to have a European Forum; however, we also realized that voices from other contexts were valuable. In Israel, the MOFET Institute was, perhaps, the only governmental funded institute which focused only on teacher educators and their development, and we learned that their knowledge and experience were important to us. Thus, they were invited to join the Forum. We also realized that the Forum would benefit from American as well as Australian input, and subsequently a collaboration was created with Frances Rust from USA, and Amanda Berry from Australia. In addition, the four founding members, from Belgium, England, the Netherlands, and Norway each asked a colleague from their own country to join, and later Ireland and Scotland became active in the Forum in the first years. So, the founding group had developed into a Forum of 15 enthusiastic teacher educators who willingly invested time and money to attend meetings and to disseminate the claim that the black box of teacher educators' praxis and practice should be opened and defined by teacher educators themselves.

InFo-TED represents a relatively unique outcome of what can be understood as new, promising forms of international scholarly collaboration, research, policy development and innovative practices. It not only acknowledges difference and diversity of contexts and educational systems, but actually embraces them as sources for intellectual, political, and practical action on a common, public interest: the professional development of teacher educators (Kelchtermans et al., 2018, p. 131).

WHAT CHANGES TOOK PLACE WHEN YOU GOT SOME FUNDING THROUGH ERASMUS+?

Kari and Ruben

InFo-TED worked without funding for three full years before we decided to apply for Erasmus+ funding. Finances were limiting our meeting opportunities and our plans to reach out to teacher educators outside our own contexts and countries. Writing the Erasmus+ application became the focus of our activities in 2015. A core group of three people did most of the writing. However, there was constant dialogue with the whole Forum. When funding was secured in 2016, we were able to have biannual meetings and four regional seminars to which colleagues in our own and neighboring countries were invited. We organized a European Summer Academy for teacher educators in Trondheim, Norway which was a huge success and new European networks were created. A second, well-attended Summer Academy was hosted online by the University of Limerick in Ireland in 2021 (due to Covid-19 restrictions), and we hope to be able to continue with the Summer Academies for teacher educators in the future.

Another major factor supporting the dissemination of InFo-TED's message and work was the creation of our website www.InFo-TED.eu. We invested in a professional website creator from the hosting university of InFo-TED, and the success of the website was happily surprising. In addition to information about the Forum, the website has an interactive blog, the model is presented, and the various areas for professional development mentioned in the model are illustrated by brief informative texts, short video clips and suggestions for readings. All InFo-TED's publications are presented on the website, including presentations at various conferences. The significant international attention that the website received reconfirmed the need for teacher educators internationally to have a place which nurtures their own professional development.

Because we had funding from the Erasmus+ grant, there were more opportunities for meetings, and InFo-TED members had time to discuss how we wanted to examine the need for teacher educators' professional development more closely. A group of dedicated Forum members, in close collaboration with the whole Forum, designed a survey questionnaire which was administered to 1,158 higher education-based teacher educators in Belgium, Ireland, Israel, the Netherlands, Norway, and the United Kingdom. The findings indicated that teacher educators are only moderately satisfied with their professional development experiences and opportunities. However, they exhibited a strong desire to expand their professional learning (Czerniawski et al., 2017). Findings from the respective national contexts have also been published (Czerniawski et al., 2018; Ulvik & Smith, 2018), as well as a further qualitative exploration of teacher educators' professional learning needs (MacPhail et al., 2019). Moreover, the survey questionnaire is being used for surveys in other contexts beyond Europe. InFo-TED is currently analyzing data from a similar survey examining school-based teacher educators' professional learning needs. The supported opportunities to meet to develop the research instruments as well as discussing the findings have been essential to the dissemination and advancement of InFo-TED's work.

WHAT ARE THE PLANS FOR THE FUTURE OF INFO-TED?

Kari and Ruben

When the funding period ended in 2019, InFo-TED members collectively expressed a desire to continue the work, even though it was now back in the unfunded conditions we had during the first 3 years. However, we also decided to seek further funding, and again an Erasmus+ application seemed to be the best opportunity. This time a different university acted as the host university. However, the application writing, efficiently led by the host university, was again a joint assignment by the Forum as a whole. In addition, the Forum was expanded, with Finland, Austria, and Portugal becoming new active members. Unfortunately, we were unsuccessful in securing funding from Erasmus+ in 2020. But a new application was submitted in 2022, and we are currently waiting for the outcome. In our new application we strongly focus on diversity, inclusion and social justice as we feel in our practice and policy work that these huge and important themes are not always on the agenda of teacher education institutions, and that teacher educators feel unprepared in dealing with these themes.

Covid-19 invaded the world in March 2020, and all InFo-TED activities went online, which was not too difficult for us as we did not have any means to travel to meetings or conferences. However, the worked continued, and especially the writing by InFo-TED members increased, reflecting the work of the Forum. We had time to complete the InFo-TED book with contributions from Forum members from USA, Japan and Australia. The four founding members of InFo-TED are the editors for the Routledge book: *Teacher Educators and Their Professional Development: Learning From the Past, Looking to the future* (Vanderlinde et al., 2021). During the Covid-19 pandemic, we continued our work and organized three online worldwide accessible webinars: one on conceptualizing teacher educators' professional development, another on the professional learning needs of teacher educators, and the third about the professional identities of teacher educators in diverse contexts.

The sustainability of InFo-TED is promising as it attracts younger teacher educators and researchers. Some of the initial Forum members are retiring, and even though they will follow the work of InFo-TED, a new generation is now taking the lead in continuing to open up the black box of teacher educators' praxis, which have become even more complex due to the unforeseen future of the world, education and teacher education. An important future task for the InFo-TED group is to have a clear voice in exploring the new norms in teacher educators' work, and to learn from their Covid-19 experiences in order to create stronger teacher education, reflecting the uncertain future we foresee. We think that teacher educators themselves can act as "good practices" by presenting their innovative practices of hybrid learning, blended learning approaches, but also their ways of supporting informal learning. Again, InFo-TED has the ambition to act as a Forum in bringing together research and practices.

CONCLUSION

In this Yearbook chapter, we have called the praxis of teacher educators a hidden profession (Livingstone, 2014), and a black box (Card, 2017) profession. We have pointed to the lack of clarity about the work and responsibilities of teacher educators, referring to various authors who have discussed different aspects of teacher educators' work (e.g., Cochran-Smith et al., 2018; Lunenberg et al., 2014; Smith, 2011). An additional ongoing challenge is defining who the teacher educators are, both those based at the university or colleges of higher education and those based in schools. The definition of who teacher educators are, is, perhaps, in itself, not the main issue. But it is useful place to start when exploring their professional learning needs, and not in the least, in preparing teacher educators for their specific roles. Different types of teacher educators will have specified learning needs tailored to their particular responsibilities as teacher educators. The vague perception of our profession led to the establishment of InFo-TED. The InFo-TED Forum was founded by experienced teacher educators who were motivated to learn more about their own profession. We realized that teacher education is a combination of generic as well as contextual factors, and by sharing experiences and practices we developed a model for our work (Vanassche et al., 2015).

There is still a lot to uncover in the black box of teacher education. In InFo-TED, we have acquired some knowledge about teacher educators' learning and development needs (Czerniawski et al., 2017; Guberman et al., 2021). Clearly, this research is only in its beginning phase, and needs to be continued and supported. InFo-TED has found that in many contexts, the research and publication aspects of teacher educators' responsibility is a challenge. However, we still know little about how to empower teacher educators as researchers, even though some work has been done in Belgium on this topic (Tack & Vanderlinde, 2014). The work of the MOFET Institute in Israel, as well as the work of the National Research School in Teacher Education in Norway (NAFOL) (Smith, 2022), are prime examples of successful practices related to empowering teacher educators as researchers. These initiatives are unfortunately few and deeply contextualized, mainly due to national needs and funding sources.

The praxis of teacher educators goes far beyond external requirements to conduct research. Czerniawski et al. (2017) found that teacher educators first of all see themselves as teachers and educators, preparing teachers for coming generations. Yet, knowledge about how teacher educators themselves are prepared, if they are prepared at all for the complex role as teacher educators, is scarce. InFo-TED's future task could be to focus on developing new knowledge about the preparation of members of our profession by collecting and sharing experiences from teacher educators globally, and perhaps suggesting a framework for the education of teacher educators which is open enough to be adjusted to national and local contexts. Within such a framework, attention should also be drawn to the induction of new teacher educators, how they are inducted into their new role in the workplace, what kind of support systems exist, for example, mentoring. Also, research is scarce, but a study from Norway points out the lack of support for novice teacher educators (Langøren & Smith, 2018).

We, two of the founders of InFo-TED, have added a modest contribution by sharing our individual narratives of becoming teacher educators, and why we became involved with InFo-TED. We have discussed the work of the InFo-TED Forum as well as its future. As we have both acted as coordinators of InFo-TED (Kari as the first one; Ruben as the current one), we find there are two main challenges InFo-TED faces when planning for the future: (1) securing long-term funding and, (2) changing InFo-TED from a Forum into an association. As we see it, these two issues might well be linked to each other. As a Forum we are a group of enthusiastic people who can focus on our main interest, to strengthen the profession of teacher educators. We have no bureaucratic regulations to follow, as we have no income, and we pay the expenses ourselves. However, this might not be sustainable in the future, just as we felt when we received the first Erasmus+ grant. At the same time, bureaucracy increased. The external accountability required a very strict reporting system, which allowed us to work more systematically and to widen our activities and reach out to more colleagues internationally. However, we also spent valuable time reporting, time which could have been spent promoting teacher educators' professional work, especially since most of the Forum members do not include their work for InFo-TED as part of their official job descriptions. Any financial support would, rightfully so, require detailed reports on how the money is spent. The question is, do we want this or not?

The second issue is if we move from a Forum to an association with open paid memberships that might attract funding, this will also require a great deal of bureaucracy, for example, registration, taxes, and full accountability to the association's members. An association would be more inclusive than the current Forum, which is, as mentioned earlier, is a rather convenience-based group. The impact of an association is likely to be much stronger than the current Forum, and thus, strengthen our professional group globally. We are, however, also afraid that the essence of our message, *How I teach is the message* by being critical and inquiry oriented, self-regulated, caring, contextual responsive, and research informed (InFo-TED conceptual model, https://InFo-TED.eu/knowledge-bases/) might be lost in administrative issues and bureaucracy, if we become too big. Neither of us has the answers to these challenges. Yet, we strongly believe they must be discussed. A major goal of InFo-TED is to clarify the distinction between the structure of teacher education and teacher educators' work by strengthening the voices of the profession itself to prevent policy makers taking over and defining the profession. As such, we plea again for all teacher educators to have stronger voices and to engage in the public and political debate on education and teacher education (Vanderlinde et al., 2021).

REFERENCES

Berry, A. (2007). *Tensions in teaching about teaching: Understanding practice as a teacher educator* (Vol. 5). Springer Science & Business Media.

Berry, A. (2016). Teacher educators' professional learning: A necessary case of "on your own"? In B. De Wever, B. R. Vanderlinde, M. Tuytens, & A. Aelterman (Eds.), *Professional learning in education: Challenges for teacher educators, teachers and student teachers* (pp. 39–56). Ginko Press & Academia.

Boyd, P. (2014). Using "modelling" to improve the coherence of initial teacher education. In P. Boyd, A. Szplit, & Z. Zbróg (Eds.), *Teacher educators and teachers as learners: International perspectives* (pp. 51–73). Wydawnictwo Libron.

Card, D. (2017). The "black box" metaphor in machine learning. *Towards Data Science, 5*.

Cochran-Smith, M., Stringer Keefe, E., & Carney, M. C. (2018). Teacher educators as reformers: Competing agendas. *European Journal of Teacher Education, 41*(5), 572–590.

Czerniawski, G., Gray, D., MacPhail, A., Bain, Y., Conroy, P., & Guberman, A. (2018). The professional learning needs and priorities of higher-education-based teacher educators in England, Ireland and Scotland. *Journal of Education for Teaching, 44*(2).

Czerniawski, G., Guberman, A., & MacPhail, A. (2017). The professional developmental needs of higher education-based teacher educators: An international comparative needs analysis.

European Journal of Teacher Education, 40(1), 127–140. https://doi.org/10.1080/02619768.2016.1246528
European Commission. (2013). *Supporting teacher educators for better learning outcomes* (Brussels).
Guberman, A., Ulvik, M., MacPhail, A., & Oolbekkink-Marchand, H. (2021). Teacher educators' professional trajectories: Evidence from Ireland, Israel, Norway and the Netherlands. *European Journal of Teacher Education, 44*(4), 468–485. https://doi.org/10.1080/02619768.2020.1793948
Kelchtermans, G., Smith, K., & Vanderlinde, R. (2018). Towards an "international forum for teacher educator development": An agenda for research and action. *European Journal of Teacher Education, 41*(1), 120–134. https://doi.org/10.1080/02619768.2017.1372743
Langøren, K., & Smith, K. (2018). Støtte og utvikling i jobben som lærerutdanner. (On job support and development working as teacher educators). *Uniped, 41*(3). https://www.idunn.no/uniped/2018/03/stoette_og_utvikling_i_jobben_som_nylaererutdanner_i_norge. Artikkel 14 av 14.
Livingston, K. (2014). Teacher educators: Hidden professionals? *European Journal of Education, 49*(2), 218–232. https://www.jstor.org/stable/26609215
Loughran, J. (2006). *Developing a pedagogy of teacher education. Understanding teaching and learning about teaching*. Routledge.
Lunenberg, M., Dengerink, J., & Korthagen, F. (2014). *The professional teacher educator: Professional roles, behaviour and development of teacher educators*. Sense Publishers.
Lunenberg, M., Murray, J., Smith, K., & Vanderlinde, R. (2016). Collaborative teacher educator professional development in Europe: Different voices, one goal. *Professional Development in Education*, 1–17.
MacPhail, A., Ulvik, M., Guberman, A., Czerniawski, G., Oolbekkink-Marchand, H. W., & Bain, Y. (2019). The professional development of higher education-based teacher educators: Needs and realities. *Professional Development in Education, 45*(5), 848–861. https://doi.org/10.1080/19415257.2018.1529610
Murray, J., & Male, T. (2005). Becoming a teacher educator: Evidence from the field. *Teaching and Teacher Education, 21*(2), 125–142.
Oolbekkink-Marchand, H., Meijer, P. C., & Lunenberg, M. (2021). Teacher educators' professional development during an international Summer Academy: Storylines as a powerful pedagogy. In R. Vanderlinde, K. Smith, J. Murray, & M. Lunenberg (Eds.), *Teacher Educators and their professional development: Learning from the past, looking to the future* (pp. 92–105). Routledge.
Richter, E., Lazarides, R., & Richter, D. (2021). Four reasons for becoming a teacher educator: A large-scale study on teacher educators' motives and well-being. *Teaching and Teacher Education, 102*, 103322.
Smith, K. (2011). The multi-faceted teacher educator: A Norwegian perspective. *Journal of Education for Teaching, 37*(3), 337–349. https://doi.org/10.1080/02607476.2011.588024
Smith, K. (2022). Balancing teacher educators' researcherly and pedagogical dispositions—An example from Norway. *Asia-Pacific Journal of Teacher Education*. https://doi.org/10.1080/1359866X.2022.2073868
Smith, K., & Flores, M. A. (2019). The Janus-faced teacher educator. *European Journal of Teacher Education, 42*(4), 433–446. https://doi.org/10.1080/02619768.2019.1646242
Smith, K., Hakel, K., & Skjeldestad, K. (2020). (University lecturers-a neglected professional group?) [Universitetslektorer-en neglisjert profesjonsgruppe]. *UNIPED, 43*(4), 280–297. https://doi.org/10.18261/issn.1893-8981-2020-04-02
Tack, H. (2017). *Towards a better understanding of teacher educators' professional development: Theoretical and empirical insight into their researcherly disposition*. Faculty of Psychology and Educational Sciences, Ghent, Belgium.
Tack, H., Rots, I., Struyven, K., Valcke, M., & Vanderlinde, R. (2017). Uncovering a hidden professional agenda for teacher educators: A mixed method study on Flemish teacher educators and their professional development. *European Journal of Teacher Education, 41*(1), 86–10.
Tack, H., & Vanderlinde, R. (2014). Teacher educators' professional development: Towards a typology of teacher educators' researcherly disposition. *British Journal of Educational Studies, 62*(3), 297–315. https://doi.org/10.1080/00071005.2014.957639
Tack, H., & Vanderlinde, R. (2019). Capturing the relations between teacher educators' opportunities for professional growth, work pressure, work related basic needs satisfaction, and teacher

educators' researcherly disposition. *European Journal of Teacher Education, 42*(4), 459–477. https://doi.org/10.1080/02619768.2019.1628212

Ulvik, M., & Smith, K. (2018). (Teacher educators' professional development) [Lærerutdanneres profesjonelle utvikling]. *Uniped, 44*(4). https://www.idunn.no/uniped/2018/04/laererutdanneres_profesjonelle_utvikling. Artikkel 5 av 8.

Vanassche, E., Rust, F., Conway, P., Smith, K., Tack, H., & Vanderlinde, R. (2015). InFo-TED: Bringing policy, research, and practice together around teacher educator development. In C. Craig & L. Orland-Barak (Eds.), *International teacher education: Promising pedagogies* (pp. 341–364). Emerald Publishing.

Vanderlinde, R., Smith, K., Murray, J., & Lunenberg, M. (Eds.). (2021). *Teacher educators and their professional development: Learning from the past, looking to the future.* Routledge.

InFo-TED, NORTH AMERICA: ADDRESSING A PROBLEM OF PRACTICE

Frances Rust and Diane Yendol-Hoppey

ABSTRACT

This chapter examines the professional background, trajectories, and learning of a broad group of teacher educators involved in initial teacher education. The work specifically identifies those who shape the practice of teaching. The authors who are members of the International Forum on Teacher Educator Development (InFo-TED) were key to the creation of InFo-TED, NA (North America), which has used Zoom technology to launch and spread its efforts. Its central purpose is to spur teacher educators and policymakers to embrace new ways to educate all children.

Keywords: InFo-TED; NA (North America); International Forum on Teacher Educator Development; teacher educator preparation; problems of practice; bridging theory and practice

In this chapter, we take up the issue of professional learning by teacher educators. High quality teacher education is fundamental to all types of education reform. It follows that effective and dedicated teacher educators are essential determiners of teacher education quality. Yet there is little clarity about who teacher educators are, what they do, and how they shape the practice of teaching. We draw on the contributions of ISATT scholars, of the International Forum on Teacher Educator Development (InFo-TED), and of North American (NA) scholars who focus on teacher learning, teacher leadership, and educational reform. The chapter highlights coordinated international efforts to reframe teacher education as critical to school reform and to re-envision teacher educators as architects of the teaching profession. We conclude with a call for action to engage teacher educators and policymakers in developing new possibilities for educating all children.

IDENTIFYING THE PROBLEM

Teacher educators are those who are engaged in the preparation and support of teachers throughout their professional lives (Rust, 2010; Snow et al., 2022; Yendol-Hoppey & Dana, 2019). We do not confine the purview of teacher educators to the initial stages of teachers' professional learning. Rather, we see teacher educators as professionals engaged in both the university and the school in a variety of roles (Snow et al., 2022), supporting the work of teaching and learning. In many ways, teacher educators are change agents.

The scholars of the International Forum on Teacher Educator Development (InFo-TED) (see https://info-ted.eu/), a group engaged in the initial and on-going education of teacher educators, have developed a conceptual framework (see Fig. 1) that describes the work of teacher educators as a dynamic learning process. That process "starts from a full appreciation of the work teacher educators are doing and of the way they are doing it: their enacted practice" (Vanassche et al., 2015, p. 349). It is situated in "a temporal context that recognizes that teacher educators enter the profession at different moments in their careers – with different experiences and different learning needs" (p. 349). InFo-TED offers this conceptual framework as a "tool to map the professional development of teacher educators" (p. 349) and a catalyst toward developing a common language "that demonstrates and makes public (i.e., opens up for critical debate) the richness of the professional expertise that it aims to describe" (p. 358).

This dynamic model captures the complex scope and fragile environment of the teacher education landscape. The teacher educator is framed as an individual standing for the profession so that the big ideas, the enduring principles that undergird teaching can be seen as core to understanding practice (the knowledge base) and as essential concerns for each practitioner. At the same time, the InFo-TED model situates the teacher educator in the local context and within the multiplex of local, state, national, international thinking about teaching and learning. The fragility implied has to do with the multiplicity of players and their grasp of and engagement with the dynamic issues described by and within each of the circular arrows.

How are teacher educators prepared and supported? This is the essential problem of practice that we and the participants of the International Forum on Teacher Educator Development in North America (InFo-TED, NA) are currently engaged (Snow et al., 2022). Berliner (1986) claims that it takes 10 years to become a competent teacher and that few will move beyond competence to becoming proficient and even expert. What is the time frame for teacher educators? Goodwin and Kosnik (2013) have written, "One becomes a teacher educator as soon as one does teacher education, but one's professional identity as a teacher educator is constructed over time" (p. 334). To understand the complexity of the role and work of a teacher educator requires "a comprehensive

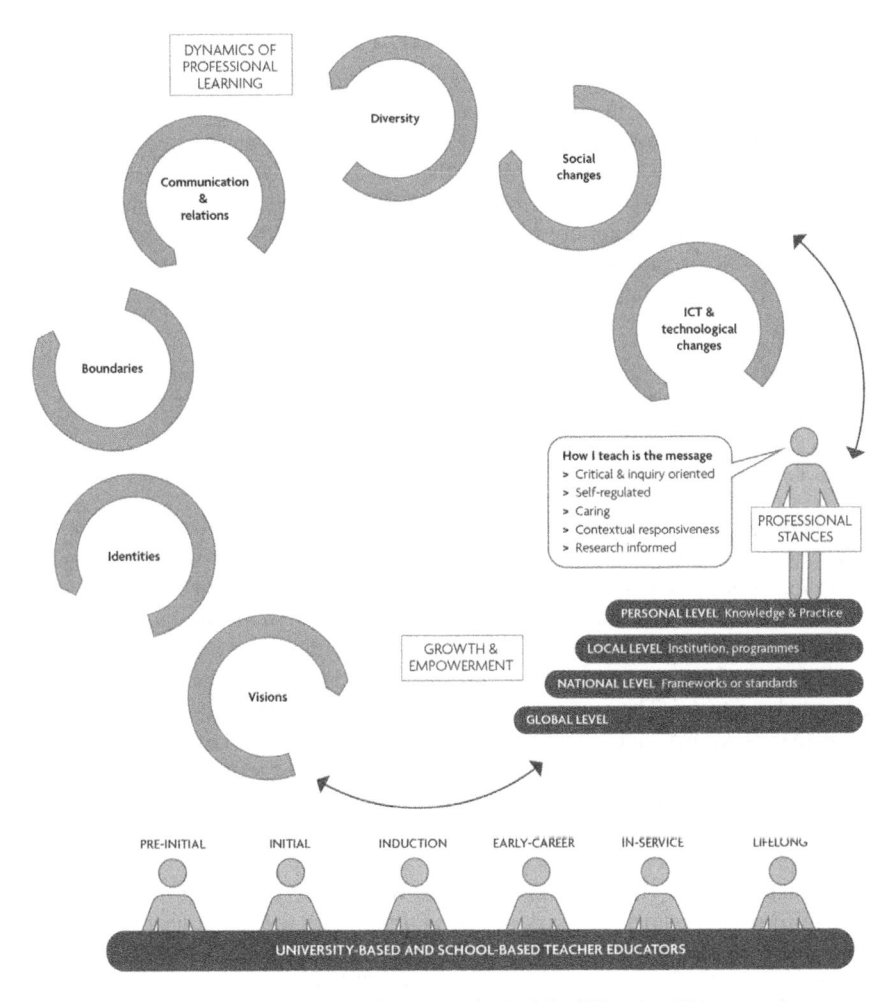

Fig. 1. The InFo-TED Conceptual Model of Teacher Educators' Professional Development.

re-conceptualization of what effective teacher education can be; an empirically based and radically local framework that addresses the two major issues confronting teacher educators: *the problem of practice* and *the challenge of succession*" (Rust, 2010, p. 2). The problem of practice refers to undoing a "…conception of teacher education as a relatively stable and replicable enterprise that, given the right sets of resources, could successfully produce new teachers capable of entering today's schools as highly competent professionals" (Rust, 2010, p. 4). The challenge of succession refers to the professional preparation and support of the next and future generations of teacher educators.

ADDRESSING THE PROBLEM

In every profession, there is concern about bringing theory and current research together with practice in ways designed to equip beginners and sustain practitioners. For beginners, the task is laying down the fundamental knowledge and practice of the field. For practitioners, the task is iterative and episodic, calling for professional recertification over time. While imperfect, this framework for professional learning generally seems to work in most fields to maintain and even improve levels of practice. Not so in teacher education. As Tatto and Clark (2019) describe it in their overview of the field of teacher education in the United States,

> A bifurcation exists between research that is done by teacher educators to inform theory and practice and the research that is done by others about teacher education, which has served to shape policies increasingly dominated by market models. [The net result is an] ...increased questioning of the worth of teacher education [that] has devalued the knowledge taught in teacher education programs and the research knowledge produced by teacher educators. (p. 234)

There are three reasons for this failure of professional learning in teacher education. All are related to a lack of understanding of how knowledge of teaching about teaching is developed and supported. The first relates to misunderstandings about teaching and learning to teach that emerge in settings where there is universal education and a concomitant low regard for teacher preparation: either some people are just "born teachers" or anyone who has been educated can teach. The second reason has to do with the absence of a knowledge base that is known and shared among teacher educators (Hollins & Warner, 2021; Ping et al., 2018). Not being able to draw from a shared understanding of what is necessary for the preparation of new teachers and the support of teachers in the field ultimately affects the entire field. Without the coherence implied by shared goals and a common language of practice, there is no chance of systemic educational reform (Darling-Hammond & Bransford, 2005; Whitcomb, 2003). The third reason relates to a lack of clarity about who teacher educators are and how they come to learn the practice and embrace the field of teacher education (Flores, 2018; Murray et al., 2021; Ping et al., 2018).

The question of how to support teacher educators' ongoing-professional learning in ways that enable both their professional vitality and their capacity to affect improvements in the field of teaching, keeping it current and responsive to a changing world – this question is at the heart of efforts to make teacher education matter in educational reform (Ben-Peretz et al., 2011; Davey, 2013; Lunenberg et al., 2014; Tack et al., 2021; Tack & Vanderlinde, 2019; Vanassche & Kelchtermans, 2014). The field has been through a number of ways of addressing professional learning.

Clark (1988) envisioned a consultancy model for connecting research and the practice of teacher education: "In this relationship, members of the research community behave as *consultants* to the community of teacher educators. To work well as a consultant, one must come to see the client's (teacher educators) problems from the perspective of a sympathetic insider" (pp. 5–6). Clark was confronting two issues: (1) a positioning of research, particularly research on teaching, that was top down, process-product oriented and (2) the concomitant positioning of teacher educators and teachers as passive recipients of the wisdom of research. The idea of a consultancy offered the possibility of a shift in the relationship between researchers and teacher educators and between teacher educators and teachers. He proposed that researchers become teacher educators and that teacher educators become co-researchers engaged in the work of developing deeper understandings of the complexities of teaching. A decade later, Cochran-Smith and Lytle (1999) moved the field toward understanding teacher education as the work of a community of practice. In their view, teacher educators operate as co-researchers *with* teachers and are positioned as thoughtful, reflective, and agile in their enactment of the core principles of a practice that embraces a commitment to social justice and equity. Their distinctions between knowledge-*for*-practice, knowledge-*in*-practice, and knowledge-*of*-practice helped educators appreciate the complementary domains of expertise that reflective teacher educators and practicing teachers bring to the table.

Murray and Male (2005) describe teacher educators as *second order practitioners*:

> Teacher educators are conceptualized here as moving from being first-order practitioners—that is schoolteachers—to being second-order practitioners (Murray, 2002). Where they once worked in the first order setting of the school, they now work in the second order setting of HE (higher education). For those working mainly as initial teacher educators their academic 'discipline' is their knowledge of schooling, of the first- order context. . . As second-order practitioners, teacher educators induct their students into the practices and discourses of both school teaching and teacher education. (p. 126)

Few teacher educators have been prepared for this work. As Murray and Male (2005) note:

> They enter HE with their experiential knowledge and understanding of school teaching as a major strength. Since this knowledge base has been generated in large part through professional practice, it is often tacit rather than explicit, and is inevitably permeated by that practice and by individual ways of understanding the processes of teaching and learning. These ways of understanding in turn are saturated by personal values, beliefs, and biographies. (p. 126)

Essentially, they move into the preparation of new teachers teaching as they were taught.

How then do teacher educators develop those second-order understandings of "learners, learning, pedagogy, and content" (p. 65) described by Hollins and Warner (2021) as the essential components of a knowledge base for teaching? How do they come to the inter-related competencies that Murray and Male (2005), synthesizing from Dutch research (Koster & Dengerink, 2001; Koster et al., 2005), claim as essential to educating teachers?

> These relate to knowledge and understanding of the subject(s) or area(s) being taught (content competencies), the ability to teach in ways to develop teacher understanding (pedagogical competencies), organisational competencies, group dynamic and communicative competencies, and developmental and personal growth competencies for working with adult learners. (p. 136)

Pressing the point even further: If, the classrooms of colleges and universities *are the* places wherein teacher educators situate their preparation of new teachers, and if teacher educators' learning must accommodate to and embrace the requirements of the university setting, how do they become teachers of teachers: How is the deep knowing of teaching that pushes the good teacher toward apprehending what Dewey (1904, 1977) called the "soul life" of the classroom to be nurtured and sustained not only for their students who are learning to teach but also for themselves as teachers of teachers? How is their role as third order practitioners – one foot in higher education, the other in school – acknowledged as essential in these radically different settings? How can teacher educators, without the benefit of professional preparation and ongoing professional learning, develop a knowledge base for teaching and teacher preparation – the "high-stakes endeavor that places teacher educators in the role of *architects for the teaching profession?*" (Hollins & Warner, 2021, p. 65) and "the linchpins in educational reforms of all kinds" (Cochran-Smith, 2003, pp. 5–6)?

There are no easy answers to these questions. Various reports from the European Union (see European Commission, 2013, 2015) suggest that efforts to improve the preparation and support of teachers to improve schools requires that attention be given to the development and learning of those who prepare teacher candidates and those who support the professional learning of practicing teachers. There have been no similar policies signaling attention to the preparation and support of teacher educators forthcoming from policymakers at the federal and state levels in the US and Canada. Zeichner (2005) writes that, "Many universities today treat teacher education as a self-evident activity both for school- and university-based teacher educators who mentor prospective teachers in clinical experiences and for the instructors and faculty who teach courses in a teacher education program" (p. 118). As Tatto and Clark (2019) see it,

> While the United States had seen a generally steady progression from teaching considered as a craft, towards technical and professional conceptions of teaching, recent accountability-driven policies and legislation have pushed the field away from conceiving teaching as a profession and towards celebrating craft and technical notions of teaching. As these policies diminished the professional status of teaching, they also eroded the role that scientific research plays in informing the knowledge base of teacher education. (p. 234)

Though Canadian and American scholars have written about the role and work of teacher educators (Beck & Kosnik, 2006; Ducharme, 1993; Ducharme & Ducharme, 1996; Russell, 1997; Zeichner, 2005), and more recently about developing a pedagogy of teacher education (see, for example, Grossman, 2018; Henning et al., 2018; Hollins, 2015; Yendol-Hoppey & Dana, 2019) few have made the explicit connection between a knowledge base for the profession and the professional learning of teacher educators that Whitcomb (2003) signaled: "I argue that even if we build teacher education programs differently, if we do not attend to the development and practice of teacher educators, such structural reforms are not likely to reach their full potential" (p. 29). Missing in all is the broad national conversation about how teacher educators are being prepared and supported to engage in this work. Instead, we look to well-established European research and scholarship for inspiration and example.

ATTENDING TO TEACHER EDUCATORS' PROFESSIONAL LEARNING

We begin with InFo-TED and move from there to the work of InFo-TED, NA. Neither group is intent on forming yet another organization focused on some aspect of teacher education. Rather, both represent efforts to raise awareness among researchers, policy-makers, and educators at all levels to the importance of teacher educators' professional learning. Thus, their work is made known through publications in journals – *European Journal of Teacher Education, British Journal of Educational Studies, Studying Teacher Education, Journal of Teacher Education, Professional Development in Education* – and book chapters and books. As well, participants in both groups regularly make presentations about the research undertaken by InFo-TED and InFo-TED, NA at meetings of professional organizations such as the BERA (British Education Research Association), ISATT (International Association on Teachers and Teaching), EARLI (European Association of Research on Learning and Instruction), ATEE (Association for Teacher Education in Europe), ECER (European Conference on Educational Research), NAFOL (Norwegian National Research School in Teacher Education), TEPE (Teacher Education Policy in Europe), AERA (American Education Research Association), the S-STEP (Self-Study of Teacher Educator Practices Special Interest Group of AERA), and others.

InFo-TED

The work of InFo-TED began with a group of 4 experienced European teacher educators meeting at AERA 10 years ago. Their concern was, as now, the professional learning of teacher educators. They put out a call to several other teacher educators and brought together a group of 20 or so representing 6 European countries (Norway, England and Scotland, Ireland, the Netherlands, Belgium) plus the United States and Israel for a meeting in Amsterdam. From that initial two-day meeting, the model we describe above (see Fig. 1) took shape, and the multinational work that has become synonymous with InFo-TED began. The first step was to seek funding for a dissemination project. Work groups developed and more meetings held with the goal of developing an Erasmus + proposal. Two years and one rejection later, the group received an Erasmus + grant (2017–2019) and began the process of website development and outreach.

By 2019, InFo-TED had established a website (https://info-ted.eu/) focusing on the situation and practice of university-based teacher educators. The website takes up each aspect of the model with conversational blogs around the building blocks of knowledge bases, with white papers, with webinars, and with research publications documenting the needs and thinking of teacher educators. As well, the group has developed national forums and two international summer academies bringing teacher educators together in person (2017) and virtually (2021). The story of the work of InFo-TED is available through the publications listed on the website and in a 2021 book, *Teacher Educators and their Professional Development* (Vanderlinde et al., 2021), that "reports and analyses the approach, processes and results of this six-year long (and still ongoing) international co-operation... across an experienced group of academics and practitioners" (p. i).

What InFo-TED has done through publication of its research projects and its website initiative is to create a powerful resource for those interested in teacher educators' professional learning. This has been especially important vis-à-vis education policy in Europe as InFo-TED research combined with local initiatives and summer institutes has brought policymakers and practitioners together regarding the critical role of teacher educators in EU-sponsored and local educational reform. It has also enabled a broad conversation beyond the EU among teacher educators from different countries and a variety of settings – both university and school – to come to know one another and to engage around practice, norms, and exploring our own journeys into the field of teacher education.

The conversation enabled by InFo-TED raised awareness of the important work of teacher educators and drew attention to their professional learning. As described in the InFo-TED white paper (see *White Paper* on https://info-ted.eu/),

> The main message of InFo-TED is that teacher educators continue to play a central role in the effort to improve education at all levels and that their professional development cannot be overlooked if educational outcomes are to be improved overall. The importance of this occupational group and the support for their development is not, in our view, sufficiently acknowledged by policymakers at national levels or at pan-European level. There is then a need for national, European, and wider international cooperation to disseminate the awareness that 'Teacher Educators Matter'. (p. 8)

InFo-TED in North America

Building on the growing interest sparked by the work of InFo-TED as well as that of the Self-Study of Teacher Education Practices SIG of AERA (see Garbett & Ovens, 2014; Loughran et al., 2004; Loughran, 2007), and members of ISATT (Berry, 2016; Russell, 1997) in the issues surrounding teacher educators' professional learning, US and Canadian teacher educators began coming together in 2015 to consider ways to shape a North American initiative around teacher educators' professional learning. We began with informal meetings in New York and at AERA annual meetings. Ours was a diverse group of colleagues from OISE and Nippissing University in Canada, and in the United States from NYU, Teachers College, City University of New York, University of North Florida, University of Pennsylvania, Alverno College, Montclair State University, and Seton Hall University.

We were aware that adopting the InFo-TED model in the United States and Canada would be different from the European approach because our systems are so different from those of Europe. However, we thought that, given the contested territory of teacher education in North America and the general lack of preparation and support given to teacher educators, the time had come to consider how something akin to InFo-TED might benefit the field and help to shift education policy agendas within and beyond the university in a positive and constructive direction. Initially, we tried using the same survey that helped InFo-TED to shape its outreach to the teacher education community (see Czerniawski et al., 2017, 2018). Each of us interviewed three teacher educators and came back to a next meeting six months later with findings that echoed those of InFo-TED: the teacher educators whom we interviewed were largely engaged in field-related/clinical aspects of teacher education and did not see themselves as engaged in research – that was what they had done for their dissertations. These were echoes of the findings of Czerniawski et al. (2017, 2018) that we wanted to take further but, with scant support, the completely voluntary and episodic nature of our meetings suggested that carrying forward with a project like that was beyond our capacity. Our focus then, became how to gather enough funding to enable us to move forward.

We made a proposal to AERA in 2019 to bring together a group representing our broad constituency of teacher educators from across the USA and Canada for an AERA-supported Research Conference[1] as a 3-day collaboration wherein we could develop a framework for implementation of high-quality opportunities for continuing professional development conceived to meet the specific needs of teacher educators and effective professional collaboration between teacher educators working in different settings (university subject departments, university education departments, schools, local authorities, private sector, etc.) – in essence, a North American version of InFo-TED or InFo-TED, NA. The group of 20 whom we initially called together in support of participating in the proposed conference as a working group were, like the initiators of InFo-TED, situated in higher education: The group includes deans of schools of education, teacher education faculty from public and private universities and community colleges, and educators whose focus is teacher professional learning.

Using Engeström and Sannino's (2010) theory of *expansive learning* which places "primacy on communities as learners, on transformation and creating of culture, on horizontal movement and hybridization, and on the formation of theoretical concepts" (p. 2), we looked at the initiative supported by such a conference as an opportunity for radically reshaping the landscape of teacher education in North America. "The basic argument for such a focus on work settings," write Engeström and Sannino (2010), is that

> when whole collective activity systems, such as work processes and organizations, need to redefine themselves, traditional modes of learning are not enough. Nobody knows exactly what needs to be learned. The design of the new activity and the acquisition of the knowledge and skills it requires are increasingly intertwined. In expansive learning activity, they merge. (p.3)

The processes and outcomes cannot be prescribed. Rather, the processes that a group engages in emerge from collaborative interactions shaped by the participants and by the context, making realization of goals and insights more expansive and surprising than anticipated.

Our intent was, and is, to draw together teacher educators who, as practitioner researchers, are focused on the professional learning of teacher educators and who are committed to an agenda of re-thinking (Rust, 2010), re-mixing (Ladson-Billings, 2014, 2017), and re-imagining (Greene, 1995) a way forward around teacher educators' professional learning and thus, of teacher education itself. We were, and are, focused on reshaping and refreshing the narrative around teacher education that moves us away from a predominantly "how to" enterprise for beginners, to a place where teacher educators see themselves and their work embracing the whole of teachers' professional lives (Rust, 2010), and as essential leaders shaping the quality of education (Hollins & Warner, 2021; Murray, 2017; Tack & Vanderlinde, 2019). We hoped that our proposed research conference would provide space to build a collective approach to supporting the work of teacher educators in universities, schools, and other professional organizations. The conversation that we imagined would focus on the preparation of the next generation of teacher educators and on how to support the professional learning of those who currently identify as teacher educators. Then Covid-19 happened. The Research Conference was not to be, and the group that we had called together in anticipation of the acceptance of our conference proposal came together anyway without funding on Zoom.

Being forced to convene online turned out to be a boon, for it enabled us to shift toward developing a research agenda that would help us to clarify how we think about and practice teacher education. We might not have taken that step had we experienced days together in person, but it has been a catalyst for developing a common understanding and shared language for our work as teacher educators.

As InFo-TED-NA, our group has engaged in a variety of activities over the course of 20 months on-line. Artifacts from our meetings included videos of our meetings, meeting agendas, meeting notes, Flipgrid video introductions, interviews of one another, and individual memos. As we discussed our work, we intuitively and individually began sharing the unique lens we each bring to teacher education. Each of us described a feeling of professional loneliness within our own contexts and the value we found connecting with one another in a dialogue about our shared work. That said, our conversations remained at a general level, and we needed to push ourselves toward finding a way to deepen our thinking and collaboration. We wanted to find ways to make our work as teacher educators more visible to one another. We were interested in understanding the extent to which our work and conceptual orientation toward that work was shared. We needed to identify a project or projects that, like the proposed research conference, were of sufficient importance to keep us meeting together virtually.

Exploring Understandings: To explore our wonderings, 12 of us chose to adapt the *Slice* protocol from the *School Reform Initiative* (http://schoolreforminitiative.org/doc/slice.pdf) to investigate a day in the life of a teacher educator and to explore the question, "What does a day in the life of a teacher educator look and sound like?" Our goal was to capture the *work* of teacher educators, the variations of the work, and what kind of whole the pieces comprise. The culmination of the Slice collaboration was a paper presented at AERA Self-Study SIG in 2022.

We worked together in pairs interviewing one another to gain insight into one another's *slice*. Then, taking the data produced, a small group did our first analysis of each of the 12 cases. Our work identified "function" as an analytic tool to capture the dynamic, cross-role teacher educator activities we identified in the data. We defined "function" as,

> an activity or purpose natural to or intended for a person or thing. Function is active and dynamic, not static. We came to see function as a lens for considering the active nature of our work as it better describes the commonality of that work better than role or activity and better than either details its impact on the field. These functions are not mutually exclusive categories. Rather, the function descriptions demonstrate or speak to the complexity of this work. (Snow et al., p. 6)

We initially identified six potential overlapping functions across the 12 cases: mentoring, design, communication, advocacy, leadership, planning. Next, using a three-phased coding process (Saldana, 2012) we were able to narrow our focus to three key functions that, irrespective of our roles, were present for each as core to our work as teacher educators. These functions were Design, Leadership, and Advocacy – all shaped, infused, and transcended by the educative nature of teacher educators' work (Dewey, 1938). Our understanding of these educative functions is informed by sociocultural learning theory (Vygotsky, 1986) wherein teaching is socially constructed through interactions with others (Moody et al., 2018).

This initial project enabled us to question, to talk about our work, and to reach new understandings. It also pushed us to think strategically about how to go forward as a group leaning into the mission we set for ourselves of enabling the conversation around teacher educators' professional learning. However, like the collaboration that is InFo-TED, we learned from our 20 months of online conversation that having a shared goal is critical to making the time to meet, especially online. We had set a presentation at the Self-Study SIG of the American Education Research Association as the target of this initial collaboration (see Snow et al., 2022). Once done, the question then became, "What next?".

Continuing to meet online, we considered how to move forward. We found that the careful work of interacting in pairs and then in small groups had enabled us to come to know one another in ways that meeting up episodically at a big conference like AERA did not give us. We determined two next steps, both involving small group work. The first was to revise the AERA paper for publication in the SIG journal, *Studying Teacher Education*. The second was to prepare for an ISATT regional meeting in Bordeaux with a pilot study digging into our *Slice* data, specifically looking at the issue of equity. The first is accomplished (see Snow et al., 2022). The second is helping us take our work deeper as we wrestle with questions about whether and how we are walking our talk.

Going Deeper: Like many teacher educators who individually and collectively struggle with the challenges of getting beyond talk to implementing and sustaining a commitment to making *Diversity, Equity, Inclusion* (DEI) live within our teacher education programs, we wanted to investigate ways in which DEI is both visible and integral in our practice. In a pilot project, four of us reanalyzed our own *Slice* and tried to explicate it as fully as possible. That examination led us to investigate the questions, "How is DEI integrated into our work as Teacher Educators?" and "What did we learn by hearing each other's stories?"

Our conversations began with the artifacts in the *Slice* that surfaced and reflected DEI initiatives. We situated those artifacts during our conversations within our broader work as teacher educators. In the same way that our initial study (Snow et al., 2022) helped us to identify key educative functions in teacher educators' work, this current "deep dive" has demonstrated the complexity of teacher educators' work as it relates to DEI. In part, this has to do with how and where our work as teacher educators happens. No two settings are alike, and neither is our work though we each carry the same title of professor/teacher educator:

- In addition to teaching courses and interacting with students, the teacher educator working in a Community College[2] setting provides faculty support regarding program alignment/coherence related to DEI in an early childhood program.
- The university educator whose content area is English as Second Language/Second Language Learning engages teacher candidates in deep focus on equity and culturally sustaining pedagogy that situates him in conversation with practice as his students navigate the settings in which they are beginning to teach.
- The private university educator whose work is situated in a unique independent school-university partnership is part of an effort of the partnership to engage teacher candidates with pedagogical tools that support deep investigation and inquiry around equity- and justice-oriented practice in settings that are not normally associated with DEI.
- The dean of a public university is focused on creating teacher preparation program contexts where structures are initiated to build in DEI and DEI is made more visible.

While only at the beginning of this inquiry, we have with these four *Slices* exposed some of the myths of teacher preparation, for example, the myth of its being neatly situated in coursework and program design in higher education, of experience with teaching and/or having a doctoral degree being sufficient preparation for being a teacher educator, and of teacher education as monolith. This small study has shown us that, in seeking to answer local questions about the ways in which race/ethnicity, class, gender, sexuality, religion, citizenship, ability, and age shape our work as teacher educators, a lens of intersectionality (Tefara et al., 2018) is essential to informing and expanding our knowledge and understanding. If we are to move toward "principled practice" (Kroll et al., 2005), we must open space for dialogue, reflection, and analysis wherein we can learn from one another and together imagine possibilities for collaborative work toward addressing the complex demographic, social, economic, and cultural transformations shaping education.

NEXT STEPS

The questions that emerge for us now relate to how to enlarge the conversation of practice drawing attention to the critical role of teacher educators as "architects" of the teaching profession (Hollins & Warner, 2021) and "linchpins" of educational reform (Cochran-Smith, 2003). Our next steps involve taking this initial *Slice* work to the ISATT regional conference in Bordeaux in 2022 and then expanding to similar deep study among the 12 for a presentation at the ISATT international conference in Bari, Italy in 2023. As the researchers who have come together around InFo-TED have found, there is no procedural blueprint to follow in raising awareness of teacher educators' significant role among teacher educators themselves and among policy-makers. We are not interested in promoting a specific model process or creating another organization. Yet, any effort to move the field toward change suggests that teacher educators must seek out platforms for discourse like those provided by ISATT in its meetings, publications, and authentic conversations. At the same time, we aspire to move beyond academia and into advocacy around education policy. If the professional learning of teacher educators in universities and in schools is to become a priority, it will require work on many fronts. Tatto and Clark (2019) write, ". . . teacher education must continue to see as its raison d'etre teacher learning, and that learning to teach must be considered as complex and demanding as preparing for and mastering other respected professions" (p. 234). To accomplish this goal, the professional learning of teacher educators, in universities and in schools, must become a priority among teacher educators and at all levels of policymaking in North America as it has in Europe.

AUTHOR'S NOTES

1. *From AERA website 2019:* AERA's Research Conferences Program awards grants of up to $35,000 for conferences intended to break new ground in substantive areas of inquiry, stimulate new lines of study on issues that have been largely unexplored, or develop innovative research methods or techniques that can contribute more generally to education research. The program aims to foster the accumulation of knowledge, enhance dissemination, encourage innovation, and advance studies of the highest quality in education research.

2. In the United States, community colleges, sometimes called junior colleges, technical colleges, two-year colleges, or city colleges, are primarily public institutions providing tertiary education, also known as continuing education, that focuses on certificates, diplomas, and associate degrees. After graduating from a community college, some students transfer to a liberal arts college or university for two to three years to complete a bachelor's degree (Wikipedia).

REFERENCES

Beck, C., & Kosnik, C. (2006). *Innovations in preservice teacher education: A social constructivist approach*. SUNY Press.

Ben-Peretz, M., Kleeman, S., Reichenberg, R., & Shimoni, S. (2011). Educators of educators: Their goals, perceptions and practices. In T. Bales, A. Swennen, & K. Jones (Eds.), *The professional development of teacher educators* (pp. 119–137). Springer.

Berliner, D. (1986). In pursuit of the expert pedagogue. *Educational Researcher, 15*(7), 5–13.

Berry, A. (2016). Teacher educators' professional learning: A necessary case of 'on your own'? In B. DeWeaver, R. Vanderlinde, M. Tuytens, & A. Aelsterman (Eds.), *Professional learning in education: Challenges for teacher educators, teachers, and student teachers* (pp. 39–56). Academia Press.

Clark, C. M. (1988). Asking the right questions about teacher preparation: Contributions of research on teacher thinking. *Educational Researcher, 17*(2), 5–12. https://w.w.w.jstor.org/stable/1174582

Cochran-Smith, M. (2003). Learning and unlearning: The education of teacher educators. *Teaching and Teacher Education, 19*, 5–28.

Cochran-Smith, M., & Lytle, S. (1999). Relationships of knowledge and practice: Teacher learning in communities. *Review of Research in Education, 24*, 249–305.

Czerniawski, G., Gray, D., MacPhail, A., Bain, Y., Conroy, P., & Guberman, A. (2018). The professional learning needs and priorities of higher-education-based teacher educators in England, Ireland and Scotland. *Journal of Education for Teaching, 44*(2), 133–148.

Czerniawski, G., Guberman, A., & MacPhail, A. (2017). The professional developmental needs of higher education-based teacher educators: An international comparative needs analysis. *European Journal of Teacher Education, 40*(1), 127–140.

Darling-Hammond, L., & Bransford, J. (2005). *Preparing teachers for a changing world. What teachers should know and be able to do*. Jossey-Bass.

Davey, R. (2013). *The professional identity of teacher educators. Career on the cusp?* Routledge.

Dewey, J. (1904, 1977). The relation of theory to practice in education. In J. A. Boydston (Ed.), *John Dewyey: The middle works, 1899–1924, Vol. 3 (1903–1906)* (pp. 249–272). Southern Illinois University Press.

Dewey, J. (1938). *Experience and education*. Collier Books.

Ducharme, E. R. (1993). *The lives of teacher educators*. Teachers College Press.

Ducharme, E., & Ducharme, M. (1996). Development of the teacher education professoriate. In F. Murray (Ed.), *The teacher educator's handbook: Building a knowledge base for the preparation of teachers* (pp. 691–714). Jossey-Bass.

Engeström, Y., & Sannino, S. (2010). Studies of expansive learning: Foundations, findings and future challenges. *Educational Research Review, 5*, 1–24.

European Commission. (2013). *Supporting teacher educators for better learning outcomes*. https://ec.europa.eu/assets/eac/education/policy/school/doc/support-teacher-educators_en.pdf

European Commission. (2015, June 2015). Strengthening teaching in Europe: New evidence from teachers compiled by Eurydice and CRELL. *Education and Training*. https://ec.europa.eu/assets/eac/education/library/policy/teaching-profession-practices_en.pdf

Flores, M. A. (2018). Linking teaching and research in initial teacher education: Knowledge mobilisation and research-informed practice. *Journal of Education for Teaching, 44*(5), 621–636. https://doi.org/10.1080/02607476.2018.1516351

Garbett, D., & Ovens, A. (Eds.). (2014). *Changing practices for changing times: Past, present and future possibilities for self-study research. Proceedings of the tenth international conference on self-study of teacher education practices*. Auckland University Press.

Goodwin, A. L., & Kosnik, C. (2013). Quality teacher educators=quality teachers? Conceptualizing essential domains of knowledge for those who teach teachers. *Teacher Development, 17*(3), 334–346. http://dx.doi.org/10.1080/13664530.2013.813766. Accessed on June, 2020.

Greene, M. (1995). *Releasing the imagination. Essays on education, the arts, and social change*. Jossey-Bass.

Grossman, P. (Ed.). (2018). *Teaching core practices in teacher education*. Harvard Education Press.

Henning, J. E., Gut, D. M., & Beam, P. C. (2018). *Building mentoring capacity in teacher education: A guide to clinically-based practice*. Routledge.

Hollins, E. R. (2015). *Rethinking field experiences in preservice teacher preparation: Meeting new challenges for accountability*. Routledge.

Hollins, E. R., & Warner, C. K. (2021). *Rethinking teacher preparation program design*. Routledge.

Koster, B., & Dengerink, J. (2001). Towards a professional standard for Dutch teacher educators. *European Journal of Teacher Education, 24*(3), 343–354.

Koster, B., Korthagen, F., Wubbels, T., & Hoornweg, J. (2005). Roles, competencies and training of teacher educators: A new challenge. In E. Befring (Ed.), *Teacher education for quality* (pp. 397–411). Association of Teacher Education European.

Kroll, L., Cossey, R., Donohue, D. A., Galguera, T., LaBoskey, V. A., Richert, A. E., & Tucher, P. (2005). *Teaching as principled practice: Managing complexity for social justice*. SAGE.

Ladson-Billings, G. (2014). Culturally relevant pedagogy 2.0: a.k.a. the remix. *Harvard Educational Review, 84*(1), 74–84.

Ladson-Billings, G. (2017). The (R)evolution will not be standardized. Teacher education, hip hop pedagogy, and culturally relevant pedagogy 2.0. In D. Paris & H. Samy Alim (Eds.), *Culturally sustaining pedagogies: Teaching and learning for justice in a changing world* (pp. 141–156). Teachers College Press.

Loughran, J. J. (2007). Learning through self-study: The influence of purpose, participants and context. In *International handbook of self-study of teaching and teacher education practices* (pp. 151–192). Springer.

Loughran, J. J., Hamilton, M. L., LaBoskey, V. K., & Russell, T. L. (Eds.). (2004). *International handbook of self-study of teaching and teacher education practices*. Kluwer Academic Publishers.

Lunenberg, M., Dengerink, J., & Korthagen, F. (2014). *The professional teacher educator: Professional roles, behavior and development of teacher educators*. Sense Publishers.

Moody, S., Hu, X., Kuo, L.-J., Jouhar, M., Xu, Z., & Lee, S. (2018). Vocabulary instruction: A critical analysis of theories, research, and practice. *Education Sciences, 8*(4), 180. https://doi.org/10.3390/educsci8040180

Murray, J. (2002). Between the chalkface and the ivory towers? A study of the professionalism of teacher educators working on primary initial teacher education courses in the English education system. *Collected Original Resources in Education (CORE), 26*(3), 1–503.

Murray, J. (2017). Defining teacher educators: International perspectives and contexts. In D. J. Clandinin & J. Husu (Eds.), *International handbook of research on teacher education* (pp. 1017–1033). SAGE.

Murray, J., & Male, T. (2005). Becoming a teacher educator: Evidence from the field. *Teaching and Teacher Education, 21*, 125–142.

Murray, J., Smith, K., Vanderlinde, R., & Lunenberg, M. (2021). Teacher educators and their professional development. In R. Vanderlinde, K. Smith, J. Murray, & M. Lunenberg (Eds.), *Teacher educators and their professional development. Learning from the past, looking to the future* (pp. 1–14). Routledge.

Ping, C., Schellings, G., & Beijaard, D. (2018). Teacher educators' professional learning: A literature review. *Teaching and Teacher Education, 75*, 93–104. https://doi.org/10.1016/j.tate.2018.06.003

Russell, T. (1997). Teaching teachers. How I teach is the message. In J. Loughran & T. Russell (Eds.), *Teaching about teaching: Purpose, passion and pedagogy in teacher education* (pp. 32–47). Falmer Press.

Rust, F. O'C. (2010). Shaping new models for teacher education. *Teacher Education Quarterly, 37*, 5–18.

Saldana, J. (2012). *The coding manual for qualitative researchers*. Sage.

Snow, J., Jacobs, J., Pignatosi, F., Norman, P., Rust, F., Yendol-Hoppey, D., Nepstad, C., Naiditch, F., Kosnik, C., & Pointer-Mace, D. (2022). *Making the invisible visible: Who are teacher educators and what is seen in our work?* Paper Presented at the Self-Study SIG, AERA, San Diego, CA, April 2022.

Tack, H., & Vanderlinde, R. (2019). Teacher educators' professional development: Towards a typology of teacher educators' researcherly disposition. *British Journal of Educational Studies, 62*(3), 297–315.

Tack, H., Vanderlinde, R., Bain, Y., Kidd, W., O'Sullivan, M., & Walraven, A. (2021). Learning and design principles for teacher educators' professional development. In R. Vanderlinde, K. Smith, J. Murray, & M. Lunenberg (Eds.), *Teacher educators and their professional development. Learning from the past, looking to the future* (pp. 51–64). Routledge.

Tatto, M., & Clark, C. (2019). Institutional transformations, knowledge and research traditions in US teacher education. In M. T. Tatto & I. Menter (Eds.), *Knowledge, policy and practice in learning to teach: A cross-national study* (pp. 234–253). Bloomsbury Academic. https://www.researchgate.net/publication/334704912

Tefara, A. A., Powers, J. M., & Fischman, G. E. (2018). Introduction: Intersectionality in education: A conceptual aspiration and research imperative. *Review of Research in Education, 42*, vii–xvii.

Vanassche, E., & Kelchtermans, G. (2014). Teacher educators' professionalism in practice: Positioning theory and personal interpretive framework. *Teaching and Teacher Education, 44*, 117–127.

Vanassche, E., Rust, F., Conway, P. F., Smith, K., Tack, H., & Vanderlinde, R. (2015). InFo-TED: Bringing policy, research, and practice together around teacher educator development. In *International teacher education: Promising pedagogies (Part C)* (pp. 341–364). Emerald Group Publishing Limited.

Vanderlinde, R., Smith, K., Murray, J., & Lunenberg, M. (2021). *Teacher educators and their professional development. Learning from the past, looking to the future*. Routledge.

Vygotsky, L. (1986). *Thought and language, revised*. MIT Press.

Whitcomb, J. A. (2003). Practice matters. Reflections on the importance of teacher educator's practice. In D. M. McInerney & S. Van Etten (Eds.), *Sociocultural influences and teacher education programs. Research on sociocultural influences in motivation and learning* (Vol. 3, pp. 15–33). Information Age Publishing.

Yendol-Hoppey, D., & Dana, N. F. (2019). *Preparing the next generation of teacher educators for clinical practice*. Information Age Publishing.

Zeichner, K. (2005). Becoming a teacher educator: A personal perspective. *Teaching and Teacher Education, 21*(2), 117–124.

InFo-TED: BRINGING POLICY, RESEARCH, AND PRACTICE TOGETHER AROUND TEACHER EDUCATOR DEVELOPMENT[*]

Eline Vanassche, Frances Rust, Paul F. Conway, Kari Smith, Hanne Tack and Ruben Vanderlinde

ABSTRACT

This chapter is contributed by InFo-TED, the International Forum for Teacher Educator Development. This newly established community brings together people from across the world to exchange research, policy, and practice related to teacher educators' professional learning and development. We define teacher educators broadly as those who are professionally involved and engaged in the initial and ongoing education of teachers. Our contention is that while there is general agreement about the important role played by teacher educators, their professional education is understudied and undersupported. Here, we elaborate the rationale for this initiative, delineate our conceptual framework, and provide examples of steps taken in Belgium, Ireland, and Norway to develop the professional identities and knowledge bases of those who educate and support teachers, and conclude with implications for a scholarly study agenda having to do with research, policy, and practice relating to teacher educators' professional development.

---

[*]This chapter is reprinted from *International teacher education: Promising pedagogies* (pp. 341–364), Vanassche, E., Rust, F., Conway, P., Smith, K., Tack, H., & Vanderlinde, R., InFo-TED: Bringing Policy, Research, and Practice Together Around Teacher Educator Development, 2015, Emerald Publishing.

Teaching and Teacher Education in International Contexts
Advances in Research on Teaching, Volume 42, 211–229
Copyright © 2023 Emerald Publishing Limited, with the exception of InFo-TED: Bringing Policy, Research, and Practice Together Around Teacher Educator Development © Emerald Publishing.
All rights of reproduction in any form reserved
ISSN: 1479-3687/doi:10.1108/S1479-368720230000042022

Keywords: InFo-TED; teacher education research; teacher education policy; teacher education practice; teacher educators' identities; knowledge base of teacher education

INTRODUCTION

Teacher educators are key players in international educational systems as they impact the quality of teaching and learning in our schools. However, those who teach the next generation of teachers – the teacher educators – have, until recently, largely been ignored by researchers and policymakers who have focused instead on structures of teacher education and on relationships between teacher education programs and student achievement in schools. In this chapter, we focus squarely on the professional learning and development of teacher educators whom we define broadly as those who are professionally involved and engaged in the initial and ongoing education of teachers. Our contention is that while there is general agreement about the important role played by teacher educators, their professional education is understudied and undersupported (e.g., Loughran, 2014; Lunenberg et al., 2014).

This chapter is contributed by a group of experienced teacher educators from Ireland, Scotland, England, the Netherlands, Belgium, Norway, Israel, and United States, who have come together over the past two years to develop the International Forum for Teacher Educator Development or InFo-TED. Our purpose is to promote professional education for educators in the field of teacher education. Spurring our work has been the increased interest in teacher education around the world and especially in Europe where the European Union (European Commission, 2012, 2013) has stressed the important role of well-prepared and highly qualified teacher educators to prepare the next generation of teachers at both the elementary and secondary levels and to support those already at work in schools and other related educational settings.

As we have met together in the various participating countries and studied the landscape of research around teacher educator development, we have come to understand the need for a specific focus on developing and supporting the professional expertise of teacher educators. We have seen that although the vast majority of practicing teacher educators have one or more postgraduate degrees in education or a cognate discipline, worldwide, those responsible for the education of future teachers have rarely been formally prepared for their vital role (Zeichner & Conklin, 2005). With the exception of Israel's MOFET Institute (https://eng.mofet.macam.ac.il/about-us/),[1] there has not been a systematic effort to develop a formal induction or continuing professional development framework for teacher educators. Our study suggests that moving from teaching in a content area to teaching that fuses content knowledge with knowledge of how to teach that content requires a fundamental shift in understandings of expertise and of instructional practice (e.g., Ball & Cohen, 1999; Grossman, 2005; Shulman, 1986, 1987) as well as in teacher educators' sense of professional identity (e.g., Berry, 2007; Zeichner, 2005). To support the development of a new conception of professional expertise among teacher educators, a common set of commitments has emerged among members of InFo-TED. These include:

- Developing a shared vision and common understanding of what is meant by quality in educating teachers;
- Access for teacher educators to high-quality opportunities for continuing professional development conceived to meet the specific needs of teacher educators;
- Effective collaboration between teacher educators working in different settings (university subject area departments, university teacher education departments, schools, local authorities, etc.).

In the next parts of our chapter, we further elaborate the rationale for this initiative, delineate our conceptual framework, and describe the initiatives that have been taken up by InFo-TED to date.

HISTORY AND RATIONALE OF INFO-TED

The foundations of InFo-TED were laid through a "coming together" of a group of experienced teacher educators at the 2012 Annual meeting of the American Educational Research Association in San Francisco. The group informally connected around a shared interest in some of the questions we perceived as needing to be answered: "What is the nature of the professional knowledge involved in the work of educating teachers to teach?" and "How do teacher educators build and develop that knowledge?" These questions were not necessarily new. In fact, similar questions have been raised by Ducharme (1986) and by Lanier and Little (1986) as early as the 1980s and have, since then, consistently been reiterated (see, for example, the 2011 Special Issue in the *Journal of Education for Teaching*). What was new, however, is the fact that these questions were being seriously considered and collectively acted upon by those involved in the field of teacher education across the globe. In a sense, then, InFo-TED can be read as a public and organized response to earlier and persistent calls for research focusing specifically on the professional lives, work, and development of teacher educators.

The very fact that these questions were raised as in need of specific attention by policymakers, practitioners, and researchers, highlights our fundamental starting premise: the work of educating teachers requires knowledge, skills, and beliefs that are qualitatively different from those developed as an experienced classroom teacher. "Although the work of teaching has much in common with the work of teacher education, the two positions are significantly different in important ways" (Dinkelman et al., 2006, p. 6). This starting premise contrasts starkly with the implicit assumption that a teacher educator is someone who simply teaches (his/her subject) to students in higher education instead of to students in elementary or secondary education. Underlying this premise is the idea that "educating teachers is something that does not require any additional preparation and that if one is a good teacher of elementary or secondary students, this expertise will automatically carry over to one's work with novice teachers" (Zeichner, 2005, p. 118). In keeping with assumptions like these, little research attention has been paid to the specific nature of teacher educators' professionalism in terms of what they define as their role as a teacher educator and how they construct the knowledge and skills for this role. Similarly, in line with such assumptions, there has been little need to pay any specific attention to teacher educators' induction or to their on-going professional learning and development needs.

There is strong evidence from the research literature that such observations have had international acceptance. Zeichner (2005), for example, wrote about what he called the "seat of the pants approach" to the preparation of new teacher educators in the U.S. context; Berry (2007) published a self-study of her struggles to coming to know what and how to teach her students about teaching as she moved from classroom teaching into teacher education in Australia; and Murray and Male (2005) conducted research on the challenges faced by successful classroom teachers in establishing their professional and scholarly identities as teachers of teachers in higher education in England. Similar research has been conducted in Israel by Ben-Peretz et al. (2011); by Davey (2013) in New Zealand; by Lunenberg et al. (2014) in the Netherlands; by Smith (2011) in Norway; and by Vanassche and Kelchtermans (2014) and Tack and Vanderlinde (2014) in Belgium. This lack of attention to the induction and professional development needs of teacher educators as well as the absence of a public and codified knowledge base in teacher education is also, in part, what led to the emergence of the Self-Study of Teacher Education Practices (or S-STEP) movement (Loughran et al., 2004). In distinguishing between the work of teaching and the work of teacher education, Murray and Male (2005) conceptualize teacher educators as second-order practitioners, that is, teacher educators induct their students into the practices and discourses of both the first-order context of schooling and the second-order context of teacher education. As second-order practitioners, teacher educators draw on second-order knowledge to teach in the second-order context of higher education (e.g., Murray, 2005, 2008). Understood in this way, teaching about teaching requires the ability to hold two perspectives simultaneously: the perspective of the classroom teacher and the perspective of the teacher educator. For teacher educators, content knowledge (knowledge about teaching) and pedagogical knowledge (teaching about teaching) are inseparable (e.g., Loughran, 2007; Russell, 1997). Teacher educators design instructional environments conducive to students' learning, they support learning processes, and select curriculum materials, pedagogies, and assessment strategies, but this teaching is always intended to support student teachers' learning about teaching (e.g., Kelchtermans, 2013). Put differently, teacher educators' distinctive expertise or disciplinary knowledge is teaching. "It is teaching teachers about teaching, rather than a specific subject discipline (i.e., physics, mathematics, English) that commands teacher educators' loyalty" (Vanassche, 2014, p. 3). Therefore, second-order practice demands extended pedagogical expertise, the capability to teach the subject of teaching in the higher education setting, and a specific understanding of oneself as a teacher of teachers.

Building an understanding of oneself as a teacher educator (e.g., Davey, 2013; Murray & Male, 2005; Swennen et al., 2010) and constructing a personal pedagogy of teacher education (e.g., Berry, 2007; Loughran, 2007; Vanassche & Kelchtermans, 2014) is then best understood as a process of becoming.

InFo-TED is rooted in this process and desires to build and strengthen in a sustainable way the work and professional development of teacher educators globally. It aims to serve as a forum and community of practice for building a research-based understanding of what teacher educators know and how that knowledge may be conceptualized and made public as well as actively supported and developed.

DEVELOPING A CONCEPTUAL MODEL

In the preceding section, we presented a short history and rationale for establishing InFo-TED. Among the first activities we carried out in the InFo-TED community was developing a conceptual model that describes how we see teacher educators' professional development. We developed this conceptual model with a twofold purpose: On the one hand, to provide a map to explain the object of our interest – which is teacher educators' professional development; and, on the other hand, to provide a common language to frame the issue of teacher educator professional development – a necessity given the diversity in teacher educators' work globally and our need to communicate with and understand one another. At the same time, we are very much aware that in this mapping and choosing of a language, we take a stance and that stance implies normative, political, and professional choices. Yet, the purpose of our conceptual developmental work is primarily descriptive and communicative. Hence, our model should NOT be read or understood as a normative blueprint (Kelchtermans, 2013). On the contrary, with our conceptual model, we react against mainstream "blueprint" approaches and plea for a "practice-based" approach (e.g., Kelchtermans et al., 2015; for a fuller elaboration of this point as well as of the model itself). Fig. 1 presents this conceptual model. It is our attempt to visualize what we understand about teacher educators' professional development. The core elements and assumptions of our conceptual model are presented at the right side of Fig. 1. In our opinion, the starting point for the professional development of teacher educators has to be their practice. This is what we mean by a practice-based approach (Kelchtermans, 2013). Our assumption is that acting teacher educators have good reasons for doing their job in the way they are doing it. This practice-based approach – as contrary to the blueprint approach – starts from a positive appreciation of the practice in which teacher educators "enact" their expertise. As InFo-TED, we do not want to compare individual teacher educators with a norm, fixed standards, or a list of competencies. The practice-based approach that we support starts with the idea that a teacher educator's actual practices reveal "who" a teacher educator is, and what s/he really stands for. Such a position implies that the professional actions and decisions teacher educators undertake are professional messages, for, as Russell (1997) writes: "How I teach is the message." In our understanding of research and our own experience in the field, we understand that such messages are reflections of a teacher educator's professional stance and likely to include

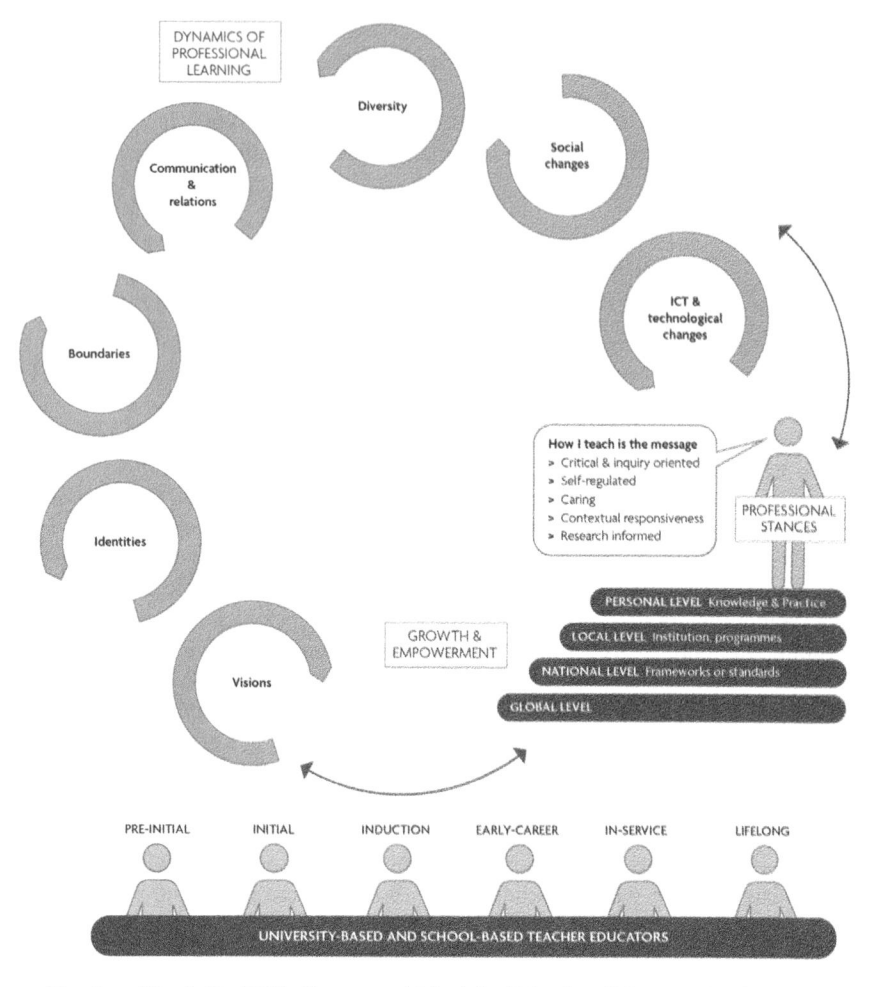

Fig. 1. The InFo-TED Conceptual Model of Teacher Educator Professional Development (e.g., Kelchtermans et al., 2015).

being critical and inquiry-oriented, self-regulated, contextually responsive, and research-informed.

In the InFo-TED conceptual model, teacher educators' practices are situated in the concrete context of the local teacher education institute and/or in the national or regional policy context. The local level refers to, for instance, the culture of the teacher education institute, the existing teacher education programs, or teacher education curricula. This level can also refer to relations with placement schools or other partnerships. The national level refers to national policy measurements, existing frameworks, or standards for teacher educators.

Finally, teacher educators' practices are situated in a global level stressing their relation with supranational and societal change.

As a next step in developing our model, we situated these messages in what we called "dynamics of professional learning." These are presented in the left-hand side of our model where we present a nonexhaustive list of possible content domains that we believe ought to be included in opportunities for teacher educators' professional development. These domains are related to, for instance, social and technological change, diversity in society, communication, and relations between teacher educators and different stakeholders, the multiple identities teacher educators have (i.e., teacher of teachers, researcher, gatekeeper, broker; Lunenberg et al., 2014), and the broad visions teacher educators have about the nature and future of "good" education. Given our practice-based approach to teacher educators' professional development, we present these content domains as nonexhaustive, or, to put it differently, providing set parameters for these domains would imply a choice for a blueprint approach. Under the circles in Fig. 1, our conceptual model further contains a continuum. It reminds us that thinking about teacher educators' professional development means thinking broadly about teacher educators as both university-based and school-based. This arrow prompts an inclusive definition of teacher educators (e.g., European Commission, 2013) encompassing a wide spectrum of positions in the educational system and field and implies that we are aware that teacher educators enter the profession with different backgrounds. Some, for example, enter having worked as teachers, some as researchers with or without a PhD, and others may come from a variety of education-related roles. At the same time, the continuum implies that we stress the importance of thinking of teacher educators' practice and professional development as situated in a temporal context that recognizes that teacher educators enter the profession at different moments in their careers with different experiences and different learning needs.

To conclude, the conceptual model of InFo-TED that we have developed illustrates that our starting point for teacher educators' professional development should lie in teacher educators' lived practice. With our conceptual model we take a stance against a blueprint approach that would attempt to identify as well as assess professionalism via an exhaustive list of standards or competencies (knowledge, attitudes, and skills) that teacher educators need to have in order to rightfully consider themselves to be "professional." Contrary to this approach, the InFo-TED conceptual model starts from a full appreciation of the work teacher educators are doing and of the way they are doing it: their enacted practice.

In the next section, we present three cases that describe how teacher educators' professional development is organized in three different countries: Flanders (Belgium), Ireland, and Norway. By presenting these country cases, it becomes clear that who teacher educators are differs from country to country, inevitably implying that professional development activities, initiatives, and structures are likely to differ from country to country. As such, the presentation of the three country cases illustrates the need to develop a conceptual model of teacher educators' professional development – a tool to map the professional development of teacher educators and a common language to frame this issue.

MAPPING THE TERRAIN: TEACHER EDUCATOR DEVELOPMENT IN DIFFERENT NATIONAL CONTEXTS

The Professional Development of Flemish Teacher Educators: A Lonely Enterprise?

Flemish teacher education in 2015 is framed by the 2006 Decree on Teacher Education that was the culmination of debates that began in 1989 about the reform of teacher education. These debates began when Belgium became a federalized state and the Flemish government received full authority for educational policy in Flanders. The 2006 Decree (re-)organized initial teacher education into two types of programs, both of which result in the same teaching certificate, but are provided by different institutes each aiming at particular student teacher populations. First, the Decree describes "integrated programs" provided by Colleges of Higher Education, which combine extended internships in schools with general educational theory and subject matter knowledge. These programs result in the bachelor's degree in education (i.e., kindergarten, primary education, or lower secondary education). Second, so-called "specific programs" that can be taken either during an initial subject-oriented study at university as part of one's master's program or as a separate program at Centers for Adult Education. These programs are for candidates with relevant work experience who want to become teachers mainly in the practical training areas of vocational and technical secondary education. These different institutional contexts inevitably shape the staff positions of teacher educators working in these institutes – including their opportunities for professional development. For example, in contrast to research-intensive settings, Colleges of Higher Education and Centers of Adult Education have traditionally taken a much more utilitarian approach to knowledge and have not developed strong research agendas nor required staff to engage in research. Teacher educators working in these nonuniversity settings generally have not had opportunities to develop the necessary conceptual and methodological expertise to actively conduct research themselves, including research on their own practice as a means of their own professional development. In this respect, Flemish teacher educators' professional development has been a lonely enterprise.

Furthermore, teacher education in Flanders has not typically been an intentional career choice. Broadly speaking, three pathways typify the entry of Flemish teacher educators into the profession: (1) successful classroom teachers become teacher educators and focus for the most part on the practical training components; (2) subject specialists with an initial degree in a subject discipline (i.e., science, mathematics) enter teacher education often without having taught in elementary or secondary schools for extended periods of time themselves; and (3) so-called "general educationalists" with master's degrees in educational sciences enter but generally have limited practical teaching experience.[2] Clearly, the work of educating teachers was generally not thought of as requiring any specific expertise or preparation and, in the absence of any organized induction or continuing professional development measures, these entry pathways have had an enormous impact on teacher educators' understanding of their new role as well as the knowledge they bring to the profession.

Frustrated with this situation and inspired by various forms of practitioner research, several Flemish regional teacher education consortiums started organizing small scale, ad hoc initiatives – but nevertheless systematic professional development trajectories for Flemish teacher educators – often in close collaboration with universities. In 2008, for example, the University of Leuven collaborated with the School of Education[3] on a two-year professional development project in which six experienced teacher educators from different institutes (one university-based program, one Centre for Adult Education, and three Colleges of Higher Education) conducted research on their own practices using the S-STEP approach (Vanassche & Kelchtermans, 2015a). This was the first enactment of the S-STEP approach in Flanders and its pedagogical rationale and outcomes have been subjected to rigorous research (e.g., Vanassche & Kelchtermans, 2015b).

Building on these understandings, a second and more recent example involves the organization and implementation of a seven-month "Masterclass" for teacher educators on practitioner research. This project is funded by the Expertise network AUGent,[4] and involves a collaboration between a College of Higher Education, a Centre of Adult Education, and a University with a shared interest in improving teacher educators' professional development. A central goal of the Masterclass is understanding and meaningfully conceptualizing teacher educators' professional development as the development of a research-oriented disposition (Tack & Vanderlinde, 2014). At the start of the project (2013–2014), 16 teacher educators from two different teacher education programs participated in this professional development experience using practitioner research. Currently (2014–2015), 30 teacher educators at work in eight different teacher education programs are taking part in this Masterclass.

Underpinning both projects is the idea that the active engagement of teacher educators in studying their own practice is a valuable approach not only to improve their own practice but also to inform the development of a public knowledge base of teacher education in Flanders and elsewhere (Cochran-Smith & Lytle, 2009; Hadar & Brody, 2012; Rust, 2009; Tack & Vanderlinde, 2014; Vanassche & Kelchtermans, 2015a). Embedded in this idea is recognition of teacher educators' professional autonomy and responsibility in (organizing) their own professional development. Clearly, the establishment and sustainability of such small-scale and local projects depends on the goodwill of the different stakeholders involved as well as the prolonged structural support that is implicit in the funding of these projects. The S-STEP research group in the first project, for example, did not continue its activities after 2010 when the funding which was used to "buy out" research time (i.e., 10% or four hours a week) from the teacher educators' daily job to participate in this project ended. However, a major benefit of the small-scale and local character of these projects and others is the opportunity to acknowledge and give central place to the contextualized nature of teacher educators' work and development. Both projects clearly illustrate how teacher educators' individual experiences, questions, commitments, or professional development always need to be interpreted and understood against the background of the working conditions in the teacher education institute. They highlight the fact that the context in which teacher educators work and develop matters.

The different institutes, in which Flemish teachers are educated as well as teacher educators' professional identities, different student teacher populations, teacher education curricula, and program structures – all clearly influence teacher educators' understanding of their work and professional development and these factors are increasingly receiving attention in Flemish policy circles. Recently, for example, as part of a large-scale evaluation study funded by the Flemish government to evaluate the implementation of the 2006 Decree on Teacher Education (EVALO, 2012), six policy groups were initiated to discuss possible improvements of our Flemish teacher education. One of these policy groups had an explicit focus on teacher educators. This group discussed whether organizing formal initiatives on teacher educators' induction and ongoing professional development might be desirable and questioned how such initiatives might be implemented.

The Flemish case suggests that if teacher education is to improve, it is essential to acknowledge and commit to the understanding that educating teachers cannot be ad hoc, that it requires specific expertise and nurturing of that expertise, and that the context of teacher educators' work must be central to their professional education and support (there cannot be a "blueprint" approach to teacher educator professional development).

The Professional Pathways of Teacher Educators in Ireland: New Opportunities to Prepare for Work in Teacher Education?

Teacher education in Ireland has been significantly reconfigured over the last decade due to a number of factors. First among these was the establishment of the Teaching Council (professional regulatory body) in 2006. Second, in response to a marked drop in reading literacy scores among 15-year-olds as measured in PISA 2009 (Department of Education & Skills [DES], 2011; i.e., a drop from 5th in 2000 to 21st in 2009), was the issuing of new guidelines for all teacher education programs (Teaching Council, 2011a, 2011b) and, as Conway and Murphy (2013) point out, the redesign since then of all initial teacher education programs. Third, as part of wider rationalization of higher education, was a review and subsequent initiation of radical restructuring of the way in which teacher education is made available in Ireland (Hyland, 2012; Sahlberg et al., 2012). The key point with regard to teacher education in Ireland is that, while teacher education has become a policy priority in the last decade, the professional preparation of those working in teacher education has not been a policy focus per se, and the multiple professional pathways into the work of teacher education has remained similar to a historic pattern of entry by two different groups: a minority of early starters typically with strong research backgrounds and possibly some experience teaching in schools, and a mid-career entry for the majority with professional practice in schools. However, with the recent and ongoing Government initiated restructuring and system rationalization, the goal of which is to reduce the number of teacher education providers from 19 to 6, and to concentrate teacher education in these six sites as centers of excellence, there have been inevitable implications for the status, work, and future professional preparation of those working in teacher education.

As a case in point, as this section of the chapter was being written, a strike was being called for by teacher educators in one small dedicated college for post-primary home economics teachers. The background of this strike call had to do with the way in which the new policies were being interpreted relative to the formation of the six centers of excellence. In keeping with the proposed amalgamation of a teacher education college program with a university into a teacher education center of excellence (as recommended by the Sahlberg Report (2012) and accepted by the Higher Education Authority), it is proposed that all the teacher educators from the colleges (here, read the home economics college) should be re-titled "university teachers" thereby losing their "university lecturer" title and their academic research status in one fell swoop. However, those already working as teacher educators in the university will retain their status as "university lecturers." This single case of a call for a strike illustrates a number of tensions in relation to the professional preparation of teacher educators in Ireland, tensions that are especially acute in a context of increased rankings pressures on universities. In the university involved here, there was concern that the university's research score would be lowered by the inclusion of the 60 staff members from the home economics college whose considerable professional practice expertise was perceived to be not strong enough to outweigh their lack of research outputs. While a significant number of the teacher educators in the home economics college do have PhDs as well as research publications, the majority of those being transferred have followed the dominant professional pathway in which professional experience as teachers along with a master's degree is the typical entry profile for new full-time teacher educators.

Although the calling of a strike in this case has not been typical of how the current restructuring is unfolding in Ireland, it starkly illustrates the implications of differing entry points and professional preparation pathways for the work of teacher education – especially when, as recommended by the Sahlberg Report (2012), teacher education is increasingly seen as optimal in a university setting. It further suggests that despite the current policy focus on the quality of initial teacher education program provision, there has been a relative lack of focus on professional learning for teacher educators as evidenced in the early 2000s review of primary teacher education (Kellaghan, 2002) as well as in post-primary teacher education (Byrne, 2002). As such, the prioritization of teacher education in the last decade and even more so in the last five years is evident in the significant Teaching Council prioritization of a labor-intensive accreditation of all initial teacher education programs in the country since the publication of binding national initial teacher education regulations by the Council in 2011.

In conclusion, there are a number of key points in the case of Ireland. First, like the Flemish case described earlier, entry into teacher education is most likely a mid-career opportunity. Second, given mid-career entry for most teacher educators, there are ensuing implications for the potential opportunities to learn to be a teacher educator. Third, the joint influence of the more complete universitization of teacher education recommended in the recent Sahlberg Report (2012) along with increased rankings pressure on universities has meant that there is more pressure on teacher education academics as they work in higher educational institutions to acquire a PhD and publish in peer-reviewed research outlets. Fourth, in the absence of particular required qualifications for work in teacher education, most teacher educators look to doctoral study in jurisdictions other than their workplaces (the United Kingdom, the United States typically) and other higher education institutions in Ireland. Fifth, the increasing diversity of the school system (Heinz, 2008) and attention to the complexity of schooling and how best to re-imagine teacher education (Waldron & Smith, 2012), with attendant implications for the professional preparation of teacher educators, has led to an emphasis on the up-skilling of staff (especially part-time teacher educators who are often retired teachers – a point noted in the Sahlberg Report) to meet the demands of the current policy focus on inquiry-oriented teacher education program provision. Sixth, this upskilling has, since early 2000, seen increasing involvement of teacher educators in self-study (e.g., Farren, 2005; MacPhail, 2014), and, since the 1998 Good Friday Peace Agreement, in a vibrant cross-border network of teacher educators (Standing Conference on Teacher Education North and South or SCoTENS) (Furlong et al., 2011).

NAFOL, A Dream Comes True

NAFOL (Norwegian Research School of Teacher Education), is the story about how a dream of making a change, a dream of moving teacher education in Norway from a seminar level into a research-active, dynamic, academic field, is coming true.

To understand why we Norwegians started to dream, some background information might be useful. Norway has a population of about five million people spread out in a long country with a coastline of 100,915 km. This explains why, per today, the country has 30 teacher education institutions in university colleges and universities. Many of the university colleges are too small to develop a strong research agenda on their own. However, they play an important role with regard to Norway's policy to keep remote districts alive and each region self-sufficient with qualified teachers. Another incentive for our dream was a shocking report published in 2004 by the Norwegian Research Council (NFR, 2004) in which Norwegian educational research was harshly criticized. The authors of the report challenged the higher educational institutions to strengthen efforts around key five areas: (1) research leadership and organization, (2) internationalization, (3) thematic efforts and prioritization, (4) recruitment, and (5) national coordination and cooperation.

Furthermore, a White Paper from the parliament, Will to Research (White paper 20, 2004–2005), suggested that national graduate schools should be created with the purpose of strengthening quality and increasing the doctoral completion rate in universities offering advanced education. As a follow-up, in 2009, a new White paper, The Teacher, the Role, and the Education (White paper 11, 2008–2009), stated that national doctoral schools were to be established to empower teacher educators' research and development. Within this context, the dream about NAFOL developed. It was presented to the National Council for Teacher Education which strongly recommended it to the government, and, after a year of planning, NAFOL was launched in 2010 as a national doctoral school for teacher education.

What Does NAFOL Offer?
NAFOL is a research school providing additional support to teacher educators engaging in doctoral studies. It is part of Norwegian educational research policy to transform a practice-based teacher education into research-informed teacher education. Nearly all of the country's relevant teacher education institutes have established a network which forms NAFOL, and they provide funding for four years to teacher educators' doctoral studies. Each student has to be accepted into a doctoral program at one of the universities or one of the few university colleges offering doctoral education. When accepted into a regular doctoral program, they can then apply to NAFOL to receive extra support, supervision, and beyond that, belong to a cohort of doctoral students from all over the wide-spread country. The cohort meets four times for two days per year during the four-year period NAFOL offers support, which means that NAFOL administrates 16 seminars (four for each cohort currently in the program) every year. Each cohort will have 16 seminars within the four-year period dealing with themes such as academic writing, methodology, communicating research, theory of teacher education, and subject didactic research. The theme leaders are prominent national and international teacher educator researchers and theoreticians. However, the heart of the seminars is the feedback sessions where the students present texts from their doctoral work to a small group of peers and a national and international senior researcher for the purposes of getting feedback on work in progress. NAFOL works strongly to pull the doctoral students out of isolation, and to avoid writing a full thesis based on feedback from only one's supervisor(s). Two times during the four years each cohort participates in NAFOL initiated seminars abroad with professors and their doctoral students from a foreign university, to enable students to create international networks, and to discuss the doctoral work with international voices. NAFOL also supports study periods abroad, and two international conferences per year for the students if peer-reviewed presentations are accepted. In addition, NAFOL financially supports PhD courses offered by the network institutions, and pays for NAFOL students' travel, accommodation, and fees to attend these courses. The idea is to encourage all NAFOL's network institutions to stretch beyond initial teacher education. NAFOL acknowledges the importance of quality supervision in

doctoral education and therefore organizes two seminars per year for supervisors of the doctoral students.

However, not all teacher educators want to engage in doctoral studies, yet, they are still working within a teacher education system in which an attitude of inquiry and publications are expected. Thus, NAFOL offers three seminars per year for teacher educators who want to develop their practical expertise informed by self-studies, action research projects, and curriculum development. This alternative leads to a broader qualification, called 1st lecturer (førstelektor). These teacher educators can also participate, if they wish, in NAFOL's PhD supported doctoral courses, and during the seminars they are invited to present texts for feedback from peers and professors.

Current Status

The original plan approved by the Norwegian Research Council in 2010 granted funding for four cohorts of 20 students (altogether 80 teacher educators) during the four years from 2010 to 2016 (the last cohort would then be accepted in 2013 to graduate by the end of 2016). However, things developed beyond our expectations due to an extremely positive mid-project international evaluation, an increasingly positive reputation around Norway's education system, and a policy shift that will, beginning in 2017, situate all teacher education at the master's level (i.e., research-based master's degree). This requires teacher educators with research competence to supervise master's theses. As a result, NAFOL's project period has been extended and fully funded until the end of 2019, and the number of cohorts yearly has grown to six. Each cohort has about 20 students (some cohorts are bigger). Two cohorts have already graduated. By 2019, we anticipate that NAFOL has supported around 160 teacher educators in the completion of their doctoral degree. That is, we believe, a significant number in a country of 5 million people. We fully anticipate that Norway's remarkable investment in teacher educators and their professional development will lead to a substantial enhancement of Norwegian research in, on, and with teacher education.

Innovation and Challenges

In Norway, an innovative aspect of NAFOL is the double aim of the research school to scaffold doctoral work and to support practicing teacher educators in developing an identity as researchers. The dialogue between the two levels is strengthened through networks formed by the students as they become integrated in national and international communities of researchers. Being systematic, yet dynamic in structure, and sensitive to the needs of the students and the society, NAFOL presents an innovative concept of doctoral studies in which students' voices are integral to shaping the doctoral program.

The impact of the graduate school is under constant evaluation with one of the most important factors being how many students will complete their doctorates (PhD programs). So far, the results from the two graduated cohorts (cohort 2010 and cohort 2011) show that the majority of students have graduated or are in the process of completing their doctoral work. Another outcome indicator is the number of publications by NAFOL students in peer-reviewed national and international journals. Here, too, we see a sign of success as the list is impressive. So is the number of presentations by NAFOL students at international conferences. However, by the end of the day, the main question we need to seek answers to is whether the quality of Norwegian teacher education has improved and whether there will be concomitant improvement in Norwegian education and schools become a better place for students. This question cannot yet be answered by counting numbers of PhDs in teacher education or by lists of publications. So, we in NAFOL still dream about improving education, and NAFOL is, for us, a means on the way to make the dream come true.

CONCLUSION AND DISCUSSION

This chapter constitutes a report on Info-TED's commitment to create a shared language for teaching about teaching that demonstrates and makes public (i.e., opens up for critical debate) the richness of the professional expertise that it aims to describe. As a network of experienced teacher educator researchers embarking on this commitment, we have taken the stance that the work of educating teachers requires a distinct professional repertoire as well as a distinct understanding of oneself as a teacher educator. We envisioned our role as very much like that of a broker as defined by Lunenberg et al. (2014) in their extensive review of teacher educators' professional roles: actively sustaining dialogue across different institutional contexts and across policy, research, and practice, as well as creating a shared vision and approach concerning teacher educator development. Embedded in this commitment are several issues or concerns that are clearly illustrated in the country cases, and which will need to be dealt with on the level of policy, practice, and research.

To conclude this chapter, we have formulated these issues as a series of questions that can be read both as guiding questions for building a research program on teacher educator development and which can serve as "touchstones" for the development of policies regarding teacher educator professional development as well as initiatives and induction programs.

First, how can we conceptualize and meaningfully support processes of professional development that serve to improve action as well as help teacher educators to develop a refined understanding of personal beliefs and their impact on practice? Underpinning our conceptual model is an understanding of teacher education as a "pedagogical" practice in which the central goal is to "educate" a future generation of teachers who have been entrusted to us as teacher educators. Therefore, the work of educating teachers inevitably implies normative choices that, as the Ireland case suggests, potentially involve political consequences. Hence, teacher educator development cannot suffice with the upscaling of instrumental knowledge (i.e., "how to"-questions: how to teach; identifying the most effective approaches); professional learning and development must also address "what"-questions (i.e., selecting curriculum materials), "why"-questions (i.e., defining goals and purposes), and "who"-questions (i.e., expertise and professional responsibility of teacher educators) (Kelchtermans, 2012). This was clearly illustrated in, for example, the Flemish case in which it was found that the professional value for teacher educators actively conducting research on their own practices and in their own institutes hinges on the ways in which this process influences one's personal beliefs and assumptions.

Second, who is to be served by research conducted by teacher educators on teacher education and, following from this, what are the necessary methodological qualities of the research conducted by teacher educators? Looking across the country cases, the answer seems to lie in conceptualizing teacher educator development as a process of inquiry (or teacher educators becoming active scholars as the result of professional development processes). If our interpretation is correct, the cases fit in nicely with the broader research literature (e.g., Cochran-Smith & Donnell, 2006). Yet, as the cases of Flanders and Ireland demonstrate, there are different understandings of research operating in these cases that clearly intersect with differing research paradigms among teacher educators at different levels across institutional contexts. What these cases highlight is a tension between relevance and rigor (e.g., Vanassche & Kelchtermans, 2015a) and associated decisions about data collection and analysis as well as knowledge outcomes: Moving too far to the side of relevance produces research that could open up new understandings for the individual teacher educator in his/her local context, but its value does not reach beyond that context. Moving too far to the side of rigor may result in concessions to methodological issues that steer the teacher educator away from the concern that triggered his/her interest to begin with and eventually leave the teacher educator without any real benefit from his/her efforts. The question then relates to where on the continuum studies deemed most valuable in moving both teacher education practice and research might be placed. Here the case of Norway may be instructive.

Third, how are teacher educators' understandings of their roles as teacher educators, as well as their development, shaped by the contexts in which they enact their expertise? Teacher education across the globe is organized in a wide range of programmatic, curricular, and institutional models. This contextual situatedness inevitably influences teacher educators' understanding of their work and professional selves as well as their (opportunities for) professional development. Adding an additional layer to this already complex situation is the body of research that indicates that the micro communities of practice within these already diverse organizational and institutional settings are central shaping forces in teacher educators' work lives and development (Murray, 2005, 2008). There is clear evidence in the three country cases that the organizational and institutional contexts in which teacher educators enact their practice matters. This understanding is neither new, nor ground-breaking. Yet, it is absolutely vital for teacher educators themselves to become aware of the organizational and institutional working conditions in which they enact their practice (and the affordances and constraints offered by these working conditions) as well as for educational researchers to develop the theoretical conceptual tools to tap into the mediating role of context in teacher educators' work lives and development.

As a consequence, in building a knowledge base for teaching about teaching (including the education of teacher educators) it is necessary to combine theories of professional learning and development – which traditionally take the individual (or the team) as the focus of attention – with "systematic" or institutional frameworks that allow for a more refined conceptualization of the working conditions in teacher education institutes and the ways in which these conditions interact with teacher educators' personal understandings of their work (e.g., Kelchtermans, 2012). In our plea for a practice-based approach with an emphasis on actual teacher education practices for conceiving of teacher educator professionalism and development, we have tried to operationalize this contextualized character of teacher education in a manner in which teacher educators globally can identify and instantiate.

NOTES

1. See http://www.mofet.macam.ac.il/eng/about/Pages/default.aspx for MOFET's mission statement and core practices.
2. This illustrates the fact that having a teaching certificate is legally not required for teaching in Flemish teacher education.
3. The School of Education is a regional consortium of 15 Flemish teacher education programs and provides a structural platform for collaboration between five Colleges of Higher Education, nine Centers for Adult Education, and the KU Leuven.
4. The Expertise network AUGent is a regional consortium of nine Flemish teacher education programs and provides a structural platform for collaboration between three Colleges of Higher Education, five Centers for Adult Education, and Ghent University.

REFERENCES

Ball, D. L., & Cohen, D. K. (1999). Developing practice, developing practitioners: Toward a practice-based theory of professional education. In G. Sykes & L. Darling-Hammond (Eds.), *Teaching as the learning profession: Handbook of policy and practice* (pp. 3–32). Jossey Bass.

Ben-Peretz, M., Kleeman, S., Reichenberg, R., & Shimoni, S. (2011). Educators of educators: Their goals, perceptions and practices. In T. Bales, A. Swennen, & K. Jones (Eds.), *The professional development of teacher educators* (pp. 119–137). Springer.

Berry, A. (2007). *Tensions in teaching about teaching: Developing practice as a teacher educator.* Springer.

Byrne, K. (2002). *Advisory group on post-primary teacher education.* Department of Education and Skills.

Cochran-Smith, M., & Donnell, K. (2006). Practitioner inquiry: Blurring the boundaries of research and practice. In J. Green, G. Camilli, & P. B. Elmore (Eds.), *Handbook of complementary methods in education research* (pp. 503–518). Lawrence Erlbaum.

Cochran-Smith, M., & Lytle, S. (2009). *Inquiry as stance. Practitioner research for the next generation.* Teacher College Press.

Conway, P. F., & Murphy, R. (2013). A rising tide meets a perfect storm: New accountabilities in teaching and teacher education in Ireland. *Irish Educational Studies, 32*(1), 11–36.

Davey, R. (2013). *The professional identity of teacher educators. Career on the cusp?* Routledge.

Department of Education and Skills. (2011). *Literacy and numeracy for learning and life: The national strategy to improve literacy and numeracy among children and young people 2011–2020.* Department of Education and Skills.

Dinkelman, T., Margolis, J., & Sikkenga, K. (2006). From teacher to teacher educator: Reframing knowledge in practice. *Studying Teacher Education: A Journal of Self-Study of Teacher Education Practices, 2*(2), 119–136.

Ducharme, E. R. (1986). *Teacher educators: What do we know?* ERIC Clearinghouse on Teacher Education.

European Commission. (2012). *Supporting the teaching professions for better learning outcomes.* Commission Staff Working Document 374. European Commission.

European Commission. (2013). *Supporting teacher educators for better learning outcomes.* European Commission.

EVALO. (2012). *Als het krijtstof neerdaalt ... Een bijdrage aan de beleidsevaluatie van de lerarenopleidingen in Vlaanderen [When the chalk dust settles. A contribution to policy regarding evaluation of teacher education in Flanders].* Bestuurlijke samenvatting.

Farren, M. (2005). *How can I create a pedagogy of the unique through a web of betweenness.* Unpublished dissertation, University of Bath.

Furlong, J., Pendry, A., & Mertova, P. (2011). *SCoTENS: An evaluation of the first 8 years.* Department of Educational Studies.

Grossman, P. (2005). Research on pedagogical approaches in teacher education. In M. Cochran-Smith & K. Zeichner (Eds.), *Studying teacher education* (pp. 425–476). Lawrence Erlbaum.

Hadar, L., & Brody, D. (2012). The interaction between group process and personal professional trajectories in a professional development community for teacher educators. *Journal of Teacher Education, 62*(2), 145–161.

Heinz, M. (2008). The composition of applicants and entrants to teacher education programmes in Ireland: Trends and patterns. *Irish Educational Studies, 27,* 223–240.

Hyland, A. (2012). A review of the structure of teacher education provision in Ireland: A paper for the international review team. *Higher Education Authority.* www.hea.ie/files/AineHyland FinalReport.pdf

Kelchtermans, G. (2012). Dilemmas, theory, pedagogy, and learning in teachers' work lives. *Teachers and Teaching. Theory and Practice, 19*(1), 1–3.

Kelchtermans, G. (2013). Praktijk in plaats van blauwdruk. Over het opleiden van lerareno- pleiders [Practice instead of blueprint. Educating teacher educators]. *Tijdschrift voor Lerarenopleiders, 34,* 89–99.

Kelchtermans, G., Smith, K., & Vanderlinde, R. (2015). Towards an 'international forum for teacher educator development': An agenda for research and action. *European Journal of Teacher Education, 41*(1), 120–134. https://doi.org/10.1080/02619768.2017.1372743

Kellaghan, T. (2002). *Preparing teachers for the 21st century: Report of the working group on primary preservice teacher education.* Department of Education and Skills.

Lanier, J. E., & Little, J. W. (1986). Research on teacher education. In M. C. Wittrock (Ed.), *Handbook of research on teaching* (3rd ed., pp. 527–569). MacMillan Publishing.

Loughran, J. J. (2007). *Developing a pedagogy of teacher education. Understanding teaching and learning about teaching.* Routledge.

Loughran, J. J. (2014). Professionally developing as a teacher educator. *Journal of Teacher Education, 65,* 1–13.

Loughran, J. J., Hamilton, M. L., LaBoskey, V. K., & Russell, T. L. (Eds.). (2004). *International handbook of self-study of teaching and teacher education practices.* Kluwer Academic Publishers.

Lunenberg, M., Dengerink, J., & Korthagen, F. (2014). *The professional teacher educator: Professional roles, behavior and development of teacher educators.* Sense Publishers.

MacPhail, A. (2014). Becoming a teacher educator: Legitimate participation and the reflexivity of being situated. In A. Owens & T. Fletcher (Eds.), *Self-study in physical education teacher education* (pp. 47–62). Springer.

Murray, J. (2005). Re-addressing the priorities: New teacher educators and induction into higher education. *European Journal of Teacher Education, 28*(2), 67–85.

Murray, J. (2008). Towards the re-articulation of the work of teacher educators in higher education institutions in England. *European Journal of Teacher Education, 31,* 17–34.

Murray, J., & Male, T. (2005). Becoming a teacher educator: Evidence from the field. *Teaching and Teacher Education, 21,* 125–142.

Norwegian Research Council. (2004). *Norwegian pedagogical research. An evaluation of research from selected universities and university colleges*. Norwegian Research Council.

Russell, T. L. (1997). Teaching teachers: How I teach is the message. In J. J. Loughran & T. L. Russell (Eds.), *Teaching about teaching: Purpose, passion and pedagogy in teacher education* (pp. 32–47). Falmer.

Rust, F. O. C. (2009). Teacher research and the problem of practice. *Teachers College Record, 111*(8), 1882–1893.

Sahlberg, P., Furlong, J., & Munn, P. (2012). *Report of the international review panel on the structure of initial teacher education provision in Ireland: Review conducted on behalf of the department of education and skills*. Higher Education Authority of Ireland.

Shulman, L. S. (1986). Those who understand: Knowledge growth in teaching. *Educational Researcher, 15*, 4–14.

Shulman, L. S. (1987). Knowledge and teaching: Foundations of the new reform. *Harvard Educational Review, 57*, 1–21.

Smith, K. (2011). The multi-faceted teacher educator – A Norwegian perspective. *Journal of Education for Teaching, 37*(3), 337–349.

Swennen, A., Jones, K., & Volman, M. (2010). Teacher educators: Their identities, sub-identities and implications for professional development. *Professional Development in Education, 36*(1–2), 245–262.

Tack, H., & Vanderlinde, R. (2014). Teacher educators' professional development: Towards a typology of teacher educators' researcherly disposition. *British Journal of Educational Studies, 62*(3), 297–315.

Teaching Council. (2011a). *Initial teacher education: Criteria and guidelines for programme provider*.

Teaching Council. (2011b). *Initial teacher education: Strategy for the review and professional accreditation of existing programmes*.

Vanassche, E. (2014). *(Re)constructing teacher educators' professionalism: Biography, work-place and pedagogy*. University of Leuven.

Vanassche, E., & Kelchtermans, G. (2014). Teacher educators' professionalism in practice: Positioning theory and personal interpretative framework. *Teaching and Teacher Education, 44*, 117–127.

Vanassche, E., & Kelchtermans, G. (2015a). The state of the art in self-study of teacher educa-tion practices: A systematic review. *Journal of Curriculum Studies, 47*(4), 508–520.

Vanassche, E., & Kelchtermans, G. (2015b). Facilitating self-study of teacher education prac-tices: Toward a pedagogy of teacher educator professional development. *Professional Development in Education*.

Waldron, F., & Smith, J. (Eds.). (2012). *Re-imagining initial teacher education (ITE): Perspectives on transformation*. Liffey Press.

Zeichner, K. M. (2005). Becoming a teacher educator: A personal perspective. *Teaching and Teacher Education, 21*(2), 117–124.

Zeichner, K. M., & Conklin, H. G. (2005). Teacher education programs. In M. Cochran-Smith & K. M. Zeichner (Eds.), *Studying teacher education: The report of the AERA panel on research and teacher education* (pp. 645–735). Lawrence Erlbaum.

SECTION 5
PARTNERSHIPS

INTRODUCTION

Özge Hacıfazlıoğlu

The collection of five chapters shared in this section is a wonderful example of how international communities of practice have been created between and among ISATT members. ISATT has celebrated partnerships and collaborations for more than four decades through the regional and biennial conferences, which have provided ample opportunities for collaborations and partnerships among teachers and teacher educators. Although the stories of the teachers and teacher educators presented in each chapter have distinct qualities, they all share the common goal of revealing the power of synergistic relationships among researchers/authors/practitioners who are committed educators and members of the ISATT community.

The first chapter *Communities of Practice with Visiting Scholars* shares the accounts of scholars who served as visiting scholars at Leysin American School in Switzerland with the lead author Paul Magnuson, who has been the director of Leysin American School Educational Research Center, which opened its doors to visiting scholars all around the world. Stories of visiting scholars shared in this chapter highlight the value of connection and creating communities of practice for nurturing our souls.

The second chapter *Collaborative Reflection, Knowledge, and Growth: Exploring Ongoing Teacher Learning Within Knowledge Communities* focuses on experiences of the Portfolio Group that shows how teacher collaborative groups have the capacity to be safe spaces, where critical professional dialogue, reflective exchanges, and generous scholarship are cultivated. Based on two US-based knowledge communities (the Faculty Academy is the second one), Gayle Curtis and Michaelann Kelley provide snapshots of how longitudinal collaborations among teachers (Portfolio Group) and cross-institutional faculty members (Faculty Academy) enabled them to seek their best-loved selves (Schwab 1954/1978).

The third chapter is a rich example of a long-standing international collaboration among ISATT colleagues; Maria Assunção Flores from Portugal and her colleagues from Canada, Brazil, and the United States. The four-country study illuminates policies and practices in the post-Covid-19 period. The chapters reveal neoliberal approaches to policymaking and education, which ensure that the technicalities of teaching received heightened attention to the neglect of the well-being of teachers and the agency that they should be afforded them. In such an anxiety-ridden atmosphere, "turmoil and crisis" became the two critical words that described the overarching educational context, which are clearly illustrated in the media and in research.

The fourth chapter *International Forum on Teacher Education as an Educational Research Partnership Space* focuses on the development of the International Forum on Teacher Education (IFTE Conference) and its developing partnership with ISATT. The International Forum on Teacher Education, organized at Kazan Federal University, is an example of the ways in which conferences can offer unique spaces and platforms for partnerships to develop and transform. In the regional conference held at Kazan in the Russian Republic, ISATT members continued to build connections and partnerships with colleagues from widening parts of the world both to grow the research culture and to extend the scope of future ISATT biennial conferences.

ISATT members continued their scholarly work in spite of the challenges and barriers they encountered due to the unexpected Covid-19 circumstances. They continued to collaborate from distant places; they reflected deeply on their experiences and stayed connected as colleagues and friends. The fifth chapter, *Cultivating Teacher Resilience Through Intercultural Interaction and Collaboration,* reveals the stories of teachers working at international schools in Türkiye and the United States and shares accounts of how international teachers developed resilience in times of difficulty and uncertainty.

The chapters in this partnerships section are powerful exemplars of ISATT's approach to creating international communities of practice through embracing the goals of reciprocal mentoring, caring leadership, sustained teamwork, and ongoing collaboration in field-based inquiries.

COMMUNITIES OF PRACTICE WITH VISITING SCHOLARS

Paul J. Magnuson, Özge Hacıfazlıoğlu, Steven Carber and Rae Newman

ABSTRACT

A boarding school research center annually invites students, professors, and others to collaborate with faculty members, forming interconnected communities of practice. The authors interviewed visitors to determine how their experience contributed to their identity as a scholar and the extent to which they felt part of a community of practice. Categorizing emergent themes according to Wenger's (1998) categories of communities of practice, we identified six subthemes that characterize their experience. All participants valued their stay and expressed a desire to remain connected to the school, visiting scholars, and other people they met and now consider part of their network.

Keywords: Communities of practice; visiting scholars; high school; professional development; collaboration; networking

As teachers we are in a sense constantly building communities of learners at many levels, from students' paired work during a simple classroom activity to organized professional learning communities among faculties. Educators are often encouraged to make their schools learning organizations, which may sound odd to an outsider since what are schools if not learning organizations? Yet the sentiment makes sense to most educators, since many have perhaps experienced the creeping stagnation within a school that stops being a learning environment, where teachers may close their classroom doors, keep to themselves, and experience little professional talk in the teacher lounge. In fact, the structure of schooling may inadvertently contribute to the environment from being a non-learning one for teachers, as they are assigned to large classes and work on a packed schedule with little discretionary time. Further, teacher roles are defined by the hours spent teaching, which again may seem like common sense. Yet at a university level, it is clear that roles are defined more broadly, including, for example, research, networking, and further development of ideas.

A boarding school in Switzerland has over the last decade built the possibility for faculty members to engage, if they choose, in a learning environment that promotes and rewards involvement in academic scholarship related to teaching and learning. In the last six years, the activities of the school's faculty has been augmented by the development of a visiting scholar program, in which people from around the world stay at the school for an extended period of time to observe, collaborate, and work in the existing learning organization. The school promotes the program so that its teachers can rub shoulders with academics and connect with a steady stream of new ideas. In the process, the visiting scholars have come to learn that they, too, have much to learn from the school's teachers, and the resulting social and professional orbits have repeatedly coalesced into interesting and useful communities of practice.

Now, with an established record of success hosting visiting scholars and building the school's capacity for continuous professional development through collaboration, a deeper look at the experience of the visiting scholars is warranted. Defining the interaction of visiting scholars with each other and with the school's faculty members as communities of practice nicely describes an important aspect of the visiting scholar experience, both during and after their stay at the school.

CONTEXT AND BACKGROUND TO THE VISITING SCHOLAR PROGRAM

In an idyllic setting in a ski station in the Swiss Alps, 275 international students, aged 12 to 18, attend boarding school. The views from the classroom windows are magnificent and the opportunities for travel and winter sports are nothing short of amazing. Students study, ski, and tour Europe with friends from every corner of the world. The tagline on the school's original professional development website for its first in-house professional learning program was *Continually becoming the professionals we already are*. At the time, the research center didn't exist, though this first program remains one of several opportunities the research center now offers teachers. The idea at the time was to stop paying external experts to deliver one-shot professional development and to pay faculty members instead. Professional development changed from largely ineffective one-shot workshops to ongoing collaborative and classroom-based experiences. Thus, the school sent the message that faculty members were already professionals who should learn from and teach each other, who were worthy of being paid for their efforts, and that, although a boost from an outside source could be useful from time to time, the school's own teachers were the number one resource for professional expertise and school improvement.

Over the years, the number of programs and opportunities grew. A second program used classroom observations to inform teachers about the balance of teacher talk and student talk in their classes. The research center added professional development for the pedagogical use of technology, working with ESL students in mainstream classes, accommodating students with special needs, mindfulness, assessment, and more. Programs have come and gone depending on need, interest, and the availability of skilled lead teachers.

With the formal establishment of the center in 2013, the center's leader was given a boost in flexibility and credibility – and a generous operating budget. As was the case with the original program, when professional development funds were directed to the school's teachers instead of to outside experts, much of the budget was again directed to those faculty members who chose to be involved with the program. These teachers were called resident scholars. Resident scholars proposed year-long investigations into their own teaching or curriculum development, and if their projects were selected by school leadership, the resident scholar was paid a stipend and allocated a budget for expenses related to the project. In the early years resident scholars had to be recruited; five years into the program there were more applications than the budget could support, making the selection competitive and the overall quality of the projects arguably higher.

From resident scholars to visiting scholars was not a great jump. The school's first visiting scholar, a former international school administrator, interviewed faculty members and wrote about the IB program in Fall 2014. Simultaneously, he served as a proof of concept, and the visiting scholar program was launched the following academic year. The lure of a sabbatical in the Swiss Alps, coupled with free room and board for visitors, removed any major obstacles to begin receiving scholars from around the world. In 2019–2020, 20 visiting scholars collaborated on studies and articles, created curriculum, and offered return stays in their home countries, complete with school visits and conference presentations. In sum, the research center, having started with a single program for a handful of faculty members, had grown into what could be described, perhaps with just a little hyperbole, as a laboratory school or a small university functioning inside a grade 7–12 boarding school. Faculty members were teaching, of course, but also collaborating on research, traveling to present their work, and writing articles and book chapters, all while collaborating and networking with visiting scholars from around the world.

Loosely grouped by the type of activity, recent visiting scholars have participated in the following areas:

Curriculum projects: Design thinking, Linguistics, Place-based learning in the Alps, Simulations and Theater

Studies using LAS teachers and students as research participants: Cyber bullying, Pedagogical technology, Professional development observation tools, Translanguaging, and Robotics.

The small-town boarding school environment, with its wide range of activities stretching across the day with multiple shared meals in the cafeteria, brings people into the community very quickly. It's probably fair to say that visiting scholars are more or less "adopted" by faculty members into the school community. Those visiting scholars who stay multiple weeks or make more than one visit (many do) tend to make individual friendships and find collaborative partners that transcend any particular project. They soon have independent connections among our faculty members and, not uncommonly, in the town as well.

In the early years of the program, the school scrambled for participants. Five years in, the demand by visiting scholars to stay at the school began to require advance booking to ensure that no more than two or three visiting scholars were on campus at one time. Furthermore, since many visiting scholars wanted to return a second or third time, the growing pool of collaborators created greater demand each year.

Finally, the program brought many reciprocal opportunities, initially with the director of the research center, but increasingly with other faculty members as well. Faculty members have made informal exchanges with visiting scholars by traveling to England, Spain, Russia, Taiwan, Turkey, and the United States. It is expected that this wider community of practice will grow as collaborative projects continue and additional visiting scholars spend time on campus.

LITERATURE REVIEW

We first introduce communities of practice as a framework for understanding the social nature of engaging in practice, reflection, and continuous improvement. Then we look at the extent to which visiting scholars are welcomed at institutions of learning to potentially expand and join communities of practice. We find that hosting visiting scholars is a common practice at the university level, but much less common at the high school level, mostly due to the reward structure of the two types of institutions but also, of course, due to factors such as tradition, inertia, and available time.

Communities of Practice

Wenger (1998) and Wenger et al. (2002) emphasize the value of creating communities of practice in which each member of the community is engaged in social practice with others in the community, creating a continuous loop of learning among members. Active interaction and cooperation enable teachers to develop a sense of belonging to specific practices and they learn new ways to collaborate and to enact the practice itself. Therefore, in this double loop process (Argyris, 1991), teachers co-construct their identities as both learners and practitioners (Clark et al., 2021). As Olson and Clark (2009) and Painter and Clark (2015), relying on Wenger (1998), put it:

> ...people construct and develop their identities and transform their thinking through their active participation and engagement with others in cultural-historical practices that are situated in social communities. Thus, members of a community of practice interact, share, and

participate in the creation and re-creation of the practice and, through that engagement, develop, reify, and transform their identities (p. 217).

Wenger (1998) identifies four components of learning: "Meaning, practice, community and identity": (1) teachers and teacher educators talk about the *meaning* of their professional contexts, using reflection as a means of professional development; (2) teachers relate their views and experiences in the process of mutual engagement in actual *practice*, in which (3) teacher participation and commitment is recognizable as *community*. Finally, (4) teachers who are learning within communities of practice re-construct their *identity* as a teacher. This structure is based on social learning theory and provides the basis for establishing communities of practice in school settings. Each of the four interrelated components reinforces the others. This perspective is derived in an early study by Lave and Wenger (1991), underlying the importance of "shifting the analytic focus from the individual as learner to learning as participation in the social world" (p. 12).

Craig's recent study (2020) on knowledge communities in teacher education recounts the shared experiences of five teachers and teacher educators in which collaborative professional development laid the groundwork for teacher growth in practice, leadership, and careers. Based on Schwab's conceptualization of "best loved self," Craig and her colleagues' long-standing Portfolio Group serve as an example for knowledge communities that continually grow as they receive feedback from trusted friends and colleagues. As asserted by Clandinin et al. (1997), teachers are constantly growing as new knowledge and experience enrich their practical knowledge. From this perspective, the notion of communities of practice is based on reflective practices in which members are given the opportunity to self-reflect and reflect as a group through discussion of past experiences as they construct meaning for their present situations.

The research center creates a community of practice by hosting visiting scholars representing a broad spectrum of educators with different cultural backgrounds. The stories of visiting scholars, who range from individuals outside the field of education through graduate students and professors, highlight rarely seen perspectives on the journey of teaching. The Communities of Practice described in this study provide a safe and encouraging context for visiting scholars to reflect on their past experiences and articulate a conceptual synthesis of their own professional development.

Research and Teaching Priorities

The school's faculty members are generally rewarded for being good at teaching classes. Additional professional rewards involve leading sports and clubs, and shouldering the duties associated with residential life supervision. University faculty members are rewarded through a combination of successful teaching, research, and outreach (securing grants, presenting, and collaborating with others). While a high school's *raison d'être* is to teach course content, "knowledge creation, not just knowledge dissemination, is one of the fundamental roles of universities" (Rosowsky, 2020). Knowledge creation and outreach are in fact stressed to the point that they can at times overshadow teaching responsibilities at the university, since research and service, in addition to teaching, are usually part of tenure decisions (Harris, 2019).

Faculty exchanges between universities support the built-in reward system of higher education and are therefore a manner of creating and supporting communities of practice among faculty members. This is much less the case at the secondary level, where full teaching loads comprise an overwhelming majority of a teacher's responsibilities. In K-12 environments, engagement with research is something usually done in professional development programs (if at all), or through the individual initiative of teachers, often propelled by a desire to complete a graduate degree. Their reward is the prestige of the degree and perhaps a change in salary and, hopefully, greater satisfaction as a professional. There is usually no expectation, however, that teachers continue to do research at the school. In fact, there is little time for research in the context of a busy teaching and extracurricular schedule.

Exchanges Between Educational Institutions

It is not surprising, then, that there is limited literature about visiting scholars at the high school level, while there is plenty at the university level. Heinz and Lewis (2009) describe a program at the University of Colorado at Boulder that invited over 60 visiting scholars over a six-year period to support student learning. To support faculty members, Shimmi (2014) argues that networking strengthens scholarship through the sharing of ideas. Others emphasize the importance of exchanging scholars to gain greater international understanding (Bano, 2020; Farrell, 1978; Guo-Brennan & Wei, 2012; Zhang, 2016). Visiting scholar programs at the high school level are less common, though there are programs that support teacher exchanges (AFS in your country, n.d.).

Well-Developed Visiting Scholar Programs at the K-12 Level

There are a few more fully developed visiting scholar programs at the high school level that look more like their university counterparts. For example, Park School in Baltimore, Maryland has a well-established visiting scholar program for visitors in certain domains, namely artists, journalists, and writers. The program's aim is to bolster the student experience. In their own words, "visiting scholars meet with students for discussions and workshops, in large and small groups, revealing worlds of excitement and possibility beyond the classroom" (Visiting Scholars, n.d.). The program reaches out to its own alumni, at least in part, creating specialized communities of practice that include hands-on student workshops and presentations. The program at the Leysin American School is also robust, with a multiyear history and several completed and ongoing projects, publications, and collaborations (Educational Research, n.d.).

It is perhaps worthwhile to establish a working definition of visiting scholar, since we have introduced a few types and purposes of visiting scholars and exchange programs in both secondary and tertiary institutions. We define visiting scholars as individuals working in education or interested in education who are not employed by the host school but who visit it, often for an extended period, and who experience some degree of integration into the host community through the activities they are involved in while on site, whether teaching, writing, conducting research, developing curriculum, or some other pursuit. This study shares experiences of visiting scholars and the ways in which creating and being part of a community of practice shape their identity as scholars and teachers.

METHODOLOGY

Design

In this study, reports of experiences of visiting scholars, who have all spent time visiting the same high school, were analyzed using a phenomenological design qualitative research methodology. The goal of the study is to "illuminate the specific, to identify phenomena through how they are perceived by the actors in a situation" (Lester, 1999, p. 1). We selected 10 visiting scholars from the pool of all visiting scholars who visited the school in the last six years, deliberately choosing individuals with a variety of backgrounds and experiences. We then interviewed them about their experiences as visiting scholars.

Data Collection

We arranged remote, face-to-face interviews with former (and in one case, current) visiting scholars. Each prospective interviewee received an invitation letter explaining the research and listing the questions we intended to ask. Each interviewer followed a simple set of guiding questions as prompts, allowing the conversation to take its course after each prompt. Interviews lasted from 45 minutes to well over an hour. Interviews were recorded and transcribed and/or notes were taken during the interview. In one case, a participant with whom we had trouble setting an interview time sent responses to the question prompts by email.

Participants

Participants lived on campus for stays that ranged from several days to nearly two months, between Fall 2016 and Spring 2020. Participant ages range from their twenties to their sixties, and their backgrounds include small business owners, teachers, graduate students, and seasoned professors. They represent five nationalities (American, British, Icelandic, Russian, and Turkish) working in seven different countries (Australia, Finland, Iceland, Spain, Turkey, and the United States) (Table 1).

Their motivations to visit the school varied. One researcher prepared a specific study and collected data during her stay. Two individuals came to observe existing programs in which they were interested. Some visiting scholars came with no particular agenda other than completing their own work – a sabbatical, more

Table 1. Visiting Scholar Demographics.

	Position	Teaching Experience NA, New (1–5 years), Experienced	Home Institution	# of Stays at the School
1	Researcher	NA	MIT, USA	1
2	Professor	Experienced	University of Iceland	1
3	Professor	Experienced	University of Iceland	1
4	Consultant	Experienced	Self-employed, USA	5
5	Graduate Student	NA	City, University of London	1
6	Recent PhD holder	Experienced	In transition, maternity leave	3
7	Small business owner	Experienced	(name withheld for anonymity), Spain	1
8	Teacher	New	College de l'Humanité, Switzerland	1
9	PhD Candidate	Experienced	Adjunct Faculty, (name withheld for anonymity), Turkey	1
10	Researcher	Experienced	JAMK University of Applied Sciences, Finland	1

or less – but during their time on campus participated in curriculum writing, teaching, and program advising. Most visiting scholars in this study were only at the school once, though one made three visits and one made a total of five visits, the first visits as a paid consultant. They represented diverse fields, including teacher education, sociology, environmentalism, language instruction, alternative education, and economics.

Data Analysis

The interviews were first transcribed. Written transcripts of the responses to the semi-structured interviews were then color-coded by one of us, by reading each interview and highlighting themes that seemed most important to the interviewee. After coding all interviews, seven strong common themes emerged, which expanded to 12 after a second reading of all 10 transcripts, and which was then pared down to six by combining themes that were similar enough that it was difficult to delineate where a particular comment best fit. For example, while themes of having a "rewarding" stay and a "productive" stay were originally classified as separate categories, they were later merged. The iterative process of returning to previously coded interviews to add or combine themes helped form a summary of the visiting scholar experience, which is an amalgamation of all the experiences, though we also provide quotes and examples from specific visiting scholars. This is not to say that the experience is the same for all visiting scholars – that is not the case. But it does identify commonalities across most visiting scholars' experiences.

The first compilation of the emerging sub-themes was shared with the other researchers who had interviewed visiting scholars to check whether the amalgamated description of the visiting scholar experience corresponded to their impressions and notes from the interviews they had conducted. Comments from those researchers were integrated into the results. We then analyzed the extent to which the themes we discovered in the interviews fit in the framework proposed by Wenger, cross walking his four components: meaning, practice, community, and identity, with the themes – now more properly called subthemes, that we discovered in the interviews. As Wenger notes, the areas overlap and mutually support one another, so we were not surprised to see that, when mapped to Wenger's four areas, a single theme of ours could arguably fit in two, or even three or four, areas. It is perhaps easiest to see the relationships in a cross tabulation of Wenger's four areas of communities of practice and the six sub-themes that emerged in the analysis of the interviews of the visiting scholars. As mentioned, these components of communities of practice are not discrete and each reinforces the other.

FINDINGS: EXPERIENCES OF VISITING SCHOLARS

The communities of practice described in this study provided visiting scholars with opportunities to reflect on the process of co-creating communities of practice and on the content of their own interests and work while at the school. The 10 visiting scholars are earnest professionals, bound together by an interest in education and the physical setting of a boarding school in the Swiss Alps. They either sought a connection with the school or were recruited by the school, or, in one case, recruited by another visiting scholar. They came to the school with a general desire to share their expertise with the school's faculty members, whether through a particular agenda (i.e., a pre-arranged research study) or through presenting their fields and interests in classes or presentations. They also came prepared to learn from the school, though what they were going to learn might not have been apparent to them before they arrived. For example, visiting scholars with little international school exposure tended to comment more about the international nature of the school community and how its members interact. As one would expect, the business owner and the consultant focused on different learnings (school operations and new ways of thinking, respectively) than did those who worked on research and curriculum development, and the graduate students tended to be quite focused on their particular subjects of study, while others more readily adapted their learning to the context in which they found themselves. First-time visiting scholars seemed less likely to get deeply involved in ongoing projects and were more dependent on the directors of the center and visiting scholars on their third and fifth visits operated quite independently, leveraging friendships and working relationships that integrated them quite naturally into many different aspects of the school, both professionally and socially.

We identified six subthemes as common among the visiting scholars we interviewed. Each subtheme fits in one or more of Wenger's areas (Table 2).

We discuss the emergent sub themes in the context of each of Wenger's four components, which were predetermined in line with his notion of community of practice. Some subthemes appear in more than one of Wenger's components; we discuss the subtheme only the first time it appears but remind the reader that the subtheme is important in other components of Wenger's community of practice by including it after the relevant section header. Throughout, the voices of the visiting scholars can be heard across Wenger's components, as participants were encouraged to tell their stories in an illuminating and memorable way (Seidman, 1998). All quotations are from the transcripts but are not attributed to specific speakers.

Theme 1: Identity: Learning as Becoming

- Unsure of what to expect
- Personal growth and having a productive stay

Entering a new environment as an outsider for an extended period was a little uncomfortable for some of the visiting scholars. "I felt a little bit intimidated," admitted one visiting scholar, who also recommended that future visiting scholars "don't feel stressed and don't feel intimidated." Another expressed that he "was unsure what would be expected from me." Despite an orientation regarding expectations of the research center well before arrival, visiting scholars generally felt that they were supposed to give back to the school – a theme taken up further below – and often tried to plan more involvement than the director of the research center was looking for. The message to come to the school first and get familiar before contributing – or even the message of not having to contribute at all – was difficult for some visiting scholars to understand and they arrived feeling

Table 2. A Crosswalk of Communities of Practice and Emergent Themes in the Interviews.

Communities of Practice (Wenger, 1998)	Emergent Subthemes in the Interviews
Identity: learning as becoming	• Unsure of what to expect
	• Personal growth and having a productive stay
Practice: learning as doing	• Personal growth and having a productive stay
	• Specific takeaways and transfer of learning
Meaning: learning as experience	• Personal growth and having a productive stay
	• Specific takeaways and transfer of learning
	• Giving back to the school
Community: learning as belonging	• Feeling connected to the school
	• Networking

unsure of their role. One veteran visiting scholar recommended that first time visiting scholars take longer to understand the environment before beginning to collaborate, a luxury for those who have a long enough stay and for those who do not come with a specific project to accomplish with the school, for example a research study.

"Being there pushes me," reported the consultant, who had been at the school several times, referring to collaborative work she did with faculty members in language classes, the middle school, and with the school's assessment system. "It is a place to experiment" and it helped me "break down my own barriers," said another, who had recently received her masters' degree and was getting some initial experience in the classroom. "I did a lot" and "we were really productive" and the experience was a "massive accomplishment" were further responses, each from different individuals, about their time at the school.

"I was surprised how I could be alone, and I think the amazing view and the nature affected me a lot," said one professor. The sentiment about the natural setting was common to nearly all participants. From the lodging provided them, visiting scholars have a view across the valley to the next range of mountains, with beautiful sunrises and constantly changing light and clouds. The stunning setting may well play a role in the desire of visiting scholars to return – it may not just be the program and the various opportunities the school affords. However, the same scholar who felt the natural beauty affected her so much also reported that one of the school's faculty members took her work "to another level," meaning her curriculum project exceeded her own expectations, quite apart from the setting in which she worked on it.

Younger visiting scholars expressed personal growth in terms of their confidence as academics. "For me as a new academic it was a real boost to be seen differently," one (now former) graduate student reflected. "It was quite inspiring to know that my research was of interest to other academics and researchers." Another younger visiting scholar specifically mentioned the word confidence six times during her interview, saying that the experience "helped me develop confidence about my own ideas" and that because the school's faculty members were curious about her work, it "gave me confidence that I can bring value to international communities."

Younger visiting scholars also mentioned the intellectual and practical value of their experience. "I had rigorous and stimulating conversations at the same level of the conversations that I was having in grad school," said one, while another reported that he had learned better how "to communicate with a wider range of audiences," perhaps because he had more than once found his graduate level vocabulary and understanding needed to be modified for high school economics students. Another visiting scholar reported on her experience being interviewed by students in front of an invited audience: "The speaking experience was great – you can never get enough of that. I'm a bit more reserved and shy, but my ambition to break out of that is what gives me motivation to do these sort of things, so it helped break my own barriers."

More experienced visiting scholars explored areas they hadn't known they were going to explore, outside of their usual academic milieus. "I was trying to understand the culture among the teachers," said one professor, and another: "I managed to get into an area of research that I hadn't had the time to dig into before, which is about writing and academic writing, the sociological sides of academic writing." Still another said that the experience "motivated me" and that she "got into this whole hack learning movement and what that means," and that the experience has "given me a lot of freedom and encouragement to try new things and to look through a different lens."

Their experiences were supported by what other visiting scholars noted about the school. There is "a community of teachers who are curious and confident," said one. "It is such a rich and thriving environment, and I just love being in it," said another. It is perhaps, in the end, the "role of innovation amid the traditional structure of a big international school" which is the underlying affordance the visiting scholars were noticing. "I haven't really seen that before."

Theme 2: Practice: Learning as Doing

- Personal growth and having a productive stay
- Specific takeaways and transfer of learning

The visiting scholars interviewed here experienced the school community and the activity they were involved in through their individual lenses and their motivation to spend time at the school. The youngest, an alumna, wanted to maintain the connection with the school's faculty members in addition to sharing her experiences in the working world post university. The oldest wanted to catch up on reading and some academic writing in a quiet environment, while being open to learning whatever presented itself during his stay. Some specific takeaways in the range between these two visiting scholar profiles include the following:

- Learning about the application of Agile in education (from the world of software)
- Learning about how the school runs its summer program and the academic year student orientation
- Data collection for a research study
- Creating a video, with students, about sustainability
- Experience in the classroom
- Creating curriculum and teaching about the United Nations Convention on the Rights of the Child
- Creating curriculum and teaching about the ideal school
- Writing about introducing students to Esperanto
- Consulting and presenting in areas of personal expertise, e.g., language teaching, assessment, writing centers, approaches to studying poverty, economics, progressive schools, and diplomacy
- Incidental, unexpected learning, for example, about the nature of international schools

Embedded in the emerging themes of sharing expertise, having time to work, and learning about the school are many additional stories. Visiting scholars often got to know school faculty members and other visiting scholars, sometimes to the extent that new acquaintances become friends and trusted colleagues. All the visiting scholars expressed interest in staying connected to the school, for both personal and professional relations.

Theme 3. Meaning: Learning as Experience

- Personal growth and having a productive stay
- Specific takeaways and transfer of learning
- Giving back to the school

Visiting scholars were interested in sharing their work and expertise at least as much as they were interested in gaining personally from the experience, perhaps even more so. Some visiting scholars discussed initial feelings of not knowing how best they could contribute to the community and others came prepared with ways to be involved that hadn't been requested and weren't necessarily a good fit for the school. "I started thinking about how I can contribute, even though I was told that I do not have to justify my presence. But you feel like you need to contribute to the school." Many visiting scholars expressed an interest in sharing their expertise by speaking with groups of teachers and students. "We presented our findings to the LAS community," and "I wanted to talk about my own experience ... to dispel some of the myths and pressures that they tell you in high school about how important it is to know what your path is." A third visitor enjoyed speaking to students "from a position of some experience beyond what they've done..." in order to inspire them.

"It was great for me, and I gave something to the school," said a visiting scholar who co-created a simulation with the center director. Finally, "I was happy to present my ideas about the writing center," reported another, because "It's nice to feel helpful to your colleagues."

Theme 4. Community: Learning as Belonging

- Feeling welcome and feeling connected to the school
- Networking

Except for one visiting scholar who arrived at night to a small town that closes many of its restaurants early, making her, in her own words, "alone without anything to eat," nearly all the visiting scholars felt properly welcomed and introduced to the school in their first days and beyond. One mentioned the "interesting rapport" she had with the director before arriving for her first visit and that by her second and third visit she "felt I could just walk in and start straight away." She also mentioned that having a nameplate on the office door when she arrived was "a treat," a small thing that others mentioned as well, in addition to seeing their photos and short bios on screens around campus. "Right from the beginning, people, the students, they are welcoming you because they have seen you on the digital screens."

Another mentioned that "teachers were very helpful" and that "people didn't feel like we were there to create problems for anyone." Another reported that the director of the Alpine division was "an amazing host" and that "everyone went out of their way" and that "everyone invited me into their classroom."

Interestingly, the equivalent of work chats by the water cooler is found in the school cafeteria, where visiting scholars are invited to eat breakfast, lunch, and dinner. Because most of the faculty members take their meals in the cafeteria, often with their spouses and children, the cafeteria is a central location for relaxing and socializing. Nearly every visiting scholar talked about "those chats in the dining hall" and how they are brought "around to the cafeteria so you can converse with the teachers." The visiting scholar who arrived without any dinner arrangements mentioned how in the cafeteria she "was part of a very big family." A first-time visiting scholar who didn't meet as many people as he would have liked to, mentioned that he and his wife "got acquainted with some people in the cafeteria, but we didn't meet many people apart from that." In other words, the unstructured, or very lightly structured, environment of the cafeteria makes visiting scholars feel welcome and is probably the most significant mechanism for integration into the community. In fact, no single visiting scholar mentioned the rather expensive dinner at the Swiss Chalet that everyone is invited to once; it is rather the cafeteria, with regular cafeteria fare, that puts out the widest welcome mat.

The net effect is a desire on the part of the visiting scholars to return to the school, as two of them had already done. "I am sure that I will be there again," said one, and another expressed that "it would be invaluable to come again." The veteran all agree, as one expressed when she realized her first year jitters were gone and that she knew she was part of the community and could always get right to work if she visited again.

One of the visiting scholars was recruited by a previous visiting scholar, and another visiting scholar was introduced to two previous visiting scholars, whom she subsequently visited at their schools. Another visiting scholar was an alumna of the school, who expressed the desire to stay in contact with the school for that reason, and two others were from the same university, far from the school, who grew to know each through the visiting scholar experience, even though their stays did not overlap.

"It's about building relationships," said the one who connected through school visits with previous visiting scholars. "The strength of the visiting scholar program is the diversity and variety of people that come." The visiting scholar who completed her data collection while on campus had practical reasons to maintain the relationship, namely finishing the paper together and submitting it for publication. One mentioned how she enjoyed "sharing intellectual curiosity with other people" and "maintaining an intellectual connection with the school." Another expressed it a bit differently: "You find yourself in the center of a melting pot which is intellectually stimulating and interesting." These are perhaps the most direct statements of the value found in the interconnected communities of practice that grow out of the visiting scholar experience.

"The opportunity to collaborate with teachers and students with meaningful projects" was valuable to one visiting scholar. Her work with the local community and region made her lifelong friendships with faculty members, noting that the colleague she worked with most is now "practically a family friend" and that her work with local residents required "so much networking" and talking to "so many people." It is a common theme that not only do visiting scholars develop working relationships with the school's teachers and others but also friendships that go far beyond simple professional interests. The small business owner commented on meeting other teachers and administrators "with whom I'm still connected." He recommends future visiting scholars "meet as many people as you can and find a way to collaborate with them, but most importantly, learn their story." It isn't unheard of for visiting scholars to host school faculty members when they travel abroad, and more than once school faculty members have been invited to present and write with past visiting scholars on new projects, created long after the visiting scholar has returned home. This study is, in fact, an example of that.

DISCUSSION

Based on the emergent subthemes of the interviews, the visiting scholar program at Leysin American School does seem to fit the description of a community of practice as defined by Wenger (1998). While traveling to the school is simply a given if a visiting scholar is going to stay at the school, it turns out that the experience of being away from one's everyday setting, including all its comforts, colleagues, and familiar rituals, may play a role in refreshing one's own identity. The experience, though full of community and natural beauty, is also personally disruptive. Visiting scholars are indeed outsiders who are aware that they are visitors, particularly at the beginning of their stay, and they know that some of their own expert understanding of school and academic settings may not apply in their new context. This disruption is of course social in that visiting scholars must also find a way to fit in, and it is perhaps just enough of a jolt to one's regular routine to allow new ideas and new ways of thinking about school and schooling to take hold.

That being in a new environment and interacting with new people leads to personal growth seems self-evident, although it isn't always the case. Perhaps important is that visiting scholars noticed and remarked on the vibrant community (of practice) already in place at the school, with many teachers interested in talking about and reflecting on practice, inviting visiting scholars into their classrooms and other learning spaces, and interacting socially. Learning and growth are made possible, in other words, by the school's existing communities of practice, composed of interlocking smaller groups, into which the visiting scholar is invited by creating yet another interlocking community of practice. The one or two visiting scholars who expressed a desire to interact more with the school faculty members and to get involved more in the future perhaps felt that they were missing full access to these networks. Most of the visiting scholars expressed their satisfaction with being interconnected in many ways, often stating that they felt socially integrated, and therefore were able to also be included in work discussions, classes, and other school activity.

During their stay, visiting scholars moved among Wenger's four components of meaning, practice, community, and identity. Arguably, the quality of their learning experience during their time as a visiting scholar was enhanced by the degree to which they experienced each of the four components. Being involved in practice at the school, reflecting on that practice with others, and gaining membership status in a social group interested in that practice seems to have led to deeper learning experiences. Those few visiting scholars who experienced the school mostly as an outsider – save perhaps during meals in the cafeteria – had a less rich learning experience and consequently might be less likely to want to return a second time. The enthusiasm of the veteran visiting scholars, those who came three and five times to the school, speaks volumes. Becoming, and continually becoming, part of a community of practitioners fills both social and intellectual needs, and fuels a desire to repeat or continue the process.

For this set of visitors, it seems clear that the principal physical locus for community building is the school cafeteria. Once again, there is a strong social element at play. People are in the cafeteria to eat, relax, and talk with each other. Interestingly, whom a visiting scholar eats with is mostly random, particularly at first, and therefore the connections are quite natural. Over time visitors and teachers seek each other out, and in most cases visiting scholars receive invitations, or even invite faculty members, to eat together off campus.

Personal growth is evident in comments about learning new ways to operate in a familiar context, e.g., boarding school, or having completely new experiences, like being at a school with dozens of nationalities instead of the homogenous culture of the visiting scholar's home country. Visiting scholars learned to take their cues from their host environment, moving from an assumption that they themselves had to teach or otherwise justify their stay to a mindset with a greater emphasis on learning from the school. For professors who have worked their entire careers preparing teachers for their jobs in K-12 education, a fairly radical mindset shift is required, in that they have come to a high school to learn from high school faculty members, not to tell high school faculty members how to teach. In other words, experienced professors may arrive with an expectation of being an instructor of others, as might a consultant, whereas a graduate student might view the experience much more readily through the lens of someone visiting to learn. No matter where on the spectrum, however, most visiting scholars reflected that they learned a great deal while at the school through what they observed and the conversations they had with faculty members. Perhaps the length of their stay is quite important. Something new that they might miss or interpret mostly through their own pre-existing lens can come up again and again during a stay of many days, with plenty of time for reflection in the cafeteria and elsewhere, effectively granting the time and space to formulate and test new ideas.

Finally, several visiting scholars mentioned specific personal takeaways ranging from learning about existing curriculum, creating new curriculum, exploring different approaches to instruction, working with multiple languages, and understanding the nature of boarding school. Among the group of visiting scholars we interviewed, two individuals regretted not immersing themselves more (i.e., making more social connections and collaborating with more faculty members), though they were pleased with how much of their own "homework" they were able to get done. The experience varied across individuals, shaped by their personalities and working styles, made possible through the social and in situ nature of being part of a working school.

CONCLUSION

A community of practice is something that forms over time, through shared experiences, as people develop mutual respect and trust. In this sense the visiting scholar program creates for the school a community of practice not unlike John Dewey's laboratory schools, which were created to study, in one of today's current terms, the *ecosystem* of a school. This laboratory school, however, is unique because of its independence from an affiliation with any particular university and the steady introduction of external guests, the visiting scholars, who become part of that ecosystem (or not) as they wish, with no required agenda. As is apparent in their reflection on the experience, each visiting scholar approaches the experience differently and has different takeaways based on differing personal backgrounds, personal goals, activities available at the school during the period of their stay, and so on. Also apparent are commonalities in their experiences, from feeling welcome and connected, to experiencing personal growth and being able to provide value, in their own ways, to the school community.

There are at least a few interesting next steps as we learn about the effects of the visiting scholar program. One important step is to research the impact the program has on current faculty members who interact, host, and collaborate with visiting scholars. What are faculty members learning and how does the experience affect their practice? Another interesting step is the consideration of applying the program to other schools. To date, our experience has been that educators are quite interested in hearing about the model but reluctant to set up their own program. Despite the perceived value, in other words, the bar to getting started is perceived as too high. We hope through the shared experience of this group of visiting scholars that other schools may take an initial, small step toward supporting visiting scholars. In this school's case, it was only a matter of saying "yes" to the program's first visiting scholar, a professor who approached the school himself, and perhaps the spark of imagination his visit lit, encouraging us to pursue the possibility of robust and interlocking communities of practice.

AUTHOR'S NOTES

The LASER Visiting Scholar Project is supported and funded by Leysin American School Switzerland. The authors would like to thank the visiting scholars who gave their valuable time to participate in this study. The authors would also like to thank the administrators of Leysin American School who supported the LASER Visiting Scholar Program for more than a decade.

REFERENCES

AFS in Your Country. (n.d.). Teacher. https://afs.org/tag/teacher/
Argyris, C. (1991). Teaching smart people how to learn. *Harvard Business Review, 4*(2), 4–15. http://pds8.egloos.com/pds/200805/20/87/chris_argyris_learning.pdf
Bano, S. (2020). *Becoming more visible: The experiences of Chinese visiting scholars at a U.S. university*. Michigan State University, ProQuest Dissertations Publishing.
Clandinin, J., Connelly, M., & He, M. F. (1997). Teachers' personal practical knowledge on the professional knowledge landscape. *Teaching and Teacher Education, 13*(7), 665–674. https://doi.org/10.1016/S0742-051X(97)00014-0
Clark, C. M., Olson, K., Hacıfazlıoğlu, O., & Carlson, D. L. (2021). Community of practice among faculty team-teaching education doctorate (Ed.D.) students: A reflective study. *International Journal of Doctoral Studies, 16*, 379–393. https://doi.org/10.28945/4775
Craig, C. (2020). *Curriculum making, reciprocal learning, and the best-loved self*. Palgrave Macmillan.
Educational Research. (n.d.). Leysin American School. https://www.las.ch/learning/educational-research
Farrell, R. (1978). Teacher exchange and intercultural communication: A follow-up evaluation of an attempt at international understanding and appreciation. Paper presented at the *Annual Meeting of the Speech Communication Association Summer Conference on Intercultural Communication*, Tampa, Florida, July 17–21, 1978. https://eric.ed.gov/?id=ED162371
Guo-Brennan, L., & Wei, W. (2012). Visiting scholars: Facilitators of sustainable international strategic alliances in higher education. *Journal of International Business Education, 7*, 181–198.
Harris, M. (2019). *How to get tenure: Strategies for successfully navigating the process*. Routledge.
Heinz, A. K., & Lewis, A. C. (2009). Enhancing university summer session programs. *Continuing Higher Education Review, 73*, 163–174.
Lave, J., & Wenger, E. (1991). *Situated learning: Legitimate peripheral participation*. Cambridge University Press.
Lester, S. (1999). An introduction to phenomenological research. Taunton UK, Stan Lester Developments. www.sld.demon.co.uk/resmethy.pdf
Olson, K., & Clark, C. M. (2009). A signature pedagogy in doctoral education: The leader–scholar community. *Educational Researcher, 38*(3), 216–221.
Painter, S. R., & Clark, C. M. (2015). Leading change: Faculty development through structured collaboration. *International Journal of Doctoral Studies, 10*, 187–198. http://ijds.org/Volume10/IJDSv10p187-198Painter0954.pdf
Rosowsky, D. (2020, June 11). The teaching and research balancing act: Are universities teetering? *Forbes*. https://www.forbes.com/sites/davidrosowsky/2020/06/11/the-teaching-and-research-balancing-act-are-universities-teetering/#ed5cab2ed8a7
Seidmann, I. (1998). *Interviewing as qualitative research: A guide for researchers in education and the social sciences*. Teachers College Press.
Shimmi, Y. (2014, September 26). International visiting scholars: An underused resource. University World News. https://www.universityworldnews.com/post.php?story=20140924081517506
Visiting Scholars. (n.d.). Park School. https://www.parkschool.net/academics/visiting-scholars/

Wenger, E. (1998). *Communities of practice: Learning, meaning, and identity.* Cambridge University Press.
Wenger, E., McDermott, R. A., & Snyder, W. (2002). *Cultivating communities of practice: A guide to managing knowledge.* Harvard Business School Press.
Zhang, L. (2016). *Intercultural competence development: The perceptions of Chinese visiting scholars sojourning abroad.* University of Nottingham. https://ethos.bl.uk/OrderDetails.do?uin=uk.bl.ethos.689859

COLLABORATIVE REFLECTION, KNOWLEDGE, AND GROWTH: EXPLORING ONGOING TEACHER LEARNING WITHIN KNOWLEDGE COMMUNITIES

Michaelann Kelley and Gayle A. Curtis

ABSTRACT

Teacher retention and continued teacher growth and development have long been critical global issues in education. The recent pandemic crisis and subsequent "great resignation" (Lodewick, 2022) have returned our attention to the need for positive and enriching educational landscapes that promote teacher collaborative reflection, knowledge, and growth in order to sustain teachers in the field. This chapter explores the ongoing teacher learning that has occurred within two knowledge communities (Craig, 1995b) in the United States. It begins with an overview of Craig's early work with teachers, during which her conceptualization of knowledge communities emerged. According to Craig, knowledge communities are safe, collaborative spaces that cohere around teachers' intra/inter-school dialogue and their storying/restorying (Clandinin & Connelly, 1996, 1998) of experiences. Additionally, knowledge communities (Craig, 1995b) begin with originating events, allow teachers' experiences (Dewey, 1938) to resonate with others in the group, feature reciprocity of members' mindful responses, and promote the development of shared ways of knowing. Equally important, knowledge communities evolve and change, fuel ongoing reflection in community, and bring moral horizons into view. Employing these knowledge community qualities as our lens, we examine the interactions of the Portfolio Group and the Faculty Academy. The Portfolio Group is a teacher/teacher educator/researcher group formed in 1998 during a US education reform era (Craig, Curtis et al., 2020).

Its sister group, the Faculty Academy, is a cross-institutional, cross-discipline higher education group of teacher educators/researchers formed in 2002 (Craig, Turchi et al., 2020). Employing a parallel stories representation (Craig, 1999), exemplars (Mishler, 1990) from both groups show how teacher collaborative groups have the capacity to be safe spaces in which critical professional dialogue, reflective exchanges, and generous scholarship occur among members. Furthermore, they are nurturing spaces in which teachers can thrive and be their best-loved selves (Craig, 2013; Schwab, 1954/ 1978). These two groups exemplify the ways in which knowledge communities support teacher collaboration, promote ongoing teacher growth and development, and foster teacher sustainability.

Keywords: collaboration; critical friendship; generous scholarship; knowledge communities; reflection; storying/restorying

Teacher retention and continued teacher growth and development have long been critical global issues in education. The recent pandemic crisis and subsequent "great resignation" (Lodewick, 2022) have returned our attention to the need for positive and enriching educational landscapes that promote teacher collaborative reflection, knowledge, and growth, all of which is critically important to sustaining teachers in the field. While there has long been tension between the ideas of teachers-as-curriculum-implementers and the lived experiences of teachers in classrooms as curriculum-makers (Connelly & Clandinin, 1988), recent social and political pressure-groups have triggered additional tensions about how race and sexual orientation should be taught, and more. This has exacerbated the conditions under which teachers work, leaving many feeling as though they are on the receiving end of a conduit down which flows mandates and prescribed programs to be implemented in classrooms (Craig, 1995a), which eventually lead to teacher attrition (Craig, 2017; Kelchtermans, 2017). Laying alongside these issues is the perceived theory-practice divide between schools and higher education, with some believing that professors and school-based teachers cannot work alongside one another because of different knowledge bases, different power bases, and different populations/communities served.

Recent research on teacher attrition in the United States shows a direct correlation between "the quality and comprehensiveness of mentoring and induction" (Bailey et al., 2021, p. 42) and "teachers' intentions and decisions" on whether to stay or leave. In particular, beginning teachers are "the most at risk for experiencing social isolation and the most dependent on meaningful collaboration with colleagues" (Shernoff et al., 2011, p. 465). Where both novice and veteran teachers are concerned, scholars agree that teacher professional growth and continued development is strengthened when schools maintain a culture of learning (Darling-Hammond, 2010; Feiman-Nemser, 2012).

With these situations in mind, we (the authors) reflected upon the ways in which we have benefited from our participation in two collaborative teacher/teacher educator groups in the United States: the Portfolio Group (a teacher/teacher educator/researcher group of 25 years) and the Faculty Academy (a teacher educator/researcher higher education group of 21 years). Uniquely, both long-standing groups are cross-institutional/cross-disciplinary knowledge communities that function outside of formal institutional affiliations. In this chapter, we turn our attention to the ways in which the Portfolio Group and Faculty Academy promote teacher learning through collaborative reflection, knowledge co-construction, and professional growth.

CONCEPTUAL FRAMEWORK

Personal Practical Knowledge

Connelly and Clandinin (1988) contend that teacher knowledge is not "something given to people, but [is] something narratively embodied in how a person stands in the world; and that knowledge as attribute can be given; knowledge as narrative cannot. The latter needs to be experienced in context" (p. 137). They define personal practical knowledge as "a moral, affective, and aesthetic way of knowing life's educational situations" (p. 59). Olson (1995) suggests that personal practical knowledge is "embodied within the individual as well as embedded within the individual's socio-historical contexts. Students [and teachers] construct and reconstruct meaning based on this knowledge" (p. 120). This concept allows us to talk about and better understand the ways in which "our knowledge shifts and changes and is multiple within the multiple worlds we inhabit" (Cain et al., 2021, p. 37). Gayle expressed our collective thoughts on personal practical knowledge, saying, "Coming to the term personal practical knowledge was an 'aha' moment for me. It named what I had sensed but could not succinctly verbalize about how education-related knowledge and personal experience coalesced in my teaching" (Kelley et al., in review).

Narrative Authority

Conceptualized by Margaret Olson (1995), narrative authority "is rooted in the personal practical knowledge of teacher education students, university teachers and classroom teachers as they interact within the contexts of teacher education" (p. 119). Drawing on Dewey's (1938) perspective of experience as educative, narrative authority adopts the perspective that knowledge is constructed and reconstructed through contextualized social experience.

> Because the narrative version of knowledge construction is transactional, authority comes from experience and is integral as each person both shapes his or her own knowledge and is shaped by the knowledge of others. Knowledge is personally and socially constructed and reconstructed in situations as people share their ideas and stories with others. Since everyone is a knower who deserves to be heard, all voices become authoritative sources. (Olson, 1995, p. 123)

Social Capital

Whereas human capital in education refers to the expertise held by individuals and often connected to student achievement (Amrein-Beardsley, 2008), social capital in education has to do with teacher networks and interactions that promote professional growth (Panuel et al., 2009). Social capital speaks to "the importance of individuals associating with one another" (Plagens, 2011, p. 41) – an idea put forward by Dewey in 1915 in *The school and society* (and taken up in "My pedagogic creed" 1897/2000 and *Experience and education* [1938]). For Dewey (1916/1996), "A man really living alone (alone mentally as well as physically) would have little or no occasion to reflect upon his past experience to extract its net meaning" (p. 197). Interactions among individuals is a stimulating educative experience that brings about personal growth. He asserted,

> ...the very process of living together educates. It enlarges and enlightens experience; it stimulates and enriches imagination; it creates responsibility for accuracy and vividness of statement and thought. (Dewey, 1916/1996, p. 197)

Critical Friendship

A critical friend is described as "a trusted person who asks provocative questions, provides data to be examined through another lens, and offers a critique of a person's work as a friend" (Costa, 2008, p. 124; see also Stenhouse, 1975). A critical friend is further described as one who "engages with another person in a way which encourages talking with, questioning, and even confronting, the trusted other, in order to examine [their practice]" (Hatton & Smith, 1995, p. 41). This process "can give voice to teacher thinking while at the same time being heard in a sympathetic but constructively critical way" (p. 41). Utilized in various forms of teacher communities of learning and in self-study research, the feedback of critical friends helps us to reframe our experiences by providing a different lens through which to view our experiences (Schuck & Russell, 2005).

Knowledge Communities

The conceptualization of knowledge communities emerged from Craig's (1995b, 1995c, 2007; see also Craig, Curtis et al., 2020, Ch. 2) work with Canadian teachers, Benita and Tim (pseudonyms). She observed how Benita and Tim organically came together over their practice and, in particular, the ways in which their sharing of teacher stories with one another in a safe space promoted reflection and knowledge development. Thus, the concept of knowledge communities took shape.

According to Craig (1995b), knowledge communities begin with originating events and are safe, collaborative spaces that cohere around teachers' intra/inter-school dialogue and their storying/restorying (Clandinin & Connelly, 1996, 1998) of experiences (see Fig. 1). Knowledge communities (Craig, 1995b) allow teachers' experiences (Dewey, 1938) to resonate with others in the group, feature reciprocity of members' mindful responses, and promote the development of shared ways of knowing. Equally important, knowledge communities evolve and change, fuel ongoing reflection in community, and bring moral horizons into view.

Knowledge Communities

- begin with originating events
- enable teachers' intra/inter-school dialogue
- allow teachers' experiences to resonate with one another
- evolve and change
- cohere around teachers' storying/ restorying of experience
- fuel ongoing reflection in community
- develop shared ways of knowing
- feature reciprocity of members' responses
- bring moral horizons into view

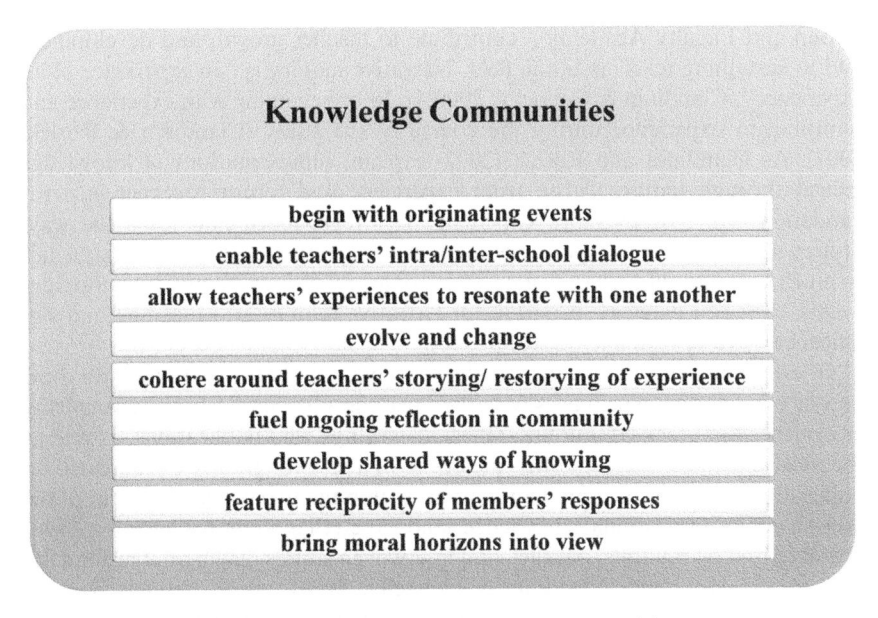

Fig. 1. Qualities of Knowledge Communities.

There are multiple forms of successful and sustained collaborative teacher and teacher educator groups, many of which focus on teacher practice, dialogue, reflection, critical friendship, and collaborative work. Not all, however, exhibit the characteristics of knowledge communities. A distinguishing factor is often that they are mandated groups following a prescribed pathway rather than the voluntary participation and no predetermined pathway found in knowledge communities. As will be illustrated in this chapter, the Portfolio Group and Faculty Academy are two exemplars of knowledge communities (which we are intimately familiar with) that exhibit the aforementioned qualities and allow the work to determine each group's pathway, leading to sustained collaboration and ongoing teacher learning.

PURPOSE

This chapter explores the collaborative reflection, knowledge construction, professional growth, and ongoing teacher learning occurring over time within two long-standing knowledge communities (Craig, 1995b) – the Portfolio Group and the Faculty Academy.

METHODS

Narrative inquiry methods (Clandinin & Connelly, 2000) are employed in this chapter to explore the ways in which two knowledge communities – the Portfolio

Group and Faculty Academy – contribute to teacher growth and development and to sustaining teachers in the field. Narrative inquiry is "an experience of an experience" (Clandinin & Connelly, 2000, p. 189); beginning with experience and returning to experience during the course of the study (Clandinin & Rosiek, 2007). As Clandinin and Rosiek (2007) explain, representations of knowledge gained through inquiry "arise from experience and return to experience for validation" (p. 39). In short, experience is foregrounded and leads the way. Stories of experience, therefore, are integral to narrative inquiry, as story "is not so much a structured answer to a question, or a way of accounting for actions and events, as it is a gateway, a portal, for narrative inquiry into meaning and significance" (Xu & Connelly, 2010, p. 356).

In examining these two long-standing teacher collaborative groups, we drew on our own storied experiences with the Portfolio Group and Faculty Academy as evidenced in archived journals, reflective writings, and publications, as well as the storied experiences of other members of the two groups documented in publications. We reflected on interrelations within the two groups, mindful of the ever-changing professional knowledge landscape (Clandinin & Connelly, 1996) characterized by multiple, parallel, and interwoven stories playing out around the two groups over time (Clandinin & Connelly, 2000), which harkens back to Dewey's (1916/1996) notion of continuity in education and what Connelly and Clandinin (2006) call the three-dimensional research space (sociality–interaction; place–location; and temporality–past, present, future).

We employed Craig's (1995b, 2007) nine qualities of knowledge communities (see Fig. 1) as a lens through which to identify similarities and differences between the two knowledge communities. Exemplars (Mishler, 1990) were specifically selected to show "how a practice works" (Lyons & LaBoskey, 2002, p. 6) and to capture the intent and meaning making of the individual group members (Lyons & LaBoskey, 2002). The purposeful inclusion of storied experiences or exemplars that give a sense of "lifelikeness" (Bruner, 1986, p. 11) promotes trustworthiness by addressing "credibility, transferability, dependability, and confirmability" (Gay et al., 2006, p. 403).

THE PASSAGEWAY TO KNOWLEDGE COMMUNITIES

Introducing the Groups

To illustrate how the qualities of knowledge communities play out in different, yet sometimes similar ways in the Portfolio Group and the Faculty Academy, we use Craig's (1999) concept of parallel stories, laying the two groups' stories alongside one another, and sometimes intertwining the retelling of their stories, around emergent themes.

Portfolio Group

The Portfolio Group is a teacher/teacher educator/researcher group that was formed in 1998 during the late 1990s education reform era in Houston, Texas

(Craig, Curtis et al., 2020). Eleven of the city's urban schools (elementary, middle, and high school) serving diverse student populations received Annenberg Foundation Beacon School grants to support the various change efforts unique to each site. For the purposes of improving student learning, some schools focused on different approaches to literacy development, while others centered their work on art integration across the curriculum, and still another anchored reform efforts in two-way immersion (Spanish/English) dual language instruction. Based on the Houston Annenberg Challenge theory of action, grants included three imperatives of teacher learning, personalizing instruction, and breaking down barriers of isolation (Craig, Curtis et al., 2020, p. 52) with each school individualizing their plans to meet the needs of their students.

University professor Cheryl Craig was selected as the Formative Evaluator by five schools (two elementary, two middle, and one high school) whose principals determined that they wanted to employ school portfolios as formative grant evaluation pieces in order to show the broad (and deep) story of their reform efforts. Reflecting on her earlier work when Benita and Tim (Craig, 1995b) formed a knowledge community, Cheryl proposed the formation of the Portfolio Group which would bring together grant coordinators and teacher representatives from each of the five schools for the purpose of learning about and collaborating on the development of school portfolios.

> Cheryl would only agree to work with the schools who selected her if they would, in turn, agree to work collaboratively to document their own work and their collective work. She did not want to mediate rivalries between and among the schools and personalities of the teachers in the group. Nor did she want people or schools competing for her attention. She wanted everyone to focus their full attention on improving schooling for urban youth. (Gray, 2008, p. 17)

In addition to participation in the larger Portfolio Group of 18, each school formed its own Campus Portfolio Group comprised of representatives in the Portfolio Group and other campus teachers, thereby broadening the perspectives and voices contributing to each school portfolio.

Faculty Academy
With reform initiatives going on in schools, the reform movement had also concluded that "the local universities and faculties needed to improve how they partnered with schools and teachers" (Craig, personal communication, 2022). With the support of a small, short-term grant, in 2002 Cheryl Craig established the Faculty Academy – the Portfolio Group's sister group – with the purpose of breaking down the barriers between PK-12 and higher education and promoting teacher learning. Although now best described as a cross-institutional, cross-discipline higher education group of teacher educators/researchers, the Faculty Academy's early membership "brought together eight university-based faculty with eight community school-based teachers who met bi-monthly to discuss current issues in schooling and particular challenges confronting Greater Houston's urban schools" (Curtis & Craig, 2020, p. 19). Faculty Academy members represented different universities and content areas; school-based

teachers represented various levels of PK-12 urban schools and varied subject disciplines.

In the beginning years, Cheryl led and facilitated the monthly meetings of both groups, with the Portfolio Group rotating locations from school to school and the Faculty Academy from institution to institution. Over the years, facilitation of meetings was passed on to others, always with Cheryl's guidance and mentorship. During the middle and later years of the groups' collaborative histories, meetings continued to be held at schools and universities, but also at restaurants, coffee shops, and even at members' homes in the case of the Portfolio Group. Thus, the notion of a table became symbolic for the two groups, serving as a metaphor for the members' experiences of sharing their stories, reflections, tensions, challenges, and ideas, while learning together and working collaboratively on varied areas of group interest.

Critical Friendship

Since the beginning, critical friendship has had a prominent "place at the table" for both Portfolio Group and Faculty Academy in so much that both groups provide space and time for intra/inter-school/institution dialogue and feedback to occur in meaningful and equitable ways, allowing experiences to resonate between/among members. The members of both groups subscribe to the ontology of "being there" – being present to one another – around the table (Hlebowitsh, 2012).

Portfolio Group

From our perspectives as long-time Portfolio Group members, critical friendship is integral to the members' interactions, relationships, and professional growth. It anchors our collaborative work in practice, reflection, and continued improvement, offering the support and feedback needed to navigate our journeys in the educational landscape. For Michaelann,

> My time in the Portfolio Group has been the single most influential learning community in my professional career. This was/is a safe place to reflect upon the challenges and dilemmas in my practice: first in my high school teaching, then as a doctoral student, then as a district administrator, and now as a university professor. My critical friends were always a part of my learning and growing along the way.

Gayle also shared,

> My experiences in the Portfolio Group have made an indelible mark on my practice, learning, and professional growth—all of which starts with the authentic relationships and meaningful interactions with trusted colleagues. Whether sharing an aspect of practice or a contentious situation, I feel assured that the thoughtful critical feedback given by others is offered with care, support, and my best interest, and that of my students, in mind—it has been the most crucial factor in sustaining me in education.

The reflection, sharing of stories, and learning from one another always found their way back into our everyday practices, helping to improve our teaching and collaboration with others in order to better meet the needs of students.

Faculty Academy
Like the Portfolio Group, the Faculty Academy's safe environment enabled teacher educators/researchers to engage in authentic dialogue and for members to cohere around the storying and restorying of experiences that resonated among members. The critical feedback exchanged within the group was enhanced by the members representing early, middle, and later career experiences in higher education and holding different areas of content expertise. Talking about the role of critical friendship in the group, long-time Faculty Academy member Carrie Markello (2020) shared,

> The process-oriented work of the Faculty Academy has been key to the group's functioning. The group used three main strategies: constructive critical feedback, collaboration, and reflection. These intentional strategies reinforced its collaborative leadership and supported a cornerstone of the relational leadership style. (p. 38)

For her, and other Faculty Academy members, these interactions "created an environment where listening, learning, and the development of trust enabled strategies for professional development" (p. 39) which "strengthened the group's ability to take on professional challenges and enable growth."

Evolution of the Two Groups

The evolution of the two groups is perhaps best evidenced in their shifting leadership and changing focus of collaborative work. Cheryl Craig initially served as the helmsman for the groups – the Portfolio Group and Faculty Academy educator ships, if you will – thereby fulfilling the requirements of the reform agency. Like most sea-going vessels in which all crewmembers must be able to guide and navigate when needed, leadership within the two groups has been taken up by others along the way.

Portfolio Group
The Portfolio Group was the first in the Houston area to look at data in an alternative way through the development of school portfolios. "The Group's school portfolio work acted as a counterbalance to testing and school accountability at a time when accountability pressures were mounting in Texas" (Craig et al., 2016, p. 135). Michaelann reflected on using school portfolios as alternative data to state-mandated testing, explaining,

> The beginning years of the Portfolio Group were all about showing the work—not just to our [Houston Annenberg Challenge] funder but also to our school districts and community. We wanted everyone to be aware of the quality of our scholarship of teaching on our home campuses. (Craig, Curtis et al., 2020, p. 56)

In the school portfolios, Gayle saw "the unique characteristics of both the schools and the portfolio-makers at each school" (Craig, Curtis et al., 2020, p. 50). She "[came] to see the portfolios as the telling and showing of each school's change story within which [her] personal narratives of experience could be embedded."

During a 2001 presentation on "School Portfolios by Reform Practitioners," we and other Portfolio Group members recall a pivotal moment. "When an audience member asked for a recap of the group's reform efforts, Gayle, to the surprise of the entire Portfolio Group, quickly rattled off a description of each individual school's education reform initiatives with precision and accuracy" (Craig, Curtis et al., 2020, p. 59); after which Michaelann commented, "I realized that my stories were her stories and her stories were mine." It was then we realized that over the three years of our working together we had formed a knowledge community. As the group began to share their experiences and work at local, national, and international conferences, their educator identities shifted to include both teacher and researcher selves. As Gayle recounts,

> Looking at our work through the eyes of others affirmed the value of our portfolio work and encouraged us to show a deeper school story. At [Nona Lyons' [Portfolio Conference], the Portfolio Group formed a bridge to the academy. It was a watershed experience because we began to think of ourselves, not only as teachers, but as bonafide "researchers." (Craig, Curtis et al., 2020, p. 62)

When the school grants ended in 2002, the Portfolio Group continued its collaborative endeavors (albeit with a much smaller group). Over the years, Portfolio Group membership has ebbed and flowed, with members coming, going, and returning. Such is the case of one member who left because of a job change and returned to the group in 2021 after almost 20 years away. Some members moved out of the classroom into administrative positions, some stayed in the classroom, some left for district positions then returned to the classroom, and others moved on to higher education.

In an ever-changing education environment, the group has continuously endeavored to undertake work of common interest, delving into online blogging, traveling journals, narrative inquiries into education, and self-study of their individual practices and the group's collaboration. The Portfolio Group's collaborative efforts on numerous articles, presentations, papers, and even a book (Craig, Curtis et al., 2020) document not only the group's work over 25+ years, but also how we have walked alongside one another throughout our professional and personal journeys (Curtis et al., 2012, 2013). Many of the group would agree with us when we say that our identities as narrative inquirers were and are shaped by our membership in the Portfolio Group.

Faculty Academy
The evolution of the Faculty Academy has not had as many twists and turns compared to the Portfolio Group in large part because its original mission is still very much in place today. When their small grant ended just a couple of years

into the formation of the group, Faculty Academy members chose to continue their collaborative work. Cheryl Craig shared,

> In the final report to the Houston Annenberg Challenge, the Faculty Academy group summarized its activities. Each member then outlined why they joined the group and what they each had learned from membership. They also stated their intent to continue the group—without funding. (personal communication, 2022)

The members have changed over the years because of new positions, new institutional locations, and/or retirements. As Denise, an original member and long-time group leader who is now retired, points out "we, as Faculty Academy members, continue to progress through proliferating possibilities of who we are and where we aspire to go as academic leaders" (McDonald et al., 2020, p. 69). Although she is no longer affiliated with an academic institution, Denise continues her work with the Faculty Academy, continuing to mentor and guide junior academics.

Graduates of one of the Faculty Academy founding universities, group members Jane Cooper, Leslie Gauna, and Christine Beaudry – known as "Las Chicas Críticas" (the Critical Girls) to denote their "commitment to critical theory and pedagogy" (Cooper et al., 2020, p. 328) – began working together during their doctoral studies in order to examine and support one another's practice. Jane shared, "We became members of the Faculty Academy not long after completing our doctorates in order to broaden our collaborative opportunities and to learn from the collective knowledge of the group" (p. 328).

Individual growth and development is an integral part of the Faculty Academy, as indicated by Carrie when she said, "As a member of the Faculty Academy I experienced opportunities to address professional identity and insecurity through encouragement and creative activity; together, we were *doing* and *undergoing*" (Markello, 2020, p. 43, echoing Dewey, italics in the original). Jackie and Irma shared, "The opportunity to share and reflect with like minds in supportive settings like the Faculty Academy has been invaluable in our leading and learning" (Sack & Vazquez, 2020, p. 269).

Career Pathways

Opportunities and challenges in career pathways seem to pop up from unlikely places, but what some members of the Portfolio Group and Faculty Academy discovered was that it is easier to navigate professional waters and stormy seas with the authentic experiences, collegial guidance, and the critical friendship of their colleagues from other schools and institutions.

Portfolio Group
The Portfolio Group members seem to be on an upward and stellar route. Once asked why she never applied for any of her district's open assistant principal positions, Michaelann quickly responded with, "I don't want to count keys and direct buses." Although this remark is a huge generalization of the responsibilities of the position, it reflects that Michaelann was very aware of the limitations such

a position held for leadership and curriculum development. As it would happen, a little over a year later she found what she calls her "perfect job," moving to higher education as an assistant professor of art and design. Other members have had similar stories of recognizing their "dream" jobs because their membership in the Portfolio created a space for them to understand their chosen path through learning and reflection.

Not all the members have had that North Star to guide them. One member decided to retire from education and then realized that it was not the right choice for them and returned to education albeit on the university level rather than PK-12. Another member found themselves laid off from their "perfect job" and was searching to find a new position only to find out that they were rehired and the layoff was an administrative political move rather than a performance issue. The support of other Portfolio Group members when navigating contentious work environments, job insecurities, and challenging situations is immeasurable.

Faculty Academy

The group's distributive leadership (Spillane, 2005) became an unexpected treasure for members along their career path, especially when preparing to go up for tenure. "Unexpectedly, we found that our leadership skills also developed through stories shared and collegial support graciously supplied by members. Leadership proficiency was a surprising boon to Faculty Academy participation" (McDonald et al., 2020, p. 47).

Since many Faculty Academy members join the group as junior faculty, support from other members has been essential to their road to tenure. As Pohl (2020) shared,

> The tenure-track phase is a pivotal and transformative moment in the life of a university academic... a period of undeniable anguish, despair, and desperation. Buried beneath all these emotions lies the responsibility to fulfill the three main pillars of the tenure-track process: teaching, scholarship, and service. (p. 113)

Jackie Sack, a former middle school mathematics teacher turned professor, "who credits her work with the Faculty Academy as the reason for reaching tenure" (personal communication, Craig 2022) illustrates the rich learning available in the "swampy lowlands" (Schön, 1995, p. 28). Vazquez, a middle school teacher collaboratively writes with Jackie, "We have led and learned about leading in many ways in our collaborative project, which is also informed through Jackie's participation in Faculty Academy. Engaging in classroom-based research at the outset was an opportunity for both of us to lead each other toward our learners' mathematical growth" (Sack & Vazquez, 2020, p. 266). She continued, "Jackie's association with the Faculty Academy has additionally provided us with the opportunity to further develop our personal understandings of this collaborative work" (Sack & Vazquez, 2020, p. 269).

The words of Faculty Academy members speak to the group's continued support. "As a supportive professional community, Faculty Academy offer[s] members sustenance for exploring career passions, connections with other educators, validation as practitioners and researchers, personal encouragement, and when needed, professional patronage as promising academic leaders" (McDonald et al., 2020, p. 48).

Cross-Pollination and Extended Collaborations

Although not explicitly cited in Craig's nine qualities of a knowledge community, we consider the ideas of cross-pollination and extended collaborations part of the last quality: bringing moral horizons into view. As long-time members who have benefited greatly from our associations in knowledge communities, we feel it is our privilege and moral obligation to share our knowledge, skills, and provide opportunities for others.

Portfolio Group

The initial school grants included the charge to break down the barriers between schools and others (school-school, school-district, school-community, school-university, and even among the stakeholders in the schools). With this in mind, we wanted to offer learning opportunities for others in our broader education community; thus, the Epiphany Lecture Series was born. Series speakers included educational scholars such as Bill Ayers, Roland Barth, David Berliner, Coach Herman Boone (*Remember the Titans* movie subject), Larry Cuban, Elliot Eisner, Michael Fullan, A. Lin Goodwin, Carl Glickman, Andy Hargreaves, Gloria Ladson-Billings, and Nona Lyons.

Each speaker gave a large-scale keynote lecture and a smaller session with a select group of targeted participants in a more intimate setting. Michaelann recalls Carl Glickman talking with Eagle High School students about working toward a more democratic society in and out of schools. A few years later, students at Eagle High School organized a walk out to shed light on immigration and needed immigration reform. Although a direct correlation could not be made between Glickman's visit and walkout, the student discipline for the walkout was managed very differently than it would have been before the lecture.

Faculty Academy

Over the past 20 years, the Faculty Academy has disseminated their work in over 26 conference presentations and numerous collaborative publications (see Craig, Turchi et al., 2020). Additionally, various extended collaborations have sprung out of the Faculty Academy within institutions (i.e., *teach* HOUSTON), with other institutions (i.e., University of Houston – Clear Lake), and with local schools (i.e., T. P. Yeager Middle School). These collaborations enrich the work of the Faculty Academy, providing multiple perspectives and diverse points of view. Cross-pollination and extended collaborations are embedded as part of the foundation of the work.

BRINGING IT TOGETHER

Collaboration, professional growth, and relationality among members characterized by both the Portfolio Group and the Faculty Academy has been key to the groups developing and sustaining knowledge communities (Craig, 1995a, 1995b, 1995c, 2007). Both groups consider themselves participant observers where our colleagues are concerned, with relationship and ethics firmly embedded in our face-to-face work. The ways in which both groups exhibited care in nurturing and maintaining relationships made it possible for individuals to choose which collaborative projects of interest they would participate in, without judgment from other members. Cooper et al. (2020) emphasize the importance of learning together,

> As one of our members said, *It's easier if we don't work together—it's easier to stay in our silos*... But we came to treasure our [collaborative] learning and believe that this is the kind of work that can benefit the ongoing functioning of the institution. (p. 324, italics in original)

These two groups also show how educators within knowledge communities continuously strive to bring moral horizons into view in their work. Cooper et al. (2020) suggest,

> When we adopt the ethical stance of our teacher educator identities, we align our critical values to teaching practices we enact with our students. These values include promoting a democratic, inclusive, classroom community; privileging student voices; and empowering students to make decisions and engage in critical thinking. (p. 329)

Craig's (1995a, 1995c) knowledge community concept overturns the notion that educators from different content areas, institutions, and levels of education cannot work collaboratively. When teachers, teacher educators, and researchers choose to work together with moral horizons in view, the capacity for teacher learning and growth is exponential. Striving to improve one's practice in this way brings one closer to the reality of being and living one's best-loved self (Craig, 2013; Schwab, 1954/1978). As Cheryl Craig (2020) writes,

> We are the products of the choices that ourselves make and the subsequent actions and non-actions we take. Similarly, our world is the product of our cumulative choices and actions that we collectively make and take/do not make or take as human beings. This is the reason generous scholarship is so critically important to the educational enterprise. It is a pathway to a kinder, gentler, future academy and a kinder, gentler future world. (p. 362)

CONCLUSION

As Cheryl Craig reminds us, "There is no predetermined pathway to becoming a knowledge community... We go the way that experience leads us" (personal communication, 2022). While the two groups featured here exemplify the ways in which knowledge communities support teacher collaboration, promote ongoing teacher growth and development, and foster teacher sustainability, it is important to note that they are simply two exemplars of the many knowledge communities in existence, some of which may use another nomenclature to describe their group. It is also essential to bear in mind that the Portfolio Group and Faculty Academy did not start out as knowledge communities. Sans the originating event, the nine qualities of knowledge communities emerged organically via trust-building and ongoing reflexive and relational collaboration.

While the work of the group and its membership may change, the long-reaching impact of knowledge communities is their capacity to increase teacher learning in such ways that positively shape teacher practice and affect student success. The importance of the work is in working together to mentor, guide, and lead alongside colleagues, especially early career educators, on tumultuous educational landscapes where educators are getting bombarded from inside and outside the school. Although teachers are leaving the profession by large numbers, a group of passionate educators working together as a knowledge community could be effective in sustaining teachers in the profession.

Pohl (2020) recalls the moment he made the decision to move into academia and which eventually became his work with the Faculty Academy, "he [his principal] told me that career changes are about taking *leaps of faith* [italics in original]. It is something that you have to do if you want to move forward...That day, I began my own leap of faith" (p. 131). We encourage readers to take their own leap of faith by making the reading of this article their (your) "originating event" and to start working with a small group of colleagues to promote teacher learning through collaborative reflection, knowledge co-construction, and professional growth. Begin with looking at your work, broaden to observing and working together, share stories of experience, and move into reflecting and discovering new ideas about improving your teaching and student's learning. So, take a leap of faith and start a learning community – which may become your knowledge community. We encourage you to choose your own pathway and let experience lead the way.

REFERENCES

Amrein-Beardsley, A. (2008). Methodological concerns about the education value-added assessment system. *Educational Researcher, 37*(2), 65–75.

Bailey, J., Hanita, M., Khanani, N., & Zhang, X. (2021). *Analyzing teacher mobility and retention: Guidance and considerations report 1 (REL 2021–080)*. U.S. Department of Education, Institute of Education Sciences, National Center for Education Evaluation and Regional Assistance. Regional Educational Laboratory Northeast & Islands. https://ies.ed.gov/ncee/edlabs/regions/northeast/pdf/REL_2021080.pdf

Bruner, J. (1986). *Actual minds, possible worlds*. Harvard University Press.

Cain, V., Clandinin, D. J., & Lessard, S. (2021). *Narrative inquiry: Philosophical roots*. Bloomsbury Publishing.

Clandinin, D. J., & Connelly, F. M. (1996). Teachers' professional knowledge landscapes: Teacher stories—stories of teachers—school stories—stories of schools. *Educational Researcher, 25*(3), 24–30.

Clandinin, D. J., & Connelly, F. M. (1998). Stories to live by: Narrative understandings of school reform. *Curriculum Inquiry, 28*(2), 149–164.

Clandinin, D. J., & Connelly, F. M. (2000). *Narrative inquiry: Experience and story in qualitative research*. Jossey-Bass.

Clandinin, D. J., & Rosiek, J. (2007). Mapping a landscape of narrative inquiry: Borderland spaces and tensions. In D. J. Clandinin (Ed.), *Handbook of narrative inquiry: Mapping a methodology* (pp. 35–75). Sage.

Connelly, F. M., & Clandinin, D. J. (1988). *Teachers as curriculum planners. Narratives of experience*. Teachers College Press.

Connelly, F. M., & Clandinin, D. J. (2006). Narrative inquiry. In J. L. Green, G. Camilli, & P. Elmore (Eds.), *Handbook of complementary methods in education research* (3rd ed., pp. 477–487). Lawrence Erlbaum.

Cooper, J. M., Gauna, L. M., Beaudry, C. E., & Curtis, G. A. (2020). In C. J. Craig, L. Turchi, & D. M. McDonald (Eds.), *Cross-disciplinary, cross-institutional collaboration in teacher education: Cases of learning and leading* (pp. 327–350). Palgrave Macmillan.

Costa, A. L. (2008). *The school as a home for the mind: Creating mindful curriculum, instruction, and dialogue*. Corwin.

Craig, C. (2020). Generous scholarship: A counternarrative for the region and the academy. In L. Turchi, C. Craig, & D. McDonald (Eds.), *Cross-disciplinary, cross-institutional collaboration in teacher education: Cases of learning and leading* (pp. 351–365). Palgrave Macmillan.

Craig, C. J. (1995a). Dilemmas in crossing the boundaries on the professional knowledge landscape. In D. J. Clandinin & F. M. Connelly (Eds.), *Teachers' professional knowledge landscapes* (pp. 16–24). Teachers College Press.

Craig, C. J. (1995b). Knowledge communities: A way of making sense of how beginning teachers come to know in their professional knowledge contexts. *Curriculum Inquiry, 25*(2), 151–175.

Craig, C. J. (1995c). Safe places on the professional knowledge landscape: Knowledge communities. In D. J. Clandinin & F. M. Connelly (Eds.), *Teachers' professional knowledge landscapes* (pp. 137–141). Teachers College Press.

Craig, C. J. (1999). Parallel stories: A way of contextualizing teacher knowledge. *Teaching and Teacher Education, 15*(4), 397–411.

Craig, C. J. (2007). Illuminating qualities of knowledge communities in a portfolio-making context. *Teachers and Teaching: Theory and Practice, 13*(6), 617–636.

Craig, C. J. (2013). Teacher education and the best-loved self. *Asia Pacific Journal of Education, 33*(3), 261–272.

Craig, C. J. (2017). International teacher attrition: Multiperspective views. *Teachers and Teaching, 23*(8), 859–862.

Craig, C. J., Curtis, G. A., & Kelley, M. (2016). Sustaining self and others in the teaching profession: A group self-study. In D. Garbett & A. Ovens (Eds.), *Enacting self-study as methodology for professional inquiry* (pp. 133–140). Self-Study of Teacher Education Practices.

Craig, C. J., Curtis, G. A., Kelley, M., Martindell, P. T., & Pérez, M. M. (2020). *Knowledge communities in teacher education: Sustaining collaborative work*. Springer Nature.

Craig, C., Turchi, L., & McDonald, D. M. (Eds.). (2020). *Cross-disciplinary, cross-institutional collaboration in teacher education: Cases of learning while leading*. Palgrave Macmillan.

Curtis, G. A., & Craig, C. J. (2020). Faculty academy: A new version of an established concept of collaboration. In C. J. Craig, L. Turchi, & D. M. McDonald (Eds.), *Cross-disciplinary, cross-institutional collaboration in teacher education: Cases of learning and leading* (pp. 9–24). Palgrave Macmillan.

Curtis, G. A., Craig, C. J., Reid, D., Kelley, M., Glamser, M., Martindell, P. T., & Gray, P. (2012). Braided journeys: A self-study of sustained teacher collaboration. In J. R. Young, L. B. Erickson, & S. Pinnegar (Eds.), *Extending inquiry communities: Illuminating teacher education through self-study. Self-study of teacher education practices* (pp. 82–85). Brigham Young University.

Curtis, G., Reid, D., Kelley, M., Martindell, P. T., & Craig, C. J. (2013). Braided lives: Multiple ways of knowing, flowing in and out of knowledge communities. *Studying Teacher Education*, *9*(2), 175–186.

Darling-Hammond, L. (2010). *The flat world of education: How America's commitment to equity will determine our future*. Teachers College.

Dewey, J. (1915/1897). *The school and society*. University of Chicago Press.

Dewey, J. (1938). *Experience and education*. Basic Books.

Dewey, J. (1996/1916). *Democracy and education*. The Free Press, MacMillan.

Dewey, J. (2000). My pedagogic creed. *Philosophical Documents in Education*, *2*, 92–100.

Feiman-Nemser, S. (2012). Beyond SOLO teaching. *Educational Leadership*, *69*(8), 10–16.

Gay, L. R., Mills, G. E., & Airasian, P. (2006). *Introduction to educational research*. Pearson.

Gray, P. D., Jr. (2008). *Narrative ways of knowing: Using portfolios to illuminate learning from a knowledge community perspective (3340585)*. [Doctoral dissertation, University of Houston]. Proquest. https://www.proquest.com/openview/e31be810179268f2c8a767be1109dc31/1?pq-origsite=gscholar&cbl=18750

Hatton, N., & Smith, D. (1995). Reflection in teacher education: Towards definition and implementation. *Teaching and Teacher Education*, *11*, 33–49.

Hlebowitsh, P. (2012). Being there: The ontological measure of teaching. *Curriculum and Teaching Dialogue*, *14*(1/2), 1A.

Kelchtermans, G. (2017). 'Should I stay or should I go?': Unpacking teacher attrition/retention as an educational issue. *Teachers and Teaching*, *23*(8), 961–977.

Kelley, M., Craig, C. J., & Curtis, G. A. (in review). Narrative inquiry knowledge tree: A reflective examination of shaping influences and ethical concerns in narrative methods.

Lodewick, C. (2022, April 4). The Great Resignation could last for years, says the expert who coined the term. *Fortune*. https://fortune.com/2022/04/04/great-resignation-could-last-years-expert-says/#:~:

Lyons, N., & LaBoskey, V. K. (Eds.). (2002). *Narrative inquiry in practice: Advancing the knowledge of teaching*. Teachers College Press.

Markello, C. (2020). Reflecting on growth and change: The persistence of the Faculty Academy (2002–2020). In C. J. Craig, L. Turchi, & D. M. McDonald (Eds.), *Cross-disciplinary, cross-institutional collaboration in teacher education: Cases of learning and leading* (pp. 25–44). Palgrave Macmillan.

McDonald, D. M., Divoll, K., Newsum, J. M., Williams-Duncan, O. M., Auzenne-Curl, C., & Klekel, J. (2020). Involvement in a professional community yields unexpected skills: Faculty Academy members' stories of leadership and learning. In C. J. Craig, L. Turchi, & D. M. McDonald (Eds.), *Cross-disciplinary, cross-institutional collaboration in teacher education: Cases of learning and leading* (pp. 45–82). Palgrave Macmillan.

Mishler, E. (1990). Validation in inquiry-guided research: The role of exemplars in narrative studies. *Harvard Educational Review*, *60*(4), 415–443.

Olson, M. R. (1995). Conceptualizing narrative authority: Implications for teacher education. *Teaching and Teacher Education*, *11*(2), 119–135.

Penuel, W., Riel, M., Krause, A., & Frank, K. (2009). Analyzing teachers' professional interactions in a school as social capital: A social network approach. *Teachers College Record*, *111*(1), 124–163.

Plagens, G. K. (2011). Social capital and education: Implications for student and school performance. *Education and Culture*, *27*(1), 40–64.

Pohl, B. (2020). Musing on the sidelines: Leadership and learning during the tenure track experiences. In C. J. Craig, L. Turchi, & D. M. McDonald (Eds.), *Cross-disciplinary, cross-institutional collaboration in teacher education: Cases of learning and leading* (pp. 113–134). Palgrave Macmillan.

Sack, J. J., & Vazquez, I. (2020). Learning and leading as teacher researchers. In C. J. Craig, L. Turchi, & D. M. McDonald (Eds.), *Cross-disciplinary, cross-institutional collaboration in teacher education: Cases of learning and leading* (pp. 257–270). Palgrave Macmillan.

Schön, D. A. (1995). The new scholarship requires a new epistemology. *Change*, *27*, 26–34.

Schuck, S., & Russell, T. (2005). Self-study, critical friendship, and the complexities of teacher education. *Studying Teacher Education*, *1*(2), 107–121.

Schwab, J. J. (1954/1978). Eros and education: A discussion of one aspect of discussion. In I. Westbury & N. Wilkof (Eds.), *Science, curriculum and liberal education: Selected essays*. University of Chicago Press.

Shernoff, E. S., Mariñez-Lora, A. M., Frazier, S. L., Jakobsons, L. J., Atkins, M. S., & Bonner, D. (2011). Teachers supporting teachers in urban schools: What iterative research designs can teach us. *School Psychology Review*, *40*(4), 465–485.

Spillane, J. P. (2005). Distributed leadership. *The Educational Forum*, *69*(2), 143–150.

Stenhouse, L. (1975). *An introduction to curriculum research and development*. Heinemann.

Xu, S., & Connelly, M. (2010). Narrative inquiry for school-based research. *Narrative Inquiry*, *20*(2), 349–370.

MULTINATIONAL POLICY ANALYSES: THIRD TIME AROUND

Maria Assunção Flores, Darlene Ciuffetelli Parker, Maria Inês Marcondes and Cheryl J. Craig

ABSTRACT

This chapter is a multinational policy analysis focusing on what happened in the aftermath of the Covid-19 pandemic in Brazil, Canada, Portugal, and USA. It is a follow-up to the first two analyses which were also conducted collaboratively (2019, 2022). The studies are constant-comparative. The four-country approach illuminates policies and practices in what hopefully is post-Covid-19 times. Neoliberal approaches to policymaking and education in general ensure that the technicalities of teaching received heightened attention to the neglect of the well-being of teachers and the agency afforded them. The critical situation of the teaching profession in the post-pandemic time means there are teacher shortages as well as the lowering of working conditions for teachers. Turmoil and crisis are two words that describe the education sector and are clearly illustrated in the media and in research. While the need to invest in education, and particularly teachers' education and career prospects, is reiterated in policy discourse, it is far from being a reality as the four cases show. The pandemic has exacerbated the existing problems in the field of education, causing heightening concern about teachers' recruitment, working conditions and well-being.

Keywords: Policy analysis; teachers' role; teaching profession; post-Covid-19; teacher shortage; crisis

As a diverse international author team, we conducted a comparative study of four nations in 2018–2019 (Craig et al., 2020): Brazil, Canada, Portugal, and the United States (Fig. 1). We presented our research at the ISATT Conference in

Fig. 1. A Comparative Study of Four Nations in 2018–2019 (Craig et al., 2020).

Romania because researchers in teacher education typically do not make strong connections with national educational policies, let alone with OECD (Organization for Economic and Co-operative Development) (OECD, 2020a, 2020b, 2020c) and its PISA (Program for International Student Assessment) testing program, as well as other international agencies and their measures. We followed this first study with a more recent *Palgrave Handbook of Teacher Education Research* analysis (Craig et al., 2022) where we contemplated whether the 2018–2019 trends continued or whether they lessened or became replaced by other policy efforts when Covid-19 struck in the first quarter of 2020 and continued to spread. With that study, we quickly determined that despite the pandemic being universal, teachers and students did not face it in the same way. Those who already were at a disadvantage (i.e., lack of technology, influence of poverty, underserved school contexts, etc.) experienced deeper effects. This undercurrent was felt in all four of our nations. Also, standardization, a phenomenon directly tied to the spread of neoliberalism, remained a common theme across all four countries, but had a stronger influence in Brazil and the United Ststes. than in Canada and Portugal, with the reverse being true where incremental change was concerned. In this ISATT 40th anniversary yearbook chapter, we conduct our multinational policy analysis a third time around – this time focusing on what happened in the aftermath of the Covid-19 pandemic in each country – in order to arrive at some international findings.

LITERATURE REVIEW

This third study's research pillars are the same as our first two investigations: (1) school reform, (2) role of teachers in change efforts, and (3) neoliberalism.

School Reform

Since the beginning of time, people have felt the need to improve their situations. In the field of education, the human desire to change is expressed in curricular and school reform efforts (Fullan, 2001). Adopting organized interventions – "reforms" – has become not only national passions but an international fascination as well. The achievement of students in different countries are systematically compared with one another through PISA and other international testing measures (Fullan, 2012; Sahlberg, 2021). The outcomes affect international ratings and nations' economies and may directly impact educational funding decisions.

Teachers' Roles in Change Efforts

Two pervasive metaphors capture teachers' roles in curricular and school change: teacher-as-curriculum-implementer and teacher-as-curriculum-maker (Clandinin & Connelly, 1992; Craig & Ross, 2008). Neither of the metaphors are mutually exclusive because the boundaries between them are porous. The curriculum implementer image casts teachers as "agents of the state...paid to do its bidding" (Lent & Pipkin, 2003, p. x) – that is, as "passive deliverers of pre-digested [changes]..." (Goodson, 2003, p. 72). By way of contrast, the curriculum maker image acknowledges the mindedness of teachers and how they necessarily interpret government mandates to meet the needs of their students, communities, and situations. Dewey (1908/1981) was the first to recognize teachers as being moved by "their own intelligences and ideas" (p. 16), Schwab (1954/1978) envisioned teachers as "agent[s] of education, not of ... subject matter" (p. 128), and Jackson (1968/1990) sought to understand classroom life, not through policymakers' and parents' moral admonitions, but in teachers' and students' own terms. Freire (1968) likewise championed the agency and decision-making powers of teachers despite blanket government directives.

Neoliberalism

Since the 1980s, neoliberalism is a philosophy that has become a near-ideology. It has spread through the world, most especially in developed countries (Davis & Bansel, 2007). In the neoliberal paradigm, the free-market reigns supreme and competition – particularly international competition in the face of globalization – is encouraged. The entrepreneurship of individuals and corporations is favored over the economic good of all. When neoliberalism is reduced to its essence, everything has a price tag. This includes education and teachers. Schools and education are no longer viewed as "essential to collective well-being, but are services, like any others, to be traded in the marketplace" (Peters, 1999, p. 2).

METHOD

This constant-comparative analysis burrows into local and national policy efforts and broadens to the international policy landscape (Engeli et al., 2014). It is a "serial interpretation" (Schwab, 1954/1978) that examines three identifiable data points and searches for common themes surfacing across time and place.

We adopted this serial interpretation approach (Fig. 2) because it "increases explanatory power and gives findings of multiple studies [from multiple countries] added heft. It serves as a vehicle to discuss [overarching] ideas that transcend multiple research investigations" (Craig et al., 2019, p. 344). In short, serial interpretation allows for "talking across" (Stone, 1988, p. 2) or "see[ing] across" (Clandinin, 2013, p. 131) research endeavors, rather than reporting a single country case or a single cross-country comparison. It provides a fuller picture and is able to unearth contributing factors not initially visible.

The Third Time Around

Brazil

The pandemic was experienced by teachers and students in different ways. In the Brazilian educational context, relating to the pandemic, the Ministry of Education decrees on March 17, 2020, through Ordinance no.343, resulted in the suspension of in-person classes and their replacement by non-in-person activities via digital media while the Coronavirus pandemic (Covid-19) situation continued.

The review research, *Education in the context of the Covid-19 pandemic: A systematic review of the literature* (Vieira & Seco, 2020), reveals challenges and experiences of students and teachers to mitigate the effects of the transition to remote teaching and learning and future perspectives for education. The study is based on the academic productions published on the CAPES Journal Portal, in the Scientific repositories of Open Access of Portugal – RCSSP, in SCIELO and on Google Scholar, from March/2020 to July/2020. The review research studied

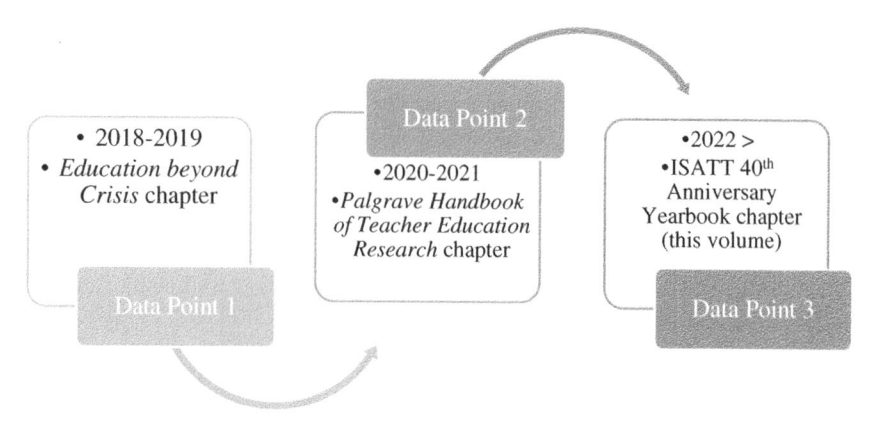

Fig. 2. Three Data Points for Comparative Purposes.

the Portuguese and Brazilian context, but in this chapter only issues related to the Brazilian context will be discussed.

The literature review's basic questions were: What are the impacts of Covid-19 on the Brazilian school education? What difficulties and challenges did teachers and students face during classes in this period of remote learning? What technologies and platforms (*Moodle, Teams, Google meet*, etc.) were adopted by schools? What methodologies and activities (video classes, synchronous web conferencing, asynchronous activities) were used by teachers? Did the adopted strategies guarantee the participation and learning of all students in the circumstances in which we live? What are the trends and dilemmas in Basic and Secondary Education after the Covid-19 pandemic?

In relation to the *prospective analyses and post-pandemic opportunities*, the review highlights the need for teacher education that enables the development of digital skills that could modify their pedagogical practices with the use of technological resources. In addition to the technological domain, it is essential to develop authorial skills to produce and share knowledge in cyber space, to move away from historically consolidated transmissive practices in education criticized by the Brazilian educator Paulo Freire (1968).

Educational measures of equality, equity, and inclusion must account for the diversity of students in the country. In particular, tools such as the Internet and a broadband network must be accessible. Also, homes must have spaces that support and monitor remote learning, as well as additional support for students needing extra assistance. It is necessary to understand diversity, accessibility, and the principles of inclusion to meet demands of students in situations where they experience social vulnerability.

In relation to prospective analysis and post-pandemic opportunities (Vieira & Seco, 2020, p. 1026), the literature review revealed that post-pandemic, hybrid education mediated by digital educational resources will prevail. However, concern and care must be focused on what really matters: the teaching working conditions, the quality of the teaching-learning process, the relevance of the topics to be addressed, the development of student-centered pedagogical practices, the awakening of students to the possibilities inherent in their learning processes, and the involvement of families in the lives and learning of children and adolescents. The Brazilian literature review asserted that the remote teaching trend produced more inequality among students, more fragility in the teaching profession, and even more disruption in public education, given teachers' limitations where digital competencies were concerned.

In relation to the students in Brazil from disadvantaged backgrounds, they will probably make up a lost generation in terms of educational gains. The percentage of children who cannot read and write even single words more than doubled in just two years. Data from the Basic Education Assessment System (Saeb), released by the Ministry of Education in October of 2022, show that the country had 15.5% of second grade children with this level of learning. In 2021, the index jumped to 33.8%. Since the beginning of the pandemic, with the closure of schools, education experts and teachers have drawn attention to the difficulty of distance literacy. These children need help and are now in third grade classes all over Brazil. It is time to intervene in overcoming this observed gap. The consequences of much lower levels of learning will be felt for a long time.

A last word related to teachers' work in a changed context: Teachers had to mobilize their skills to teach during the pandemic using different ways of communicating with children including physical delivery of learning materials to use of teaching and learning materials to teaching and learning platforms for online communication and WhatsApp messages. Unfortunately, the pandemic has most acutely harmed the poorest countries and the poorest populations in the rich countries.

Interim Analysis

Problems already prevalent in public education in Brazil deepened during the pandemic. The precariousness of many schools, the absence of many schools, the absence of sufficient professionals, the lack of support from digital networks, and the policy vacuum that was created cumulatively made it difficult to find alternatives during the pandemic. The search for solutions required dialogue between the educational community and other sectors of society.

Canada

On the front page of the *Toronto Star* the headline reads, "Province will block strike by education workers" (Roshowy, 2022). The article reports that the Education Minister will "not allow turmoil in schools after two-plus years of disruption due to the Covid-19 pandemic." Blocking educators' violation of rights poses another sort of turmoil, indeed, on an already vulnerable education context.

Turmoil is a word that has multiple meanings on how the world has played out in systems of education during the pandemic and as we approach a post pandemic landscape. In Ontario at present, imposing austerity measures on education systems is a chilling reminder of Bill 115 in 2012 when Ontario teachers' salaries were frozen, as well as the elimination of sick pay days and banking sick days. At the time, Bill 115 also removed teachers' ability to strike fully. In 2016, the Ontario Supreme Court of Justice ruled that Bill 115 violated the collective bargaining rights of teachers and school staff. This resulted in the province paying out, to date, over $210 million to teacher unions (Roshowy, 2022). This ruling has not, however, deterred the current government from introducing Bill 28, *Keeping Students in Class Act*, which if passed would also do what Bill 115 did in 2012; further, the bill would contravene the Canadian Charter of Rights and Freedoms by having "the effect of terminating any strike or lock-out that may be in effect before the Bill receives Royal Assent" (Nevison, 2022). At the time of this writing, strikes are ensuing in Ontario, with the Federal Government cautioning provincial legislation against using Canada's Constitution's notwithstanding clause to override the Charter of Rights and Freedoms.

The reality in Canada is that turmoil in school systems have ensued pre-pandemic, pandemic, and as we approach post-pandemic contexts. The increases in mental health challenges for students, teachers, and teacher candidates are specifically "attributed to months of physical distancing, growing job loss, economic uncertainty, housing and food insecurity and child-care or school closures" (Jenkins et al., 2020, para. 4). So now we have the turmoil that existed, and the turmoil with immense mental health issues for educators and students alike. Add to that the turmoil of austerity measures placed on school systems by governments which rain heavily upon otherwise well intended policies and practices in schools trying to gain traction on issues of equity, diversity, and inclusion. Undoubtedly, "at no other time during this pandemic global crisis, and as the world awaits in hope for a healthier tomorrow, is it ripe for a meaningful new normal of schooling for an equitable education for all students" (Ciuffetelli Parker & Conversano, 2021, p. 8). And yet, with all that has transpired, the topic of equity and schooling has been gripped and used for political gain, most recently in the government's *Right to Read* report.

> The *Right to Read* report, supported by the Ontario Ministry of Education, makes a persuasive case that this is an issue of social justice that requires more attention (and financial resources) than it has received up to this point. Unfortunately, the authors of the report risk undermining their own urgent and powerful message when they stray from specific challenges…into a more general condemnation of the Ontario educational system. The report makes two dubious claims to 'explain' the reading difficulties of children in Ontario schools. First it attempts to make a case that Ontario schools are failing to teach reading skills effectively for all students…Second, it attributes this 'failure' to the fact that most Ontario schools implement a 'balanced' approach to reading instruction, which they claim pays insufficient attention to teaching sound/letter correspondences…Contrary to the unsubstantiated claims…Ontario is among the top performers internationally and across Canada in reading performance. (Cummins, 2022, p. 86)

Jim Cummins, Professor Emeritus whose life's work is in literacy development, in writing this commentary response to the *Right to Read* report, lays bare the issue at hand: the report claims (without research support) that a balanced approach does not sufficiently pay attention to teaching phonemic awareness and phonics. Cummins asserts, with reasonable account, that this is simply untrue. Further, the report's recommendation is to do away with the three-cueing system (i.e., semantics, grammar, phonics) as a balanced program. The launch of the report claimed that a balanced literacy approach is an injustice to marginalized and vulnerable populations. And here is the rub. Faculties of Education and Dean's associations are currently writing position papers, and a great political debate has entrenched Ontario, leaving teacher candidates, in-service teachers, school systems, and faculties of education scrambling as to how to deliver reading instruction. The tension is palpable as educators are caught between coping in a post pandemic break-down-and-building-up of systems, on one hand, and on the other hand, dealing with political pressures and austerity measures, all for the party in political power. The reality is that teachers are caught between schooling for a democratic society while pushing a political agenda.

All this, at a time when there is, as has been described by other nations across the world and in this chapter, a severe teacher shortage. The Ontario College of Teachers (OCT) reports after the second Covid-19-affected year that,

Teacher shortages will increase for French-language boards. Many English-language boards will have insufficient French as a second language teachers to staff these high demand programs. Chronic shortages of occasional roster teachers will persist for English-language boards, and they will experience increased competition to fill some elementary and secondary teacher LTO and permanent job vacancies. (OCT, 2021)

There has been much school turbulence and turmoil for early-career Ontario teachers. Teacher education preservice programs across the province are now offering, through the Ministry of Education and OCT, temporary certificates during their two-year in-service academic program. This is an unprecedented move, given the stress on teacher candidates' academic workload and practicum evaluations. Add to that the pressure of obtaining a temporary certificate for teacher candidates to now secure a job pre-graduation as "the new normal" and the competition arising for access to desired teaching positions, given the teacher shortage. The result has amounted to academic and work stress, mental health challenges, and hundreds of teacher candidates requesting medical leaves of absence from their teacher education program or leaving their programs altogether. A Catch-22, indeed. Teacher education programs, meanwhile, are being filled to over-capacity with enrollment, but without the required administrative support of faculty or staff to administrate larger enrollment programs. The stress on leadership roles that oversee teacher education programs comes with a steep daily turmoil. The ongoing and regular deliberation with senior leadership and the university "white tower" has reached a new level of complexity, post pandemic.

Interim Analysis
The province of Ontario, and by association the nation of Canada, is at a tipping point in teaching, teacher education programs, and administrative programming. The basic human rights of education workers and the basic right of a student's proper and equitable education are both at stake. We cannot violate the rights of our workers and students for the sake of political gain. One opposition Minister was quoted, "There is no notwithstanding clause for workers who cannot afford to pay their bills…it's going to hurt them and it's going to hurt their families." Politics and education will be forever married, especially since governments fund school systems in Canada. However, toward a post pandemic view of schooling, it must be acknowledged that working conditions affect if schooling is successful, or not. Impingement on curriculum by governments, such as how to teach reading (which by the way is a century long debate in school systems), is and remains a caution, and a slippery slope too. We see what is happening in reading instruction in this iteration here and, in the former collaborative iteration, the topic was on math proficiency testing of teacher candidates (which resulted in the government forcing to eliminate it, by court ruling). These issues, and especially issues of teacher education programming, enrollment, and work recruitment require deep thinking and revision.

Portugal

> I have done my best with this situation [Covid-19], and even though I think I've only done what was possible, I have done my best. But that doesn't mean that the best has happened (...) I have done my best in exceptional circumstances and this is what teachers have to recognize when they look back at what happened. (Teacher, 26 years of teaching)

This quote from a Portuguese teacher illustrates well the feelings of many teachers during the pandemic and beyond. While teachers have dealt with the Covid-19 crisis in a quick and overall effective way in order avoid too much "learning loss," they also acknowledge a sense of powerlessness and even frustration at not being able to "reach all students."

The translocation of teaching from a classroom setting to online platforms (Ávalos et al., 2022) was an intense experience for teachers as they felt the "initial shock" but also created an opportunity for them to collaborate. This has been associated with teachers' sense of professionalism, the emergence of creative solutions and the mobilization of endogenous resources in the schools and in the local communities (Flores et al., 2021).

Yet, teachers also stress the difficulty to reconcile family and professional lives and the increased workload (non-remunerated working hours) along with the lack of support. In a national survey conducted in Portugal in 2021 (n = 2,192), when asked about the support they received and how they handled the difficulties they encountered, the majority of teachers highlight factors associated with their immediate working contexts, namely: colleagues (69.5%), tutors (teachers responsible for liaising between students, teachers and families) (63.4%), leadership team (60.9%), department/year/cycle coordinators (59.1%), the school principal (58.7%), and the support team responsible for distance teaching in the school (45.7%). Less significant was the guidance provided by the Ministry of Education (15.1%). Also, a large study of 1,479 teachers in Portugal by Alves et al. (2020) unveiled a decrease in teacher well-being, as well as a lowering of their professional commitment and long-term perspectives. Such a picture has been exacerbated in the aftermath of the Covid-19 and needs to be seen in the light of the current situation of the teaching profession.

Although the teacher shortage crisis is not new, it has been amplified recently as the figures in relation to students without teachers have marked the start of academic year in the "new normal." A look at the highlights in the media is illustrative of the dimension of the crisis:

> The school year starts with the "dark shadow" of the lack of teachers and the new normal. Next year around 110 000 students will not have a teacher in at least one subject (Lusa, 2022).
>
> Until Christmas more than 600 teachers will have retired (SIC Notícias, 2022).
>
> Back to school: more than 2000 teachers will retire until the end of the year (SIC Notícias, 2022).
>
> New school year marked by the lack of teachers, around 70.000 students have started the school year without a teacher in at least one subject (SIC Notícias, 2022).
>
> Lack of teachers: more students without classes and fewer teachers available; more than 80.000 students without a teacher in at least one subject (Diário de Notícias, 2022).

Lack of teachers: October with a record number of teachers who retired (Diário de Notícias, 2022).

The aging of the teaching workforce is also a reality (51.9% of the teachers are 50 years or above and only 1.6% are younger than 30 years of age) (CNE, 2021). According to the official statistics, there will be a need to recruit more than 34.000 teachers by 2030 (on average 3.450 per year) due to retirement (DGEEC, 2021). Although there has been an increase in the number of student teachers in the last few years, the number of qualified teachers who graduate each year does not correspond with the needs especially in given subjects. The need to recruit unqualified teachers (without a teaching degree) is a threat to the quality of education. School principals and teacher unions are concerned and, despite the initiatives developed by the Ministry of Education to mitigate the problem (i.e., bring back to school those teachers who were performing other functions within the statute of mobility; changing rules for mobility due to health issues), the structural problem of teacher shortage requires wider and more consistent measures involving all the stakeholders.

Interim Analysis
While the Covid-19 crisis has shown the fragility of the education systems (especially with respect to equipment, resources, connectivity with implications for equity and social justice), it has also demonstrated the key importance of teachers. Yet, the recognition of the teaching profession and the valorization of teachers' work need urgent and structural measures to face the crisis of teacher shortage and the low numbers of teaching candidates. Issues of social and economic status, working conditions, education, and recruitment need to be addressed in a consistent manner that brings together policy, practice, and research.

United States
This following *Facebook* post recently circulated in the United States:

> There is no teacher shortage. There are thousands of qualified experienced teachers who are no longer teaching. There's a shortage of respect and proper compensation for teachers, allowing them to actually teach. (From Other 98% website)

The question of what occurred in the United States when the pandemic died down can be summed up in two words: teacher shortage. Even the principal from the US portion of the research in our initial publication (Craig et al., 2020) joined the *Facebook* discussion. On the website, she reported that her campus would begin the 2022–2023 school year with three less teachers than needed. Wishful thinking, she queried whether there were readers who could fill those vacancies?

The truth of the matter is that Houston Independent School District (HISD), which is the fourth largest urban district in America, had 870 openings prior to the beginning of school in 2022–2023 (Serrano & Dillinger, 2022). However, when HISD's numbers were combined with the surrounding metropolitan school districts, the urban area was 3,400 teachers short. The same was also true of other parts of the United States like Los Angeles and New York. The US rural situation was equally dire.

The *Texas Tribune* observed the following about both the state's urban and rural campuses:

> Texas schools have long had two few teachers. The pandemic made the situation worse but issues like low pay, poor benefits and polarizing statewide politics all have had an impact, too. (Lopez, 2022)

The news article then declared that teachers have long sat at the fulcrum of "ongoing tensions over how race and sex should be taught" in the schools. These contentious issues have more recently been joined by high levels of anxiety about school safety after the slaying of 19 elementary school children and 2 adults in Uvalde, Texas, the deadliest school shooting in Texas to date. Texas's tragedy joins the Columbine High School massacre in Colorado and the Sandy Hook Elementary School murders in Connecticut, among school deaths elsewhere in the nation. The *Texas Tribune* underscored the fact that teachers have cumulatively been "pushed to their limits" and out of the profession (Lopez, 2022).

Much can be added, of course, about benefits for teachers – or the lack thereof. Despite Texas being a state with an economic productivity that surpasses the countries of Mexico and Canada, it also is a state that has one of the lowest paying teacher retirement plans in the country. Further to this, teachers have not received a cost-of-living increase since 2004. In short, teachers in Texas feel not only "underpaid" (under-compensated) but "undervalued" as well (Lopez, 2022).

A promising white, male teacher who recently quit the profession was interviewed for the *Tribune* report. That teacher echoed Dewey (1897), saying "the classroom is a microcosm of what is going on outside." He then said he could no longer live with the existential angst concerning the education and wellbeing of other people's children in his care. It ultimately boiled down to him putting his concerted efforts into his own kids and leaving the classroom behind.

At the national level, *The Washington Post* termed the US teacher shortage "catastrophic" (Natanson, 2022, August 3). The article then graphically outlined some details:

> Rural school districts in Texas are switching to four-day weeks this fall due to a lack of staff. Florida is asking veterans with no teaching background to enter classrooms. Arizona is allowing college students to step in and instruct students.

Unfortunately, there is no overarching federal policy dealing with teacher attrition. To be precise, the 10th Amendment (U.S. Constitution, Amend. X). states that "powers not delegated to the federal government are reserved to the States respectively or to the people." Ever since then, the courts have upheld education as a state right.

This explains why what is happening overall in the United States is limited – to a certain extent – to what individual states report. Nevada, for example, disclosed that it was 3,000 teaching and staff positions short (Adcox, 2022), whereas Illinois said 88% of its school districts were having trouble filling teaching positions, which equates to a shortage of 5,301.8 teachers as of September 25, 2022 (Illinois State Board of Education). Also, a school district in California was looking for homes where teachers could pay room and board because they could not afford to live in apartments or single-family dwellings near the schools where they teach (Hernandez, 2022). As for Wisconsin, superintendents there created a "whisper network" through which teachers moving from one state to another could be located. Like the *Texas Tribune*, the *Washington Post* referred to pandemic-induced teacher anxiety (Iati, 2021) along with low pay and teacher compensation packages (Natanson, 2022). The *Post* also noted that politicians, parents, and school board members do not respect teachers for the difficult roles the play in the "escalating culture wars" in the United States – and the increasingly restrictions placed on them concerning what they can say about American history, race, racism, sexual orientation, and LGBTQ issues (Natanson, 2022).

Interim Analysis
While policymakers pinpoint the American teacher shortage as being caused by the pandemic, the situation is much more complicated than that. The teacher shortage was not singlehandedly produced by the pandemic. The pandemic may have been the turning point, but the conditions (high stress, low pay, high stakes testing, constant intervention by the public, etc.) for the "great resignation" (Klotz, 2021) had been building for decades. In Texas, teachers had been hovering between the lower class and the middle class for some time due to low salaries and no cost-of-living adjustments. This is highly problematic as teachers are to be role models for the students they teach. Also, the pandemic changed society's overall view of work. People are fitting work into their lives, "instead of having lives that squeeze into their work" (Klotz, 2021).

SIGNIFICANCE

This four-country study illuminated policies and practices arguably post-Covid-19. Neoliberal approaches to policymaking and education in general ensured that the technicalities of teaching received heightened attention to the neglect of the well-being of teachers and the agency that should be afforded them (Hargreaves, 2021). What is clear in the four contexts is the critical situation of the teaching profession in the post-pandemic time associated with teacher shortage and the lowering of working conditions of teachers. Turmoil and crisis are two words that describe the education sector in these contexts and that are clearly illustrated in the media and in research. While the need to invest in education, and particularly teachers, their education and career prospects, is reiterated in policy discourse, it is far from being a reality. The pandemic is not the root cause, but it has exacerbated the problems that already existed in pre-pandemic times. The lack of teachers and the need to solve the problem in the short and long run raises questions about the focus and direction of the policies – with risks being associated with quick-fixes and with the tension between quantity and quality and consequently, deprofessionalization

(Flores, in press). Along with that, as the cases in this chapter demonstrate, is teachers' well-being and support in terms of career development. Accountability measures and increased external surveillance of teachers' work and what they said about social issues in their classrooms (Zuboff, 2019) also affected teachers' morale and commitment (Ciuffetelli Parker & Craig, 2017; Craig, 2020; Flores, 2012). Trust between the teaching profession and educational bureaucracies seemed mostly to wane (Evetts, 2009) and, in the extreme case, increasingly operated in a surveillance mode against a backdrop of what Ladson-Billings (2021) called the "four pandemics." Amid contradictory sets of assumptions, the nature of teachers' work significantly changed across the four nations represented in our cross-case analysis in the aftermath of the pandemic. This needs to be seriously taken into account at policy, practice and research levels as the world moves toward a future yet unknown.

REFERENCES

Adcox, A. (2022, August 7). Nevada faces teacher and staff shortage of 3000 ahead of the new school year. Washington Examiner. https://www.washingtonexaminer.com/policy/education/nevada-teacher-staff-shortage-new-school-year

Alves, R., Lopes, T., & Precioso, J. (2020). Teachers' well-being in times of Covid-19 pandemic: Factors that explain professional well-being. *IJERI: International Journal of Educational Research and Innovation, 15*, 203–217. https://doi.org/10.46661/ijeri.5120

Ávalos, B., Flores, M. A., & Araneda, S. (2022). Battling to keep education going: Chilean and Portuguese teacher experiences in COVID-19 Times. *Teachers and Teaching: Theory and Practice, 28*(2), 131–148.

Ciuffetelli Parker, D., & Conversano, P. (2021). Narratives of systemic barriers in schools: Income equity, diversity, inclusion, and the call for a post-pandemic new normal. *Frontiers in Education Journal, 6*(70466), 1–19. https://www.frontiersin.org/articles/10.3389/feduc.2021.704663/full

Ciuffetelli Parker, D., & Craig, C. (2017). An international inquiry: Stories of poverty Poverty stories. *Urban Education, 52*(1), 120–151. https://doi.org/10.1177%2F0042085914566097

Clandinin, D. J. (2013). *Engaging in narrative inquiry*. Left Coast Press.

Clandinin, D. J., & Connelly, F. M. (1992). Teacher as curriculum maker. In P. Jackson (Ed.), *Handbook of curriculum* (pp. 363–461). Macmillan.

CNE. (2021). *Estado da Educação 2020*. CNE.

Craig, C. J., Evans, P., Verma, R., Stokes, D., & Li, J. (2019). A tribute to 'unsung teachers': Teachers' influences on students enrolling in STEM programs with the intent of entering STEM careers. *European Journal of Teacher Education, 42*(3), 335–358. https://doi.org/10.1080/02619768.2018.1523390

Craig, C. J., Flores, M. A., Marcondes, M. I., & Ciuffetelli Parker, D. (2020). The impact of reform policies on teachers and their practices: Case studies from four countries. In *Education beyond crisis* (pp. 3–31). Brill.

Craig, C. J., Flores, M. A., Marcondes, M. I., & Ciuffetelli Parker, D. (2022). Cases of four international reforming contexts: Prelude to the pandemic and beyond. In I. Menter (Ed.), *Palgrave handbook of teacher education research*. https://doi.org/10.1007/978-3-030-59533-3_76-1

Craig, C., & Ross, V. (2008). Cultivating the image of teachers as curriculum makers. In F. M. Connelly, M. F. He, & J. Phillion (Eds.), *The sage handbook of curriculum and instruction*. SAGE Publications Inc. http://doi.org/10.4135/9781412976572.n14

Cummins, J. (2022). Dialogue and commentary: Ontario Human Rights Commission "Right to Read" Report: Sincere, passionate, flawed. *Journal of Teaching and Learning, 16*(1), 85–92. https://doi.org/10.22329/jtl.v16i1.7279

Davis, B., & Bansel, P. (2007). Neoliberalism and education. *International Journal of Qualitative Studies in Education, 20*(3), 247–259. https://doi.org/10.1080/09518390701281751

Dewey, J. (1897, January). My pedagogical creed. *School Journal, 54*, 77–80.
Dewey, J. (1908/1981). The practical character of reality. In J. McDermott (Ed.), *The philosophy of John Dewey*. University of Chicago Press.
DGEEC. (2021). *Estudo de diagnóstico de necessidades docentes de 2021 a 2030*. Direção-Geral de Estatísticas da Educação e Ciência.
Diário de Notícias. (2022, October 14). Lack of teachers: More students without classes and fewer teachers available. https://www.dn.pt/sociedade/falta-de-professores-mais-alunos-sem-aulas-e-menos-docentes-para-colocar-15252407.html
Diário de Notícias. (2022, October 26). Lack of teachers: October with a record number of teachers who retired. https://www.dn.pt/sociedade/falta-de-professores-outubro-com-recorde-de-aposentacoes-15287442.html
Engeli, I., Allison, C. R., & Allison, C. R. (Eds.). (2014). *Comparative policy studies: Conceptual and methodological challenges*. Springer.
Evetts, J. (2009). The management of professionalism: A contemporary paradox. In S. Gewirtz, P. Mahony, I. Hextall, & A. Cribb (Orgs.), *Changing teacher professionalism. International trends, challenges and ways forward* (pp. 19–30). Routledge.
Flores, M. A. (2012). Teachers' work and lives: A European perspective. In C. Day (Ed.), *The Routledge international handbook of teacher and school development* (pp. 94–107). Routledge.
Flores, M. A., Machado, E. A., Alves, P., & Vieira, D. A. (2021). Ensinar em tempos de COVID-19: um estudo com professores dos ensinos básico e secundário em Portugal. *Revista Portuguesa de Educação, 34*(1), 5–27. http://doi.org/10.21814/rpe.21108
Flores, M. A. (in press). Unpacking quality in teacher education. In J. Madalinska-Michalak (Ed.), *Quality in teaching and teacher education*. Brill.
Freire, P. (1968). *Pedagogy of the oppressed*. The Continuum International Publishing Group Inc.
Fullan, M. (2001). *The new meaning of educational change*. Routledge.
Fullan, M. (2012). *Change forces: Probing the depths of educational reform*. Routledge.
Goodson, I. (2003). *Professional knowledge, professional lives*. McGraw-Hill Education.
Hargreaves, A. (2021). What the COVID-19 pandemic has taught us about teachers and teaching. In *Children and schools during COVID-19 and beyond: Engagement and connection through opportunity* (pp. 138–167). An RSC Policy Briefing.
Hernandez, J. (2022, September 7). A California school district is asking families to rent rooms to teachers. National Public Radio. https://www.npr.org/2022/09/07/1120849458/a-california-school-district-is-asking-families-to-rent-rooms-to-teachers
Iati, M. (2021, December 24). The pandemic has caused nearly two years of collective trauma. Many people are near a breaking point. *Washington Post*. https://www.washingtonpost.com/health/2021/12/24/collective-trauma-public-outbursts/
Illinois State Board of Education. (2022, September 25). https://www.isbe.net/unfilledpositions
Jackson, P. W. (1990/1968). *Life in classrooms*. Holt, Rinehart & Winston.
Jenkins, E., Gadermann, A., & McAuliffe, C. (2020). Mental health impact of coronavirus pandemic hits marginalized groups hardest. The conversation. https://theconversation.com/mental-health-impact-of-coronavirus-pandemic-hits-marginalized-groups-hardest-142127
Klotz, A. (2021). On defining the great resignation. *The Verse Media*. https://www.theversemedia.com/articles/anthony-klotz-defining-the-great-resignation
Ladson-Billings, G. (2021). I'm here for the hard re-set: Post pandemic pedagogy to preserve our culture. *Equity & Excellence in Education, 54*(1), 68–78.
Lent, R., & Pipkin, G. (2003). *Silent no more: Voices of courage in America*. Heinemann.
Lopez, B. (2022). It's not just COVID-19: Why Texas faces a teacher shortage. The Texas Tribune. https://www.texastribune.org/2022/07/25/texas-teacher-shortage/
Lusa. (2022). The school year starts with the "dark shadow" of the lack of teachers and the new normal. https://eco.sapo.pt/2022/09/11/ano-letivo-arranca-com-nuvem-negra-da-falta-de-professores-e-nova-normalidade/
Natanson, H. (2022, August 14). Never seen it this bad: America faces catastrophic teacher shortage. https://www.washingtonpost.com/education/2022/08/03/school-teacher-shortage/
Nevison, C. (2022). Ontario tables significant legislation impacting school board sector. Hicks Morley LLP. https://hicksmorley.com/2022/11/01/ontario-tables-significant-legislation-impacting-

school-boardsector/#:~:text=On%20October%2031%2C%202022%2C%20the,of%20Public%20Employees%20(CUPE)
OECD. (2020a). *Education and COVID-19: Focusing on the long-term impact of school closures*. OECD Publishing. https://oecd.org/coronavirus/policy-responses/education-and-covid-19-Focusing1134 on-the-long-term-impact-of-school-closures-2cea926e
OECD. (2020b). Strengthening online learning when schools are closed: The role of families and 1136 teachers in supporting students during the COVID-19 crisis. https://read.oecdilibrary.org/1137view/?ref¼136_136615-o13x4bkowa&title¼Strengthening-online-learningWhen-schools-are1138closed1139
OECD. (2020c). The impact of COVID-19 on student equity and inclusion: Supporting vulnerable 1140 students during school closures and school re-openings. http://www.oecd.org/coronavirus/1141 policy-responses/the-impact-of-covid-19-on-student-equity-and-inclusion-supporting-vulner-a1142ble-students-during-school-closures-and-school-openings-d593b5c/#section-d1e3202
Ontario College of Teachers. (2021). *Transition to teaching 2021: 20th annual survey of Ontario's early-career elementary and secondary teachers*. Ontario College of Teachers. https://www.oct.ca/becoming-a-teacher/transition-to-teaching/previous-reports/2021-survey
Peters, M. (1999). Neoliberalism. In *The encyclopedia of philosophy of education*. http://www.vusst.hr/ENCYCLOPAEDIA/neoliberalism.htm
Roshowy, K. (2022). Province will block strike by education workers. *Toronto Star*. https://www.thestar.com/opinion/letters_to_the_editors/2022/11/01/province-not-going-to-arbitration-and-blaming-education-workers.html
Sahlberg, P. (2021). *Finnish lessons 3. 0: What can the world learn from educational change in Finland?* Teachers College Press.
Schwab, J. (1954/1978). Eros and education: A discussion of one aspect of discussion. In I. Westbury & N. Wilkof (Eds.), *Science, curriculum and liberal education: Selected essays*. University of Chicago Press.
Serrano, A., & Dillinger, H. (2022). Houston districts trying to fill thousands of teacher vacancies just 2 weeks before school starts. *Houston Chronicle*. https://www.houstonchronicle.com/news/houston-texas/education/article/Districts-across-Houston-still-look-to-hire-17343401.php
SIC Notícias. (2022). Until Christmas more than 600 teachers will have retired. https://sicnoticias.pt/pais/2022-09-15-Ate-ao-Natal-reformam-se-mais-600-professores-4c41be5b
Stone, E. (1988/2017). *Black sheep and kissing cousins. How our family stories shape us*. Routledge.
U.S. Constitution. https://constitution.congress.gov/constitution/amendment-10/
Vieira, M. F., & Seco, C. (2020). A Educação no contexto da pandemia de Covid-19: uma revisão sistemática da literatura. *Revista Brasileira de Informática na Educação, 28*, 1013–1031.
Zuboff, S. (2019). *The age of surveillance capitalism: The fight for a human future at the new frontier of power*. Profile Books.

INTERNATIONAL FORUM ON TEACHER EDUCATION AS AN EDUCATIONAL RESEARCH PARTNERSHIP

Roza Valeeva, Aydar Kalimullin and Tatiana Baklashova

ABSTRACT

This chapter focuses on a unique partnership made possible by Kazan Federal University, which has one of the largest teacher preparation programs in the Russian Republic. The partnership sponsors a scientific-practical conference known as the International Forum on Teacher Education (IFTE), arguably the most influential conference in the field of education in Eastern Europe and post-Soviet countries. Thousands of papers about different educational themes have been presented since 2015. Researchers share their views and their research results on the issues of modernization and development of the content of teacher education. Most recently, international guests have been playing a larger role. For example, ISATT partnered with IFTE and an ISATT regional conference flew under the IFTE banner in 2019. Many ISATT regional representatives attended. Since then, more researchers from the western world – including those from Europe and the United States – have been regularly attending IFTE, which is gaining an international reputation for being one of the most comprehensive teacher education conferences in the world.

Keywords: Partnership; educational research partnership; International Forum on Teacher Education (IFTE); scientific-practical conference; ISATT partnership; Volga region

One of the effective forms of improving the profession and developing the professional competence of teachers is through a scientific-practical conference, which includes dissemination and generalization of pedagogical experiences and skills. The scientific-practical conference is not only a platform for relaying pedagogical experience. It is an opportunity to study the trends and features of the modernization of education. It includes analysis and generalization of the theoretical and the practical. It furthermore includes traditional and innovative approaches to learning as well as scientific and methodological support that enriches the quality of education in accordance with the requirements of the changing times. Additionally, it provides a forum for the exchange of educational technologies, materials, and work experience.

The teachers' professional and pedagogical activities are significantly shifting. The question that becomes extremely important is: "How exactly should the teacher's professional and pedagogical activity change to provide a new quality of education able to meet the 'challenges of the time'?" Human capital in the modern world is becoming the main resource for the development of any country, a factor ensuring its stability and progress. These issues are described in the works of the researchers in the field of teacher education who participated in the International Forums on Teacher Education held annually at Kazan Federal University since 2015 (https://ifte.kpfu.ru/en/home-page/). Traditionally, the program of the forum includes pre-conference and post-conference events, three main conference themes, keynote lectures, symposium and paper sessions, as well as different roundtables and workshops. Currently, the International Forum on Teacher Education is one of the biggest platforms for discussing various educational trends and reforms in the international field of teacher education. Over the years, the Forum has grown to be one of the most influential conferences in the field of education in Eastern Europe and post-Soviet countries. Thousands of papers on different educational themes have been presented at the Forum since 2015. Researchers share their views and research results on the issues of modernization and development of the content of teacher education. They discussed questions related to values and priorities within the field of modern teacher education, to modernization processes and the content of teacher education, including the requirements of a competency-based approach. Key issues of teachers' professional development and other essential topics related to teacher education are also touched upon in the symposiums and roundtables. This is how the International Forum on Teacher Education became an educational research partnership platform.

This chapter follows the development of the International Forum on Teacher Education paying special attention to the forum organized in partnership with ISATT. Some interviews with participants of IFTE/members of ISATT will also be included in this chapter.

KAZAN FEDERAL UNIVERSITY: THE RUSSIAN CENTRE FOR RESEARCH ON TEACHERS AND TEACHING

The training of teachers is becoming a priority in the development of educational systems in many countries, accompanied by a search for new forms and content of teacher education that would most adequately meet the needs of a changing world. Russia is no exception, where large-scale reforms in the field of teacher preparation have taken place over the past three decades (Margolis & Safronova, 2018; Menter et al., 2017; Valeeva & Kalimullin, 2019a). In the 1990s, it was a departure from the socialist past and the de-ideologization of the educational process, and then the implementation of innovations in the face of economic, social, and technological challenges of the early twenty-first century. It was at this time that serious changes took place in the organization of teacher education, when a diversified system of teacher training began to take shape. This meant including higher education institutions of various types in teacher training and ending the monopoly of specialized universities and institutes (Valeeva & Kalimullin, 2019b).

As a result, the Russian system of teacher education was diversified and more than 250 higher educational institutions of various types, different in specialization, size, and forms of ownership were introduced. Among them, a group of the largest universities with strong scientific and educational potential, focused on research activities in the field of education, stood out – these are Moscow, Kazan, Tomsk universities, the Higher School of Economics and a number of others. Thanks to a large-scale state program to improve the international competitiveness of Russian higher education institutions (Project 5-100), some of them have taken a course toward the internationalization of their scientific activities. This gave a serious impetus to research work in the field of education, and allowed Russian researchers to study the world's best practices and best practices in teacher training. As a reverse phenomenon, international cooperation made it possible to provide national achievements more widely to the world scientific and pedagogical community. Indicative in this regard was the development of Kazan Federal University, which literally in a decade was able to form a new model of teacher training for Russia, which was recognized due to its scientific, educational and social productivity, as well as the high assessment of KFU in the leading international rankings in the subject area of education (QS, THE, Scimago institutions ranking) (Valeeva & Gafurov, 2017).

Kazan University was founded in 1804 by Russian Emperor Alexander I and is one of the oldest institutions of higher education in Russia. The history of the university is associated with such well-known names of prominent scientists and public figures as N.I. Lobachevsky, L.N. Tolstoy, V.I. Lenin, N.N. Zinin, A.M. Butlerov, I.M. Simonov, A.R. Luria, V.M. Bekhterev, and others. At different times, nine Nobel Prize winners worked at Kazan University.

The history of teacher training at Kazan University dates back more than 200 years to the Pedagogical Institute opened here in 1812. For a long time, it was the only educational institution of this type in the east of the Russian Empire, which prepared teachers for Siberia, the Caucasus, the Volga region, and Central Asia.

However, in the second half of the nineteenth century, the training of teachers at the university gradually ceased, and the era of specialized pedagogical educational institutions began in Russia, which dominated until the beginning of the twenty-first century. In particular, in Kazan, for almost 140 years, teachers were successfully trained at the Kazan Teachers' Institute and its historical successors.

However, in 2011, a new stage in the development of teacher education in the region began, when two specialized pedagogical higher educational institutions joined the Kazan (Federal) University. As a result, it became one of the largest teacher training centers in the Russian Federation, teaching more than 11,000 students in undergraduate, graduate, and postgraduate programs. In addition, annually more than 10,000 active teachers were trained here on advanced training and professional retraining programs. A new teacher training system was created at KFU, which included several models for entering the teaching profession and a unique modern infrastructure that allows not only to provide the educational process with all the necessary attributes, but also to create conditions for conducting a wide range of research. It includes three own schools of various types, additional education centers, a kindergarten for children with autism spectrum disorders, a planetarium, children's science centers, an educational IT technology park and much more. Numerous innovations were implemented to promote school-university partnerships.

Along with solving educational problems, the infrastructure facilities were unique and accessible scientific and experimental sites for research work. This was another positive side of the development of teacher education within the framework of a large university complex. This made it possible to bring scientific activity as close as possible to educational practice, to concentrate on the study of urgent problems of school and university education. The capabilities of the university, in particular, the presence of a wide range of scientific areas, made it possible to establish versatile research activities at the intersection of education with other sciences on the basis of numerous laboratories and experimental sites. The interdisciplinary approach implemented at KFU has increased the relevance and importance of research in the field of education, opened up unique opportunities for including representatives of a larger number of scientific fields (pedagogy, psychology, sociology, economics, political science, medicine, demography, etc.) into the process of studying educational problems.

The objective scientific metric indicators of the research activities of KFU scientists, primarily in the international databases Scopus and Web of Science, became indicators of KFU's progress in this area. Educational technologies, the quality of the educational process, scientific research in the field of teacher education allowed KFU to be the first among Russian universities to enter the top 100 best universities in the world in the subject area "Education" (Ranking Times Higher Education, 2020, 2021). In the QS Ranking, the university traditionally takes 101–150th place (2020, 2021). KFU is the only Russian university that trains teachers and was represented in the main professional and scientific national and international associations. International recognition means, first of all, the correctness of the strategy in the field of "education," aimed primarily at making the various levels of the country's educational system capable of effectively fulfilling the tasks that modern life puts forward.

One of the main missions of KFU is to unite the efforts of Russian and foreign researchers in the study of topical issues of teacher training. Unfortunately, for a number of reasons, the Russian system of teacher education was only fragmentarily represented in the international scientific and pedagogical community. Meanwhile, the historical past, traditions, features of political and socioeconomic development have formed a rather interesting educational system in Russia. Therefore, the main philosophy of our scientific activity, an important element of which is the IFTE International Forum on Teacher Education, has been and remains in cooperation with education scientists from around the world, studying the best educational practices, objectively covering the history and current state of teacher training in Russia, comparing them with global trends and processes taking place now or taking place at a particular historical stage. Each of them was unique in its own way, including today, when we observe a close interweaving of the most diverse trends. On the one hand, this is the preservation of the best traditions of the Soviet era, for example, the predominance of the public sector in teacher training, the absolute accessibility of all levels of education, broad social guarantees for students, etc. On the other hand, in the last two to three decades, international trends have naturally manifested themselves, in particular, joining the Bologna process, increasing the level of internationalization of education and student mobility, reducing the number of universities with one specialization, developing the commercial sector, etc. Productive in this regard was cooperation with scientists united within the framework of the International Study Association on Teachers and Teaching at the International Forum on Teacher Education (IFTE). This allowed us to create a harmonious scientific community of researchers from different countries, striving to make teacher education more effective at the global and national levels.

HISTORY OF THE INTERNATIONAL FORUM ON TEACHER EDUCATION (IFTE)

The International Forum on Teacher Education (IFTE), organized by Kazan Federal University, has an eight-year history. The first time it was organized was from June 3–5, 2015. A number of joint IFTE 2015 seminars played a significant role in the development of the Forum as a conference space: (1) Russian-Turkish seminar "Pedagogical education in Russia and Turkey: Results of scientific research and their use in educational practice"; (2) Russian-Dutch seminar "New approaches to the modernization of teacher education in Russia and Holland"; and (3) Russian-British seminar "Increasing publication activity in the field of education."

From the very beginning of its existence, a distinctive feature of IFTE has been a focus on international cooperation in the field of teacher education, the study of the best international practices of teacher training systems in the world. To ensure this task, Russian and international experts were invited to participate in the

Forum: Professor of Oxford University, Director of Professional Programs of the Department of Education, at that time President at the British Association for Educational Research Ian Menter (Great Britain); Professor Nick Rushby, Editor-in-Chief of the *British Journal of Educational Technology* (Great Britain); Professor at the University of Amsterdam Wilhelmina Browers (Netherlands); Professor at Balikesir University Bulent Ozdemir (Turkey). Along with international researchers, the program of the first Forum included reports by leading Russian experts in the field of teacher education, including Professor Irina Sokolova, Director of the Institute of Pedagogical Education and Adult Education of the Russian Academy of Education; Professor Irina Demakova, Head of the Department of Pedagogy and Psychology of the Academy of Advanced Training and Professional Retraining of Educational Workers (Moscow).

The IFTE organizers implemented the principle of effective linking theory and practice in the field of teacher education. It was paramount for them to ensure not only the exchange of authoritative opinion, the results of research work in the field of teachers' training, but to create conditions for the work of special methodological workshops at the Forum site, developing proposals for adjusting new modules of the main professional educational program. Thus, one of such methodological platforms within IFTE 2015 was the All-Russian Scientific and Practical Conference on the problems of developing and testing new modules of undergraduate programs in the enlarged group of specialties "Education and Pedagogy" (training area – psychological and pedagogical education), involving academic mobility of students in conditions of network interaction. This conference included scholarship around five themes: (1) content and technological mechanisms for the implementation of new modules of undergraduate programs in the direction of training, along with psychological and pedagogical education, involving academic mobility of students in conditions of network interaction; (2) international cooperation in teacher education and issues of organization of academic mobility of students; (3) modernization of teacher education in the context of network interaction, including historical-theoretical and organizational-pedagogical aspects; (4) problems of education in teacher training: history and modernity; and (5) competency-based approach in teacher education. Thus, the participants were asked to consider the essence and features of the content and procedural aspects of teacher education implemented in the context of network interaction, the historical and pedagogical prerequisites for its transformation, to assess the importance of international cooperation in the field of teacher training, the potential for academic mobility of the student body in pedagogical universities of the Russian Federation and abroad, modern challenges in relation to the professional development of student-future teachers based on a competency-based approach.

The history of the development of the Forum is regularly recorded on its website (https://ifte.kpfu.ru/istoriya-foruma/); the organizers keep track of the expansion of the geography of the IFTE participating countries, count the number of scientists, educators, and practitioners participating in the Forum; also, lists of universities are compiled, whose researchers present their reports on its site. For example, in 2015, 165 participants took part in it, of which 101 participants were in person, 22 representatives were from partner universities testing new models of the educational program, and 64 participants were in absentia with their material appearing in the collection of scientific papers of the conference. Eight reports were heard at the plenary session, 49 speeches at the section meetings. At the final plenary session, proposals were heard from section leaders, representatives of partner universities, as well as international and Russian experts on finalizing new modules of the main professional educational program. The IFTE 2015 conference was attended by 13 international participants from the United Kingdom, Turkey, the Netherlands, and Vietnam, along with 42 participants from Russian regions (Moscow, St. Petersburg, Izhevsk, Arzamas, Novokuznetsk, Cheboksary, Saransk, Krasnogorsk, Perm, Kirov, Yekaterinburg, Naberezhnye Chelny, Yelabuga, Birsk).

The II International Forum on Teacher Education (IFTE 2016) made it possible to increase the number and geography of IFTE participants. The Forum in Kazan brought together about 800 scientists from such countries as Scotland, Ireland and Great Britain, Austria, Finland, Singapore, Cuba, Vietnam, Laos, Korea, Armenia, Bulgaria, and USA. From May 19 to 21, 2016, colleagues from different countries exchanged their professional experience, discussed common problems for the field of pedagogy of education and jointly searched for ways to solve them, taking into account the peculiarities of the development and functioning of various education systems. A large number of highly qualified professionals presented their views on the system of teacher education and proposed their methods for its modernization. A distinctive feature of IFTE 2016 was the participation of editors and members of the editorial boards of 12 scientific journals indexed in the Scopus and Web of Science abstract databases, including *Critical Studies in Education*; *British Journal of Educational Technology*; *Research in Comparative and International Education*; *Journal of Baltic Science Education*; *Educational Sciences: Theory and Practice*; *Journal of Turkish Science Education*; *Eurasia Journal of Mathematics*, among others. A significant event of the II International Forum on Teacher Education was the publication of its materials in the journal European Proceedings of Social and Behavioral Sciences and the indexing of this collection in the Web of Science database (https://www.futureacademy.org.uk/publication/EpSBS/IFTE2016VolumeXII), which has become a tradition for many years.

IFTE 2016 reports, their topics, and content were determined by the goals of the Forum: (1) study of historical background, trends and features of the teacher education modernization in Russia; (2) analysis and generalization of theoretical and practical, traditional and innovative approaches to the teacher education modernization; (3) scientific and methodological support of the quality of training of a modern teacher in accordance with the requirements of new educational standards and the labor market; (4) familiarization with the practice of teacher education abroad; (5) exchange of educational technologies, materials, work experience. In accordance with the goals, the main areas of the Forum's work were identified, such as the historical formation of the system of teacher education in Russia and abroad; modeling the personality and professional activity of a new type of teacher; problems of modernization and development of the content of professional and pedagogical education, taking into account the requirements of new educational standards; implementation of a competent approach in the system of teacher education; problems of preparing a future teacher for innovative pedagogical activity in a multilevel structure of the organization of the educational process in a pedagogical university; innovative educational technologies for the personal and professional development of future teachers; integration of professional pedagogical and classical university education in the training of a new type of teacher and a number of others.

Starting in 2016, the Forum includes holding the main thematic scientific and practical conferences. The topics of IFTE conferences reflect modern trends in the development of teacher education, the challenges of high-quality training of a professional teacher. So, in 2016, the International Forum on Teacher Education at KFU included three sub-conference themes: "Children's Literature and Education in a Multicultural World"; "The Effectiveness of Teacher Education: Innovative Approaches"; "Multicultural Educational Space and Teacher Training: Integration of Russian and International Experience."

It is important to note that at the Forum site in different years, politicians, heads of ministries, universities, and academies voiced fateful decisions that have a significant impact on the development of teacher education in the Republic of Tatarstan, and in general, in Russia. Thus, in 2016, at the grand opening ceremony of IFTE in the main concert hall "UNIX" of KFU, Vice-President of the Russian Academy of Education Vladimir Laptev presented the Rector of KFU Ilshat Gafurov with an official document confirming the beginning of the organization and formation of one of the eight federal regional scientific centers of the Russian Academy of Education in Kazan Federal University. Since 2016, the Federal Regional Research Center of the Russian Academy of Education in Kazan has been training highly qualified teaching staff, forming a "gold reserve" of the educational pedagogy system, developing and implementing the latest strategies for modernizing the education system as a whole.

The directions of work of the III International Forum on Teacher Education, held from May 23 to 25, 2017, are set by the following scientific and practical conferences: (1) continuing teacher education in the modern world: from research search to productive solutions; (2) socially sustainable and safe environment for children: Psychology and pedagogy of nonviolence in the family and school; (3) transnational and regional adaptation of migrant children with a focus on modern practices and models of sociocultural and psychological-pedagogical integration. More than 600 colleagues from Russia, as well as countries near and far, took part in IFTE 2017, including leading experts in teacher education from the USA, China, Germany, Great Britain, Ireland, Slovenia, Cuba, Poland, France, etc. It is worth noting that, as a preliminary event, on May 22, 2017, an international seminar, Educational Research Methodologies, was held, which was organized by colleagues from the University of Miami and University College Dublin.

The keynote speakers at IFTE 2017 were President of the International Study Association on Teachers and Teaching (ISATT) Maria Assunção Flores, President of the European Educational Research Association (EERA) Theo Wubbels. Academic

Supervisor of the Institute of Education of the National Research University Higher School of Economics Isaak Frumin; Professor of the University of Ljubljana Andrea Istenic Starcic; Professor of the University College Dublin Conor Galvin; Director of the Department of Further Education of the Nazarbayev University Aigul Aktymbayeva; Professor of the University of Miami Dina Birman; Honorary Professor of the University of Oxford Ian Menter presented their papers at the Forum. Professor of the University of Glasgow Margery McMahon; Dean of Sofia University "St. Kliment Ohridski" Boncho Gospodinov; Professor, Head of the Scientific and Pedagogical Center of the Dresden Technical University Axel Hermann; Rector of the Maxim Tank Belarusian State Pedagogical University Alexander Zhuk; Professor of Kazan Federal University Roza Valeeva. During the three days of the forum, 16 plenary reports were presented by leading Russian and international experts in the field of teacher education; as well as 16 symposiums and 28 sections.

The publication activity of the teaching staff is a priority of Kazan Federal University, which explains the interest in holding special sessions within the framework of IFTE under the guidance of editors of leading journals that publish articles on education and teacher training. IFTE 2017 was no exception in this regard. For operational interaction with the editors of leading international journals, to increase the level of publication culture, the Forum organizers invited to Kazan the editors-in-chief and members of the editorial boards of 19 journals indexed in the Scopus and Web of Science databases. For example, *Review of Education (RoE), International Journal of Intercultural Relations, American Journal of Community Psychology, Journal of Community and Applied Social Psychology, The American Journal of Education, Teachers and Teaching Theory and Practice, European Journal of Teacher Education, British Journal of Educational Technology, TOJET (Turkish Online Journal of Education Technology)* and many others.

The public lecture was delivered by Jill Hawthorne, Director of International Development at Wiley Publishing. She talked about the reasons why many publishers reject scientific papers and how to avoid it. The lecture aroused the interest of the participants, as evidenced by the lively discussion at the end. Proceedings of the III International Forum on Teacher Education were published in the journal European Proceedings of Social and Behavioral Sciences (https://www.futureacademy.org.uk/publication/EpSBS/KazanFederalUniversityRussia).

IFTE 2018 AND ISATT 2018 REGIONAL CONFERENCE

In 2018, the International Forum on Teacher Education was organized in cooperation with the International Study Association on Teachers and Teaching (ISATT), which held its Regional Conference in Kazan. The forum attracted more than 550 Russian and more than 60 overseas participants, including eight ISATT National Representatives. The Association for Teacher Education in Europe (ATEE) also was a partner of the 2018 Forum.

Despite its young age, 3 years old, the Forum has become widely known in professional society; more than 700 best experts in the field of pedagogical science from different countries discussed the problems of modeling the personality and professional activity of a new type of teacher, the problems of preparing a future teacher for pedagogical activity in a multicultural educational space at the IFTE 2018 platform. The starting point for the IFTE 2018 was a plenary session at which reports were made by KFU Rector Ilshat Gafurov on teacher training in non-pedagogical universities in Russia, ISATT Chair Maria Assunção Flores (University of Minho, Portugal) on quality and professionalism of the teacher, the rector of the Moscow State Pedagogical University, Professor Aleksey Lubkov on teacher professionalism, professor of the University of Texas Murat Choshanov on research on the role of subject knowledge in the "teacher-student" system, Director of the Harvard University Research Institute Gil Noam on supplementary education as an innovation in education, Oxford University professor Ian Menter on determining the professional knowledge of teachers. Dina Birman, a world-famous researcher in the field of multicultural education, professor at the Department of Research in Education and Psychology, shared information on how to organize the education of migrant children. Margery McMahon, 2018 Director of the Training and Management Research and Learning Group and now Director of the School of Education at the University of Glasgow, recalled the role of ethics in teacher education. Conor Galvin (University of Dublin, Ireland) focused on the professional characteristics of a teacher. Professor and creator of the author's "Murray Method," Marilyn Murray gave a lecture and a master class on deprivation as emotional trauma.

IFTE 2018 became the most representative not only in terms of the scope of participants, but also in terms of the scope of the topics covered: 350 reports were made by scientists on the problems of modernizing and developing the content of vocational pedagogical education, modeling the personality and professional activities of a new type of teacher, integrating professional pedagogical and classical university education in training teachers of a new type, problems of improving the system of continuous pedagogical education and many other topics. The forum included a number of significant scientific events: international scientific and practical conferences "Integration of theory and practice in the subject preparation of a teacher," "Teacher training as an educator," "Children's deviations: psychological and pedagogical technologies of prevention and overcoming." As part of IFTE 2018, the ceremony of presenting the National Award "Professor of the Year" of the Russian Professorial Assembly was also held. Professor Roza Valeeva received this award. In addition, within the framework of the Forum, a conference was held by the authoritative international association for teacher training ISATT, the theme of which was "Teacher's professionalism as a condition for the quality of education." Holding the ISATT conference at the KFU site as part of IFTE 2018 made it possible to strengthen the scientific and methodological support for the quality of training of a modern teacher in accordance with the requirements of new educational standards and the labor market, provided a unique opportunity for teachers from different countries to get acquainted with the best practices of teacher education abroad and exchange educational technologies, materials, and experience. Below Juanjo Mena from the University of Salamanca, Spain, describes the IFTE/ISATT partnership from an organizational and personal perspective:

> The IFTE 2018 and the ISATT 2018 regional conferences were a combined effort to merge Russian national scholars with international teacher educators coming from different countries worldwide (i.e., ISATT members and national representatives). The conference's scope brought western and eastern perspectives together. It was a meaningful event to me as a researcher since I could learn from my international colleagues (something I always have the chance to do when attending conferences worldwide) and additionally, I could discover the current Russian and Eastern trends in education that were less familiar to me. This constructive learning enabled me to enhance my perspective and critical views of my research field.

Over the three days of the Forum, more than 20 key reports were presented from leading Russian and international experts in the field of teacher education; 14 symposiums, 90 sections, 5 round tables, 4 plenary discussions, 4 international conferences, 2 master classes were also held. As part of the Forum, there was a presentation of DAAD programs, a round table with coordinators and alumni of the Global Education program, an interactive discussion via video link with the Chechen Republic and Kazakhstan of the problems of a safe educational environment at school, roundtables and discussion platforms. The "parade of pedagogical projects" conducted by scientists of the Institute of Psychology and Education of KFU, including the forum-theater "Child on the Net: the danger of suicide," "Another" child in the classroom also aroused great interest of the forum participants. Editors of the KFU scientific journal *Education and Self-Development*, Professor Nick Rushby and Professor R.A. Valeeva held a traditional round table on the requirements and problems of preparing articles for publication in high-ranking international journals. Its participants were Olga Kirillova (President of the Association of National Editors and Publishers), editors and members of the editorial boards of international journals indexed in the Web of Science and Scopus databases.

IFTE 2019: THE PARTNERSHIP CONTINUES

In 2019, the V International Forum on Teacher Education became a platform for events of various levels and scales: plenary and breakout sessions, round tables, seminars, master classes, panel discussions, etc. Well-known Russian and international experts, outstanding teachers, representatives of metropolitan and regional educational institutions acted as section leaders and moderators at the forums. Representatives of the universities of Oxford, Dublin, and other universities acted as speakers at the forum. In total, scientists from 140 Russian and 60 international universities from more than 30 countries of the world took part in the forum.

The main topic of IFTE 2019 was "Development of Teacher Professional Competencies: Key Issues and Values." Within the framework of the forum, four major international scientific and practical conferences were held: "Continuing teacher education: New concepts and technologies," "Young teacher: Adaptation and professional development," "Research-oriented teacher education," and "Janusz Korczak's ideas in the preparation of a future teacher." Their topics included consideration of all aspects of the teacher's work: from education to digital technologies and the integration of education into state development programs of various countries. The importance of the International Forum on Teacher Education in his welcoming speech was quite succinctly revealed by KFU Rector Ilshat Gafurov, emphasizing that in times when the professionalism of a teacher is an extremely important problem for educational systems in almost all countries of the world: "Our forum is, first of all, a scientific platform, where we can study advanced Russian and international experience, present our own models of teacher education, which we have been successfully developing at KFU since 2011." Attention to pedagogy, the allocation of this area of knowledge as a priority for the development of KFU, decent funding and the right goal-setting have made the Institute of Psychology and Education of KFU one of the world leaders.

During the three days of IFTE 2019, 10 key reports were presented; 13 symposiums, more than 100 sections, 2 round tables, 4 international conferences, 2 master classes were held. During the work of the Forum, the most pressing problems were put on the agenda, and, importantly, the scientific community showed unity in an effort to find their solution, and also showed commitment to the basic values of humanity in the approach to finding answers to the most important questions facing the world education today. The forum included a number of significant scientific events. Thus, a discussion was held at KFU with the participation of academicians of the Russian Academy of Education, the topic of which was changes in textbooks and curricula, support for rural schools and motivation for young teachers to remain in the profession. Among the participants of IFTE 2019 were the members of the International Korczak Association, headed by its President Marek Michalak who held the ceremony of awarding the International Order of the Smile to Professor Irina Demakova. Professor of the Department of Education and Innovation at the University of Arizona, Maria Teresa Tatto; Professor Emeritus of the University of Oxford Ian Menter and KFU Professor Roza Valeeva presented to the participants of the International Forum on Teacher Education the international monograph "Knowledge, Policy and Practice in Teacher Education: a Cross-National Study," which they co-authored. The Forum also included a seminar for young teachers in the TeachMeet format, an informal meeting of young teachers from Kazan, and a presentation of projects for the professional development of teachers at the Bala City International Pre-School. In the showroom of the Higher School of Journalism and Media Communications of KFU, an international discussion on the practice of adaptation of migrant children unfolded. The guests of the Forum had a chance to see the performance of the Children's Theater of the Institute of Psychology and Education "Rainbow" named "Vivat, KFU!"

IFTE DURING PANDEMIC AND POST-PANDEMIC TIMES

2020 was marked by new conditions for the interaction of people with each other. The Covid-19 pandemic that swept the world had contributed to the rapid development of distance learning formats, the professional work of specialists in various fields of activity, and scientific and academic cooperation. Many leading associations of the world this year refused to hold traditional conferences, officially rescheduling them for 2021. Kazan Federal University accepted a new challenge and organized IFTE 2020 entirely online. The VI International Forum on Teacher Education was held for 2 working weeks due to the specificity and novelty of the new mode of organization of the conference space. The main theme of virtual IFTE 2020 was "Perspectives and priorities of teacher education in the era of transformations, choices and challenges." Three conferences were held within the framework of the Forum: "Informatization and digitalization in teacher education," "Pedagogical education for social justice, equality and culturally appropriate pedagogy," "Global trends and prospects for bilingual and language education in teacher training." The main areas of work of virtual IFTE-2020: digitalization of modern teacher education, advanced training and retraining of teaching staff in the context of the "digital divide," digital technologies in the preparation of future teachers, and others. About 50% of all applications were related specifically to the organization of education, including the problems that teachers, children, and parents face during distance learning. Key reports were made by 17 well-known international researchers from leading universities in Russia, Great Britain, USA, Ireland, Australia and other countries. Speakers and guests of honor include Moscow State Pedagogical University Rector Alexei Lubkov, Ian Menter (University of Oxford, UK), Margery McMahon (University of Glasgow, UK), Maria Assuncao Flores (University of Minho, Portugal), Conor Galvin (University of Dublin, Ireland), Murat Choshanov (University of Texas at El Paso, USA), etc.

The remote format of the Forum contributed to the attraction of a record number of participants – about 900 scientists from 29 countries of the world. The number of international participants was fixed at around 120 people. The Forum participants were able not only to present the results of their work and research, but, most importantly, to communicate, reflect, argue, despite the virtual format of the Forum. Microsoft provided technical support to the Forum. Video lectures by key speakers, synchronous virtual round tables, international online symposiums, research group meetings, and poster presentations were held on the Microsoft Teams corporate platform. In addition, according to Microsoft's analytics, more than 32,000 online entries to section sessions, symposiums and master classes were registered. Thus, in the context of the pandemic, the Forum has become one of the world's largest scientific platforms in the field of education.

The architecture of the Forum in 2020 has become more flexible, reflecting the rapid development and diversity inherent in the modern education system. The meaningful agenda of the forum included the work of 74 sections, where recognized Russian and international experts discussed the current challenges facing Russia and the world in the new decade in the field of education. Work was carried out in 14 study groups, 39 meetings were held within these groups. IFTE 2020 has become the most representative not only in terms of the scope of participants, but also in terms of the scope of the declared topics: 575 reports were made by scientists from 275 universities, scientific and educational organizations, including 79 international universities, on the problems of modernizing and developing the content of vocational and pedagogical education, personality modeling and professional activity a new type of teacher, the integration of professional pedagogical and classical university education in the training of a new type of teacher, the problems of improving the system of continuous pedagogical education, etc. The lecturers and students of Russian universities acted as listeners. According to IFTE President, Professor, Academician of the Russian Academy of Education, Rector of KFU Ilshat Gafurov.

Severe shocks such as a pandemic should not separate researchers representing Russian and international universities in solving the problem of improving the quality of teacher training. The capabilities of Kazan University allowed Russian and international participants to successfully present and discuss the results of scientific research in teacher education remotely.

IFTE Co-Chairman, Director of the KFU Institute of Psychology and Education, Professor Aydar Kalimullin noted that

> ...the virtual IFTE-2020 was the first experience of holding a large-scale conference in a virtual format for KFU. And this experience did not come up short. For the sixth time, IFTE has provided an opportunity for teacher education scholars to share their concerns and plans, exchange views, and develop new insights to address the challenges of pedagogy, especially in the context of active digitalization.

It is noteworthy that it was in 2020 that KFU received a high assessment of the transformations in the field of teacher training that have been carried out at the university in recent years: one of the leading international rankings of the best universities in the world, *Times Higher Education*, included KFU among the 100 best in the subject area "Education."

The informational support of the Forum was richer than ever. Several international associations in the field of education posted information about IFTE 2020 on their websites. Press releases about the Forum were also published on the websites of federal and regional ministries. Congratulations were sent by the Minister of Science and Higher Education of Russia, the Minister of Education of the Republic of Tatarstan, the President of the Russian Academy of Education, the Presidents of the Academies of Education of Russia and Kazakhstan, the presidents of international scientific associations. Every day, at least 4 news about the work at the Forum were published on the official website of the Forum ifte.kpfu.ru and on Facebook pages. Since May 27, ifte.kpfu.ru has been visited by 5,400 unique users from 88 countries (including Russia). The number of international visitors to the site amounted to 20% of the total number of unique users.

As part of the closing of the forum at the KFU Institute of Psychology and Education, a press tour "VR Tour to the Future with Kazan University" was held, during which virtual reality technologies for training future teachers were demonstrated to media representatives. Journalists were introduced to the innovative teacher training system at KFU, which combines the capabilities of a specialized pedagogical institute and a classical university. There was also a unique opportunity to test a virtual reality helmet on yourself in order to see with your own eyes how classes are held in VR format.

Continuing the online tradition of a conference space that can attract a large number of participants from different parts of the globe, the organizers of IFTE in 2021 and 2022 used a hybrid format, where offline mode was combined with a remote form of meetings. The main theme of the VII International Forum on Teacher Education (IFTE 2021) was "Pedagogical Education: New Challenges and Goals." It was held from May 26 to May 28, 2021; more than 500 participants came to Kazan, and about 1,000 took part remotely. For three days, over 1,500 Russian and international scientists from over 200 universities shared their pedagogical practices with each other. A feature of IFTE 2021 was the holding the International Conference for Young Researchers within its framework, because among the 1,500 offline and online participants of the Forum, there were 340 young scientists.

The agenda of the forum included the work of 81 sections, where recognized Russian and international experts discussed the current challenges facing Russia and the world in the new decade in the field of education. Work was carried out in 18 SIGs and 41 meetings were held within the groups. During IFTE 2021 three major international scientific and practical conferences were held: "Teachers for children with special educational needs," "Trajectories of education in the era of extreme events," "Teacher-educator training in the twenty-first century." Key reports were prepared and voiced by 17 well-known international researchers from leading universities in Russia, Great Britain, USA, Ireland, Australia, and other countries.

IFTE 2022 was also organized and held in a hybrid format. The main topic of the 2022 Forum was "Education, professional development and health preservation of teachers in the twenty-first century." Key conferences of the VIII International Forum on Teacher Education were "Psychological well-being and teacher effectiveness," "Teacher education and testing by Covid-19 pandemic," "Research-oriented teacher education as a phenomenon of pedagogical anthropology." It is noteworthy that the meetings of the Forum in 2022 were built into the architecture of the program, taking into account the preferences of the initiators and participants of scientific projects, research groups created on the electronic platform of the International Community of Researchers in the Field of Teacher Education, a KFU project aimed at strengthening cooperation between scientists, practicing teachers of the Russian Federation and neighboring abroad.

More than 1500 scientists from 29 countries representing 214 higher educational institutions and scientific organizations became participants in IFTE 2022, organized jointly with the Russian Academy of Education. An innovation was cooperation with the association "Forum of Russian Educators," which made it possible to involve more than 10,000 teachers from most regions of the Russian Federation in the discussion of topical problems of education. Thus, the Forum has become one of the largest events in the field of teacher education not only in our country, but also in the world. The work of IFTE 2022 was organized in offline, online, and mixed formats. Moreover, more than 800 scientists took part in various meetings. For three days of work, 10,077 entries from Russia, China, India, Brazil, Turkey, Kazakhstan, Uzbekistan, and other countries were made to various Forum sites. In total, 203 various meetings were held within the framework of the Forum – panel discussions, symposiums, round tables, master classes, open podiums, lectures, at which more than 1000 reports were made by researchers in the field of teacher education.

IFTE 2022 once again fulfilled its most important task – to be a scientific bridge between Russian and international scientists, on the one hand, promoting the traditions and modern achievements of Russian education to the international community, and on the other, studying the best international practices and adapting them to our realities. Kazan Federal University, in this regard, as one of the largest teacher training centers in Russia, was able to demonstrate its achievements in modernization of teacher education and to show the potential of the Russian education system at the world level. Traditionally, at the end of the Forum, the key issues of IFTE 2023 were identified. As part of its general theme "Quality of Teacher Education Under Modern Challenges," the following topical issues will be considered: (1) Education in modern socio-cultural conditions: traditions, new challenges, responsibility; (2) Teacher training as a factor in the effectiveness and efficiency of teacher education; (3) Historical and pedagogical heritage and teacher training: national values, modern understanding, and best practices.

CONCLUSION

The International Forum on Teacher Education, organized by Kazan Federal University, is a unique conference space, the hallmark of which is the ability to develop and transform. In recent years, it has acquired the characteristics of a hybrid academic space, opened its doors to talented young people who are fond of scientific research in the field of psychological and pedagogical issues, contributed to the development of interaction between Russian and international scientists, practicing teachers in the field of teacher education, and made it possible to publish collections of hundreds of IFTE conference papers (indexed in the RSCI, Scopus database, WoS), dozens of scientific articles in a special issue of the journal "Education and Self-Development." Today, IFTE is the hallmark of Kazan Federal University, which is rapidly developing in terms of teacher training, one of the brightest, most anticipated events in the field of Russian and international teacher education.

REFERENCES

Margolis, A. A., & Safronova, M. A. (2018). The project of modernization of teacher education in the Russian Federation: Outcomes 2014–2017. [Psikhologicheskaya nauka i obrazovanie] *Psychological Science and Education*, *23*(1), 5–24. https://doi.org/10.17759/pse.2018230101. (In Russ., abstr. in Engl.).

Menter, I., Valeeva, R. A., & Kalimullin, A. M. (2017). A tale of two countries – Forty years on: Politics and teacher education in Russia and England. *European Journal of Teacher Education*, *40*(5), 616–629. https://doi.org/10.1080/02619768.2017.1385060

Valeeva, R., & Gafurov, I. (2017). Initial teacher education in Russia: Connecting practice, theory and research. *European Journal of Teacher Education*, *40*(3), 342–360.

Valeeva, R. A., & Kalimullin, A. A. (2019a). Learning to teach in Russia: A review of policy and empirical research. In M. Tatto & I. Menter (Eds.), *Knowledge, policy and practice in teacher education: A cross-national study*. Bloomsbury.

Valeeva, R., & Kalimullin, A. (2019b). Teacher education in Russia. In *Oxford research encyclopedia of education*. Oxford University Press. https://doi.org/10.1093/acrefore/9780190264093.013.446

CULTIVATING TEACHER RESILIENCE THROUGH INTERCULTURAL INTERACTION AND COLLABORATION

Özge Hacıfazlıoğlu, Bilge Kalkavan, Chunyan Yang, Gökçe Ünlü and Serra Gürün

ABSTRACT

This collaborative effort aims to reduce international teacher attrition. Findings from the data are meant to be shared with principals to reduce the number of international teachers leaving teaching. The study revolves around three important research questions: What challenges do international teachers encounter and how do they meet them? What individual strengths help international teachers develop resilience in the transition process? and What support mechanisms help international teachers develop resilience in the adaptation process? The chapter ends with recommendations and implications for school leaders as they create conditions that will help retain new teachers.

Keywords: International teacher attrition; intercultural interaction; collaboration; resilience; adaptation process; support mechanisms

CULTIVATING TEACHER RESILIENCE THROUGH INTERCULTURAL INTERACTION AND COLLABORATION

This chapter draws on analyses of semi-structured face-to-face interview data collected from 15 teachers in different stages of their careers in a range of international schools in Türkiye and the United States. The story of each teacher is unique and is shaped by their personal experiences and by the particular sociocultural context of each host school. The data were analyzed with a view to identifying aspects of resilience that are necessary for making a balanced transition through the stages of adapting to a new school and regional culture. We conclude with recommendations and implications for school leaders as they create conditions that will help them retain new teachers.

With the increasing number of international schools worldwide over the last few years, the issue of recruiting and retaining international teachers has become increasingly important. Internationalization of education has opened pathways for qualified teachers to travel to distant places and discover new lands and cultures while working as teachers. This has created a new market for education stakeholders who deal with teacher recruitment. However, the conditions provided for international teachers in schools where there are limited resources for supporting teachers' well-being are insufficient for teacher retention. In such a competitive arena, to retain international teachers, international schools should prioritize full disclosure recruitment processes and put in place retention strategies, which may include support mechanisms for teachers' families as well as benefits. No matter how generous these benefits may be, teachers and their dependents pass through phases of adjustment to a new social context. Ward and Kennedy (1996) and Ward et al. (1998) assert that starting a new life in a new culture brings lots of stress and anxiety. Roskell (2013) describes the adjustment phase as "sojourners learning the culture-specific skills necessary to interact successfully and integrate with the host environment" (p. 157). Nevertheless, helping the visiting scholar off to a good start as an honored guest is crucial to all that follows.

The purpose of the study is to share accounts of international teachers as they adjust to working in a new country. They share the ways they balance their academic and private lives and how this leads to developing resilience, enabling them to adjust. The study also looks at the notion of being an international teacher through the lens of intercultural communication. Documenting the experiences of international teachers provides rich examples and unique insights that can help inform teacher retention strategies. We sought to answer the following research questions:

(1) What challenges do international teachers encounter and how do they meet them?
(2) What individual strengths help international teachers develop resilience in the transition process?
(3) What support mechanisms help international teachers develop resilience in the adaptation process?

Lysgaard's (1955) study on culture shock relates to risk and resilience factors, in which an individual's feelings of satisfaction and wellbeing progress through three stages. This was later refined by Oberg (1960), who documented four stages of adaptation, which are: the honeymoon, crisis, recovery, and adjustment stages. The excitement of being in a new culture can shift into a crisis phase in which the teacher feels homesick that can lead to regret and depression. Roskell (2013) highlights the conceptual confusion over the definition of adjustment and proposes two critical domains in the cross-cultural adjustment process, psychological and socio-cultural, which aligns with Ward and Kennedy (1999), who describe sociocultural adjustment as the ability to "fit in," communicating effectively with the host environment. Scholarship on international teachers highlights the ways in which they compensate while adjusting to a new school context and culture. However, the voices of teachers relating how they maintain balance when dealing with multiple spheres of adjustment have rarely been addressed in teacher education literature, and teachers' stories of challenge, resilience, and the ways in which they are supported has rarely been investigated. From a distance, it may appear that visiting teachers enjoy a wealth of advantages when working in privileged private schools. However, our experiences as teachers and scholars visiting such schools shows that each setting is unique in the challenges it presents.

In the literature, teacher retention has been connected to successful leadership. In schools where trust and sincerity are evident, teacher motivation appears high, promoting long term retention of teachers. Even in challenging contexts, retention can be maintained through teacher resilience (Burghes et al., 2009; Castro et al., 2010; Day & Leithwood, 2007; Gu & Day, 2013). The value of trust and sincerity is even more important where teachers must adjust to a new school in an unfamiliar culture, since the initial stages involve feelings of uncertainty, anxiety, and risk (Bakioglu et al., 2010). The study we report here is based on the theory of resilience, which recognizes the importance of individual circumstances and changing environments, and posits that resilience is a dynamic state that is dependent on an individual's "adjustment domains in time" (Luthar et al., 2000, p. 551). The nature and extent of resilience in a person's work and life span needs to be interpreted within a social system of interrelationships (Benard, 1995; Gu & Day, 2013; Luthar et al., 2000). Moving to a new school in a new culture presents many complications on a wide spectrum from settling in a new home and new office as well as adjusting to a new sociocultural context of school life. The decision to accept an offer in another country is risky, involving many interrelated challenges. Although the intensity of these barriers and constraints can be felt differently depending on a teacher's individual personal dynamics, everyone encounters significant challenges on the path to adjustment. In this study, we use Gu and Day's (2013) conceptualization of teacher resilience:

> ...teacher resilience [is not defined as] the capacity to 'bounce back' or recover from highly traumatic experiences and events but, rather, the capacity to maintain equilibrium and a sense of commitment and agency in the everyday worlds in which teachers teach. (p. 26)

Challenges in the Adjustment Process

Given the influences of globalization, intercultural competence has become an essential survival skill. With the constant demand for teachers around the world, teachers have become more mobile and are required to rapidly adjust to a new culture so they can support learners in the classroom. However, cross-cultural transition is widely accepted as a challenging, life-changing event (Roskell, 2013). Many international teachers struggle with this, despite the benefits they are offered, and need to develop the capacity to survive and thrive through the stages of cultural adjustment. The adjustment stage, the final stage of a successful cross-cultural transition, comes after the honeymoon, crisis, and recovery stages (Oberg, 1960). International teachers' adjustment entails managing two critical dynamics, sociocultural, and psychological.

Sociocultural Factors in Cultural Adjustment

A study by Roskell (2013) describes and assesses the experiences of 12 teachers who relocated to Southeast Asia to teacher in an international school. This longitudinal, ethnographic study revealed how international teachers are required to adjust to a new host culture and an unfamiliar work culture simultaneously, creating a double-culture shock. The findings show that dimensions of host-culture characteristics such as food, weather, transport, local people, and environment have real positive effects as teachers enjoy the experience of life abroad. The dimension of relationships with co-nationals, leadership, support staff, and children was positive upon arrival but became increasingly negative around the fourth month, becoming more positive after the seventh month. The third dimension, work characteristics, revealed difficulties with timetable, environment, roles, expectations, and assessment as the teachers began to worry about a perceived lack of professional knowledge and skills. The study found that participants adjusted to the unfamiliar host nation culture more easily than they adjusted to the unfamiliar work culture and that they found socio-cultural adjustment easier than psychological adjustment (Roskell, 2013).

Research focusing on the personal experiences, benefits, and challenges faced by a group of 22 visiting faculty in the United States revealed that they faced challenges related to language barriers, interaction with native speakers, classroom management, lack of support from school administrators, and separation from family (Ospina & Medina, 2020). Data collated through questionnaire, written narrative, and semi-structured interview revealed three main categories: intercultural issues, professional issues, and personal issues. Sociocultural challenges with socializing, language barriers, and professional issues such as classroom management, parent conferences, lack of support from schools, and ineffective mentoring all affected the ability of teachers to adapt to the community and the school system, greatly impacting their professional lives (Ospina & Medina, 2020), for instance, their ability to apply strategies for managing their classrooms.

Other research has focused on the relationship between job satisfaction and other job related factors and international teachers' adjustment. A study by Richardson et al. (2006), conducted with 196 international teachers from North America, the United Kingdom, and the Caribbean revealed that these factors are clearly related to the ability to adjust given that they are concrete motivational tools (Richardson et al., 2006).

Psychological Factors in Cultural Adjustment

Roskell (2013) demonstrated a close connection between sociocultural factors and psychological factors. Difficulties that present as sociocultural factors such as workplace or culture adjustments may lead to stress or worry for international teachers. This can become highly stressful when cross-cultural transition is perceived from the perspective of loss.

Ospina and Medina (2020) state that when teaching internationally, teachers also face challenges with personal issues. Being away from family, for instance, can be one of the biggest difficulties for teachers and settling down in a new environment is another source of psychological challenge. Teachers reported that establishing new living arrangements is one of the biggest challenges when arriving in a new country, making their adaptation to American life very stressful. Also, some teachers also stated that they felt abandoned by school administrators and worried about a lack of trust from administrators, colleagues, and parents (Ospina & Medina, 2020). Richardson et al. (2006) state that high self-esteem correlates with better adjustment. They also found a positive correlation between self-esteem and pay satisfaction. Moreover, with strong self-esteem, international teachers' transition is less stressful. While positive self-esteem may help people feel good about themselves, it does not solve all problems involved in adapting to a new culture smoothly and successfully.

Teacher Resilience

Gu and Day (2013) suggest that "to teach, and to teach at one's best over time, has always required resilience" (p. 22). Their research aimed to provide empirical evidence about the significance of resilience in teacher's work. They analyzed twice yearly semi-structured face-to-face interview data from 300 teachers in different phases of their careers in primary and secondary schools in England over a three-year period. The teachers agreed that resilience was a necessity for teachers to be successful. Their resilience capacity was affected by their personal biographies and the strength of their educational values. Sociocultural factors and policies embedded in their teaching contexts and personal, relational, and organizational situations in which they worked and lived also made a difference. For teachers, resilience is much more than the capacity to survive and thrive under adversity and is not a mere option but is a necessity. Gu and Day's study (2013) illustrates that resilience in teachers is the capacity to manage the unavoidable uncertainties inherent in the realities of teaching. Teacher resilience is driven by teachers' educational purposes and moral values, which are influenced by their biographies and the situations in which they work and live.

Volet (1999) underlines the complex and dynamic contexts in which individuals are expected to adapt, act, and live. In this context, resilience lies at the "interface of person and contexts, where individuals use strategies to enable them to overcome challenges and sustain their commitment and sense of wellbeing." Context is one of the main elements in developing resilience. Beltman and Mansfield (2011), Bobek (2002), and Gu and Day (2013) consider the importance of personal capacities and agency but highlight the risk factors individual teachers face that could affect their ability to adjust to challenging contexts and their competence in dealing with challenging circumstances. Gu and Day (2007) assert that "... resilience can develop over time and manifests itself as a result of a dynamic process within a given context" (p. 1305).

Following the perspectives of adjustment and resilience, our study focuses on international teachers' experiences of adjustment into new cultural contexts while developing resilience in response to initial challenges.

METHOD

This study utilizes a phenomenological research design in which adjusting to a new culture as an international teacher in a new sociocultural context is the focus and phenomenon of interest. High school teachers working in international schools were asked to tell their stories of adjustment as they made their way in a new school culture and sociocultural context through relating what they considered critical incidents. Through open-ended questions, they were invited to share their experiences of adjustment and resilience in a visualizable and memorable way (Seidman, 1998). This in-depth study of the stories of 15 international teachers allowed us to develop a deeper and more contextualized understanding of their ideas and experiences.

Data Collection

The interview process began with an invitation letter asking for voluntary participation. The interview questions were prepared based on Chunyan Yang's (2021) project on "Pre-service and first-year teachers' experiences with school violence and subjective well-being?" The letter informed prospective participants of our expectations of volunteers and the safeguards in place and asked that those who chose to take part confirm their informed consent. The interviews were conducted by the researchers, who used a reflective listening approach and took care not to lead the participants in any way. Most of the interviews were conducted in person, which lasted from 30 to 45 minutes. Follow up online meetings were also held with some of the participants. After each interview, a contact summary form was used to highlight main themes that emerged during the conversations and researchers worked together to identify emergent themes related to adjustment and resilience.

Participants

The sample for this study involved teachers from two countries working at international schools. A convenience sampling procedure was used and the participants were chosen from two large cities, Reno, Nevada in the United States and Istanbul, Türkiye both were home to diverse populations of different cultures and ethnicities. Both cities have international schools hosting teachers from many parts of the world. Seven participants from Istanbul and eight participants from Reno took part in the study. Half had experience working in a different country before working in Istanbul and Reno, while the other half indicated that it was their first experience as an international teacher in another country. The majority of the participants were female teachers ($n = 13$). Almost all the teachers ($n = 14$) were married and had children ranging from 3 to 15 years old. They all confirmed that their relocation decisions had been made as a family. Participants were reassured that their identities would remain confidential. Pseudonyms were used on all documents and data related to this research.

Data Analysis

We divided the analysis procedure into the five phases, as suggested by Marshall and Rossman (1999): (1) organizing data; (2) identifying themes, patterns, and categories; (3) testing the emergent hypothesis against the data; (4) searching for alternative explanations of the data; and (5) writing the report. One of the researchers who holds a PhD. The senior student researcher conducted the interviews in Istanbul while a doctoral student researcher conducted the interviews in Nevada. All the recordings were transcribed and coded by the research team members. As a first step, the research team reviewed three transcripts to develop a codebook. Then as a follow-up step, two graduate students and two researchers separately coded the same transcript and met to resolve inconsistencies to maintain inter-rater reliability. Researchers coded the remaining transcripts separately, paying specific attention to select excerpts from the transcripts and placing them into broad categories to identify thematic connections within and among the transcripts (Seidman, 1998). This chapter features interview data that captures the challenges encountered by international teachers during their transition to a new culture. We incorporated short narrative summaries to capture a few pertinent highlights from the teacher's perspective (Maxwell, 1996).

EMERGENT THEMES AND SUBTHEMES

The phenomenological design of the study and the semi structured interviews with 15 international teachers provided important insights about teachers' experiences in different cultures. The interviews were transcribed, and codes were used to identify the main theme and the subthemes. The data exploration yielded *Challenges Encountered in the Adjustment Process* and *Developing Resilience through Intercultural Interaction* as the two main themes. Subthemes that emerged from the data, listed in Table 1, will be elaborated in the following section.

Theme 1. Challenges Encountered During the Adjustment Process

Starting a new life brings many interrelated challenges, no matter how rewarding the benefits provided by the school. Teachers' stories showed that the first experiences of starting a new life is the most challenging. Our participating stories recalled many wonderful and tragi-comic stories. This adjustment process involves the process of transition to a new school culture and also into a new

Table 1. Emergent Themes and Subthemes.

Theme 1: Challenges Encountered during the Adjustment Process
1.1. Unknown school culture
1.2. Unfamiliar social environment
1.3. Maintaining balance in an unfamiliar setting
Theme 2. Developing Resilience through Intercultural Interaction
2.1. Reflection and mindfulness in cultivating resilience
2.2. Professional/interaction rituals in cultivating resilience

sociocultural context. Their personal stories revealed that they all overcame the challenges they encountered in the process of adjustment into a new culture, which led them to take on new adventures in different parts of the world. One of the teachers, Tom, referred to this journey as follows: "I had the opportunity to pursue my graduate studies. Instead, I followed a career trajectory which involved changing a country every 3–4 years. I am lucky that my fiancée has the same perspective on life, who is eager to discover new experiences in different parts of the world." Motivation to encounter enriching experiences in a new culture appears to be the primary source of support in the adjustment process. However, the teachers' stories involved inevitable roadblocks on their journey, illustrating how the professionalism of the school context made a huge difference in helping them navigate during times of uncertainty.

Unknown School Culture
All the voices of the international teachers described their initial days using words and phrases contrasting "unknown culture" and "unfamiliar culture," as illustrated by Zeynep in the following excerpt:

> Being unfamiliar with students' background was the biggest challenge for me. Understanding what is right or wrong to do or say in the classroom took some time, and I realized that no matter how much research you do about the culture, you can only learn about it by actually living there.

These stories mostly focused on coping with uncertainty and the process of adjusting to a new administrative order. Jack related an interculturally interesting experience. He found the number and duration of meetings quite intensive, particularly as they were initially conducted in Turkish and then repeated in English. He suggested having shorter meetings either in Turkish or English, making them half as long. He also found it surprising to have meetings in Turkish since in every other school he had worked at meetings were conducted in English. Alice shared how she found the lines between work and home life became blurred when teaching online, which made it challenging to maintain a balance between school and home life. She said that arriving in a new country during the pandemic was tough and it was difficult to find housing and adjust to the new work environment once the school term started. She also noted that it was more difficult than in pre-pandemic times to establish relationships with colleagues and students online as opposed to face to face. The difficulty of making sense of the school context during the pandemic is echoed in most of the voices: "It is difficult to establish a complete picture of how a school works online... both students, teachers and the wider school community were very welcoming." Teaching in a different time zone (connected to visa issues exacerbated by the pandemic) was also challenging for her. Victoria talked about the extra responsibilities that teachers have besides teaching. She shared her experience in a different cultural setting with these words:

> There is the time that goes into planning a lesson, making sure that the curriculum is being followed and implemented, marking homework assignments and essays, providing feedback, etc. Not all of this can be covered during the school day as teachers must teach the lessons, do duties throughout the day, attend meetings, etc. I think it is important to manage your time and set achievable goals. Amongst these goals, setting time to relax and step away from work is crucial in order to recover and continue to enjoy the work.

She suggested that as an international teacher, she needed additional time for considering different cultural backgrounds and teaching approaches, for example, "How would students react or interact with certain lesson plans, how should she change certain aspects of the course to make ideas more accessible to students whose first language is not English?" It was also difficult for her to live in a foreign country "with no familiarity with the area, customs, and language can add further stress and complications."

The interviews with the teachers show that each school provided orientation to teachers when they arrived. They all noted that the orientation process was carried out effectively, being introduced to a group of experienced teachers in the orientation team, which provided them with choices as to whom to approach and how to navigate school policies and procedures as well as teaching practices. However, the possibility for the orientation to raise potential bias was articulated by Zeynep:

> Usually, the orientation teams consist of experienced teachers. I think there could be another team consisting of students only as we mostly interact with students rather than teachers. I felt this need when I discovered some mismatch between the way teachers describe the learner profile and the actual profile in the classroom. I realized that teachers may have some prejudices because of their own cultural background.

The experience of teaching during Covid-19 was slightly different for Stephanie, who spent a few months teaching online in Mexico when the pandemic first started. A new challenge for all teachers worldwide, she and others in her school worked hard to ensure that education continued seamlessly. However, teachers were encouraged to step away from the computer once the online lessons finished and to physically rest. In Uzbekistan, however, unlike most other countries, teaching continued in person. She felt very fortunate to be able to be in the classroom with her students, albeit wearing masks and with social distancing regulations in place. She believes that this definitely helped her to maintain a better work-life balance as the two aspects of her life were physically separated. She added that she feels it is vital to work in and be a part of a community that values teachers' social and emotional needs. She thinks it is of utmost importance to work at a school where the administration understands how teachers work and what they need to recharge their energy, as it is a very different beast, compared to a 9-to-5 job. She also feels that teachers need more flexibility and trust in order to do their jobs well.

It was initially hard for Stephanie to create a routine around the school day, and she found herself working long into the evening and not taking enough breaks. She was dealing – as we all were – with an overload of new platforms and applications that we had to learn in order to adapt to online teaching and this became her sole focus for the first few months. She explained that once an initial panic stage subsided and she began to get used to online teaching, she found it relaxing to be able to sleep a little longer in the morning, have time for a good breakfast, take walks outside (when appropriate) between lessons, and make her own lunch. She also began to develop a healthy routine of dieting and exercising. She made herself switch off her laptop at 5 p.m., when school finished, and tried not to work at night. Similarly, Jack was also not working beyond 5 p.m. and was walking for exercise every day.

Among the challenges of adjustment, Stephanie pointed to student behavior. "I think our school deals with a lot of behavioral issues and very little effective consequences and rules. This needs to be changed through consistent and effective management." While all teachers need to deal with classroom management problems, it appears to be one of the crucial problems for international teachers. This is especially the case when school leaders fail to maintain healthy relationships between teachers and parents. At times, the teachers complained about the ways in which they were questioned by parents who try to use their community status. At some schools, this is managed professionally, but there are incidents in which teachers start to develop feelings of loneliness, which may lead them to resign.

Other teachers also mentioned problems with classroom management. Sophia said, "It is very difficult to control my classes and I have a hard time to cover my content," while Jennifer said, "I have some classroom management problems in my classes and in one of those days, the vice principal came into my class." These experiences point to a particular problem some schools might experience in embracing internationalization. The pressure to accommodate parents' demands and the problem of problematic students seem to affect the well-being of some teachers, as well as conflicting with their values as teachers. The adjustment process ends with stories of success while a few cases reflect the extent to which this process could be traumatic when there is a lack of effective school leadership. As Victoria stated:

> School should be a safe, fun, and welcoming place to be. I think that schools improve when they have better organization, a sense of school spirit, and focus on mental wellbeing. Too often, hours and classes are added on in the belief that it will result in better grades or accomplishments. However, it tends to result in tired students who do not want to learn and tired teachers who have no time to improve their lessons or rest.

As Victoria suggests, the wellbeing of teachers and students is crucial. For many, the hours of duty become exhausting. As Sophia says, they must come to school early and leave late to help to maintain control. Without breaks, they feel exhausted.

Unfamiliar Social Environments

Teaching and living in an unfamiliar social environment can be experienced as being continually out of one's comfort zone. Although this unfamiliarity might be discomforting for many who relocate to a new country, for international teachers the effect is much deeper as each and every classroom they enter constitutes a representation of that unfamiliar society. Teachers must transform their beliefs, expectations, and values. And they must come to understand a new world very rapidly, so that they can adapt to the new culture quickly and support their learners in the classroom. For instance, a teacher may act in a way that is considered very sympathetic in their own culture but that is unacceptable in the host society. This can have an impact, as clearly reflected by Sara:

> When I first taught in high school in the US, I made a cake with walnuts in it, and I served this to my students without hesitation. I later found out that some of my students had severe allergies to nuts, but this is not a problem in my culture [at least I was unaware of this] so I learned the hard way that I should never serve any food to my students ... In my culture offering food is sign of hospitality and it is never considered unsafe for a teacher or school to offer homemade baked goods but here in the US, this is a major problem and there is a regulation regarding this. I was very surprised by this when I first had this experience in the US. (Interview with Sara)

Observing all these distinct approaches in a society, international teachers inevitably develop resilience either consciously or subconsciously.

> I don't take anything personally and whatever they do or say, I have empathy towards them – I try to think that it is something cultural and I try to look from their own cultural perspective. I think this is something that I do to protect myself. (Interview with Lidya)

> I had to develop resilience, as nothing was the same! I believe you need to develop resilience even if you are only changing your institution – however this is not that! All your classroom environment, colleague environment, culture, approach, methods, techniques need to be changed, even transformed! Because although you were considered to be very successful in your own profession as your comfort zone, you do not even know what comfort means in a new country. The role of a teacher and the meaning of a teacher may even change from culture to culture. This is not a job you can conduct on a computer screen; you are directly in collaboration with humans in a classroom. (Interview with Lidya)

Maintaining Balance in an Unfamiliar Setting

The majority of the participants in this study were mothers who struggled to establish balance between their family lives in a new city and culture along with all the responsibilities they had to shoulder at their new school context. Their stories revealed that their perceptions of balance and the ways in which they reach a harmonious balance between their home and work lives differed from one teacher to another. Teachers appreciated the support provided by the school of their children's education along with accommodation opportunities close to school campus, which made their lives easier. All the participants mentioned the initial two months as the most challenging time, feeling lost in multiple roles and adjustment processes. After the first six months, almost all felt that the situation was under control. They could now allocate time for their personal and family priorities whilst performing effectively in their roles as teachers.

> It is exhausting. If you have children, you need to create a lot of opportunities for your kids to talk about what they go through. I think I achieved this by giving priority to my own family. (Interview with Zeynep)

All participants emphasized the support they have received from their family members.

> One of the participants shared his story of why he had to resign from his previous school due to the mismatch between his son and the school. The voices of the teachers echoed each other, confirming the importance of "fit with the school," which may also require it to be a good fit for the kids who become students in that school setting:

> As a teacher, I do not spend long hours at work anyway. We are a team as a family, and we support each other. My wife and my kids have been quite understanding. My professional life does not bring about any challenges that cannot be solved with a phone call or an e-mail message. (Interview with Mehmet)

> I don't think I was good at maintaining the balance between my private and professional life in the transition process. Having close friends and sharing help a lot. (Interview with Irene)

> I kept my private life separate from work and always kept boundaries so the two don't consume each other. I only worked part-time for the first 15 years so that I could be home with my young family, I only started teaching full time when I felt that I was ready to do so. Otherwise, it is very hard to maintain that balance. One reason is that there aren't any efficient ways to provide childcare in the US in most workplaces and this makes it very hard for moms to work outside the house for an extended period of time. (Interview with Sara)

All the participants noted that they had a smooth transition to the new way of life. None of them seem to be affected in a negative way. Instead, they used it as an opportunity to develop resilience for all members of the family. The excitement to discover new culture helped them to interpret all the experiences in a constructive manner, which led them to establish stronger connections with friends and other families. Each one of them tailored their own recipes for a seamless transition that leads to balanced life.

Theme 2. Developing Resilience through Intercultural Interaction

The teachers' experiences were categorized under personal-focused, process-focused, and context-focused perspectives. The way in which each of these elements emerge and interact with the other elements changed from teacher to teacher. It is evident in all the stories that person-focused and context-focused elements serve as counterparts that complement one another in a constructive way. Intercultural interaction appears to be the main theme that embraces all these patterns and dynamics in the process of developing resilience. None of the teachers had a specific strategic plan to follow critical steps to build resilience. However, awareness of their wellbeing helped them to take important actions in dealing with challenges, enabling them to develop resilience. It was clear in all the stories that they were courageous in embarking on new adventures and were therefore prepared to address risks and challenges they would face. This is reflected as follows:

> I usually accept things as they are rather than expecting something. This has helped me a lot. This happens when you can disregard your expectations, give time to yourself to observe your environment and the people without responding.

No matter how experienced each of the participants was, they all gave themselves time to "take a breath" and "observe what is going on," which enabled them to make sense of their school context as well as the new cultural context.

Reflection and Mindfulness in Cultivating Resilience

All the teachers emphasized the power of reflection and mindfulness in cultivating resilience. They struggled to allocate sufficient time to sustain their wellbeing in their new contexts. They all saw new challenges as opportunities to support their wellbeing. For this reason, they prioritized activities supporting reflection and mindfulness. However, they also mentioned the difficulty they had in being mindful and reflective in the first days of adjustment since they had to deal with multiple and urgent life adjustments along with taking on their professional roles at the school. They were aware of the necessity to create opportunities to support their wellbeing, as reflected in here:

> I think it's important to create a routine and to manage your time in such a way that work and home life remain separate as much as possible. Eating well, getting enough sleep and exercise is crucial. Keeping in touch with colleagues, family and friends is essential and asking for help when you need it. I found keeping a diary helped me empty my head and helped when feeling anxious and helpless.

Teachers also prioritized being organized and managing their time during the adjustment process. Their stories show that they developed these skills over time and the more experience they had as teachers, the easier it was. The teachers' voices reflected cycles of reflection: self-reflection, peer reflection, and group reflection (Schön, 1987). Their experiences implicitly or explicitly acknowledge the power of reflection and constructive interaction with their students and their colleagues.

> I think I am approachable as a teacher and treat my students as equals. I believe this makes them feel comfortable around me and allows us to have a better relationship. That said, I have high expectations and I consider myself quite strict in the classroom. I think as a teacher you need to create a balance of respect and friendship, and students need to know their boundaries. These strengths are acquired with experience, being confident in what you are teaching and knowing your own strengths and weaknesses.

The teachers felt that there needed to be more professional development opportunities on how schools can better create "community" within the school environment. Their words and expressions seem to fall under the category of reflection in which they "nurture each other's souls" (Clark, 2001). The following excerpt reflects the ideas of most of the teachers:

> Much of the time we are so focused on the academic side of teaching that we forget the humanistic side of it and creating an environment of respect/tolerance and well-being amongst students and staff.... Awareness is vital in order for teachers to be better educated and informed in order for them to take that knowledge into the classroom.

One-third of the participants had previous international experiences. This seems to have a positive impact on their adjustment process. Also, initial adjustment to a new setting was helped by participation in an active community of practice supporting other international teachers who were new to the school. Victoria appreciates her upbringing in an international setting as follows:

> I was able to gain these strengths as my upbringing [was] in an international setting. I myself attended an international school and was always surrounded by people from different backgrounds. Furthermore, I have always moved around and thus been comfortable with changing my settings. These experiences helped fortify my strengths.

Professional Interaction Rituals in Cultivating Resilience
Professional interactions established in this study seem to align with the features of interaction rituals, as described by Kadar and House (2021). International teachers seem to be engaged in building communities of interaction as well as developing professional interactional rituals that helped them to feel a part of the professional community. The international teachers shared their experiences focusing on intercultural interaction with colleagues, school staff, and students as means that helped them develop resilience. They focused most on collaboration with colleagues and the welcoming attitude of the host culture. Zeynep's words echo most of the teachers' experiences as to how students served as facilitators for them to understand the culture:

> My students wanted to celebrate National Day in the classroom. They arranged everything. They brought traditional food, decorated the classroom, and prepared presentations. I was a genuine listener for them as I had no idea about their culture. This was a very important learning moment for me. I realized that the best source of learning for international teachers is the students.

Half of the teachers who contributed to this study indicated that they changed schools just before the Covid-19 crisis. The initial days of adjustment made their struggle more difficult since their process of adjustment held additional risks, though all of them mentioned the support they received from their colleagues as well as from parents during times of remote teaching. Jack felt that one of the crucial factors that helped him develop resilience during Covid-19 was support from his wife and colleagues. He explained: "The colleagues that I taught classes with were also super helpful and supportive." He also explained the support he had from his students' families:

It was an exercise in empathy for everyone. Parents were more supportive and empathetic than I'd experienced before. Colleagues were also very willing to listen, share resources and help in any way they could. Students also developed more autonomy in communicating with setting up...online meetings, staying after class in a meeting [room] or taking initiative to send emails.

Alice suggested "ultimately, being an international teacher creates resilience – moving to a new country, creating new social networks, adapting to a new work environment and new colleagues – doing that during the pandemic was a little too much!" She also explained how her new school made their new staff feel welcome and found that international teachers at her school were fortunate to have such welcoming staff, students, and student families. She said that her school made a good job of making staff feel welcome and the administration reached out to staff to let them know they were looking forward to their arrival and provided lots of information. Regular communication from the administration team prior to arrival was very reassuring. She underscored the importance of good communication and shared her experience as follows:

> ... I do not see [different] racial/ethnic backgrounds, I see individuals with a passion for learning [embracing cultural richness] ... My experience of teaching in many different countries has been positive. Good communication and an understanding of the local culture is key.

This was echoed in most of the voices of the teachers who appreciated the unwritten interactional rituals created within the school setting. Routines such as tea talks, coffee gatherings, celebrations and authentic dialogues among teachers formed the basis of interactional rituals, enabling teachers to be recognized and appreciated in the host culture. Teachers noted that these professional interactional rituals helped them to feel no longer the guest but the host in the school setting.

Alice says that throughout her teaching career, she has been invited to courses on peer coaching and management. These courses have helped her to understand how to bring out the best in her students. Along with collaboration with colleagues, successful intercultural communication and peer coaching can be considered gateways to teacher resilience. Victoria said:

> It is a joy as an international teacher to have the opportunity to be a part of a global community – teachers and students alike being able to learn and share. At times, the stress comes from clashing cultural customs or when people are unwilling to learn their socially engraved stigmas. However, it is the job of the teacher to keep an open mind and approach all students and conversations with sensitivity and respect.

She shared her experience as an international teacher:

> I believe that I am a patient and adaptable person. I do not easily get ruffled and am able to listen to others with a collected and open mind. I am respectful to my students as I consider them individuals capable of making their own decisions and having their own valuable opinions. I try to see something good and unique in each student – I think that most of my students know that I listen to them, and, in turn, they listen to me. I was able to gain these strengths as my upbringing in an international setting. I myself attended an international school and was always surrounded by people from different backgrounds. Furthermore, I have always

moved around and thus been comfortable with changing my settings. These experiences helped fortify my strengths.

Victoria also shared the collective strengths that she and other international teachers have gained as a group. She suggests that most international teachers are accepting and open-minded. She has met colleagues who have lived and taught in a variety of different countries. They all have rich experiences and advice to share – they love their international background, and it has given them tolerance and appreciation. They develop these collective strengths because she says, "we bond over our profession – we believe that teaching is an important calling and seek to help our students in both their academics but also personal growth."

Stephanie explained that the process enabled her to develop resilience by being immersed in uncertainty:

> I was living on my own and had to adapt to a completely surreal experience in such a short time. I think as a school we managed to adapt very quickly and the support that was given to us by the school was unprecedented. I was also constantly thinking about my family in Italy when Italy was going through its worst days of the pandemic. It was often difficult to focus and forget and carry on [with my] teaching.

She emphasized the importance of cultivating intercultural communication skills in times of uncertainty and crisis by keeping in touch with friends and family. Creating a safe community among colleagues who can identify with similar issues and difficulties can be a support system for them. She related her experience in different countries:

> I have taught in Japan, Zambia, India, and Türkiye. It is very important to be aware of cultural/religious/social norms. One needs to be sensitive to student's personal/family backgrounds and... [disclosing] your own values and beliefs in the classroom [should wait] until you have established a close relationship with your students and understand the social dynamics that you are teaching in.

What Stephanie recommended also gives significant insights for intercultural communication and gaining resilience:

> You gain a wealth of experience living in a different country with diverse cultures and traditions. A new language can be daunting and the inability to express oneself fluently can be stressful at times. I believe it is important to adapt as much as possible and to take every 'uncomfortable' situation with a sense of humor! Working with colleagues from different backgrounds should be seen as a learning experience and one should never impose their own beliefs and methods on others ...

She thinks the ability to listen and work as a team is essential. You cannot impose your own way of doing things but need to be accepting of others, taking on board their ideas and suggestions. For her, having worked with so many people from different countries, she learned to adapt to different thought processes and learned to mediate, even when in disagreement. She considers flexibility crucial to working well with others. Sophia also believes that collaboration with local teachers helped her develop resilience. The advice of experienced teachers in her new intercultural setting had a healing effect during the process of adjustment. Intercultural communication with school administration, students, and their families helped as well. Jennifer shared her challenge within a story in which she had a hard time communicating during a teacher-parent conference. However, in collaboration with an L1 Turkish teacher, she had an amazing experience, and this gave her more confidence.

The teachers' experiences highlight the critical role school leaders play in creating a culture of collaboration and connection, serving as role models of respectful interactional dialogue. Rosa's words underline the importance of school leadership in playing an essential role in international teachers' adjustment process. The guidance and mentorship provided helped her to overcome initial challenges, giving her confidence and courage, which eventually helped her to develop agency. Rosa's words echoed in all the voices: "Teachers shouldn't feel lonely and insecure and therefore the first contact or communication with the school administration is very important...."

CLOSING COMMENTS

Utopias and dystopias exist even in privileged school contexts. While working on this study, each of us continued our overarching project of creating more equitable pathways for teachers and leaders. This study gave us insights about how intercultural interaction can serve as means to support teachers' adjustment to new cultures. Also, stories of teachers implied and highlighted the importance of successful school leadership in this challenging process. Case studies focusing on experiences of successful schools can give in depth data which can inform practices at the schools. Action research projects can also be implemented at school sites to create research-informed, local improvement-oriented practices. Finally, stories can be collected in authentic settings in different countries to hear teachers' immediate experiences and the ways in which they can navigate in different cultural contexts. As Clark (2001) notes, "authentic dialogues can enable teachers to articulate their own experiences, implicit hopes and fears, in the intellectual and emotional company of others whom they trust" (p. 177). We hope that stories shared in this study will be heard by other ISATT members who can channel the voices of teachers and leaders in their own local contexts in future collaborative studies.

AUTHORS' NOTES

The authors thank Christopher M. Clark, who read and commented on drafts of this chapter. The authors also thank the teachers who gave their valuable time to participate in this study.

REFERENCES

Bakioglu, A., Hacıfazlıoğlu, Ö., & Ozcan, K. (2010). Influence of trust in principals mentoring experiences at different career phases. *Teachers and Teaching: Theory and Practice, 16*(2), 245–258.

Beltman, S., Mansfield, C., & Price, A. (2011). Thriving not just surviving: A review of research on teacher resilience. *Educational Research Review, 6,* 185–207.

Benard, B. (1995). *Fostering resilience in children.* ERIC/EECE Digest, EDO-PS-99.

Bobek, B. L. (2002). Teacher resiliency: A key to career longevity. *The Clearing House, 75*(4), 202–205.

Burghes, D., Howson, J., Marenbon, J., O'Leary, J., & Woodhead, C. (2009). *Teachers matter: Recruitment, employment, and retention at home and abroad.* Politeia.

Castro, A. J., Kelly, J., & Shih, M. (2010). Resilience strategies for new teachers in high-needs areas. *Teaching and Teacher Education, 26*(3), 622–629.

Clark, C. M. (2001). *Talking shop.* Teachers College Press.

Day, C., & Leithwood, K. (Eds.). (2007). *Successful principal leadership in times of change: An international Perspective.* Springer.

Gu, Q., & Day, C. (2007). Teacher's resilience: A necessary condition for effectiveness. *Teaching and Teacher Education, 23,* 1302–1316.

Gu, Q., & Day, C. (2013). Challenges to teacher resilience: Conditions count. *British Educational Research Journal, 39*(1), 22–44.

Kadar, D. Z., & House, J. (2021). Interaction ritual and (im)politeness. *Journal of Pragmatics, 179,* 54–60.

Luthar, S. S., Cicchetti, D., & Becker, B. (2000). The construct of resilience. A critical evaluation and guidelines for future work. *Child Development, 71,* 543–562.

Lysgaard, S. (1955). Adjustment in a foreign country: Norwegian Fulbright grantees visiting the United States. *International Social Science Bulletin, 7*(1), 45–51.

Marshall, C., & Rossman, G. R. (1999). *Designing qualitative research.* Sage Publications.

Maxwell, J. (1996). *Qualitative research design.* Sage.

Oberg, K. (1960). Culture shock: Adjustment to new cultural environments. *Practical Anthropology, 7*(3), 177–182.

Ospina, N. S., & Medina, S. L. (2020). Living and teaching internationally: Teachers talk about personal experiences, benefits, and challenges. *Journal of Research in International Education, 19*(1), 38–53. https://doi.org/10.1177/1475240920915013

Richardson, W., Kirchenheim, C. von, & Richardson, C. (2006). Teachers and their international relocation: The effect of self and pay satisfaction on adjustment and outcome variables. *International Education Journal, 7*(7), 883–894.

Roskell, D. (2013). Cross-cultural transition: International teachers' experience of 'culture shock'. *Journal of Research in International Education, 12*(2), 155–172.

Schön, D. A. (1987). *Educating the reflective practitioner: Toward a new design for teaching and learning in the professions.* Jossey-Bass.

Seidman, I. (1998). *Interviewing as qualitative research: A guide for researchers in education and the social sciences.* Teachers College Press.

Volet, S. (1999). Motivation within and across cultural-educational contexts: A multi-dimensional perspective. In T. Urdan (Ed.), *Advances in motivation and achievement* (pp. 185–231). JAI Press.

Ward, C., & Kennedy, A. (1996). Crossing cultures: The relationship between psychological and socio-cultural dimensions of cross-cultural adjustment. In J. Pandey, D. Sinha, & D. P. S. Bhawuk (Eds.), *Asian contributions to cross-cultural psychology* (pp. 289–306). Sage Publications, Inc.

Ward, C., & Kennedy, A. (1999). The measurement of socio-cultural adaptation. *International Journal of Intercultural Relations, 23*(4), 659–677.

Ward, C., Okura, Y., Kennedy, A., & Kojima, T. (1998). The U-curve on trial: A longitudinal study of psychological and sociocultural adjustment during cross-cultural transition. *International Journal of Intercultural Relations, 22*(3), 277–291.

Yang, C. (2021). *Pre-service and first-year teachers' experiences with school violence and subjective well-being project*. University of California Berkeley. Institutional Review Board (IRB#2020-08-13553).

AFTERWORD

A few years ago, we imagined that this 40th Anniversary ISATT Yearbook would be a volume featuring incremental change in ISATT members' research agendas since our last celebratory volume, which was published 10 years earlier (Craig et al., 2013). How wrong we were! In between our 30th and 40th Yearbooks, a cataclysmic pandemic rocked the world. Our regional conference in Bordeaux, France, was canceled for two years. The same thing happened to our international conference scheduled for Bari, Italy. And what would be the purpose of undertaking a mammoth 40th Anniversary Yearbook project, if there was no international conference at which to celebrate ISATT's illustrious past, pandemic-riddled present, and bright future? Then, things lightened up (a bit) and both our regional and international conferences were reinstated. At that point, our backburner 40th Anniversary ISATT Yearbook Project took on warp speed because we no longer had the luxury of time. Our book prospectus was accepted by Emerald Publishing without revision. However, what we imagined would be one volume patterning the 30th Anniversary Yearbook, became four books, each with its own title:

Volume 1: Teaching and Teacher Education in the Wake of Covid-19
Volume 2: Teaching and Teacher Education in International Contexts
Volume 3: Approaches to Teaching and Teacher Education
Volume 4: Studying Teaching and Teacher Education

In this four-book series, themes emerged that never previously headlined ISATT's work. For example, readers found themselves introduced sections on (1) preparing teacher educators (InFo-TED), (2) excessive entitlement, (3) technology, and (4) accountability. Also, we included tributes to past members which were threaded throughout the four-volume set. These tributes showcased the plurality of career paths that ISATT members have taken and the collaborative relationships and friendships that developed. We additionally addressed vulnerable populations throughout the globe due to the current focus on equity (phrased differently depending on countries and organizations). We also added a whole section on Covid-19, which launched the first book. It opened up collaborative partnership research conducted globally by 29 ISATT regional representatives, *which is a first of its kind*. Further to this, the first volume of the four-book set had Covid-19 in its title – and the Covid-19 pandemic section, and the technology and education section fit together like hand-in-glove in a way never previously imagined.

Also, the Covid and technology themes naturally spilled over to other chapters in the other three volumes because, like the pandemic itself, they leaked into other topics of inquiry.

Finally, without the hard work of many individuals working quietly behind the scenes, this ISATT four-book project would have never made its submission deadlines. As projected, ISATT's four volumes of the 40th Anniversary Yearbook will be officially launched in Bari, Italy, at our study association's 20th Biennial International Conference, which is anticipated to be the largest attendance to date. Our dream of landing our four-volume print and electronic copy chapters/yearbook in the world's libraries – as the most representative global publication to date – has been realized. ISATT's future is on solid ground.

REFERENCE

Craig, C. J., Meijer, P. C., & Broeckmans, J. (Eds.). (2013). *From teacher thinking to teachers and teaching: The evolution of a research community*. Emerald Publishing Limited.

INDEX

Accountability, 34, 37, 56, 71, 75, 145
Accountability demands, 30, 61–62
Accreditation, 29, 56, 58, 69, 74–75, 77–78
Accrediting bodies, competition between, 73–74
Agency, 35, 37, 52, 94–95, 123, 233–234, 275, 284–285, 309, 311–312, 323
Alienation, 106
Alternative certification, 76–77
American Educational Research Association (AERA), 7, 177–178, 186–187, 201
Assessment, 42–44, 54–55, 74–75, 123, 162–163, 310
Attrition, 8, 71–72, 145–146, 256, 283
Authority of the principal, 170
Autonomous innovation, 164, 168, 170
Autonomy, 29–31, 34, 36, 84, 91, 103–104, 119, 125, 161–162, 166–168, 321

Black box, 178, 182
Blended learning, 190
Butterfly under a pin, 134, 141, 147, 149, 151–152

Cliff-hanging story, 154
Clinical practice, 62–64, 66–67
Collaboration, 4, 8, 12–13, 48, 66, 84, 107, 204, 236, 256
    cultivating teacher resilience through intercultural interaction and, 307–312
Commitment, 35, 53, 67–68, 119, 183, 205–206, 284–285, 311–312
Communities of practice, 45–46, 226–227, 236

Competency based curriculum, 30, 39–40
Conceptions, 101, 196–197, 200, 212–213
Conceptual model, 178–179, 186–187, 215, 217, 225–226
Contexts of teaching, 8, 23, 132–133
Continuing professional development (CPD), 53–54
COVID-19, 190, 204, 273–274, 315–316
Critical thinking, 268
Curriculum, 39–40, 161–162, 237

Democratic, 123–124, 126, 152, 279
Dewey, 23–24, 46, 107, 132–133, 257
Digital technologies, 299–301
Diploma teacher education, 42
Distance teaching, 281
Diversity, 36, 67, 69–71
Diversity, Equity, Inclusion (DEI), 205–206

Educational polyphony, 110
Emotion in education, 102, 137
Empowerment, 31, 91–92
Equity, 67, 71, 119
Erasmus funding, 188–189
Ethics, 164, 268, 298
Every Student Succeeds Act (ESSA), 70–71, 73, 136–137
Existential importance, 153–155
Eye of the storm, 143–144, 147, 152

Financial dilemmas, 101–102
Functional dilemmas, 101–104

General Teaching Council of Scotland (GTCS), 52, 56, 58

Hidden blessings, 154
Hidden profession, 177, 181–182
Holmes Group, 63–64

Identity, 48–49, 250
In-service training, 89
Inclusion, 37, 162–163
Inclusive education, 8, 162–163
Induction, 13, 54–55, 225, 256
Innovation, 168–169, 224–225
Integration, 45, 240–241, 248, 301–302
Integrity, 57, 132
International Forum on Teacher Educator Development (InFo-TED), 177–179, 181–182, 195–196, 212
International Study Association on Teachers and Teaching (ISATT), 4, 24, 233, 293, 296–297
   community, 12–13
   conference, 11–12, 16
   regional conference, 297–299
Internationalization of education, 308

Journal of Community, 297
Journal of Educational Administration (JEA), 20

Kenya, 8–9, 30, 39–41, 43, 45
Kenya National Examination Council (KNEC), 41–42
Knowledge dilemmas, 101–102

Leadership, 19, 55, 142–143, 265–266, 310
Legitimacy, 34, 161–162
Lesson study for learning communities (LSLC), 102–104, 106, 108
   listening in, 108–112
Lifelong learning, 83–84, 89
Listening relationships, 102–103, 106–109

Managerial professionalism, 34–35
Managerialism, 34–36, 101
Measuring Quality in Initial Teacher Education project (MQuITE), 52, 58
Miseducative experiences, 132–133
Monkey's paw approach, 139–140, 147
Multiculturalism, 34, 36, 38

NAFOL, 191, 201, 222–224
Narrative inquiry, 7–8, 132, 134–135
Neoliberal strategies, 153
No Child Left Behind Act (NCLB), 66, 70
Norwegian Research School of Teacher Education, 222
Novice teachers, 15, 67, 71, 144–145

Organization for Economic and Co-operative Development (OECD), 58, 153, 155, 273–274
Orientation dilemmas, 101–102

Pandemic, 31, 90, 94, 273–274, 276, 278–279, 301, 304
Paradigm dilemmas, 101–102
Pedagogical knowledge, 214
Pedagogical practices, 169, 277, 303
Pedagogy, 48–49, 67, 75, 84, 162–163, 167, 200–201, 296, 302
Personal communication, 139–140, 261–262, 265–266
Perspective, 13, 15, 29, 37, 61–62, 109, 214, 301
Policy gatekeepers, 162
Policy implementation, 34, 162
Political dilemmas, 101–102
Politics, 280
Portugal, 23, 35, 103–104, 164, 189–190
Probation, 57
Problem of practice, 196–197
Professional collaboration, 203
Professional community, 320

Index

Professional development, 4, 62, 83–84, 91, 183, 186–187, 236–237
Professional Development Assessment System (PDAS), 145–146
Professional engagement, 55–56
Professional learning, 8, 31, 111, 195–196, 201, 207
Professional standards, 53, 56–57
Professionalism, 35

Reflective practitioner, 111
Reforms, 39–40, 154
Research training, 88–89
Resilience, 318–323
Resources dilemmas, 101–102
Retention, 54, 68, 309

School as learning community, 63–64
School experiencing policy, 154
School principals, 162, 164–168, 282
School reform, 103, 106, 117–118, 161–162, 275
Schooling, 30, 52, 117–118, 214, 280
Schwab, 135–136, 153, 233, 239
Scotland, 30, 51, 55–56, 58, 201
Self-education, 91
Self-efficacy, 84, 88–89
Self-learning, 91
Self-positioning, 93
Self-Study of Teacher Education Practices (S-STEP), 201, 214, 219–220
Serial interpretation, 135
Social constructivism, 46
Social justice, 30, 67, 69, 71, 84, 301
Social market model, 101

Sociality, 132–133
South Africa, 8, 103, 117–118
Special education teachers, 42
Standard for Career-long Professional Learning, 55, 57
Standard for headship, 57
Standard for provisional registration, 54, 57

Teacher attrition, 8, 256
Teacher education, 29, 31, 34, 36, 38–41, 43
Teacher educators, 29, 61–62, 177, 181–183, 185, 195–196, 199, 212
Teacher induction, 54–55
Teacher Induction Scheme (TIS), 52–55
Teacher knowledge, 132–133
Teacher preparation, 29, 44–45, 61–62, 66, 73–74, 291
Teacher professional development, 35
Teacher professionalism, 34
Teacher quality, 101
Teacher turnover, 67
Teaching metaphors, 153
Teaching profession, 29–30, 49, 281
Technology, 45–48
Temporality, 132–133

Values, 3, 31, 108–109, 123, 268, 322
Virtual, 302
Visible phenomena, 154
Vulnerability, 106, 277

Workforce modernization, 54